Teyler's Foundation in Haarlem and Its 'Book and Art Room' of 1779

Scientific and Learned Cultures and Their Institutions

Editor

Mordechai Feingold (*California Institute of Technology*)

VOLUME 29

The titles published in this series are listed at *brill.com/slci*

Teyler's Foundation in Haarlem and Its 'Book and Art Room' of 1779

A Key Moment in the History of a Learned Institution

Edited by

Ellinoor Bergvelt and Debora Meijers

BRILL

LEIDEN | BOSTON

Cover illustration: Wybrand Hendriks, *Group Portrait of the Board of five Directors of Teyler's Foundation, with their Secretary and the Architect Leendert Viervant*, 1786, oil on canvas, 258 x 311 cm. Teyler's Museum, KS 282.

The Library of Congress Cataloging-in-Publication Data is available online at http://catalog.loc.gov
LC record available at http://lccn.loc.gov/2020041404

Typeface for the Latin, Greek, and Cyrillic scripts: "Brill". See and download: brill.com/brill-typeface.

ISSN 2352-1325
ISBN 978-90-04-44099-9 (hardback)
ISBN 978-90-04-44144-6 (e-book)

Copyright 2021 by Koninklijke Brill NV, Leiden, The Netherlands.
Koninklijke Brill NV incorporates the imprints Brill, Brill Hes & De Graaf, Brill Nijhoff, Brill Rodopi,
Brill Sense, Hotei Publishing, mentis Verlag, Verlag Ferdinand Schöningh and Wilhelm Fink Verlag.
All rights reserved. No part of this publication may be reproduced, translated, stored in a retrieval system,
or transmitted in any form or by any means, electronic, mechanical, photocopying, recording or otherwise,
without prior written permission from the publisher. Requests for re-use and/or translations must be
addressed to Koninklijke Brill NV via brill.com or copyright.com.

Brill has made all reasonable efforts to trace all rights holders to any copyrighted material used in this
work. In cases where these efforts have not been successful the publisher welcomes communications from
copyright holders, so that the appropriate acknowledgements can be made in future editions, and to settle
other permission matters.

This book is printed on acid-free paper and produced in a sustainable manner.

Contents

Acknowledgements   VII
List of Illustrations   VIII
Abbreviations   XIII
Notes on Contributors   XIV

PART 1
Introduction and Background

1   Purpose and Structure of the Book   3
    Debora J. Meijers and Ellinoor S. Bergvelt

2   Teyler's Foundation and the Two Societies: Emergence and
    Development up to *c.* 1800   19
    Debora J. Meijers

3   A Museum within the Foundation, 1779–2020   46
    Debora J. Meijers

PART 2
Teyler's as a Case in a Re-Reading of the History of Science

4   'The World We Have Lost': In Praise of a Comprehensive Concept of
    Science and Scholarship   69
    Wijnand W. Mijnhardt

5   The First Museum in the Netherlands? The Establishment of Teyler's
    Oval Room in Historical Perspective (*c.* 1600–1800)   87
    Eric Jorink

6   How to Collect Minerals, Rocks and Fossils for a Museum: The
    International Networks of Martinus van Marum (1750–1837)   109
    Bert Sliggers

PART 3
Teyler's between the Natural Sciences and the Visual Arts

7   'Truth-to-Nature' in the Museum? Wybrand Hendriks, Martinus van Marum and the 'Reasoned Image'   131
    Koenraad Vos

8   An Asset to Art. The Purchase of Italian Drawings by Teyler's Foundation in 1790 and the Context of Art Theory in the Netherlands   168
    Paul Knolle

9   Collecting and Displaying Art in Teyler's Museum, 1778–1885: The Usefulness of Drawings, Prints and Contemporary Paintings, and the Development of Public Access   190
    Terry van Druten

PART 4
Teyler's in an International Perspective

10   Visiting Haarlem: August Hermann Niemeyer, the Cabinet of Artefacts and Natural Curiosities at the Halle Orphanage, and Teyler's Museum   219
     Holger Zaunstöck

11   The Rise of the Modern Romantic Concept of Art and the Art Museum   239
     Arnold Heumakers

Bibliography   253
Photo Credits   280
Index   281

Acknowledgements

This volume, published to mark the occasion of the 240th anniversary of Teyler's Foundation, has grown out of an international conference, 'Museums and the (loss of?) the Encyclopedic Ideal', wich took place in Teyler's Museum on 20–22 April 2017. During the preparation of the book, attention focused on this Museum and the Foundation of which it was a part from 1779 to 1981, and the title changed accordingly. The book contains a selection of the papers delivered at the conference, with four new contributions. The conference and the publication were supported by Teyler's Foundation and Teyler's Museum.

The text was revised at various stages during the editing process. The editors are grateful to Emily Lane for her extensive contribution as English editor and corrector. Their thanks also go to Tessel Dekker, who did indispensable work as a researcher for the illustrations in this book. From Teyler's Museum, Trienke van der Spek, Terry van Druten and Herman Voogd provided information and photographs. Finally, thanks are due to Francis Knikker, Editor History, and Ester Lels, Production Editor at Brill, for their support during the publication process.

Illustrations

Figures

1.1   Taco Jelgersma, *Portrait of Pieter Teyler van der Hulst as Collector, c. 1760.* Teyler's Museum   4

1.2   The Oval Room, seen from the Library gallery. Photo 2011   6

1.3   Charles Howard Hodges, *Portrait of Martinus van Marum,* 1826. Teyler's Museum   9

1.4   Façade of the new wing by the Austrian architect Christian Ulrich (opened in 1885) seen across the Spaarne River. Photo *c.* 1900   14

2.1   Wybrand Hendriks, *Group Portrait of the Board of five Directors of Teyler's Foundation, with their Secretary and the Architect Leendert Viervant,* 1786. Teyler's Museum   26

2.2, 2.3   Johan George Holtzhey, *Prize medal of the Theological Society, awarded in 1784 to William Laurence Brown in Utrecht,* designed in 1778. Teyler's Museum   32

2.4, 2.5   Johan George Holtzhey, *Prize medal of the Second Society, awarded in 1846 to Pieter Otto van der Chijs,* designed in 1778. Teyler's Museum   35

3.1   The Foundation House and Teyler's Museum: ground floor in 1791   47

3.2   Wybrand Hendriks, *The Oval Room of Teyler's Museum with the electrostatic generator in the foreground stored in a case, c.* 1810. Teyler's Museum   48

3.3   The Foundation House and Teyler's Museum: ground floor in 1839   50

3.4   First Paintings Gallery (1839). Photo 2015   51

3.5   Second Paintings Gallery (1893). Photo 2015   52

3.6   Second Fossil Room (1885). Photo 2015   52

3.7   The Foundation House and Teyler's Museum: ground floor in 1909   53

3.8   The Auditorium (1885). Photo 2011   54

3.9   The extension of the Library (1885). Photo 2011   54

3.10   The Pieter Teyler House, formerly the Foundation House, Damstraat 21. Photo 2011   56

3.11   The Exhibition Room in the extension by Bureau Henket. Photo 1996   56

3.12   Aerial view of the entire complex. Photo 2014   57

3.13   The café by Bureau Henket (1990). Photo 2019   58

3.14   An example of the transparent connection between the new wing by Bureau Henket (1990) and the existing building by Adriaan van der Steur (1880–85). Photo 1996   59

3.15   The Lorentz Lab. Photo 2017   60

ILLUSTRATIONS

3.16 The copy of Martinus van Marum's electrostatic generator made in 2016–17. Photo 2017 61
3.17 The Pieter Teyler House and Teyler's Museum: ground floor in 2020 62
3.18 View from the 'Large Room' to the Oval Room. Photo 2011 64
3.19 The Spaarne façade (1885) of Teyler's Museum. Photo 2011 66
4.1 Jacob Ernst Marcus, *Interior of the Drawing Academy in the Amsterdam Town Hall, during a session of drawing after a male nude model*, between *c.* 1790 and 1822. Amsterdam City Archives 70
4.2 Dutch engraver, *Animals and plants*, second half of the eighteenth century, print published by the Maatschappij tot Nut van 't Algemeen. Rijksmuseum, Amsterdam 71
4.3 Bernard Picart (workshop), *La Dédicace de la Synagogue des Juifs Portugais, à Amsterdam en 1675*, from J. F. Bernard and B. Picart, *Cérémonies et coutumes religieuses de tous les peuples du monde* (Amsterdam 1723–43). Rijksmuseum, Amsterdam 79
4.4 Pieter Oets, *Portrait of Joannes de Mol* (1726–1782). Castle-Museum Sypesteyn, Nieuw-Loosdrecht 80
4.5 Cup and saucer, multi-coloured painted porcelain, Oud-Loosdrecht Manufacture (1774–84). Castle-Museum Sypesteyn, Nieuw-Loosdrecht 80
4.6 Reinier Vinkeles, after a drawing by Jacques Kuyper and Pieter Barbiers, *A Public Presentation by the Amsterdam Professor Jan van Swinden for the Felix Meritis Society in Amsterdam ('Physica')*, 1801. Amsterdam City Archives 82
4.7 Adriaan de Lelie, *The Drawing Gallery of the Felix Meritis Society*, 1801. Rijksmuseum, Amsterdam 83
4.8 Hendrik Antoon Lorentz (1853–1928). Photo *c.* 1925. Museum Boerhaave, Leiden 85
5.1 'The Museum of Ferrante Imperato', from Ferrante Imperato, *Dell' historia naturale di Ferrante Imperato Napolitano libri XXVIII* (Naples 1599). Royal Library, The Hague 92
5.2 Illustration from Levinus Vincent, *Wondertooneel der Nature* (Amsterdam 1706). Allard Pierson, Amsterdam 95
5.3 Drawers of a wooden cabinet, from Levinus Vincent, *Wondertooneel der Nature* (Amsterdam 1706). Allard Pierson, Amsterdam 96
5.4 Gerrit Rademaker, *The Cabinet of Levinus Vincent in Amsterdam*, *c.* 1680–1709. Rijksmuseum, Amsterdam 98
5.5 Collector's cabinet with a miniature pharmacy, *c.* 1720. Rijksmuseum, Amsterdam 99
5.6 One of the drawers of the collector's cabinet (figure 5.5), containing minerals and petrified materials. Rijksmuseum, Amsterdam 100

5.7	Leendert Viervant, *Longitudinal section and ground plan of the Oval Room*: final design, signed 'Viervant' lower right, undated (1779?). Teyler's Museum 103
6.1	The Oval Room of Teyler's Museum, opened in 1784. In the centre is the 1802 display case, with rocks and minerals. Photo 2011 110
6.2	Label with the writing of Johannes le Francq van Berkhey (1729–1812) concerning a piece of malachite that reached the Museum via the collection of Martinus Houttuyn (1720–1798). Teyler's Museum 114
6.3	A piece of malachite acquired via Martinus Houttuyn (1720–1798), from the collection of Johannes le Francq van Berkhey (1729–1812). Teyler's Museum 115
6.4	The same piece of malachite, illustrated as fig. 5 in Martinus Houttuyn, *Natuurlyke Historie of uitvoerige beschrijving der dieren, planten en mineralen volgens het samenstel van den Heer Linnaeus*, Amsterdam 33 (1783). Teyler's Museum 115
6.5	Label with the writing of Martinus van Marum concerning the fragment from the summit of Mont Blanc collected by Horace-Bénédict de Saussure (1740–1799) and acquired by Van Marum in 1802 from his son Théodore de Saussure (1767–1845). Teyler's Museum 117
6.6	Fragment chipped from the summit of Mont Blanc in 1787 by Horace-Bénédict de Saussure (1740–1799), acquired in 1802 from his son Théodore de Saussure (1767–1845). Teyler's Museum 117
6.7	Five of a set of 597 models of crystals by René Just Haüy, ordered between 1802 and 1804 by Martinus van Marum. Teyler's Museum 120
6.8	Label with the writing of Martinus van Marum (1750–1837). Teyler's Museum 123
6.9	Label with the writing of Barthélemy Faujas de Saint-Fond (1741–1819). Teyler's Museum 124
6.10	Wooden box with tin ores from Malacca, a gift from Cornelis Matthieu Radermacher to Martinus Houttuyn, acquired after Houttuyn's death in 1798 by Martinus van Marum. Teyler's Museum 124
6.11	Label of 'Schaalstein', no. 13 in the 'Suitensammlung' of 120 rocks and minerals from the Heidelberger Mineralien Comptoir, assembled in 1826 by Karl Cäsar von Leonhard, bought by Van Marum in 1828. Teyler's Museum 126
7.1	Wybrand Hendriks, *Self portrait*, 1807. Rijksmuseum Twenthe, Enschede (on loan from Frans Hals Museum, Haarlem) 132
7.2	Wybrand Hendriks, *The Wonder Tree on the Spanjaardslaan in the Haarlemmerhout, Haarlem*, 1819. Noord-Hollands Archief, Haarlem 134
7.3	Wybrand Hendriks and Elias van Varelen, *The Wonder Tree on the Spanjaardslaan in the Haarlemmerhout, Haarlem*, 1819. Noord-Hollands Archief, Haarlem 134

ILLUSTRATIONS

7.4 Wybrand Hendriks, *Path through the Village of Manen near Ede*, 1783. Rijksmuseum, Amsterdam 135

7.5 Wybrand Hendriks and H. Schwegman, the mosasaur fossil, 1790, in *Verhandelingen van Teyler's Tweede Genootschap* 8 (1790) 140

7.6 Wybrand Hendriks and Barent de Bakker, *Large electrostatic generator: situational view of the Oval Room*, 1787. Teyler's Museum 142

7.7 Wybrand Hendriks and Barent de Bakker, *Apparatus for the production of carbon dioxide*, 1798, in *Verhandelingen van Teyler's Tweede Genootschap* 10 (1798) 142

7.8 C. H. Koning, *Large electric spark*, 1787, in *Verhandelingen van Teyler's Tweede Genootschap* 8 (1790) 143

7.9 J. Basire and Michael Angelo Rooker, *A View of the Apparatus and part of the Great Cylinder in the Pantheon*, 1778, in *Philosophical Transactions of the Royal Society of London* 68 (1778) 149

8.1 Claude Lorrain (*c.* 1600–1682), *View in Rome, c.* 1630–35. Teyler's Museum 170

8.2 Hendrick Goltzius, *Portrait of Giovanni da Bologna*, 1591. Teyler's Museum 171

8.3 Jakob-Ferdinand Voet (1639–*c.* 1700), *Portrait of Livio Odescalchi*, 1676–77. The Walters Art Museum, Baltimore, Maryland 171

8.4 Michelangelo Buonarroti (1475–1564), *Figure study of a walking man*, between *c.* 1527 and 1560. Teyler's Museum 173

8.5 Raphael (Raffaello Sanzio, 1483–1520), *Putto holding the Medici ring, c.* 1513–14. Teyler's Museum 174

8.6 Giovanni Battista Franco, called Il Semolei (1498–1561), *Discovery of Achilles among the daughters of Lycomedes, c.* 1545–50. Teyler's Museum 175

8.7 Wybrand Hendriks, *The chamber of the former Burgher-Society in the Golden Lion*, 1795. Noord-Hollands Archief, Haarlem 176

9.1 Wybrand Hendriks (1744–1831) after Pieter van Bloemen (1657–1720), Nicolaes Berchem (1620–1683) and Herman Saftleven (1609–1685), *Dune Landscape with Ruins,* n.d. Leiden University Library 197

9.2 Pieter van Bloemen (1657–1720), *Two Horses and an Open Carriage*, n.d. Teyler's Museum 197

9.3 Nicolaes Berchem (1620–1683), *Landscape with Shepherds near a Ruin (Brederode?), c.* 1670–83. Teyler's Museum 198

9.4 Herman Saftleven (1609–1685), *Ruins*, 1649. Teyler's Museum 198

9.5 Wybrand Hendriks, *Directors and Members of the Haarlem Drawing College Kunstmin en Vlijt*, 1799. Teyler's Museum 200

9.6 Johan Conrad Greive (1837–1891), *The First Paintings Gallery of Teyler's Museum*, 1862. Teyler's Museum 204

9.7 Postcard showing the façade of Teyler's Museum (1885), *c.* 1925. Geert-Jan Janse Collection 207

10.1	Franz Gareis, *Portrait of August Hermann Niemeyer (1754–1828)*, 1800. Franckesche Stiftungen, Halle 220
10.2	Franz Gareis, *Portrait of Agnes Wilhelmine Christiane Niemeyer, née von Köpken (1769–1847)*, 1800. Franckesche Stiftungen, Halle 220
10.3	Johann Georg Mauritius, *Das Hällische Waysenhaus* (The orphanage in Halle), 1740. Franckesche Stiftungen, Halle 222
10.4	Front view of the main building of the Orphanage, *c.* 1750. Franckesche Stiftungen, Halle 224
10.5	View into the 'Kunst- und Naturalienkammer' (Room for art and *naturalia*) of the Francke Foundations with the geocentric world system according to Tycho Brahe. Photo 2015 225
10.6	Johann August Gottlob Eberhardt, *View from the City Wall of Halle to the West, c.* 1800. Franckesche Stiftungen, Halle 225
10.7	Title page of August Hermann Niemeyer, *Beobachtungen auf einer Reise durch einen Theil von Westphalen und Holland*, Halle 1824. Franckesche Stiftungen Library, Halle 229
10.8	*Ex libris* of the library of the Franckeschen Stiftungen, pasted in Caspar Heinrich von Sierstorpff, *Bemerkungen auf einer Reise durch die Niederlande nach Paris im eilften Jahre der grossen Republik*, vol. 2, Hamburg 1804. Franckesche Stiftungen Library, Halle 234
11.1	Karl Franz Jacob Heinrich Schumann, *Portrait of Karl Philipp Moritz*, 1791. Das Gleimhaus, Halberstadt 244
11.2	Julien-Léopold Bouilly, *Portrait of Antoine-Chrysostome Quatremère de Quincy. Chevalier de St Michel, de la Légion d'honneur, élu Secrétaire perpétuel de l'Académie des Beaux-Arts en 1816*, 1820. Bibliothèque nationale de France, Paris 244
11.3	Title page of Quatremère de Quincy's *Considérations morales sur la destination des ouvrages de l'art*, 1815. Bibliothèque nationale de France, Paris 245
11.4	Gerrit Jan Michaëlis, *Landscape at Vogelenzang*, 1824. Teyler's Museum 248
11.5	Johannes Christiaan Schotel, *Storm at Sea, c.* 1825. Teyler's Museum 250
11.6	Johannes Christiaan Schotel, *Calm Water*, 1829. Teyler's Museum 250

Tables

7.1	List of Wybrand Hendriks' Scientific Images 154
9.1	Artists who signed Teyler's Visitors' Books from 1789 to 1900 208

Abbreviations

ATS   Archief Teylers Stichting (Teyler's Foundation Archive), Teyler's Museum, Haarlem

NHA   Noord-Hollands Archief, Haarlem

Notes on Contributors

Ellinoor S. Bergvelt

Ellinoor Bergvelt is a specialist on collections and museums. She is Associate Professor Emeritus of Cultural History of Europe, University of Amsterdam, and Guest Researcher at the same university. She is also Research Fellow of Dulwich Picture Gallery (London), and Associate Researcher of the RKD (Netherlands Institute for Art History, The Hague). Ellinoor Bergvelt studied Art History at the University of Amsterdam. She wrote a PhD on the nineteenth-century history of the Rijksmuseum, Amsterdam, *Pantheon der Gouden Eeuw* (Waanders, Zwolle 1998). She was co-editor of the two volumes on Dutch collecting in the seventeenth century, accompanying the exhibition *De wereld binnen handbereik* (Distant worlds made tangible; Amsterdam Historical Museum, 1992), and of the Dutch Open University volume *Kabinetten, galerijen en musea* (Waanders, Zwolle 2013³, 2005² and 1993¹). With Debora Meijers, Lieske Tibbe and Elsa van Wezel, she led *National Museums and National Identity (c. 1760–1918)*, a collaborative research project of the Huizinga Institute, Amsterdam, and the Institut für Museumsforschung der Staatliche Museen, Berlin.

Terry van Druten

Terry van Druten studied Art History and Curatorial Studies at the University of Amsterdam, after finishing at the Willem de Kooning Academy of Fine Art in Rotterdam. In 2008 he was appointed as curator of the Art Collections at Teyler's Museum, where he has been chief curator since 2019. He specializes in Dutch nineteenth-century art, resulting in exhibitions of Dutch and Russian Romantic painting (with L. A. Markina and B. Naarden, *De romantische ziel*, nai010 publishers, Rotterdam/Teylers Museum, Haarlem 2014) and Dutch watercolours (with M. van Dijk and J. Sillevis, *De aquarel. Nederlandse meesters van de negentiende eeuw*, Thoth, Bussum 2015) and others. In addition he was responsible for exhibitions about the botanical art of Pierre-Joseph Redouté (2013) and Franz and Ferdinand Bauer (2019).

Arnold Heumakers

Arnold Heumakers is a literary critic for the daily newspaper NRC *Handelsblad* and until recently taught cultural history and philosophy at the University of Amsterdam. He has published several (volumes of) essays, including (with A. Mertens and P. van Zonneveld (eds)) *Een nieuwer firmament. Hella S. Haasse in tekst en context* (Querido, Amsterdam 2006) and 'Schiller und der homo ludens – eine comedy of errors', in C. Moser, E. Moesker and J. Umlauf (eds), *Friedrich Schiller und die Niederlande* (Aisthesis, Bielefeld 2012, 137–50). His most recent publication is *De Esthetische Revolutie – hoe Verlichting en Romantiek de Kunst uitvonden* (Boom, Amsterdam 2015).

Eric Jorink

Eric Jorink is Teyler Professor of 'Enlightenment and religion' at Leiden University and researcher at the Huygens Institute for Dutch History (Royal Netherlands Academy of Arts and Science) in Amsterdam. In 2012–13 he was Andrew W. Mellon visiting professor at the Courtauld Institute of Art, London. His publications include *Reading the Book of Nature in the Dutch Golden Age, 1575–1715* (Brill, Leiden 2010), and with B. Ramakers (eds), *Art and Science in the Early Modern Netherlands* (*Netherlands Yearbook for History of Art*, 61; WBooks, Zwolle 2011).

Paul Knolle

Paul Knolle is Curator of Fine Arts and Head of Collections at the Rijksmuseum Twenthe, Enschede, since 1997. Previously he was a lecturer and researcher in Art History at Utrecht University. He has published extensively on eighteenth-century Dutch art theory and art education in an international perspective, e.g. ' "Edele eenvoudigheid". De waardering voor klassieke kunst bij Nederlandse kunsttheoretici, 1750–1800', in F. Grijzenhout and C. van Tuyll van Serooskerken (eds), *Edele Eenvoud. Neo-classicisme in Nederland 1765–1800* (Waanders, Zwolle 1989, 33–43), and ' "The most amusing studies": Thomas Rowlandson en Nederland', *Leids kunsthistorisch jaarboek* 12 (2002), 177–204. He has curated several exhibitions on eighteenth-century Dutch artists in the Rijksmuseum Twenthe, including *Cornelis Troost: Works from the Collection of the Koninklijk Oudheidkundig Genootschap* (2008–9), *Nicolaas Verkolje (1673–1746): The Velvet Touch* (2011), and *At last! De Lairesse* (2016–17).

Debora J. Meijers

Debora Meijers' field of expertise is the history of collecting, ordering and presenting of objects of art and nature, especially in the eighteenth and nineteenth centuries. Her publications include *Kunst als Natur. Die Habsburger Gemäldegalerie um 1780* (Skira, Milan 1995), and (with R. Kistemaker and N. Kopaneva) *The Paper Museum of the Academy of Sciences in St Petersburg, c. 1725–60* (Edita, Amsterdam 2005), and 'Magnets, minerals and books for Teyler's Museum. Martinus van Marum's Russian aspirations in the period c. 1800', *Journal of the History of Collections* 29/2 (2017), 291–308. She was winner of the gold medal of the 1995 Teyler prize competition, and since 2006 she has been a member of the Royal Netherlands Academy of Arts and Sciences. Since her retirement from the University of Amsterdam as Associate Professor of Art History in 2012 she has been active as a Guest Researcher.

Wijnand W. Mijnhardt

Wijnand W. Mijnhardt held a personal Chair of Comparative History of Sciences until 2019 and is founder and past director of the Descartes Centre for the History and Philosophy of Sciences at Utrecht University. He was a member of the Institute for Advanced Studies at Princeton and in 2006–7 a Senior Research Fellow at the Getty Research Institute. From 2001 to 2005 he was a visiting professor of Dutch intellectual history at UCLA. At present he co-directs an international research programme entitled *The Global Knowledge Society (1450–1800)*. In the 1970s Mijnhardt was one of the first to subject Teyler's rich archives to historical research, resulting in *Tot Heil van 't Menschdom. Culturele genootschappen in Nederland, 1750–1815* (Rodopi, Amsterdam 1988). Among his more recent publications are (with L. Hunt and M. Jacob) *The Book that Changed Europe: Picart and Bernard's Religious Ceremonies of the World* (Belknap Press of Harvard University Press, Cambridge, Mass. 2010; French transl. Geneva 2016), and (with P. Brusse), *A New Template for Dutch History* (Waanders, Zwolle 2010).

Bert Sliggers

Bert Sliggers was Head of Presentation at Teyler's Museum (1988) and from 2002 to 2013 has been curator of the Palaeontology and Mineralogy Collection. He organized numerous exhibitions, often embracing themes that lie along the interface of science and art, especially those relating to the eighteenth century. In this connection he developed a particular fascination for the history of collecting: see for instance (with M. H. Besselink (eds)) *Het Verdwenen Museum. Natuurhistorische Verzamelingen 1750–1850* (V+K Publishing, Blaricum/ Teylers Museum, Haarlem 2002). After retiring in 2013 he went on to complete his PhD at Leiden University in 2017, on the provenance and function of the Palaeontology and Mineralogy Collection at Teyler's Museum: 'De verzamelwoede van Martinus van Marum (1750–1837) en de ouderdom van de aarde. Herkomst en functie van het Paleontologisch en Mineralogisch Kabinet van Teylers Museum'.

Koenraad Vos

Koenraad Vos is a PhD candidate in History of Art at the University of Cambridge, working on the display of sculpture in the Vatican Museums between 1800 and

1822. Previously he took an MPhil from the same university, graduated *cum laude* from Leiden University with a research MA in Arts & Culture, and completed his BA in History of Art at Utrecht University, where he also did a minor in aesthetics. He was editor-in-chief of the Utrecht-based student-run journal *Article* for several years. Previous publications include 'What happens when you turn twice? Where the pictorial turn meets the material turn', *The International Journal of Arts Theory and History* 11/3 (2016), 19–29.

Holger Zaunstöck

Since 2016 Holger Zaunstöck holds the staff position for research at the Francke Foundations, Halle, following his positions as curator and project manager there from 2008 to 2015. He studied history, social history and economics at the Martin-Luther-University Halle-Wittenberg (MA 1993). He obtained his doctorate in 1998 with *Sozietätslandschaft und Mitgliederstrukturen. Die mitteldeutschen Aufklärungsgesellschaften im 18. Jahrhundert* (Niemeyer, Tübingen 1999). His recent research interests comprise the history of social and educational architecture, the social and cultural history of (Halle) Pietism, national and international Pietist networking activities, and the history of collecting in its social, educational, institutional and spatial dimensions. He also manages the scholarship programme of the Francke Foundations.

PART 1

Introduction and Background

∴

CHAPTER 1

Purpose and Structure of the Book

Debora J. Meijers and Ellinoor S. Bergvelt

This volume is concerned with Teyler's Foundation, established in 1778 in the city of Haarlem in the Netherlands and still existing today. Its roots lie in the will of the Mennonite *fabrikeur*[1] of silk textiles and banker Pieter Teyler van der Hulst (1702–1778) (figure 1.1). In that, drawn up in 1756, Teyler stipulated that a foundation was to be established in his name that would use his fortune for the welfare of his less fortunate fellow citizens and for the support of theology, the sciences and the arts. To this end, his own collections were to be expanded and two *collegien* (societies) were to be set up, one for the study of theology, the other for the study of nature, poetry, history, the art of drawing, and coins and medals. Each would have six members who were appointed for life – the first six by the testator himself, their successors by the board of the Foundation on the recommendation of the sitting members. Each society would hold an international competition every year, with the five different disciplines of the latter society varied from year to year.[2]

The focus here is on the development of Teyler's Foundation into a facility for research through these two learned societies, the collections, and eventually the Museum associated with it. The charitable function, however important, will only be discussed indirectly. The book concentrates on the first decades of the Foundation's history, in particular on an episode that occurred around 1779, when immediately after its establishment the balance between the tasks of the Foundation took a slightly different turn from the one formulated by its founder. Within a few years after Pieter Teyler's death the Foundation's board decided to add an impressive extension to the founder's former home, to dispose of part of his collections instead of expanding them, and to bring together new collections in this 'Boek- en Konstzael' (Book and

---

1   In Pieter Teyler's time, a *fabrikeur* was the organizer of the production process that usually took place at home rather than in a factory. Teyler purchased raw materials and had them processed by home workers. He then sold the end product on international markets. Vogel 2006, 63–68.

2   Sliggers 2006, Bijlage (Appendix) 2: Teyler's Testament, 200. The two societies and the board, consisting of five Directors, still exist. Chapter 2 discusses the composition of the board and the societies, and the thematic range of the competitions in the first years of their existence.

© KONINKLIJKE BRILL NV, LEIDEN, 2021 | DOI:10.1163/9789004441446_002

FIGURE 1.1   Taco Jelgersma, *Portrait of Pieter Teyler van der Hulst as Collector*, c. 1760, pastel and black chalk, 535 x 419 mm.
TEYLER'S MUSEUM, V 060L

Art Room), now usually known as the 'Oval Room' – collections that were considered more appropriate to support the research activities of the two societies (figure 1.2). This key moment, which saw older scientific and collecting traditions engage (not always smoothly) with new developments in the

PURPOSE AND STRUCTURE OF THE BOOK

direction of a research institution, and a modern public museum later on, is examined by eight authors from perspectives rooted in the history of science, history of museums, and history of art, religion and philosophy respectively. The contributions thus highlight different facets of the central theme, with some going back to the early modern period, others extending to the end of the nineteenth century.

The book has grown out of an international conference in 2017, and is published to mark the occasion of the 240th anniversary of this key moment in the Foundation's history.[3]

1   Purpose and Structure of the Book

The history of Teyler's Foundation, with its two learned societies and encyclopaedic Museum, has been considered in several publications from the 1970s to the present.[4] What deserved further attention was an examination of the specific characteristics of this institution, founded by a citizen for his fellow citizens, in the context of broader questions concerning the history of the concept of 'museum', the natural sciences, religion, and the (useful and liberal) arts. Furthermore, this institution has not been considered enough in the historical context of the turbulent 1780s and 1790s, with their political and social upheavals. Another desideratum is a thorough study of the Mennonite culture in Haarlem and the place of Teyler's Foundation there. The Theological Society, in particular, has not been sufficiently investigated.[5]

The present book gratefully builds on the previous studies, but also aims to provide new insights. It focuses on the background of the decision in 1779 to build the Book and Art Room, and what that choice meant for the subsequent history of Teyler's Foundation. This question is prompted by the still relevant theory of the *Sattelzeit* (saddle period), developed by Reinhart Koselleck in the 1970s – viewing the century between 1750 and 1850 as a period of transition

---

3   The conference, 'Museums and the (loss of?) the Encyclopedic Ideal', was held on 20–22 April 2017 in Teyler's Museum. Four contributions have been added for this publication: those by Paul Knolle, Debora Meijers and Koenraad Vos.
4   Forbes/Lefebvre/Bruijn 1969–76; '*Teyler*'1978; Mijnhardt 1988; Sliggers 1996a, 1996b; Sliggers 2006; Jonge 2006; Visser 2006; Vogel 2006a and 2006b; Ibelings 2010 (Dutch edn 2009); Janse 2010 (Dutch edn 2009); Scharloo 2010 (Dutch edn 2009); Weiss 2013a, 2019; Schmidt 2016, Ch. 6, 'Space for experiment'; Sliggers 2017.
5   These last two aspects are given some consideration in the present book, especially in Chapter 2. The religious aspect is on the agenda of the Foundation's research programme.

FIGURE 1.2 The Oval Room, seen from the Library gallery. Photo 2011.

PURPOSE AND STRUCTURE OF THE BOOK

to political modernity.[6] The book concentrates on the decades before 1800 and the run-up to 1878–85, when another extension turned the building into a public museum, and also looks back to early modern traditions of science, collecting, and the long prehistory of the concept of the 'museum'. Studying the development of the Book and Art Room can be compared with the activity of Janus as the personification of History, who was able, with his two faces, to look both to the past and to the future. That history can be interpreted in different ways, depending on the direction in which the researcher is looking, is shown by the various contributions to this volume.[7]

Following an introduction to Teyler's Foundation, its two societies and the Museum (Chapters 2 and 3), the book addresses three themes in the study of this institution. The first part considers Teyler's Foundation as a case in a re-reading of the history of science. The second part examines the way in which the Foundation balanced its interest between the natural sciences and the visual arts. And while the international connections of the institution are discussed in those parts, this aspect is highlighted in the last part of the book. The emphasis there, even more than in the other parts, is on questions for further research.

2 Teyler's Foundation as a Case Study in a Re-Reading of the History of Science

Wijnand Mijnhardt, who in the 1970s was one of the first to subject Teyler's rich archives to historical research, now places the institution in a new light. His opening chapter, ' "The World we have Lost". In Praise of a Comprehensive Ideal of Science and Scholarship', refers to the title of Peter Laslett's classic book, first published in 1965.[8] Taking the history and historiography of Teyler's Foundation as an example, Mijnhardt presents a provisional outline of the development of the concepts of science, art, and technical expertise that differs from the standard textbook account of the advance of science. Instead

---

6 Brunner/Conze/Koselleck 1972–97, 'Introduction'. Koselleck's programmatic studies of semantic change in key political concepts can also shed light on the changes in meaning of concepts like 'museum' and 'public': Meijers 2020. For current critical reception of the idea of *Sattelzeit* see e.g. Olsen 2012 and https://jhiblog.org/2015/01/09/back-in-the-sattlezeit-again/ (accessed 26 March 2019).

7 See Jorink and Sliggers below with regard to the question whether Teyler's can be called the first museum in the Netherlands; see Knolle and Van Druten below regarding the usefulness of the purchase of Italian drawings in 1790.

8 Laslett 1995.

of considering that the main criterion for scientific progress is the separation of theory formation from artisanal and technical knowledge, he argues for a fundamental historicization of these concepts. On this basis, he comes to the defence of the tenets of the early modern comprehensive ideal of science and knowledge, as represented at Teyler's Foundation at the end of the eighteenth century.[9] Measured by nineteenth- or twentieth-century standards, Teyler's is often seen as backward in the development of science (conceived as theory formation), but viewed in the light of the comprehensive ideal, the institution was perfectly in tune with its time and place. Martinus van Marum (1750–1837) offers a good example of how scientific, artisanal and technical knowledge went hand in hand, certainly until the end of the eighteenth century (figure 1.3). This member of the Second Society, co-instigator of the building of the Book and Art Room and first Director and librarian of Teyler's Museum, was more a researcher engaged in practical experiments and the design and construction of the instruments they required than a specialized scientist aiming at theory formation – which is why historians sometimes value him ambivalently.[10]

In the present volume Bert Sliggers also sees Van Marum's qualities as being mainly in the field of practical experiments, but not in a pejorative sense. His chapter, 'How to Collect Minerals, Rocks and Fossils for a Museum: The International Networks of Martinus van Marum (1750–1837)', does not concentrate as is usually the case on Van Marum the physicist, whose experiments on electricity and the composition of air and water brought him into contact with celebrated scientists such as Antoine Lavoisier (1743–1794) and Alessandro Volta (1745–1827). Instead, Sliggers is concerned with Van Marum's second field of research, also highly topical at the time, that of mineralogy and paleontology. Taking him as a case study, Sliggers examines the ways in which a museum collection of minerals and fossils could be created in the period between c. 1780 and 1810. In addition, his research enabled him to place Van Marum in the contemporary debate about the age of the Earth.

Particularly interesting, in the context of this volume, is what Sliggers' research has focused on: the presence in Teyler's Museum of a collection of

---

9   The historiography of collections has also shown that scientific developments were brought about by a combination of science, art, and technical expertise. Seventeenth- and eighteenth-century cabinets of curiosities, in particular Dutch, show the importance of practice-oriented research activities by people who were not necessarily academically trained, ranging from magistrates to merchants and pharmacists, such as Nicolaes Witsen, Levinus Vincent and Albert Seba. Bergvelt/Kistemaker 1992a, 1992b; Driessen-van het Reve 2006; Driessen-van het Reve/Bleker 2017; Peters 2009.

10   For example Wiechmann/Palm 1987, 32, 220.

FIGURE 1.3
Charles Howard
Hodges, *Portrait of
Martinus van Marum*,
1826, oil on canvas,
72 x 59.5 cm.
TEYLER'S MUSEUM,
KS 1999 004

some 6,000 labels with generic names, information about origins and other facts, which were detached from the objects over time, no doubt as new insights developed into their classification. This collection of labels provides a literal demonstration of the separation, as discussed by Mijnhardt, of artisanal and technical knowledge from what would become 'pure science': the objects in the collection were stripped of their colourful history and reduced to supposedly 'neutral' set-pieces in a theoretical classification system. At the heart of Sliggers' contribution is his attempt to undo this separation: as he himself puts it, he has sought to give the collection of minerals, rocks and fossils back its voice – that is, the voice it had in Van Marum's milieu. By combining the financial records of Teyler's Foundation with the minutes of meetings held by the Directors and Teyler's Second Society, as well as Van Marum's travel journals, written records of his public lectures, correspondence and other manuscripts, Sliggers has succeeded in tracing his purchases and matching labels to objects. This has enabled him to reconstruct the international networks that Van Marum needed to build up a scientific museum collection.

While Sliggers also highlights the future-oriented nature of Van Marum's activities for Teyler's Museum, citing the definition of a museum by the International Council of Museums (ICOM),[11] Eric Jorink, referring to the same definition, concludes that this 'museum', rather than being the start of something new, did in fact maintain an older tradition of collecting. In his chapter, 'The First Museum in the Netherlands? The Establishment of Teyler's Oval Room in Historical Perspective (c. 1600–1800)', he supports this thesis by pointing, first of all, to the fluidity of the term 'museum', which was – and still is – subject to historical changes in meaning, just like the institution for which it was and is used. Moreover, many other terms could be used to refer to collections, including *thesaurus*, *theatrum*, and *studio* or *studiolo*.[12]

Jorink further substantiates his thesis by presenting a number of characteristics of collecting in the early modern age that were still associated with Teyler's in general and Van Marum in particular at the end of the eighteenth century, such as the religious foundations of the research (based on physico-theology), the related fascination with the age of the Earth, the sometimes decorative presentation of the collections, and their limited accessibility.

However, for a better understanding of the genesis of Teyler's Museum there is a need for further research into these questions of continuity and change. Although the Museum's roots are in the early modern age, from its establishment in 1779–84 (and gradually during its self-styling as a museum) it developed in the *Sattelzeit* between the early modern and modern ages, which means between (pre-)eighteenth-century encyclopaedic scientific and collecting practices and nineteenth-century specialization, theorization and museumization. Teyler's Museum needs to be seen at the interface between the older tradition of the Dutch *kunstkamers* and *rariteitenkabinetten* (cabinets of curiosities), like the one of Levinus Vincent, also a Mennonite silk manufacturer, and the modern public museum.[13] There is certainly a connection to be made with these older examples, but in 1779, when the decision to build the Book and Art Room in Haarlem was made, a type of museum had already developed throughout Europe that had a number of new features compared to the cabinets from which it had emerged. This type of museum, or rather proto-museum, was often combined with an academy of sciences and arts and gave practitioners from different fields of study the opportunity to improve the intellectual and artistic level of the state, region or city in question, as

---

11 See Chapter 6 below, p. 128, and Chapter 5 below, pp. 87–88, n. 2.

12 Findlen 1989; Lee 1997; Meijers 2013 (1st edn 1993, 2nd edn 2005). There is a need for more semantic research into these terms.

13 See Van Druten below.

PURPOSE AND STRUCTURE OF THE BOOK

well as the production of (luxury) goods, and thus its prosperity.[14] The proto-museum found its most emphatic form in larger royal or 'national' collections including the Kunstkamera in St Petersburg (new building opened in 1728), the British Museum in London (opened in 1759), and the Museum Fridericianum in Kassel (new building opened in 1777). Its principles, however, manifested themselves also in smaller private museums such as Teyler's. The fact that Teyler's Museum was 'based on a principle, not built around a pre-existing collection',[15] is an indication of this. Initially there was little to put in the new room, due to the sale of most of Pieter Teyler's collections apart from the coins and medals within a few years after his death.[16] This *tabula rasa* offered oppor-tunities for a change of course: the acquisition of instruments, minerals and fossils, Dutch and foreign master drawings, and for the library such works as the *Encyclopédie* of Diderot and d'Alembert (28 volumes), the *Description des arts et métiers* (12 volumes), and the *Philosophical Transactions* of the Royal Society in London (4 volumes).

3 **Teyler's Foundation between the Natural Sciences and the Visual Arts**

Although Pieter Teyler had not indicated that a museum should eventually be built behind his house, for him it was essential that his collections should be added to after his death, and used for the common good. As was usual at the time for collectors with encyclopaedic interests, his collections included not only natural history specimens, coins and medals and books, but also draw-ings and prints and some paintings. Between 1780 and 1838, however, hand in hand with the building of the Book and Art Room and its expansion into a semi-public museum, the character of the art collection changed, as well as its position within the collection as a whole. This was due not only to the many purchases of drawings and prints made by the then keeper of the art collection, Wybrand Hendriks (1744–1831), and his successor, Gerrit Jan Michaëlis (1775–1857), but also to the introduction of a new field of collection: the acquisition from the early 1820s of paintings by living artists. These paintings, displayed in an unused lecture room in 1829 and then in a picture gallery newly built in

---

14   Meijers 2013 (1st edn 1993, 2nd edn 2005). Dolezel 2019.
15   Eric Ebbinge, Introduction to Sliggers 1996b, 9.
16   Most of Teyler's books, paintings, drawings and prints were apparently no longer consid-ered suitable and sold, as was his modest collection of birds and insects. His collection of coins and medals was left intact. Sliggers 2006, 78–79, 82, 87.

1839, took on the character of a museum collection (figure 9.6).[17] The nature of the scientific collections also changed, especially that of the instruments and apparatus. Overtaken by technological progress, they were less useful for research purposes, and effectively became museum pieces. These two developments together meant that in the first decades of the nineteenth century the Museum became more and more attractive to a new group of visitors, 'the public'.[18]

The three chapters in the following section explore different aspects of this relationship between the natural sciences and the visual arts. Koenraad Vos focuses on a field where the two are closely interlinked, that of scientific illustration. In '"Truth-to-Nature" in the Museum? Wybrand Hendriks, Martinus van Marum and the "Reasoned Image,"' Vos considers the collaboration between the natural scientist Van Marum and the draughtsman and painter Hendriks on the production of illustrations for the former's scientific publications, and attempts to understand the visual formulas used. By making an inventory and analysing this aspect of Hendriks's œuvre for the first time,[19] Vos succeeds in relating the formal and structural qualities of the drawings to the eighteenth-century norm of 'truth-to-nature'. This concept is contrasted by the historians of science Lorraine Daston and Peter Galison to the concept of 'objectivity' that developed in the course of the nineteenth century.[20] Artists and naturalists previously did not strive for 'objectivity' but produced 'reasoned images' – that is to say, they strove to highlight aspects of the object that were representative of a general type. The shift from 'reasoned' and 'true-to-nature' to 'objective' was not limited to image formulas, but went hand in hand with a change in the relationship between the (natural) sciences and the arts. While the two fields were still bound by the earlier pursuit of 'truth-to-nature', the new norm of 'objectivity' applied to the (natural) sciences in particular. This shifting relationship between the natural sciences

---

17 This (First) Paintings Gallery of 1839 also gave the public the opportunity to view the numerous albums and portfolios of drawings and prints. A Second Paintings Gallery was added in 1893 as an extension of the first one. See Chapter 3 for the successive extensions of the Oval Room.

18 For this process, and the audience for Teyler's Museum, see Weiss 2010, Weiss 2013a, and Van Druten below. For the genesis of 'the public' as a concept in the context of collections and museums, Meijers 2016, 2020.

19 The only monograph on Hendriks considers his work as a painter of portraits, still lifes, genre scenes and landscapes, and pays little attention to his scientific images: Regteren Altena/Borssum Buisman/Bruyn Kops 1972.

20 Daston/Galison 2007.

PURPOSE AND STRUCTURE OF THE BOOK

and the visual arts deserves further investigation, with regard to the Museum's collections as well.

A special case in the visual arts is explored by Paul Knolle in 'An Asset to Art. The Purchase of Italian Drawings by Teyler's Foundation in 1790 and the Context of Art Theory in the Netherlands', where he looks in detail at the acquisition and reception of these works. The some 1,700 drawings, by masters including Raphael, Michelangelo and Guercino, have received much international attention from art historians since the end of the nineteenth century, and to this day frequently form part of exhibitions in the Netherlands and abroad. Up to now, however, there has been little research on the motives for this spectacular acquisition. Knolle considers, and rejects, the theory that the drawings were not used because around 1800 there was already more interest in 'home-grown' Dutch art. Referring to source material that has been under-used, including several competition entries for Teyler's Second Society, and to practice in drawing academies throughout the Netherlands, he shows that the purchase of the Italian drawings harmonized with the Classicist art theory that still dominated the Dutch art world until well into the first half of the nineteenth century. He concludes that they must frequently have been used as study material during drawing sessions in the Haarlem Teekencollegie Kunstmin en Vlijt (Love of Art and Diligence Drawing Society), which had close ties with Teyler's, and during gatherings for art appreciation there and in other societies,[21] certainly more often than the rare surviving documentation would suggest.

Terry van Druten, in 'Collecting and Displaying Art in Teyler's Museum, 1778–1885: The Usefulness of Drawings, Prints and Contemporary Paintings, and the Development of Public Access', gives an overall view of the motives and ideas that informed the institution's art-collecting activities. Unfortunately hardly any documentation on the subject exists, but from what has survived he traces the development from a closed private foundation, collecting art with a utilitarian and educational idea aimed at artists, to a public museum addressing a more general audience in 1885. The decision around 1820 to collect (contemporary) paintings as well is seen by Van Druten as possibly the most significant change of course for the future of Teyler's Museum since the opening of the Oval Room.

---

21   In the eighteenth century a distinctive form of social gathering developed among artists and art lovers, *kunstbeschouwingen*; at these gatherings for art appreciation drawings and prints were passed from hand to hand, and their character and artistic qualities discussed and compared.

FIGURE 1.4 Façade of the new wing of Teyler's Museum by the Austrian architect Christian Ulrich (opened in 1885) seen across the Spaarne River. Remarkable in this and many other old photographs is the lively commercial activity right in front of the stately 'Viennese'-looking museum: this was a landing place for ships with cheese, beer and other merchandise, to be transported further via the Weighhouse (far left) to the Cheese Market – a mix of trade and culture, typical of Dutch city life. The Gothic St Bavo rises in the background. Photo c. 1900.

Here study material for artists and art to be enjoyed by a wider audience went hand in hand, the latter eventually becoming dominant.

Because documentation is scarce, Van Druten is cautious in his interpretations. That applies in particular to the famous purchase of drawings in Rome, mentioned above. Though the presumed aim of this acquisition was to provide study material for artists and art lovers from Haarlem and the surrounding area, Van Druten has found hardly any evidence that the drawings were actually used in that way. He assumes that their use was hindered by the closed character of the institution, something that only really changed with the opening of the new wing in 1885 (figure 1.4).

PURPOSE AND STRUCTURE OF THE BOOK   15

4   Teyler's in an International Perspective

The final part of this book is concerned with the international dimensions of Teyler's Foundation, societies and Museum around 1800, revealing the extent to which this institution was involved in international scientific exchange and also, to a degree, artistic exchange. Evidence for the latter includes the purchase of old master drawings in Rome mentioned above, which came about thanks to the international connections of Willem Anne Lestevenon (1750–1830), a member of Teyler's Second Society, who, as a high-ranking Patriot, was discharged from his duties after the Orangist Restoration of 1787 and travelled through France and Italy afterwards.[22] For the natural sciences, it was chiefly Martinus van Marum who gave Teyler's its international aura. His *grande machine Teylerienne*, the enormous electrostatic generator built for him by the Amsterdam-based English instrument-maker John Cuthbertson (1743–1821) in 1784, made a deep impression throughout Europe and brought him a network of international contacts, not only Lavoisier and Volta but also other noted scientists including the instrument-maker George Adams (1750–1795).[23] Knowledge of Van Marum abroad was due not only to the mineralogical collecting trips that he made to Germany, Switzerland and France but first of all to the *Verhandelingen* (Transactions) of Teyler's Second Society.[24] These publications ensured the international dissemination of information about his physical experiments and facilitated his membership of numerous European academies of sciences, including those in Paris (1783), Berlin (1787) and London (1798). Van Marum also took account of the most recent international developments in the field of museums. In 1802, for instance, he visited the revolutionary Muséum d'histoire naturelle in Paris, where the mineralogist René Just Haüy (1743–1822) showed him the application of his new crystallographic classification system. Back home, Van Marum applied this new knowledge in Teyler's Museum.[25]

As a result, the Library, which was also established by Van Marum in the early 1780s, rapidly grew to be an up-to-date international research instrument, with among its impressive holdings the transactions of the most important

---

22   More research into the (international) contacts of Teyler's Society members in these politically turbulent times would be worthwhile. See Knolle (especially p. 174, n. 9) and Zaunstöck below, as well as Chapter 2.

23   For Van Marum's correspondence see Forbes/Lefebvre/Bruijn, VI, 1976.

24   *Verhandelingen, uitgegeeven door Teyler's Tweede Genootschap* (Transactions, published by Teyler's Second Society), vols 1–28 (1781–1857); new series, vols 1–19 (1873–1975).

25   See Sliggers below, and Meijers 2017.

academies of science in Europe, Russia (St Petersburg) and the United States (Philadelphia). In addition, Van Marum purchased numerous catalogues of collections and large-format botanical and zoological albums with hand-coloured plates. When a reading room was built in 1825 and public access was granted, visitors from outside the immediate Teyler circle could also benefit from it.[26]

The remit of the two Teyler societies was also pursued at both national and international levels. The competitions that they held remain a rich area for further research. Announced internationally, they drew entries from foreign scholars as well, as was customary in the large academies of science abroad.[27] In contrast to the Hollandsche Maatschappij der Wetenschappen (Holland Society of Sciences), also in Haarlem, founded in 1752, the Teyler societies did not have an international membership. This was not a major drawback, however, because from 1794 Van Marum was also secretary of the Hollandsche Maatschappij, allowing him to engage several important scientists with Haarlem.[28]

Another theme that merits further research is the foreign visitors who showed an interest in and ensured international recognition of Teyler's Foundation.[29] This is considered here by Holger Zaunstöck. In 'Visiting Haarlem: August Hermann Niemeyer, the Cabinet of Artefacts and Natural Curiosities at the Halle Orphanage, and Teyler's Museum' he draws on the account that Niemeyer, a Pietistic theologian and educationalist from Halle (currently in Saxony-Anhalt), published of the journey through the Netherlands that he made with his wife in 1806. As co-director in Halle of the Franckesche Stiftungen, the

---

26   See Jorink, and Van Druten below, p. 202, n. 34. The Library is now a treasure trove for historians of science.

27   The foreign scholars were mostly German. Dietrich Georg Kieser (since 1812 in Jena), for example, won the Second Society's gold medal in 1808 with his entry on 'L'Organisation des plantes'. It was published in abbreviated form in the *Verhandelingen* 18 (1814); Van Marum had part of the text deleted because he did not agree with Kieser's Romantic, metaphysical, approach. Kraayenga 1985.

28   For other societies in Haarlem, and for Van Marum's further positions at the Hollandsche Maatschappij, see Chapter 2. Foreign members of the Maatschappij in Van Marum's time included the chemist Claude-Louis Berthollet (1748–1822, member from 1786), the physician and anthropologist Johann Friedrich Blumenbach (1752–1840, member from 1792), and the architect and hydraulic engineer Carl Friedrich von Wiebeking (1762–1842, member from 1798).

29   For research on visitors see Janse 2010 and Weiss 2013a. The 23 visitors' books, kept from 1789 to 1947, can be consulted on the Teyler website: http://beeld.teylersmuseum.nl/digital_library/Webs-Gastenboek/Gastenboeken/Gastenboeken.html. For comparison with the Hollandsche Maatschappij and the Frans Hals Museum, both in Haarlem, see Beer 2014 and Chu 1987 respectively. See also Van Druten's Table 9.1, pp. 208–215.

PURPOSE AND STRUCTURE OF THE BOOK

Francke Foundations (founded in 1695), that included the Royal Pädagogium for children of the nobility and well-to-do citizens combined with an orphanage, Niemeyer visited Teyler's Museum and its Director. Martinus van Marum, in turn, had been to Halle in the 1780s. But while Niemeyer was impressed by the Museum in Haarlem, Van Marum had ignored the 'school town' in Halle, despite its collections being expressly open to visitors. By the time he visited Halle, two kinds of collections had been established at the Francke Foundations: on the one hand, a popular and popularizing 'Cabinet of Artefacts and Natural Curiosities', which also provided an insight into Pietism and the missionary activities of the Foundations; and on the other hand, a group of collections, including a cabinet of minerals and instruments for mathematics, physics and astronomy, intended for the education of both the students at the Royal Pädagogium and the children in the Orphanage. Collections with such purposes evidently had little appeal for Van Marum, focused as he was on communicating with colleagues and expanding the collections at Teyler's, which were geared to scientific research.

Niemeyer, for his part, did not come to Haarlem especially for Teyler's Museum. His primary objective was a meeting with Josué Teissèdre l'Ange (1771–1853), a clergyman, school reformer and member of Teyler's Second Society since 1797, who translated Niemeyer's *Grundsätze der Erziehung* (Principles of Education) into Dutch. Furthermore Niemeyer met the school reformer Adriaan van den Ende (1768–1846), also a member of Teyler's Second Society, who gave him an insight into the Dutch school system. Niemeyer characterized him as being 'at the forefront of all the national education in the Netherlands', which was no exaggeration, since Van den Ende had drafted the Education Law of 1806, which from a European perspective had made the Netherlands a very progressive country.[30]

The account of the Niemeyers' travels does shed light on various aspects of Teyler's Foundation, the societies and the Museum, especially the social ones, and consequently on Teyler's relationship with the Haarlem community – another field that holds much promise for future research.

---

30 This law governed public primary education from 1806 to 1856. Teachers had to be qualified and to obtain an education certificate. They were required to teach in a classroom. Every child in the Netherlands had to receive a good education. A distinction was made between public education, which received a subsidy from the government, and special (confessional) education. The doctrinal education, in which children had to memorize psalms and Bible texts, made way for general Christian education, which was seen as neutral. The various churches had to provide extra religious lessons. See also Zaunstöck in this volume, p. 230, n. 38.

Arnold Heumakers, the author of the last chapter, also shows that an international perspective can offer new insights. In 'The Rise of the Modern Romantic Concept of Art and the Art Museum' he considers the collection of contemporary Dutch paintings built up by Teyler's since the early 1820s in a different light than usual. It shows that the idea of visual art as classicist and utilitarian, which was predominant in Haarlem and elsewhere in the Netherlands until the mid-nineteenth century,[31] was in stark contrast to attitudes in France and Germany. Drawing on canonical publications by Abbé Jean-Baptiste Du Bos (1670–1742), Abbé Charles Batteux (1713–1780), Alexander Baumgarten (1714–1762) and Immanuel Kant (1724–1804), Heumakers shows how an aesthetic revolution took place in the course of the eighteenth century. A new concept of art emerged that expressed itself fully for the first time in the early German Romanticism of Karl Philipp Moritz (1756–1793), Friedrich Schiller (1759–1805) and others. Heumakers demonstrates a clear relationship between this new Romantic concept of art and its main characteristics, such as aesthetic autonomy and aesthetic education, and the modern art museum that developed in the early nineteenth century. He doubts whether traces of this development can be found in or around Teyler's Museum, where no such aesthetic debate seems to have taken place in relation to the collection of contemporary paintings.

Heumakers' contribution touches on the question, often raised but never satisfactorily answered, whether there was a Romantic movement in the arts in the Netherlands in the first decades of the nineteenth century. If the answer is indeed in the negative, then that prompts several questions: on what grounds are the paintings by masters alive at the time, especially in the First Paintings Gallery of Teyler's Museum, now often classified as Romantic? How were they perceived at the time? Little is yet known about the experiences of the visitors to these galleries. More research is needed, a starting point for which could be the inventory of artist-visitors included in this book (pp. 208–215).

So much for the structure of the book. Chapters 2 and 3 will outline the origin and development of Teyler's Foundation, the associated societies and the Museum, as a background for the various aspects treated in the book.

---

31   Bergvelt 1998, and Knolle below.

CHAPTER 2

Teyler's Foundation and the Two Societies: Emergence and Development up to *c.* 1800

Debora J. Meijers

Following the brief sketch of the creation of Teyler's Foundation in Chapter 1, here we examine the circumstances of its founding in greater detail – more specifically, the motivation that Pieter Teyler drew from the poor economic conditions that prevailed since the mid-eighteenth century, from the life of societies in Haarlem, and from his Mennonite faith. Then we introduce the first Directors of the Foundation, and give an impression of the two societies and their activities, especially the competitions in the Foundation's first decades. Finally we will make a closer acquaintance with the artist who had to keep the Foundation House and the collections in order.

With this overview we return to the interpretation of Pieter Teyler's aims by the executors of his will, which led not only to the building of the Book and Art Room known as the Oval Room, but also to differences of opinion regarding the purpose of this costly extension and the kind of collections that were considered appropriate for it.

•••

1   Pieter Teyler in Haarlem

Pieter Teyler van der Hulst[1] (1702–1778) came from a family that had roots in England and in Flanders, from where respectively his great-grandfather and great-grandmother had to flee at the end of the sixteenth century because of their Protestant faith. They met in Haarlem, where they joined the Mennonite Church. Their profession could not be determined, but it is certain that their son, Pieter's grandfather, was successfully active in Haarlem's textile industry. The same was true for Pieter's parents, Isaac Teyler (1669–1750) and Maria van der Hulst (d. 1721), who had started to specialize in the manufacture of silk fabrics, and then for Pieter himself and his wife, Helena Wijnands Verschaave (d. 1754).

---

1   For Pieter Teyler's ancestry and biography see Sliggers 2006, 15–45. Teyler extended his surname by adopting his mother's family name, Van der Hulst, after her early death in 1721, something that was not uncommon in families of social standing at the time. Another example is Gerrit Willem van Oosten de Bruyn, who will be discussed below as a member of Teyler's Second Society. Bunge 2003, 752.

© KONINKLIJKE BRILL NV, LEIDEN, 2021 | DOI:10.1163/9789004441446_003

In addition to the family business, Teyler inherited the family capital when his father died in 1750. The company was no longer profitable then, due to the decline of the silk industry that had already begun around 1735 as a result of competition from elsewhere.[2] In 1756, when Teyler's company finally collapsed, his banking activities (providing loans) had already become more important. This was also the time when he drew up his will, two years after the death of his wife.

The years of Pieter Teyler's life span a period of radical political, economic and social developments in the Republic. His year of birth, 1702, saw the start of the Second Stadholderless Age (1702–47), when the provinces of Holland, Zeeland, Utrecht and Overijssel chose not to accept the sovereignty of the Stadholder of Groningen and Friesland and to remain independent. This period, characterized by economic and social stagnation and even decline, ended in 1747 under the influence of the Austrian War of Succession (1740–48). In that year, panicked by the advance of the French armies in the Austrian Netherlands, the United Provinces decided to appoint Willem IV (1711–1751) as captain-general, as admiral-general of the Republic and as Stadholder of all the provinces. This considerably extended his powers compared to those of his predecessors. The expectations of the restored stadholderhood were not fulfilled, however, nor would they be under the last Stadholder, Willem V (1748–1806), who would be deposed in 1795 by the Patriot revolution.[3]

In 1778, the year of Teyler's death, the Republic was on the eve of this Patriot movement. As a Haarlem entrepreneur, he will have experienced how the tension between the Stadholder, the States, a strongly divided city administration and the citizens had increased in the preceding decades. The decline of the textile industry in particular had led to unemployment and poverty among large groups of the population. Already in the first years after the appointment of Willem IV in 1747 various Dutch cities, including Haarlem, were the scene of rioting and looting, prompted by deteriorating economic conditions and maladministration. The silk weavers were also among the groups who protested against increased taxes and lowered wages.[4]

---

2   Vogel 2006a; 2006b, 63–68, 73. In the eighteenth century Haarlem producers were mainly dependent on markets in the German states and areas around the Baltic Sea (e.g. Leipzig, Frankfurt, Danzig). There, however, they encountered competition with products from France, and also more and more from Prussia, where a protectionist policy was pursued to stimulate the local (still young) silk industry.
3   Further research into the political and social context of Pieter Teyler's life is needed.
4   Jongste 1984; *Deugd* 1995, 164–68. For the decline of the silk industry see Vogel 2006b, 63–68. The protests were not yet anti-Orange in principle; anti-Orangism developed after the arrival of Willem V in 1766, when the Dutch States and cities disagreed with the Stadholder about military decisions that would further harm industry and trade. The American War of Independence (1775–83) and the English declaration of war on the Republic (Fourth Anglo-Dutch War, 1780–84) played an important role.

Pieter Teyler's will of 1756 shows that he clearly perceived the economic, social and moral effects of this crisis. It is in this light that we should see not only the charitable duties that he gave to the Foundation but also the establishment of two *collegie*, as the societies were called in the will – the first, which was to address 'all sorts of substances and materials for the study of Truth and freedom in Christian Theology and the Civil State [*Burgerstaat*]', and the second, which was to address themes pertaining to the 'faculties and knowledge' of 'physics, poetry, history, drawing and numismatics'.[5]

With this decision, Pieter Teyler joined the international trend to found societies, more or less structured private associations where well situated citizens met on a regular basis to engage in specific types of activities.[6] If we only consider scholarly and amateur societies, at the time when Teyler made his will, in 1756, there were six such associations in Haarlem, while in 1778, the year of his death, the number had risen to around seventeen.[7] We shall return to some of them several times below. First of all, there was the Natuurkundig College (Physics Society), a society of amateurs that was founded *c.* 1737 and continued to function until *c.* 1788.[8] Next, there was the internationally

---

5   Teyler's will in Sliggers 2006, Appendix 2, 200. Weiss 2019a, 68–69. The names 'Theological Society' and 'Second Society' were established in 1778 in the respective meetings of their members, though the reduction to 'theological' does not do justice to the social and moral intentions of that society. Teyler's project differed from others of the time in that it was concerned with all these fields. In general, two mutually exclusive reactions were triggered in Haarlem by the deteriorating economic conditions: some saw the solution in more material or moral support for the poor and the needy, while others saw it in innovative developments of industry and the useful arts. Mijnhardt 1988, 316–17. Pieter Teyler saw the importance of both approaches.

6   Mijnhardt 1988, 78–79, distinguishes between three types of society. The first is scholarly, e.g. the Hollandsche Maatschappij der Wetenschappen (Holland Society of Sciences) in Haarlem, 1752; the Zeeuwsch Genootschap ter bevordering van Nuttige Kunsten en Wetenschappen (Zeeland Society of Useful Arts and Sciences) in Flushing, 1768, known since 1769 as Zeeuwsch Genootschap der Wetenschappen (Zeeland Society of Sciences); and the Utrechts (Provinciaal) Genootschap van Wetenschappen en Kunsten (Utrecht [Provincial] Society of Sciences and Arts) in Utrecht, 1773. The second type could be called amateur, or dilettante: e.g. the Natuurkundig College (Physics Society) founded in Haarlem *c.* 1737, Felix Meritis in Amsterdam, 1777, and the many societies for reading, poetry and theatre. The third type is reform-minded: e.g. the Maatschappij tot Nut van 't Algemeen (Society for the Promotion of Public Welfare), founded in Edam in 1784, with branches all over the Netherlands, including Haarlem. (For this society see also n. 17.) According to Mijnhardt 1988, 361, the two Teyler societies can be placed between the scholarly and the amateur types.

7   Jonge 1995.

8   Sliggers 1987, 68, 71–97. The earliest mention comes from the Leiden physicist Petrus van Musschenbroek (1692–1761), who praised the company in his *Beginselen der Natuurkunde* (Principles of Physics) of 1736 for the meteorological observations it had communicated to him for a number of years. This praise shows the importance given at the time to empirical research, carried out in a societal context by researchers who were not necessarily academically trained.

renowned Hollandsche Maatschappij der Wetenschappen (Holland Society of Sciences), founded in 1752.[9] A branch of this society, the Oeconomische Tak (Economic Branch), was founded in 1777, based on the example of the Society for the Encouragement of Arts, Manufacture and Commerce founded in London in 1754. The aim of the Oeconomische Tak was to reverse the economic decline by means of technical and practical improvements in the fields of trade, industry and agriculture.[10]

In addition, there was the Teekenacademie (Drawing Academy), with both artistic and economic concerns. In their petition to the City Council in 1771 its founders, who included Pieter Teyler, stated that 'in this current age of unemployment' they were planning to found, at their own expense, an academy of painting and drawing that would be suitable for the training of 'poor children, both from orphanages of all faiths and others showing spirit and skill', who would in time form a source of competent painters, draughtsmen, bricklayers, stonemasons, sculptors, structural engineers and architects.[11] In this we might see the motivation for the founding of many associations in the eighteenth century.

Furthermore, there were a number of societies in Haarlem that focused mainly on sociability, such as the theatrical Leerzaam Vermaak (Instructive Entertainment) society and the 'poetry-loving, nonsensical' society known as Democriet, founded in 1785 and 1789 respectively.[12]

2   Pieter Teyler's Motivation and His Choice of Directors

The fact that Haarlem was home to a large number of learned and amateur societies raises the question of what may have inspired Pieter Teyler to add

---

9   It is characteristic of the Republic that even the Hollandsche Maatschappij was a private initiative, in this case from a number of Haarlem regents. Only nine years after its founding did it acquire a patent from the States of Holland, giving it the status of a provincial institution. The Zeeland Society of Useful Arts and Sciences and the Utrecht (Provincial) Society of Sciences and Arts, both mentioned in n. 6 above, were founded on the example of the Hollandsche Maatschappij and had the same pattern of recognition by their respective provinces. Mijnhardt 1988, 90, 140.

10   Bierens de Haan 1952.

11   Sliggers 2006, 80. See also Mijnhardt in Chapter 4 below. The Teekenacademie was abolished in 1795 and succeeded in 1796 by the Teekencollegie Kunstmin and Vlijt – Love of Art and Diligence Drawing Society – that existed until 1826. After a split, a parallel drawing society was founded in 1821, Kunst Zij Ons Doel – That art may be our goal (NHA 3496: Kunst Zij Ons Doel (KZOD) at Haarlem, Introduction).

12   Both societies, founded by Adriaan Loosjes (see below) and others, had a Patriot signature and counted a considerable number of Mennonites among their members. See Jonge 1995, 22. For the concept of 'sociability' see Berg 1995 and especially Geerlings 2014.

TEYLER'S FOUNDATION AND THE TWO SOCIETIES

his own after his death. Some have argued that he did so because the existing societies would not accommodate him and his fellow believers. Several studies have shown, however, that Mennonites did in fact constitute a significant proportion of their memberships, and often even of their founders, which is all the more remarkable in view of the low (and falling) percentage that Mennonites made up of the population of Haarlem – from about 10 per cent at the beginning of the eighteenth century to about 4.5 per cent at the end.[13] This strong participation is demonstrable for the Natuurkundig College and the Drawing Academy. The case of the Hollandsche Maatschappij is more complicated. Although no Mennonite was elected as a member until 1788, from its founding in 1752 its directors frequently included Mennonites, from families including Kops and Barnaart. They probably qualified because they moved in the highest social circles, enjoying a lifestyle similar to that of Haarlem's regent families. Pieter Teyler, whose lifestyle was modest despite his wealth, did not belong to this category.[14]

There were two societies that Teyler was able (and willing) to join, however. In view of the above, it is significant that he did participate in the Hollandsche Maatschappij's branch the Oeconomische Tak immediately after its founding. His name features in the list of members in 1778, the year of his death (with the addition *Obiit*, Deceased).[15] A few years before that he had been one of the founders of the Drawing Academy, and also sat on its board.[16] The fact that he did not belong to the Natuurkundig College should be attributed to his lack of experience in that field, not his faith: no instruments for physics were found in his collections, as was usually the case with members of that society. The very founding in 1784 of the Maatschappij tot Nut van 't Algemeen (Society for the Promotion of Public Welfare) was due to Mennonites, and it would probably have appealed to him, but he had died by then.[17] All in all,

---

13   Jonge 1989, 11.

14   Verheus 1993, 293–95; Jonge 1995, 20, 24; Jonge 2006, 119–20; Sliggers 2006, 36.

15   *Naamlyst* 1778, 13–17. In addition to Pieter Teyler himself, two future Directors of his Foundation are listed as members: Antoni Kuits ('Mayor and Council'; see below, pp. 25–28) and Adriaan van Zeebergh ('Pensioner, Directing (*Dirigeerend*) member of the Oeconomische Tak'; see below, pp. 26–28). There were also four future members of Teyler's societies-to-be: Frederik Scheltinga, Johannes Enschedé (see below, p. 34), Martinus van Marum ('Medicinae Doctor and Lector'; see below, pp. 37–41) and Willem Anne Lestevenon ('Member of the Town Council [*Vroedschap*]'; see below, p. 36).

16   He also made 'De Hulst', the house where he lived before he moved to Damstraat 21, available for its meetings. Sliggers 2006, 42. See also Knolle in Chapter 8 below.

17   Founded in Edam in 1784 by the pastor Jan Nieuwenhuijzen and his son Martinus, it developed branches throughout the Netherlands, including one in Haarlem in 1789. This society, which is still in existence today, was founded with the aim of disseminating

we can conclude that society life in the second half of the eighteenth century provided an area for cooperation between Mennonites and members of the official Dutch Reformed Church, something that was to a certain degree also true of the two societies of Teyler's own Foundation.

This does not alter the fact, however, that Pieter Teyler's motivation for the distribution of his legacy was linked to his Mennonite faith. As shown by his will, the two societies formed part of an extensive package of financial support for his closest associates, employees, and various charitable institutions in Haarlem in general. The legator was thereby manifesting what his fellow believers had traditionally practised: charity as a conscious demonstration of unwavering faith.[18] This had become especially important since the mid-1730s, due to the economic decline. In this period of rising unemployment and poverty, among the merchants and manufacturers who had joined the wealthy echelons it was the Mennonites in particular who offered extensive support.[19] They not only provided assistance in the form of charity, but also contributed to the development of education for a wider range of social classes and the recovery of industry and manufacturing. It is in this context that we should see Teyler's founding of the two societies: the research that they were expected to conduct would create the conditions for an economic, religious (in the sense of moral or virtuous) and social revival. The resources that Teyler left for this purpose – 2 million guilders – were so generous that they proved sufficient until World War I not only for running the two societies but also for managing the Museum that later developed from the Book and Art Room, including a

---

knowledge to the impecunious through 'the improvement of the school system and the education of youth, as the main basis for the formation, improvement and civilization of the citizen'. The society also published affordable books and educational prints (figure 4.2). Mijnhardt 1988, ch. VI. For the branch in Haarlem see Helsloot 1989.

18 Visser 2006, 145: 'In Teyler's Mennonite milieu, practicing the works of mercy [...] was not just a Christian commitment, but a conscious demonstration of decisive faith, reflecting the high ideal of selfless and unconditional imitation of Christ. Thus everyday practice was seen as a demonstration of that belief: life preceded the doctrine – not vice versa.'

19 Visser 2006, 145, points to the way in which charity is anchored in the Mennonite faith (n. 18 above).Verheus 1993, 293–95, adds that a commitment to emancipation also played a role. Like all religious communities other than the Dutch Reformed Church, such as Remonstrants, Catholics and Jews, Mennonites had the status of second-class citizens. In the second half of the eighteenth century this gradually changed because their wealth (fostered by a modest lifestyle) and generosity increased their popularity in bad times. The first constitution of 1798, after the founding of the Batavian Republic in 1795, brought legal equality for all religions. Among other things, this meant that members of previously excluded denominations were allowed to hold public offices. Berg 1996; Sliggers 2006, 42; Oddens 2013, 123. That this equality sometimes looked different in practice than on paper is clear from Bloemgarten 2007 and Stikkelorum 2007.

TEYLER'S FOUNDATION AND THE TWO SOCIETIES

significant extension around 1880.[20] We shall return to this in the next chapter. For now, let us begin at the beginning, with the creation of the Foundation.

3   The Directors

The administrators of the Foundation and the members of the societies that Teyler appointed in his will were preferably, although not exclusively, Mennonite.[21] He had provided for five Directors (effectively trustees), selected from his circle of family and friends, who were tasked with administering his legacy. As a result, for years to come a team of five Directors had to administer the Foundation's capital, fulfil its charitable duties,[22] and manage the two societies. They were, and still are, assisted by a secretary, the first one being Koenraad Hovens (1737–1817), who is seen as 'het schoolvoorbeeld van de doopsgezinde patriot' (the textbook example of the Mennonite Patriot).[23]

The first board of Directors, who took office immediately after Teyler's death, consisted of Isaäc Brand (d. in or after 1782) and Willem van der Vlugt Sr (d. in or after 1807), both members of his family, and in addition Antoni Kuits (1718–1789), a member of the Haarlem magistrature, and the merchants

---

20   According to a rough estimate, 2 million guilders was equal to around €20 million in 2018. The income from the Foundation's assets amounted to 60,000 guilders a year in 1778, which in 2018 was approximately equal to €0,6 million. Sliggers 2006, 12; 'Teyler' 1978, 14; https://iisg.amsterdam/en/research/projects/hpw/calculate.php?back-link=1 (accessed 9 Nov. 2020). For the serious depreciation of Teyler's assets as a result of the First World War, see Weiss 2019a, 273–74.

21   New Directors had to be chosen preferably from 'relatives of the Lord Testator and Mennonites, if qualified, before all others' (Mijnhardt 1988, 299). This shows that Teyler considered ability to be more important than religious denomination. To illustrate Teyler's religious tolerance, Mijnhardt points to Bernard Picart, *Cérémonies et coutumes religieuses de tous les peuples du monde* (Amsterdam 1723–43, in several languages). Pieter Teyler owned this precious illustrated work in eleven parts, probably not only because of its encyclopaedic qualities but also because of the message of tolerance that it expressed: Mijnhardt 2006, 818–20. See figure 4.3. In practice, this tolerance did not extend to Catholics and Jews; they had their own organizations.

22   The charitable obligations of the Foundation included subsidies and loans to numerous institutions, and the maintenance of a 'hofje' (a housing complex) for impecunious, not exclusively Mennonite, women over seventy. In 1787 the board of Directors replaced this with a more impressive new building, designed by the architect of the Oval Room, Leendert Viervant. Visser 2006, 134; Sliggers 2006, 34. The complex is currently managed by a housing cooperative and is still inhabited by women, but regardless of age.

23   Jonge 2006, 123–24. Hovens was especially active in the second (democratic) phase of the Patriot movement, before and during the revolution of 1795. He even gave a speech in the Grote Kerk to celebrate the Batavian Revolution and became a member of the National Assembly. For the participation of Mennonites in the Patriot movement see also n. 41.

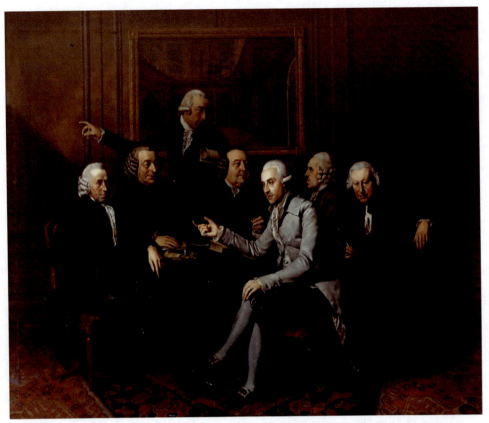

FIGURE 2.1 Wybrand Hendriks, *Group Portrait of the Board of five Directors of Teyler's Foundation, with their Secretary and the Architect Leendert Viervant*, 1786, oil on canvas, 258 x 311 cm. Seated from left to right: Willem van der Vlugt, Antoni Kuits, Gerard Hugaart, Adriaan van Zeebergh, Jan Herding(h), and the Secretary, Koenraad Hovens. Viervant, the architect of the Oval Room, is standing in the background. A painting of the Oval Room, probably by Hendriks as well (but different from the one in figure 3.2), hangs on the wall.
TEYLER'S MUSEUM, KS 282

Jacobus Barnaart Jr (1726–1780) and Gerard Hugaart Jr (d. in or after 1791). Most of them, including their secretary Koenraad Hovens, are depicted in Wybrand Hendriks' group portrait of 1786 (figure 2.1), except for Barnaart, who died in 1780, and Brand, who passed on his position to his son-in-law, Jan Herding(h) (1747–1822), around 1782. Prominently placed, in front of the table, is Adriaan van Zeebergh (1746–1824), who had replaced Barnaart.[24]

24   See Jonge 2006, 120–21; Mijnhardt 1988, 299, 305. For the preference for family members see the reference to Teyler's will in n. 21 and the case of Kuits and Van Zeebergh on p. 27 below.

TEYLER'S FOUNDATION AND THE TWO SOCIETIES

The input of Barnaart, Kuits and Van Zeebergh in particular was important for the theme that is central to this book. Jacobus Barnaart Jr was a Mennonite and a trader in piece goods (textiles).[25] His father, Jacobus Sr (1696–1762), belonged to the same generation of silk manufacturers and traders as Pieter Teyler, and like him he had grown extremely wealthy. In addition to a large library and collections of art, coins and medals and musical instruments, he had a collection of scientific instruments, including an electrostatic generator and a telescope. He and his son, who started making astronomical and meteorological observations at an early age and assembled a collection of instruments in later life, were both members of the Natuurkundig College.[26] Despite its short duration, Jacobus Barnaart Jr's role as a Director of Teyler's Foundation left indelible marks. Of particular significance was his friendship with the young physician and scientist Martinus van Marum (1750–1837). Van Marum – who we met in Chapter 1 – had moved from Groningen to Haarlem in 1776, at the age of twenty-six, attracted to the city by its scientific societies.[27] Immediately upon his arrival, two of those societies admitted him: first, in 1776, the Hollandsche Maatschappij der Wetenschappen, for which he was nominated by his tutor, the anatomist and palaeontologist Petrus Camper (1722–1789), and then the Natuurkundig College, for which he was nominated by Barnaart. In 1779 the newly established Teyler's Foundation, where Barnaart was one of the five Directors, voted Van Marum to be a member of the Second Society. In the meantime, in 1777, he had also become Director of the Hollandsche Maatschappij's cabinet of natural history (a collection consisting mainly of animal specimens).

Barnaart and Van Marum shared the ambition of using Pieter Teyler's legacy to improve the study of the natural sciences in Haarlem, especially physics and astronomy. As such they were the driving force behind the expansion of Teyler's original residence with the Book and Art Room – the Oval Room, that forms the focus of this book. Unfortunately, however, Barnaart died in 1780, and the construction of the gallery came to a stop.

Barnaart's fellow Directors had reservations about the building project. Among them was Antoni Kuits, a member of the Dutch Reformed Church,

---

25   Sliggers 1987, 88. Mijnhardt 1988, 299 calls him a broker.

26   Sliggers 1987, 87–88 (about Jacobus Barnaart Sr and Jr). For diary notes of Jacobus Jr as an eleven-year-old, see Sliggers 1987, 87–88, and http://www.egodocument.net/egodocumententot1814-2.html (no. 241).

27   Sliggers 1987, 95. For Van Marum see Forbes/Lefebvre/Bruijn 1969–76; Snelders 1980; Wiechmann/Palm 1987; Palm 1999. For a revaluation of his approach to the natural sciences, see Mijnhardt in Chapter 4 below.

who held a number of senior positions in Haarlem's City Council, including eight terms as burgomaster. Between 1757 and his death he was also one of the directors of the Hollandsche Maatschappij der Wetenschappen.[28] This dual role may have been one of the reasons why he saw other priorities for Teyler's Foundation than the construction of a new gallery. When, following Barnaart's death, a space opened up on the board of Directors in 1780, Kuits ensured that the team of five was made complete again with the addition of his son-in-law, the lawyer Adriaan van Zeebergh, Pensionary of Haarlem and a key figure in the first 'aristocratic' phase of the Patriot movement in the 1780s.[29] Initially together with Kuits Van Zeebergh tried to rein in the natural science ambitions of the Second Society, and to shift the policy towards the other research fields that had been identified by the legator and towards charity, the Foundation's other major duty. The groundwork was thereby laid for a series of conflicts with one member of the Second Society in particular, Martinus van Marum.[30] Although in 1784, when the gallery was finally completed, the board had promoted Van Marum to be Director of the incipient mineralogical and natural science collections, and had occasionally provided him with ample resources to expand these, his ambitions would encounter increasing resistance on their part.[31] It was not their intention that this 'cabinet of *liefhebberijen*', of curiosities, as the Directors continued to call the collections,[32]

---

28   Sliggers 2006, 34.

29   In the Low Countries a 'pensionary' was the leading functionary and legal adviser of a principal town's corporation. As a regent, Van Zeebergh played an important role in the Republic's attempts at administrative reform, but he was relieved of his public positions with the restoration of Stadholder Willem V in 1787. After that he devoted himself entirely to Teyler's Foundation. He was no longer involved in the second, democratic phase of the Patriot movement and the founding of the Batavian Republic in 1795. During the Kingdom of Holland (1806–10), on the other hand, he received awards from King Louis Napoleon and, after its annexation by France (1810–13), from the Emperor Napoleon. Aa 1878, 35–36. For the Patriot movement in Haarlem see Daalder 1975; in relation to Teyler's Foundation, Mijnhardt 1988, 309–11, 320–22.

30   Mijnhardt 1988 gives several examples of conflicts, *inter alia* the following: between Van Marum and Van Zeebergh, 307–8 (about Van Marum's spending pattern), 323–24, 326–29 (about Van Marum's preference for public, rather than private, lectures); between the Directors and the Second Society, 355–56 (about the Patriot movement); and within the Second Society, 306 (about the composition of the Library). There were also disagreements between Van Zeebergh and the Theological Society: 345, 349, 351 (on the assessment of several prize questions).

31   For the purchases that Van Marum was allowed to make, see Wiechmann/Touret 1987. For a reconstruction of the ups-and-downs of his career at Teyler's, Sliggers 2017 and Weiss 2019a, ch. 3.

32   By the end of the eighteenth century, *liefhebberijen* (curiosities) had come to mean a kind of collectors' items appropriate for the enthusiast or amateur, who wished to be

TEYLER'S FOUNDATION AND THE TWO SOCIETIES

should be transformed into an internationally renowned scientific institution at great expense. This point will be considered again in the context of the Second Society. Other issues, not directly connected with the Museum, played a role in the Theological Society.

4 The Theological Society

As well as the board of five Directors, Pieter Teyler appointed the first members of the two societies. He had set their number at six per society, and had determined that they should be residents of Haarlem.[33] For the Theological Society, none was a member of the Dutch Reformed Church. Teyler chose five clergymen – four Mennonites and one Remonstrant. The sixth member, also a Mennonite, was appointed by the first five and was the only non-theologian.[34] A few examples may suffice to give an impression of the company.

Among the Mennonite clergymen – or *leeraren* (teachers) as they were, and still are, known – was Klaas van der Horst. Teyler knew him because they both belonged to the Congregation of Flanders and Waterland, formed by the merging of two of the many subdivisions that had developed in the Mennonite Church over time. Van der Horst was among those who strove to overcome this state of division even further, a movement that resulted in the so-called *Vereniging* (Unification) in 1784. He became known for his sermon on that occasion, in which he called for tolerance and cooperation.[35] Pieter Teyler did not live to see the eventual unification, but given his emphasis on religious tolerance, he would have felt a sense of kinship with that ambition.[36] As early as 1735, when the Mennonite seminary was founded in Amsterdam, he had made a plea not to require the new professors to make a confession: that would only lead to dissension and conflicts.

---

introduced to, and entertained by, natural history and science. This type of collector was distinguished from the (mostly academically trained) collector-researcher who sought new discoveries and new knowledge. The present gap between amateur and expert was starting to grow in the last decades of the eighteenth century.

33 Members were appointed for life. After a death, the sitting members nominated three candidates, from whom the board made a choice. Mijnhardt 1988, 340, 344 and 354–55.

34 They were Age Wijnalda (1712–1792), Cornelis Loosjes (1723–1792), Klaas van der Horst (1731–1825), Barend Hartman van Groningen (before 1745–1806), and the Remonstrant minister Jan Verbeek (d. 1788). The sixth was Frederik Scheltinga (d. 1781). Sliggers 2006 and Jonge 2006. For Wijnalda and Van der Horst see also Verheus 1993, 114–16.

35 *Leerrede* 1784; Verheus 1993, 115–16. In addition, Van der Horst may have been an interesting candidate for Teyler due to his pursuit of the 'mathematical sciences'. See Obituary Horst 1825.

36 Mijnhardt 2006, 819: Teyler's 'mission for the Theological Society breathes the same spirit'.

Subsequent appointments to the Theological Society continued to favour Mennonites, although they did not always have to be theologians. Patriotic sympathies were no obstacle. This is illustrated by the appointment of three scions of the Loosjes family. Cornelis Loosjes (member from 1778) and his half-brother Petrus Adriaanzoon (1735–1813; member from 1788) were both Mennonite ministers; they adhered to an enlightened, tolerant version of Christianity, and showed themselves to be Patriots of a non-radical signature. The broad interpretation of their duties is shown by the monthly magazine that they founded in 1761, *Vaderlandsche Letteroefeningen* (Literary essays for the benefit of our fatherland). This instructive journal, one of the most influential in the Netherlands in the second half of the eighteenth century, drew its readers' attention to useful (also international) publications and gave them an opportunity to make their own contributions. The contents spanned a wide range of themes – just as broad, one might say, as would later be covered by the two Teyler's societies combined. The journals tended to begin with a sermon or a theological exposition. Each issue contained articles that varied, for example, from the theology of the ancient Persians and experimental physics to the fundamental principles of moral action and subjects from the belles-lettres and the arts.[37] This mix of philosophical reflections and interest in the natural sciences was typical of the Mennonites,[38] but it also drew readers from other denominations. Both Pieter Teyler and three of his future Directors read it, as shown by the readership records, written on surviving issues from the first years (1761–1762).[39]

The third descendant of this Mennonite family was Adriaan Loosjes (1761–1818, member from 1813). Rather than being a clergyman, he was a poet, writer of plays and prose, bookseller and publisher. Like his father and uncle he was socially active in the publishing world by establishing a magazine, the *Algemeene Konst- en Letterbode, Weekblad voor min en meer Geoefenden, Behelzende Berichten uit de Geleerde Wereld van alle Landen* (General

---

37 For the support of the Patriot movement by the editors: Laan 1952, 545. As they stated in the first issue, no limits were set 'to any knowledge, not even to any Civil or Religious party'. They went on to say: 'anything that can serve modestly to investigate the truth, to unfold, or to confirm, to clarify or enhance the abilities of humanity, anything that can serve to edify or amuse in a reasonable way, and thus to be useful to Religion and beneficial to the Civil State, will be pleasing to us at all times, without regard to persons'. The magazine appeared from 1761 to 1876. https://www.kb.nl/themas/boekgeschiedenis/meer-bijzondere-boeken/vaderlandsche-letteroefeningen (accessed 27 Sept. 2019).

38 Verheus 1993, 294–95.

39 The magazine was first delivered to Antoni Kuits, who passed it on to Adriaan van Zeebergh. Pieter Teyler then got it, and in turn passed it on to Jacobus Barnaart. In this way they, with a few others, constituted an informal reading society. Bosch 1999, 16–25; Sliggers 2006, 34–35. Passing on magazines and books was a common practice in the eighteenth century.

TEYLER'S FOUNDATION AND THE TWO SOCIETIES 31

messenger of art and literature, a weekly for the more or less learned, with reports from the scholarly world in all countries).[40] He was also involved in various societies, the most important being the Maatschappij tot Nut van 't Algemeen, of which he co-founded the Haarlem branch in 1784. Like his father and uncle he showed himself to be a supporter of the Patriot movement, though he was more radical. This is evident from his publications, for example his *Gedenkzuil, ter gelegenheid der vry-verklaaring van Noord-America* (Memorial column on the occasion of the declaration of independence of North America) of 1782, and also from his activities as secretary of the Burgersocieteit, a Patriot society aimed at bringing about major administrative reforms, which eventually led to the proclamation of the Batavian Republic in 1795.[41] His appointment as a member of the Theological Society in 1813, the year of the restoration, was probably due more to the anti-French and pro-Dutch attitude that he had developed during the annexation by France than to his earlier role in the Patriot movement.

5 The Competitions of the Theological Society

Both of the Teyler societies were to meet weekly, but on separate days, in what had been Teyler's house (from 1778 the Foundation House, now the Pieter Teyler House); and, as we have seen, each had to hold an annual competition. The winning entries were awarded a gold or silver medal and were published in the *Verhandelingen*, the Transactions, of the particular society. In the case of the Theological Society, the themes of the competitions, and the iconography of the medal (figures 2.2, 2.3), reflected the aim that had been formulated immediately upon its founding in 1778 – namely to address 'all manner of subjects relating to Natural and Revealed Religion, thus including treatises that are suitable for defending the Freedom of Religion and of the Civil State against

---

40   The *Algemeene Konst- en Letterbode*, founded in 1788, was more cosmopolitan than the *Vaderlandsche Letteroefeningen*, and not religious in nature. https://www.ent1815. nl/a/algemeene-konst-en-letterbode-1788–1861/ (accessed 31 Oct. 2019). The magazine also published information from the Haarlem branch of the Maatschappij tot Nut van 't Algemeen, including news about education in Haarlem by the school overseer for the district, Josué Teissèdre l'Ange – mentioned in Chapter 1 as a school reformer and member of Teyler's Second Society since 1798. For him see also Zaunstöck in Chapter 10 below.

41   Jensen 2018 (consulted 28.10.19); Daalder 1975, 220; Driedger 2007, especially 535–38, 'Radical Dutch Mennonitism in the Age of Revolution'. Visser 2006, 145 signals a certain receptivity in the Mennonite religion for the Patriot movement of the years 1780–90.

FIGURES 2.2, 2.3
Johan George Holtzhey, *Prize medal of the Theological Society, awarded in 1784 to William Laurence Brown in Utrecht*, designed in 1778, gold, d 72 mm. On the front: Freedom, with a Phrygian cap on a spear, leads naked Truth, with palm branch and scroll in one hand and a radiant globe in the other, to Religion, illuminated by light from heaven. She points invitingly to an open Bible. A broken yoke and broken shackles, symbols of prejudice and oppression, lie on the ground. There is a view of Haarlem in the background. Inscription on the front: *Waare godsdienst-kennis bloeyt door vryheyd* (True knowledge of religion flourishes through freedom).
TEYLER'S MUSEUM, TMNK 14884

all Oppression; thus, to fight persecution and to promote reasonable freedom of thought'.[42]

This aim would make the Society collide with Van Zeebergh more than once, because it assigned an important place to 'rational thinking' and rejected as 'prejudice' that this would be incompatible with 'the maintenance of the Revelation'.[43] The subject of the very first competition to be held, in 1778, was entirely in line with this. The subject was the distinguishing characteristic of Christian Revelation [the revelation of God through his incarnation in Christ] and its relation to natural and Judaic religion. The winner of the first prize, a gold medal, was Daniel Hovens (1735–1795), a Mennonite minister in Leiden and supporter of a 'reasonable religion'. His accession to the board of the

---

42 Mijnhardt 1988, 345, from Board Minutes (*Directienotulen*), ATS 5, 9 Oct. 1778. With this objective, the society responded in a more elaborate form to the assignment that Pieter Teyler had expressed in his will (see n. 5). The link in Teyler's Foundation between religion and the civil state can in turn be associated with the purpose of the *Vaderlandsche Letteroefeningen* (see n. 37).

43 Mijnhardt 1988, 345, from the programme of Teyler's Theological Society for 1783. See also n. 30.

TEYLER'S FOUNDATION AND THE TWO SOCIETIES 33

Maatschappij tot Nut van 't Algemeen, not long afterwards, points to his social involvement and pedagogical attitude. His publication of a catechism for children, written as a game of question and answer, is also evidence of the latter.[44] A silver medal was awarded to Petrus Loosjes, co-editor of the *Vaderlandsche Letteroefeningen*, as we saw above, who would be granted membership of the Theological Society a decade later when a vacancy arose.[45]

The subsequent competitions also reflected the general aim. In 1780 the Society called for a paper on 'human moral freedom', and in 1788 the subject concerned 'The founding principle of Protestantism, that every Christian of sound mind is justified and bound, in keeping with his ability, to judge for himself in matters of Religion'. Paulus van Hemert (1756–1825), a liberal reformed preacher who had switched to the Remonstrants, won the gold medal. Equally characteristic of the society's theme of freedom was the subject in 1795: 'Whether and how the civil authorities may exercise some influence in matters of Religion'.[46] This was a topical issue in the early years of the Batavian Republic, especially prior to the constitution of 1798 that finally put an end to the monopoly of the Dutch Reformed Church. However, it should not be forgotten that Pieter Teyler in his will of 1756 had charged the first society with addressing truth and freedom in Christian religion and, significantly, the civil state – already concerned with the relationship between those two entities.

On the whole, we see a coherent series of questions in the Theological Society that tie in with the theology-related ethical and social debates that were held at the time, especially among Mennonites and other religious minorities. There is no connection with the collections in the Museum, perhaps with the exception of the Library. Contrary to what one might expect, the themes addressed did not refer to, for example, physico-theology: they had more in common with the competitions held by similar organizations in the Netherlands, such as the Stolpiaansch Legaat (Stolpian Legacy) in Leiden.[47]

---

44 Zijpp 1956; Hovens 1787; *Biografisch lexicon*, III, 1988, 192–93.

45 The winning entries for this competition were published in *Verhandelingen van Teylers Godgeleerd Genootschap* 1 (1781).

46 For the prize questions of 1788 see Horst 1978, 114, and of 1795 see Vuyk 2007. Paulus van Hemert also won in 1789 (gold) and 1791 (silver). After the Mennonites, it was mainly Remonstrants who participated in Teyler's theological competitions.

47 Quay 2000, 14. The Stolpian Legacy refers to a sum of money left by Leiden merchant Jan Stolp (1698–1753) to Leiden University to award a gold medal every two years for the best essay on any subject *ter staving van de natuurlijke godsdienst of van de geopenbaarde zedenleer* (in support of natural religion or revealed [Christian] ethics). In the assessment, attention should not be paid to the religious denomination of the writer. P. P. de Quay provides an analysis of the entries to the competitions of the Stolpiaansch Legaat, Teyler's Theological Society, and the Maatschappij tot Nut van 't Algemeen. Quay 2000.

Interestingly, one of the first members of the Second Society, Gerrit Willem van Oosten de Bruyn (1727–1797), was working on an entry for the Stolpiaansch Legaat when Pieter Teyler selected him for his future institution. The treatise, which earned Van Oosten de Bruyn the gold medal in 1757, dealt with the moral merits of the Classical philosophers, demonstrating the many similarities between their ethical principles and those of the Christians. On that basis, the author concluded that these principles derive their truth directly from God; in other words, they are universal, and did not need confirmation by Christ; but, a Reformed/Walloon, he ends with a quote from Calvin, to show that in practice man cannot live without Christian revelation.[48] Pieter Teyler probably knew his friend's view of natural religion, but that was not a reason for him to assign Van Oosten de Bruyn to the Theological Society, which at the time of its foundation was intended for members of the Mennonite or at most Remonstrant churches (as demonstrated by the membership of Jan Verbeek, mentioned above). However, the case raises the question of how the relationship between the two Teyler societies functioned in practice.

6 The Second Society

There were considerable differences between the two Teyler societies from the outset in terms of membership and competitions. In both respects, the Second Society had less coherence, something that was primarily due to the fact that it spanned five fields: physics, poetry, history, drawing, and numismatics. This was not reflected in a common purpose, analogous to the Theological Society: while the iconography of the prize medal did emphasize a message of mutual cohesion, this seems to have referred more to a bygone ideal than to the reality of the 1780s and 1790s (figure 2.4, 2.5).

Furthermore, in the Second Society there was a diversity of religious convictions. Of the members appointed by Teyler himself, only two were Mennonite; the other four were Reformed or Walloon. They also varied in their professional backgrounds. There were two printers and publishers: Jan Bosch (1713–1780; Mennonite), publisher of the *Verhandelingen van de Hollandsche Maatschappij der Wetenschappen* and a member of the Natuurkundig College; and Johannes Enschedé (1708–1780; Reformed), son and partner of the founder of the famous printing house and publisher of the *Oprechte Haarlemsche Courant* (literally, the sincere, or honest, *Haarlemsche Courant*), among other

---

48   For Van Oosten de Bruyn see Mijnhardt 1988, 304–5; Bunge 2003, 753; Haar 1954. For this particular competition Quay 2000, 47.

FIGURES 2.4, 2.5

Johan George Holtzhey, *Prize medal of the Second Society, awarded in 1846 to Pieter Otto van der Chijs*, designed in 1778, silver gilt, d 73 mm. On the front: the radiant all-seeing eye, above a symbolic depiction of the five arts. From left to right, history (with books), poetry (lyre), physics (globe and compass), drawing (brush and palette) and numismatics (a medal, and tray with medals). Inscriptions: (front) *Omnes artes quae ad humanitatem pertinent*, (reverse) *habent quoddam commune vinculum* (All sciences relating to human civilization have a certain bond in common).

TEYLER'S MUSEUM, TMNK 02221

things.[49] Two other members were Jean la Clé (1738–1802; Reformed) and the above-mentioned Gerrit Willem van Oosten de Bruyn (Reformed, but Walloon after his marriage), who in 1756, the year that Teyler selected him for his future Second Society, had become city historian of Haarlem. Both held positions in public administration – something that, as noted above, was only possible for members of the official church prior to the constitution of 1798.[50] Both were Orangist, meaning that the political developments of the 1780s and 1790s led to interruptions in their public careers (as was the case for Patriots, in the opposite direction). In 1787, during the temporary restoration of Stadholder Willem V, Van Oosten de Bruyn was able to become a councillor for Haarlem City Council, and subsequently to serve two terms as burgomaster in 1789 and 1790. In 1795, however, he was stripped of his offices as a consequence of the (second) Patriot revolution.[51]

---

49 For Jan Bosch, Sliggers 1987, 89; for Johannes Enschedé, Sliggers 2006, 42.
50 See also n. 19.
51 For La Clé and Van Oosten de Bruyn, Jonge 2006, 122–25. For the Orangist colouring that the latter gave to his city history of Haarlem, see Bunge 2003, 753: 'Van Oosten de Bruyn in his history of Haarlem implicitly rejected the traditional claim of the (anti-stadholderist) States Party that the sovereignty of the States dated back to the Middle Ages'.

In addition to these Orangists, the Second Society also included a number of Patriots, such as Johannes Enschedé, mentioned above, and Willem Anne Lestevenon (1750–1830; Reformed, member from 1780).[52] Thus, aside from professional and religious differences, there were also fundamental political distinctions between the members. The 'cohabitation' between Orangists and Patriots within Teyler's Foundation could form the subject of a separate study.[53]

Aside from all the diversity, however, the first members of the Second Society shared a broad interest in the visual arts, history, and, in a number of cases, also in the natural sciences, which was expressed in the collections they had assembled. Enschedé had brought together paintings, drawings and prints, a library with incunabula, and various rarities. As well as an extensive library, Van Oosten de Bruyn had a numismatic collection and a substantial art collection, including the celebrated *Straatje* (*The Little Street*) by Vermeer (now in the Rijksmuseum, Amsterdam).[54] There was also the merchant and regent Cornelis Elout (1714–1779; Reformed), who in addition to paintings, drawings and prints also owned shells and instruments for physics, and Bernardus Vriends (1727–1791, the only Mennonite member after Bosch's death in 1780), who owned various instruments for physics including an electrostatic generator, and a planetarium. His natural history collection was even mentioned by the French writer Antoine-Joseph Dézallier d'Argenville in the latter's *Conchyliologie* (Paris 1780).[55] Pieter Teyler had selected the members of the Second Society in such a way that all fields were sufficiently covered.[56] Even when, a short while later, places became free due to deaths, they were filled in accordance with that principle. Lestevenon, for example, combined a utilitarian interest

---

52   Lestevenon played a central role in the Patriot revolution of the early 1790s and was a member of the First National Assembly (1796–97): Oddens 2012, 425. For his career, see Knolle in Chapter 8 below. See also n. 57.

53   To summarize the cases mentioned above: Patriots on the board of Directors were Antoni Kuits and Adriaan van Zeebergh, as well as the secretary, Koenraad Hovens. The Theological Society also had Patriots among its members: Cornelis and Petrus Adriaanzoon Loosjes (Adriaan Petruszoon Loosjes was not yet a member in his activist years). In the Second Society Johan Enschedé and Willem Anne Lestevenon were Patriots, in contrast to Gerrit Willem van Oosten de Bruijn and Jean le Clé who were Orangist. Martinus van Marum tried to remain more or less neutral. Among the Patriots, Kuits, Van Zeebergh and Cornelis and Petrus Loosjes can be seen as belonging to the aristocratic version, and Hovens, Enschedé and Lestevenon to the radical, democratic version that took over after 1787.

54   For its provenance (including the famous collections of Van Winter and Six, and Sir Henry Deterding who gave it to the Rijksmuseum in 1921) see RKD, no. 52501: https://rkd.nl/en/explore/images/52501; see also: http://hdl.handle.net/10934/RM0001.COLLECT.6419.

55   Dézallier 1780, 357; see also Sliggers 2006, 37, 77.

56   ibid., 35–44.

TEYLER'S FOUNDATION AND THE TWO SOCIETIES

in the natural sciences with expertise in the visual arts. After he had to leave the Netherlands in 1787, he continued to advise the Foundation's board on purchases in both fields.[57]

Not long afterwards, however, this encyclopaedic breadth would come under pressure, due to the actions of Martinus van Marum, who had been a member of the Second Society since 1779 and Director of the Museum since 1784. As we have seen, his interest was in the natural sciences, and he assembled two sorts of collections for the Museum. As early as 1782, when the new gallery was not yet complete, he started to collect minerals, rock samples and fossils, which could be used for research on the composition of the Earth's crust and the age of the Earth, themes on which he also delivered lectures to the Directors, the societies' members and other invitees.[58] In addition, he built an armamentarium for physics experiments, especially for research on electricity and the analysis of 'air' and water, topical research fields internationally at that time.[59] One milestone for Teyler's Foundation, as mentioned in Chapter 1, was the enormous electrostatic generator built for Van Marum by John Cuthbertson, an English instrument-maker based in Amsterdam, which in 1784 formed an integral part of the recently completed gallery.[60] In the following year Van Marum published his experiments in the *Verhandelingen* of Teyler's Second

57   In 1783 Lestevenon made money available for an experiment with a modern, mechanized textile factory to revive that branch of industry. The project, led by the Englishman Matthew Wilcock, was supported by the Oeconomische Tak, of which he and several other Teylerians were members: see n. 15 and Mijnhardt 1988, 304. For Lestevenon's acquisition of old master drawings for Teyler's Foundation see Knolle in Chapter 8 below. In addition, he made various proposals (not adopted) for purchases in the field of natural history from Italy, including a collection of fossils and a set of anatomical wax models by Felice Fontana (1730–1805). Forbes/Lefebvre/Bruijn 1969–76, VI, 197–219 (correspondence Van Marum–Lestevenon).

58   Unlike the Foundation's board of Directors, Van Marum was an advocate of public lectures. In addition to his practice as a medical doctor, he started his career in Haarlem in 1777 as a city lecturer, a position that existed in several cities in the Republic. His lectures at Teyler's, however, were intended for a small audience of insiders. In 1795 the board gave him temporary permission to give public lectures in the Remonstrant Church, using the Foundation's equipment. But in 1798 he was again dependent on the Museum and the limited audience selected by the Directors. This also applied to Adriaan van den Ende, who took over the lectures from Van Marum in 1804. See Wiechmann/Touret 1987, 148–49; Mijnhardt 1988, 323–24, 326–29. See also Sliggers in Chapter 6 below, and for Van den Ende Zaunstöck in Chapter 10 below.

59   See *Verhandelingen van Teyler's Tweede Genootschap* 10 (1798), on the theories of Lavoisier and Van Marum's construction of a less expensive version of a 'gazometer', a device with which the composition of water could be determined. https://adcs.home.xs4all.nl/varia/hmw/teyler.html (accessed 2 Jan. 2020).

60   The wooden base of the machine was provided by Leendert Viervant, with the same decorations that he had given to the room (figure 7.6).

Society in Dutch and French, with a sequel in 1787, which brought international renown to him and Teyler's Foundation.[61] Following the example of his tutor Petrus Camper in the field of palaeontology, Van Marum also built up an international network of contacts in his research fields (see also Chapter 1).

With the exception of the plants on his country estate, Van Marum did not have any collections of his own. Unlike the other members of the Second Society, he assembled and managed collections in the service of an institution, a practice that had been customary for centuries at princely courts. It was the procedure not only at Teyler's but also at the Hollandsche Maatschappij der Wetenschappen, where Van Marum had been head of the *naturalia* collection since 1777.[62] In parallel with his growing influence at the Hollandsche Maatschappij, which culminated in his appointment in 1793 as secretary, giving him authority on the competitions and foreign correspondence, he also made increasing demands at Teyler's. His approach did not reflect the original vision of sociability, so characteristic of citizens' societies, with its focus on cooperation between the members with their different capacities. Under his influence there was a profound shift in the emphasis of the range of fields in the Second Society: of the ten new members admitted between 1790 and 1815, seven were chiefly interested in the natural sciences.[63] As we shall see, Van Marum also forced a similar shift in the competitions. Viewed in this light, the purchase in 1790 of the first-class collection of old master drawings, proposed by Willem Anne Lestevenon in Rome and approved by Van Zeebergh on behalf of the other Directors, could almost be seen as a countermove on their part.[64] Thus, in addition to the tension between the natural sciences and charity, yet another tension emerged in the objectives of Teyler's Foundation – between the natural sciences and the visual arts. It became increasingly clear that the Museum served a different purpose for the

---

61   Marum 1785 and Marum 1787.

62   Van Marum had free residence in the building on Grote Houtstraat where the Hollandsche Maatschappij was based from 1777 to 1841, right below the natural history cabinet, so that was sometimes thought to be his own collection. See Zaunstöck in Chapter 10 below, pp. 232–233, n. 48.

63   Mijnhardt 1988, 353–54, also for the selection procedure of the new members.

64   The purchase was made not in consultation with the Second Society but directly by the board, in the person of Van Zeebergh, who had begun to play the leading role in 1788/89 (but would not become official chairman until 1807). He was advised by the keeper of the Museum's collection of prints and drawings, Wybrand Hendriks. Van Zeebergh was a supporter of the traditional encyclopaedic cultural idea in which the visual arts occupied an important place, even if they were only accessible to the Directors, the members of the two societies, and invited guests. Mijnhardt 1988, 312, 330–31, and Knolle in Chapter 8 below.

TEYLER'S FOUNDATION AND THE TWO SOCIETIES

Directors. Unlike Van Marum, they cherished a cultural ideal characterized by an encyclopaedic range of interests and broad knowledge. In addition to the other areas prescribed by the founder, their agenda included the promotion of the natural sciences, but that was based primarily on physico-theological considerations: knowledge of nature would reinforce belief in the omnipotence of the Creator. Although Van Marum also drew on such arguments, especially in his requests for money from the Directors, something else was heard in his lectures. There (in lectures on geological matters) he dared to assume the existence of rational beings before Adam,[65] or (in those on physical subjects) gave primacy to utilitarian considerations. His experiments with the electrostatic generator often revolved around potential medical applications, for example, and his research into the qualities of 'air' led to the construction of a ventilation system for ships and improved aid for people rescued from drowning. Van Marum showed no interest in the other fields of the Second Society.[66]

7   The Competitions of the Second Society

Like the membership, the Second Society's competitions followed a different pattern from that of the Theological Society, and the fact that five fields were combined is likely to have played a role in this as well. In accordance with Teyler's will, these were considered annually on an alternating basis (initially, at least). It is striking that the questions do not always appear to have been linked to particular debates, and they were sometimes formulated so briefly that the motivation behind them is not immediately clear. In 1787, when it was the turn of numismatics, the request (probably proposed by Van Oosten de Bruyn) was simply for an inventory: 'The coins of this country minted since 1579'. But was this task, tantamount to a history of the Republic told in coins, an implicit reference to the political circumstances of the day? After all, the year 1579 (the Union of Utrecht) marked an important stage in the founding of the Republic of the Seven United Provinces (1588), while in 1787, the year of the competition, that history was on the verge of taking a dramatic turn, until the battle between the Patriots and the Orangists was decided at the last minute

---

65   Sliggers in Chapter 6 below, pp. 127–128, n. 35, refers to Van Marum's interest in the theory of Isaac La Peyrère (*Prae-Adamitae*, 1655). Weiss 2019a, 165, maintains the thesis that Van Marum was a convinced adherent of physico-theology.

66   For differences in scientific approach between Van Marum and the Directors see Theunissen 1987, 19–20; Mijnhardt 1988, 307–8; Weiss 2019a, 155–72.

to the advantage of the latter, and Stadholder Willem V was restored to power. Much more explicit was the topicality of the question for history in 1800: 'The defining features of the eighteenth century with respect to enlightenment and morality, compared to the previous century'.[67]

It was Van Marum who formulated the physics questions. He had himself participated in the first competition in 1778, shortly before he became a member. The call at that time was for a paper on 'phlogisticated and dephlogisticated airs', a theme that revolved around the causes of combustion phenomena and the essential role that 'air' played in this.[68] The subsequent topics also revealed Van Marum's influence, such as 'The general changes undergone by the surface of the Earth, and the age of our planet Earth' (physics, 1783).[69] One physics competition set by the Second Society, however, distinguished itself with its explicitly physico-theological character. In 1801, the call read: 'To be demonstrated, in examples drawn from Physics, that a wise and serious consideration of the nature of things known to us is convincing proof of the Creator's existence and His perfection'.[70] As none of the other physics prize contests had religious foundations, the question arises as to whether this theme was devised by a member other than Van Marum, or whether he had formulated the question in order to ingratiate himself with the board of Directors, with its physico-theological bent. After all, in the same period Van Marum was also attempting to shift the emphasis of the competitions towards themes in physics, the same

---

67   For the competitions of the Second Society see Hoorn 1989, 1990, 1991; Meer 1992; Weringh 1992; Velde 1995. The award-winning entry by Jan Brouwer was published in the *Verhandelingen van Teyler's Tweede Genootschap* 14 (1805). For the contests with historical themes, see Porte 2019, ch. 2. Brouwer, pastor of the Mennonite Congregation in Leeuwarden and member of the Zeeland Society of Useful Arts and Sciences, had also won several medals from the Theological Society: in 1793 (silver), 1794 (gold), 1796 (gold) and 1799 (silver).

68   For Van Marum and the phlogiston theory, see Snelders 1987, 164–68. The older theory by the German doctor and chemist Georg Ernst Stahl (1659–1734), which explained incineration by the presence in every combustible substance of a flammable principle, 'phlogiston', which is released during incineration, was under discussion internationally in the second half of the eighteenth century. It was recognized that 'air' was needed for combustion and assumed that this air absorbed the phlogiston and thereby changed to 'phlogisticated air' (nitrogen).

69   The award-winning entry by François-Xavier (de) Burtin, medical doctor and mineralogist from Brussels, was published in the *Verhandelingen van Teyler's Tweede Genootschap*: Burtin 1790. See also Jorink in Chapter 5 below, p. 105; Boom 2018. Burtin also took part in the drawing/painting competition of 1806 (see below, n. 72).

70   This physico-theological theme attracted a record number of entries, twenty-four, but none was rewarded. Mijnhardt 1988, 359–60. The Theological Society competitions did not include any questions related to the natural sciences.

TEYLER'S FOUNDATION AND THE TWO SOCIETIES   41

shift that he had achieved in the recommendations for new members, as we saw above. In 1796, and again in 1801, the Second Society (read: Van Marum) requested permission from the Directors 'to be spared' the competitions for numismatics and drawing/painting in those years. The request was repeated a few more times and granted, with the result that the alternations soon came to an end. Of the eighteen competitions between 1796 and 1815, eight related to the natural sciences, four to history, three to poetry, two to drawing/painting, and one to numismatics.[71] The encyclopaedic scheme envisaged by Pieter Teyler thus disappeared altogether – and with it, in all likelihood, the appeal of the Second Society to potential respondents. This would help to explain the small number of entries compared to those for the competitions run by the Theological Society.[72]

8   The Custodian of the Foundation House and Keeper of the Art Collections

Finally we should consider yet another important functionary: a combination of custodian of the building – variously spelt *castelein, casteleyn, casteleijn or kasteleijn* – and keeper of the art collection.[73] We met the latter role in Chapter 1. Until well into the nineteenth century it was customary for the keeper or director of a museum to live in or next to the building, and in his will

---

71   Mijnhardt 1988, 358–59. Remarkably, Van Marum had been making the same shift in the Hollandsche Maatschappij competitions since 1794: see his explanation in *Natuurkundige Verhandelingen der* [since 1795 called] *Bataafsche Maatschappij der Wetenschappen te Haarlem* 1, pt 1 (1799), iii–v.

72   On average 1.8 compared to 13.4 entries per competition. Although the response at the Second Society increased to an average of 5.4 in the period 1795–1815, this was mainly thanks to the success of the physico-theological (1801), drawing/painting (1806) and numismatics (1797) competitions. Mijnhardt 1988, 348, 357 and 360. The drawing/painting competition of 1806, won by Pieter Kikkert (gold), Adriaan van der Willigen (silver) and Jacob van Manen (Adz) (silver), is discussed by Knolle in Chapter 8 below. Kikkert 1809. The entry by François-Xavier (de) Burtin, mentioned in n. 69, did not earn him a medal, but it was published, Burtin 1809; Bergvelt 1976, 16 and 62, n. 15, and *passim*. For the drawing/painting competition of 1811, which had at least one entry but no prize, see Bergvelt 2007, 277–80. For Van der Willigen, member of the Second Society since 1812, see http://www.egodocument.net/egodocumententot1814-3.html (no. 456).

73   Vos in Chapter 7 below, p. 137, n. 12: *Instructie voor den Castelein*, ATS 5, 143–44. Vincent van der Vinne (see below, p. 42) was still called *custos* when he was appointed in 1778 and had to take care of the entire collection. When Wybrand Hendriks took office (1785–1819), he was called 'Bewooner of Casteleyn van deezen Huize' (Resident or Custodian of this House), and his task as keeper was limited to the prints and drawings.

Teyler had specified that his house should be occupied by a painter or other devotee of the arts and sciences, who would not only keep the house in good order but also care for the library and the collections of *liefhebberijen* (these must have been Teyler's cabinets with stuffed birds and insects), medals, prints and drawings. This entailed conserving the objects properly, organizing them, and recording them in a catalogue or register. He would take his orders from the Directors, and also take account of the wishes of the two societies, who needed to be able to use the collections.[74]

During the first years after the establishment of the Foundation in 1778, these were indeed the duties of this official. The first *custos* (custodian/keeper), the painter Vincent Jansz. van der Vinne (1736–1811), who resigned in 1785 following a feud with Van Marum, had made a catalogue of Pieter Teyler's collections.[75] Unfortunately this has not survived, something that is all the more regrettable because his natural history specimens and most of his books, drawings and prints were disposed of between 1779 and 1784.[76] Later researchers could reconstruct only a fragmentary picture of what the founder had possessed, and what survives today. Only his numismatic cabinet remained intact.[77]

The keeper also had to admit and guide visitors, and to keep a visitors' book.[78] We know little about the extent to which the members of the societies actually made use of the collections, or about the role that he played in this. Van Marum is the only person known to have worked regularly in the Museum, sometimes accompanied by colleagues, interested parties, and even human test subjects.[79] The commotion caused by his visits would prove to be a major factor in Van der Vinne's resignation.[80] It can be assumed that the custodian/

---

74 Sliggers 2006, Appendix 2, 199 (p. 18 of the will).

75 For Van der Vinne see http://www.egodocument.net/egodocumententot1814-2.html, no. 293.

76 Teyler did not possess any scientific apparatus or instruments. Sliggers 2006, 77–78 and Appendix 2.

77 Sliggers 2006, 75, 78, 82.

78 See Vos in Chapter 7 below.

79 He once invited two medical doctors and several individuals to the Oval Room, including his own wife and Van Oosten de Bruyn and La Clé of the Second Society, to subject them successively to positive and negative electricity. The aim was to investigate the effect on their pulse rate. It turned out to be negligible. Marum 1785, 97–103.

80 Wiechmann/Touret 1987, 151, refer to Regteren Altena/Borssum Buisman/Bruyn Kops 1972, 11. Van der Vinne had written to the Directors that he and his wife 'were tired of the difficulties of living in this house, in particular those which they had been suffering from Mr Van Marum for some time, and that they had decided to give up the position of residents rather than have so much disturbance for longer'.

keeper also gave other members access to the Foundation House and the Oval Room, opened cabinets, and brought out objects and books.

The keeper was in effect a curator of visual art, but one who simultaneously continued to work as a visual artist and had his studio next to the museum, something that remained the norm until well into the nineteenth century. At Teyler's this practice even continued until the retirement of the last *kastelein* (spelt thus from the twentieth century) in 1980.

Van der Vinne's successor, Wybrand Hendriks (1744–1831; figure 7.1), painted portraits, genre scenes and landscapes for his Haarlem-based clients, and also, in the context of the Museum, produced drawings for Van Marum to illustrate the latter's publications. His services were also called upon when making new purchases. In 1790 Van Zeebergh asked his advice on the purchase of the collection of old master drawings that Lestevenon had proposed from Rome. When the drawings eventually arrived, Hendriks was responsible for conserving them. In addition, he regularly attended auctions to buy drawings and prints (mainly Dutch). From 1821 his successor, Gerrit Jan Michaëlis (1775–1857), would add paintings by living Dutch masters.[81] When separate departments with their own curators were established in 1864, the keeper's position fell into line with those of the curators of the physical and mineralogical-palaeontological cabinets. Strikingly, though, the name *kastelein* remained in use until 1980.[82]

9 Conclusion

At this point it can be established that Pieter Teyler's project, as recorded in his will of 1756, bore witness to an ambition that was more typical of a group of regents than of an individual citizen at that time:[83] to serve the common good through the promotion of religion and moral, utilitarian scientific practice and the (useful and fine) arts. This was achieved on the one hand by assigning the usual encyclopaedic subjects of physics, poetry, history, drawing and

---

81 For these tasks see the chapters by Vos, Knolle and Van Druten below.

82 The positions of *kastelein* and curator of the art collections were separated in 1951. The art historian Iohannes Quirijn van Regteren Altena (1899–1980) was given the title of 'conservator' (curator; 1952–1973). The painter Jan Hendrik van Borssum Buisman (1919–2012) was the last to be referred to by the term *kastelein*, the position he held from 1952 to 1980. After Van Regteren Altena's retirement in 1973 the position of curator was again combined with that of *kastelein*. Van Borssum Buisman fulfilled both functions from 1973 until 1980. See 'Teyler' 1978, 129.

83 As had been the case four years earlier, in 1752, with the Hollandsche Maatschappij van Wetenschappen, albeit with a slightly different purpose and scope than Teyler's project.

numismatics to the Second Society. On the other hand, the Theological Society, based on broadly formulated religious foundations which were open to both revealed and natural religion, sought to promote 'reasonable freedom of thought' and, moreover, to defend the freedom of religion and the civil state against all domination.

It is a testimony to his vision and energy that Teyler undertook this project in his minority position as a Mennonite. But it was also precisely thanks to his religious mindset, and his social position, that he designed the Foundation in this way. Moreover, it is significant that he put the institution on a sound legal footing by making it a foundation, thus ensuring its independence from political and religious institutions.

When Teyler died in 1778, however, times had changed. From the very creation of the Foundation there was tension between charity and science, and between the natural sciences and what we would now call the humanities, not only within the board of Directors and within the societies, but also between the Directors and the individual societies. How communication proceeded between the societies, and between Mennonite theologians and predominantly Reformed entrepreneurs and regents, would be a question for further investigation.[84] To a degree the various tensions reflected contrasting concepts of science, but it was also inevitable that the political differences between Orangists and Patriots, and between aristocratic and democratic Patriots, would play a role. Because all these parties were represented at Teyler's in this period, politically charged subjects could hardly be avoided.[85]

All in all, we get the impression of a game of contrasting, sometimes even opposing, forces – a different impression from the usual image of Teyler's Foundation as an Enlightenment institution where religion, science and the arts went harmoniously hand in hand, in the interests of a clear concept of the common good. This image requires further adjustment. For the moment we can surmise that within the two Teyler's societies several sorts of 'Enlightenment' were represented, varying by type, depending on the religious and political affiliation, the age, and the professional field of the individuals involved.[86]

---

84 Mijnhardt 1988, 342. The little we know about this question concerns the procedure to assess the entries for the competitions in the Second Society. The judgment of the Directors and that of the society's members was not deemed sufficient: a general meeting had to be held in which the members of the Theological Society also cast their vote, to ensure that no atheistic entries were rewarded.

85 Mijnhardt 1988, 355, was only able to give two examples. The sources seem to preserve a careful silence on this matter.

86 See also Geerlings 2014. Based on his overview of recent research into societies, he distinguishes more than one concept of the Enlightenment.

Returning to the *Sattelzeit* concept introduced in Chapter 1, it is advisable to consider the institution in its variety of backward-looking and forward-looking, locally determined, characteristics, rather than smoothing out the contrasts by considering it simply under the concept of Enlightenment. With this in mind, the construction of the Book and Art Room and its subsequent development into a modern museum will be examined in the next chapter.

CHAPTER 3

A Museum within the Foundation, 1779–2020

Debora J. Meijers

An important aspect of Teyler's Foundation is its visibility through the Museum and its collections. Starting with a single room, which revealed itself to the visitor as a 'surprise' behind Teyler's house, the Museum developed in stages into an extensive complex that presents itself clearly in the city. The key moments in this process are summarized here in four plans, which show the situation in 1791 (figure 3.1), 1839 (figure 3.3), 1909 (figure 3.7) and 2020 (figure 3.17). In this chapter the line is continued to the present day, because Teyler's Foundation, as one of the few of its kind, has survived with its original conception and housing.

•••

1 The Oval Room as a Cuckoo's Egg?

As discussed above, within two years after the death of Pieter Teyler van der Hulst in 1778 the board of his Foundation (figure 2.1) took a further step and decided to erect a new building as an extension behind his former home. At the end of his will Teyler had given permission for the executors to interpret his provisions,[1] but this building proved controversial from the start. While its initiators, the Director Jacobus Barnaart Jr and his young friend Martinus van Marum, regarded the extension as necessary for scientific development, others saw the oval construction as a cuckoo's egg, as it were, which would consume resources that would be better spent on the Foundation's charitable works.[2]

This 'Boek- en Konstzael' (Book and Art Room), designed by the Amsterdam architect Leendert Viervant (1752–1801) in 1780, opened in 1784 to a limited circle of users and visitors associated with Teyler's Foundation (figures 1.2 and 3.1).

---

1 Sliggers 2006, Appendix 2, 201: *alles ter volkomen discretie, goedvinden en arbitrage en interpretatie van de gemelte vijf Heeren Directeuren, Administrateurs en Executeurs in den tijd zijn zullende, en zoals dezelven dat in gemoeden zullen oordeelen en vinden te behooren* (all to the utmost discretion, approval, arbitration and interpretation of the aforementioned five gentlemen Directors, Administrators and Executors, now and in the future, as they will judge it and find it appropriate).

2 For fluctuations in Teyler's Foundation's spending pattern between 1778 and 1815, under the influence of changing political and economic conditions in that turbulent period, see Mijnhardt 1988, e.g. 331–39.

© KONINKLIJKE BRILL NV, LEIDEN, 2021 | DOI:10.1163/9789004441446_004

A MUSEUM WITHIN THE FOUNDATION, 1779–2020　　　　　　　　　　　　　　　　47

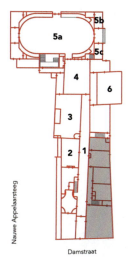

FIGURE 3.1
The Foundation House and Teyler's Museum: ground floor in 1791
Foundation House
1. Corridor, 2. 'Small Room', 3. Courtyard, 4. 'Large Room' (1778–today)
Shaded area
Living quarters of the *castelein* (1780–1980)
Museum
5a. 'Book and Art Room' or *Musaeum* (1784–today), 5b and 5c. Storage space (1784–1938),
6. Physics and chemistry laboratory used by Martinus van Marum (1791–before 1837).

Judging from its name, it was meant primarily to serve as a library and a repository for drawings and prints. It was also to be a laboratory for Van Marum's physics experiments, with the electrostatic generator (figure 3.2) installed in the same year (for his other experiments, a separate laboratory was set up elsewhere in the house: figure 3.1, no. 6).[3] On the roof of the new room there was a belvedere, intended as an observatory, but due to the wooden construction of the building it was not stable enough for that purpose (figure 3.13).

Most of Teyler's collection had been disposed of in the first years after his death, so there was initially little to be placed in the room. His cabinet of coins and medals survived, but that did not get a place in the Museum for a long time.[4] Soon the room was filled with instruments, minerals, fossils and, on the gallery, books, thanks to acquisitions by Martinus van Marum (figure 1.3), who in 1784 was appointed Director of the cabinets that were developing there. In addition, the artist and keeper of the art collection, Wybrand Hendriks (figure 7.1), ensured that

---

3　Sliggers 1996b, 90–91.
4　It remained behind closed doors until the 1870s, when it was enriched by donations and acquisitions, and moved to its present location in the Museum in 1888 (no. 8 in figure 3.7).

FIGURE 3.2 Wybrand Hendriks, *The Oval Room of Teyler's Museum with the electrostatic generator in the foreground stored in a case*, c. 1810, oil on panel, 47.7 x 62 cm.
TEYLER'S MUSEUM, KS 009

the collection of prints and drawings expanded. Due to the numerous purchases the room proved too small, not least because it also housed the large electrostatic generator, which could only be used when the long cabinet in the centre of the room was pushed aside along a rail in the floor. That the albums with prints and drawings (after 1790 probably also those from Rome) were kept in this cabinet, right next to the sparking generator, was apparently not perceived as risky.

As we saw in the previous chapter, in addition to his physics experiments Van Marum had developed a particular interest in the composition and history of the Earth's crust, which he propounded in several series of lectures. In 1824–26 the Museum (as the room was by then generally known) was extended with a fossil gallery, a lecture room and a reading room, the latter on the upper floor, connected to the library that was opened for public use in 1825.[5]

---

5 See Van Druten in Chapter 9 below, p. 201, n. 34; Sliggers 1996b, 27–28. A year later, ladies were also admitted, albeit outside opening hours: 'Teyler' 1978, 14.

A MUSEUM WITHIN THE FOUNDATION, 1779–2020

A new interest emerged in the early 1820s, marking the next turn in the institution's policy: the collecting and exhibition of paintings by living Dutch artists. Initially displayed in the lecture room, they were moved to the newly built Paintings Gallery in 1839 (figure 3.3, nos 7 and 9; figures 3.4, 9.6).[6] When the lecture room became available after the construction of the Paintings Gallery it was designated as an exhibition room for fossils and in 1886, after their removal to the next extension of the building, for drawings and prints (figure 3.3, figure 3.7, no. 7, the so-called Watercolour Gallery).[7] In the meantime the collection of paintings grew steadily, calling for the construction of the Second Paintings Gallery in 1893 (figure 3.5; figure 3.7, no. 15).

Thus about a century after the completion of the Book and Art Room an east wing had developed, where, in addition to paintings, the collection of drawings and prints had been given storage space and its own exhibition hall. Apparently it was not just a matter of providing more space, but also of establishing a department for a specific part of the collections, the visual arts.[8] The same was true of the expansion that followed, when between 1878 and 1885 a wing was created south of the Oval Room for scientific instruments and fossils; the minerals remained in the Oval Room. From then on, that room was the pivotal point between the two wings.[9] The south wing included three large galleries (figure 3.6; figure 3.7, nos 11–13), with on the upper floor a large, well-equipped Auditorium (including a laboratory bench with a sink) and an extension for the Library (figures 3.8, 3.9). From then on, the building not only reflected the specialized structure of the collections but was also aimed at a larger public. Where originally one had entered through the former home of Pieter Teyler, walking past the apartment of the *castelein* (figure 3.10), now there was an impressive new Neo-Renaissance entrance facing the Spaarne River, which must have made a remarkable addition to the buildings there (figures 1.4, 3.19, 9.7). This arrangement, with a façade by the Viennese architect Christian Ulrich (1836–

---

6 In this respect Teyler's was ahead of the Museum of Living Masters in the Pavilion Welgelegen in Haarlem, which did not show contemporary paintings from the Rijksmuseum and the Mauritshuis until 1838 (the decision to do that had, however, been taken in 1828). Bergvelt 1998, 23.

7 The lecture room was rarely used as such, since other members of the societies were less willing than Van Marum to give lectures.

8 This process was gradual. As we saw, in the 1820s space was also created on the east side for the growing collection of fossils, until that was moved to the new wing on the south side in 1884–85 (see below).

9 It may have come to be known as the 'Oval Room' after their development.

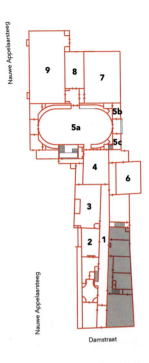

FIGURE 3.3
The Foundation House and Teyler's Museum: ground floor in 1839
Foundation House
1. Corridor, 2. 'Small Room', 3. Courtyard, 4. 'Large Room' (1778–2020)
Shaded area
Living quarters of the *castelein* (1780–1980)
Museum
5a. Oval Room (1784–today), 5b and 5c. Storage space (1784–1938), 6. Physics laboratory used by Jacob van Breda (1837–67), 7. Lecture Room (1824–29); Paintings Gallery (1829–38); Palaeontological Museum II (1839–85) / Second floor: Reading Room (1824–today), 8. Palaeontological Museum I (1839–85), 9. (First) Paintings Gallery (1839–today).

1909) and galleries by Adrianus van der Steur (1836–1899), the result of an international competition on the occasion of the Museum's first centenary, emphatically confirmed the building's status as a public museum. The inscription on the frieze of the pediment reads '1778 TEYLER'S STICHTING 1878', which just as emphatically presents the Museum as 'the building of Teyler's Foundation'.[10]

---

10 In press releases the Museum was presented as the Foundation's calling card; Jorink in Chapter 5, p. 88, n. 3, refers to *Algemeen Handelsblad*, 22 Jan. 1885. For the inscription, Ibelings 2010, 36.

FIGURE 3.4 First Paintings Gallery (1839). The interior was restored to the original colour scheme in 2014. Photo 2015.

2 Reorganization, Professionalization and Research

This architectural development was preceded by a reorganization of the Museum management that tightened its relationship to the Foundation. In 1864 the Directors of Teyler's Foundation had decided to distinguish between the Cabinet of Physics and the Palaeontological and Mineralogical Cabinet, and to appoint specialist curators for each of those departments. With that they put an end to the original situation, in which both cabinets came under one Director, Van Marum, who curated and managed this part of the Museum. After Van Marum's successor Jacob van Breda (1788–1867) retired in 1864, the Directors of the Foundation decided not to appoint a new Museum Director, and to control the general management of the Museum themselves.[11]

The division into departments and the appointment of specialist curators, characteristic of the professionalization of museums everywhere in the Western

---

11 Sliggers 1996b, 17, 21–22. The art collections (curated by the keeper) had been under the management of the Directors from the outset. The two specialist curators appointed in 1864 were Tiberius C. Winkler (1822–1897) for the Palaeontological and Mineralogical Cabinet and Volkert S. M. van der Willigen (1822–1878) for the Cabinet of Physics. For both see Weiss 2019a, 246–49, 259–72.

FIGURE 3.5 Second Paintings Gallery (1893). The interior was restored to the original colour scheme in 2013. Photo 2015.

FIGURE 3.6 Second Fossil Room (1885). In the distance is the door leading to the Instrument Room. Photo 2015.

A MUSEUM WITHIN THE FOUNDATION, 1779–2020

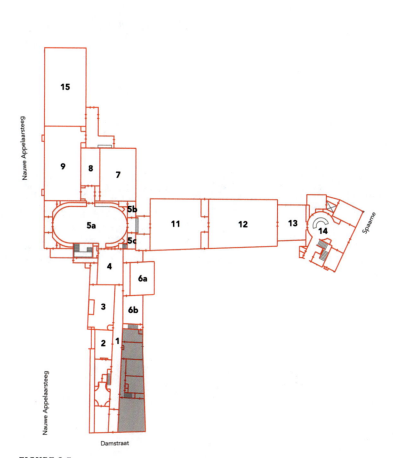

FIGURE 3.7
The Foundation House and Teyler's Museum: ground floor in 1909
Foundation House
1. Corridor, 2. 'Small Room', 3. Courtyard, 4. 'Large Room' (1778–2020)
Shaded area
Living quarters of the *castelein* (1780–1980)
Museum
5a. Oval Room, with Library at gallery level and Observatory on the roof (1784–today), 5b and 5c. Storage space (1784–1938), 6a and 6b. Physics laboratory used by Elisa van der Ven (1878–1909) and Hendrik Lorentz (1909–28), 7. Watercolour Gallery (1886–1911) / Second floor: Reading Room (1824–today), 8. Coins and Medals Cabinet (1888–today), 9. First Paintings Gallery (1839–today), 10. Observatory and laboratory used by Volkert van der Willigen (1864–78), 11. Instrument Room / Second floor: extension of the Library (1885–today), 12. Second Fossil Room / Second floor: Auditorium (1885–today), 13. First Fossil Room / Second floor: Lobby/Reception Room (1885–today), 14. Spaarne entrance (1885–today), 15. Second Paintings Gallery (1893–today).

FIGURE 3.8 The Auditorium (1885). Photo 2011.

FIGURE 3.9 The extension of the Library (1885). Photo 2011.

A MUSEUM WITHIN THE FOUNDATION, 1779–2020

world around 1850, was followed by the publication of extensive catalogues of the respective collections and articles in international scientific journals.[12] These mostly French-language publications created even more 'brand awareness' for the institution. Where scientific research was concerned, the Foundation enjoyed a boom around 1900, despite its sharply decreasing financial resources. An important milestone was reached during the service of Hendrik Jacobus Scholten (1824–1907), curator of the Art Department between 1872 and 1907. In that period, the now world-famous old master drawings purchased in Rome in 1790 were rescued from oblivion when German art historians 'rediscovered' them.[13] Furthermore, the palaeontologist Eugène Dubois (1858–1940), known for his quest for the 'upright ape-man', the *Pithecanthropus erectus*, became curator of the Palaeontological and Mineralogical Cabinet in 1898 (until 1928), a few years after his sensational (and for some: controversial) discovery of this missing link in human evolution on the island of Java. But above all, in 1909 the Foundation succeeded in appointing the Nobel Prize-winner Hendrik Antoon Lorentz (1853–1928; figure 4.8), as curator of the Cabinet of Physics.[14] A Teyler Chair was created at Leiden University in 1928 for him, but he died before he could occupy it. After the 1920s, however, there was little possibility for further development: the consequences of the First World War and the Russian Revolution caused financial loss,[15] and changes in the field of physics in particular now required facilities that Teyler's was unable to provide.

---

12 In addition to many popularizing articles, Winkler published *Musée Teyler: catalogue systématique de la collection paléontologique*, 6 vols, Haarlem 1863–67; 5 suppls 1868–96. Van der Willigen, on the other hand, was not concerned with cataloguing, but published in international journals, including the *Archives du Musée Teyler*, founded in 1866. A few decades later the first catalogue of the drawings collection followed, by the keeper Hendrik J. Scholten: *Musée Teyler à Haarlem. Catalogue raisonné des dessins des écoles française et hollandaise*, Haarlem 1904.

13 See Knolle in Chapter 8 below pp. 180–181, n. 33. The German art historians August Schmarsow, Adolf Bayersdorfer, Heinrich Brockhaus and Paul Schumann were in Amsterdam on the occasion of the fifth international art-historical congress in 1898. They visited Teyler's Museum and signed the visitors' book. Janse 2010, 14, 24.

14 For Dubois, Theunissen 1985, Shipman 2001. For Lorentz and his position at Teyler's, Weiss 2019a, ch. 5, and Weiss 2019b. A creative reconstruction of the laboratory that Lorentz had used was opened to the public in 2017, (see below).

15 Weiss 2019a, 274, mentions a number of factors. The Russian Revolution made Russian state bonds, of which Teyler's Foundation held many, worthless overnight. New taxes were levied. The German economy collapsed with hyperinflation in 1923.

FIGURE 3.10 The Pieter Teyler House, formerly the Foundation House, Damstraat 21 (the tall sand-coloured building), early seventeenth century, thoroughly remodelled in 1715. The neighbouring house to the right was until 1980 part of the living quarters of the *castelein* (by then *kastelein*). Photo 2011.

FIGURE 3.11 The Exhibition Room in the extension by Bureau Henket, interior design by Marijke van der Wijst (1990–96). Seen here is the opening exhibition, with paintings by Giorgio Morandi. Photo 1996.

FIGURE 3.12 Aerial view of the entire complex. It forms a capital T, with the Oval Room at the point where the two axes meet. To the left and right of that in the 'arms' are the Foundation House (at the extreme left of the picture) and the two Painting Galleries on the right. The long extension of 1885 with its façade on the River Spaarne forms the leg of the T. The 1990s extension is between the trees. Photo 2014.

3   A Museum of a Museum

In the 1970s and 1980s there was yet another radical reorientation, one that was also expressed in architectural form. But before that Teyler's Foundation went through another deep valley. The most critical period in its existence began after 1945, the board recalled on its two-hundredth anniversary in 1978, continuing with the warning that at the time of writing the very existence of the Foundation was in danger.[16] As a solution, a fundamental change was realized in the relationship between Teyler's Foundation and the Museum in 1981. A separate foundation was created for the management and maintenance of the Museum, so that from then on it was eligible for a subsidy from the central government.[17] In 1983 the Museum got its own Director again, in

---

16   'Teyler' 1978, 15.
17   Janse 2010, 28. The two foundations are linked by a covenant. Teyler's Foundation remains the owner of the complex, and has lent the building and the collections to the new Foundation. See the UNESCO Nomination File, in *Teylers in Haarlem* 2012, vol. 1, 137, and the corresponding Management Plan, ibid., vol. 2, 31–32.

FIGURE 3.13 The café (Bureau Henket 1990), with a view of the Observatory (Leendert Viervant 1779–80) through the skylight. Works by Haarlem schoolchildren relating to the exhibition of the moment are regularly displayed here. Photo 2019.

FIGURE 3.14 An example of the transparent connection between the new wing by Bureau Henket (1990) and the existing building by Adriaan van der Steur (1880–85). Photo 1996.

FIGURE 3.15 The Lorentz Lab, a free reconstruction in 2017 of the laboratory of the physicist Hendrik Antoon Lorentz, where visitors can follow a theatrical tour. Photo 2017.

the person of Eric Ebbinge.[18] Not entirely coincidentally, this was also the period when new perspectives opened up under the influence of growing academic interest in the history of learned societies and museums.[19] That Teyler's Museum is now one of the world's few institutions to display its collections in the original building and interiors, dating from 1784–1893, is thanks to the fact that it was one of the first museums in the Netherlands to join this trend and start to engage with its own history. On the other hand, that the building and its interiors have survived unchanged can also be attributed to the fact that they were managed by a private institution, which, moreover, did not have the financial means to keep up with developments in the museum world of the twentieth century.

The organizational and ideological reorientation after 1978 was expressed in another extension, this time with rooms to support the increasingly public function of the Museum: a gallery for temporary exhibitions (figure 3.11), rooms for educational activities, a café, and a shop, designed in 1990 and opened in

---

18 The previous directors, Van Marum and Van Breda, were only in charge of the natural science collections. Ebbinge held the directorship until 2001. He was succeeded by Marjan Scharloo.

19 Among others Mijnhardt 1978 and 1988; Impey/MacGregor 1985 (proceedings of the 1983 conference); Pomian 1987 (collection of essays, several of them first published in the 1970s).

FIGURE 3.16 The copy of Martinus van Marum's electrostatic generator made in 2016–17, placed in a 'Faraday cage' to protect bystanders. Photo 2017.

phases between 1993 and 2001.[20] This extension was thoughtfully designed by the architect Hubert-Jan Henket (again in response to an international competition) to maintain some distance, both physically and conceptually, from the existing building. Instead of being detrimental, it elevated the original building into a 'museum of a museum', breathing new life into the institution for the future (figures 3.12–3.14).[21] As a result, to this day Teyler's is not only a unique historical monument but also a living one.

A further project, the creative reconstruction of Hendrik Lorentz's laboratory (figures 3.15, 3.17, nos 6a, 6b), led to a new form of historical experience in 2017: with the use of actors to demonstrate Lorentz's discoveries to a wide

---

20 An adjoining property, the Zegelwaarden building, was purchased and renovated for offices, workshops and storage.
21 The architect had been involved with new developments in museums since the 1970s, when the destruction of historic interiors was gradually declared taboo and (parts of) the original architecture and layout were exposed or reconstructed. For a representative overview of his projects, including Teyler's, see Henket 2013. The interior was designed by Marijke van der Wijst.

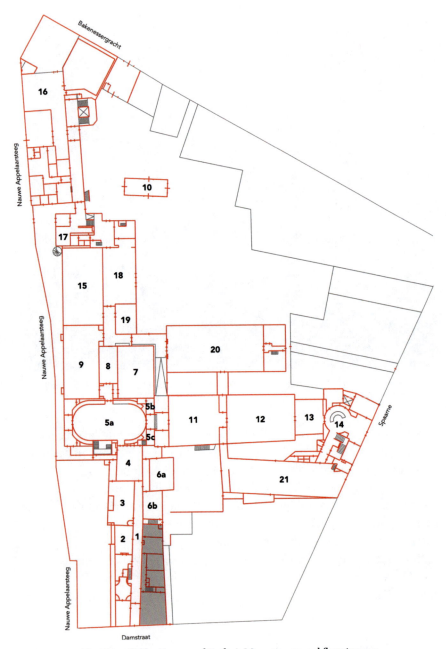

FIGURE 3.17   The Pieter Teyler House and Teyler's Museum: ground floor in 2020

A MUSEUM WITHIN THE FOUNDATION, 1779–2020 63

FIGURE 3.17 The Pieter Teyler House and Teyler's Museum: ground floor in 2020 (*cont.*)

1. Corridor, 2. 'Small Room', 3. Courtyard, 4. 'Large Room'
Shaded area
Living quarters of *kastelein* Jan Hendrik van Borssum Buisman (1952–80), later of Museum director Eric Ebbinge (1983–2001). Currently under development
Museum
5a. Oval Room (1784–today), 5b. Luminescence Room (1938–today), 5c. R. van Stolk Room (1996–today), 6a and 6b. Lorentz Lab (2017–today), 7. Exhibition room for drawings and prints (1996–today), 8. Coins and Medals Cabinet (1888–today), 9. First Paintings Gallery (1839–today), 10. 'Betalab' for School Education (1996–today), 11. Instrument Room / Second floor: extension of the Library (1885–today), 12. Second Fossil Room / Second floor: Auditorium (1885–today), 13. First Fossil Room / Second floor: Lobby/reception room (1885–today), 14. Spaarne entrance (1885–today), shop (1996–today), 15. Second Paintings Gallery (1893–today), 16. Former Zegelwaarden building: offices, store rooms and workshops (1993–today), 17. Room for education (1996–today), 18. Café (1996–today). 19. Exhibition room for books (1996–today), 20. Exhibition Gallery (1996–today), 21. Shop (2001–today).

audience, a new link was added in the chain of museological developments that had characterized the institution since its founding in 1779. At the end of the tour visitors can see a demonstration of a functioning full-size copy of Martinus van Marum's large electrostatic generator of 1784, transporting them back to the founding years of the institution (figure 3.16).

For the time being, the last of these recent building projects is the current restoration of the Foundation House, now known as the Pieter Teyler House, the place where it all began (figures 3.10, 3.17). This will entail the restoration of the passage to the Book and Art Room, so that visitors can experience what their predecessors would have felt between 1785 and 1885: the transition from the relatively dark 'Large Room' to the elegant Neoclassical Oval Room, bathed in daylight, with its scientific apparatus, scale models and minerals, and bookcases in the gallery (figures 1.2, 3.18).[22]

4 Changing Relations between the Societies and the Museum

The original purposes of the two societies have broadly been maintained: the stimulation of scientific research by holding competitions, and the propagation of knowledge for the 'common good', later for 'the public', by means of lectures, publications, and, since 1995, also via the internet.[23] Due to its increasingly

---

22 So far, no contemporary account has been found of this experience.
23 On 2 February 1995 Teyler's Museum was the first Dutch museum to have its own website: *Haarlems Dagblad en IJmuider Courant*, Bijlage (Appendix), 29 Feb. 1996, 17. In 2012, in line with the enlightened tradition from which Teyler's Foundation sprang, there was

FIGURE 3.18 View from the 'Large Room' to the Oval Room through the door that gave access to the Museum between 1784 and 1885. After the restoration of the Pieter Teyler House it will be opened to the public again. Photo 2011.

A MUSEUM WITHIN THE FOUNDATION, 1779–2020

public role since the 1880s, however, and especially since the extension in the 1990s, the Museum has more emphatically taken the latter path. As a result of this development, and of the organizational division in 1981, the societies and the Museum have grown apart, although the exhibitions are always built on solid scholarly foundations, and the central focus of the educational activities is invariably to introduce the public to what spurs science: a sense of wonder and the search for knowledge.[24] More recently, the ties between the societies and the Museum are being renewed by encouraging scientific research, for instance in partnership with Leiden University which now has two Teyler Chairs.[25] The conference held in 2017 and the present volume form part of this project.

5 Conclusion

In the introductory chapters we have aimed to paint a picture of Teyler's Foundation, with its two learned societies and Museum – a remarkable eighteenth-century institution of scientific-historical interest, one of the few of its kind, that has retained its original conception and housing. The latter is the reason why in the present chapter we have traced its history up to the present day. The book focuses on the last decades of the eighteenth century: on the decision in 1779 to build a Book and Art Room behind the founder's house, and on the meaning of that decision for the subsequent history of the Foundation up to 1885, the opening year of a fully-fledged museum of science and art, which

---

collaboration with Wikipedia on a writing contest, Teyler's Challenge, on subjects associated with the Foundation and the Museum.

24 The exhibitions in Teyler's Museum have a wide range of subjects. Past exhibitions include *De exotische mens: andere culturen als amusement/L'Homme exotique: les autres cultures sous forme d'attraction/Exotic man: other cultures as entertainment* (2009, in cooperation with Museum Dr Guislain, Ghent), *Raphael* (2012–13), *Michelangelo* (2018) and *Electricity: The Spark of Life* (2017–18, in cooperation with The Wellcome Collection, London). Further international collaboration will take place in the Alliance of Early Universal Museums, in which Teyler's Museum, the Museum of Anthropology and Ethnography (Kunstkamera 'Peter the Great') in St Petersburg and the Franckeschen Stiftungen in Halle (Germany) are joined since October 2020.

25 As we have seen, the Teyler Chair was created at Leiden University in 1928 for the physicist H. A. Lorentz, but he died prematurely. It was then held by A. D. Fokker from 1928 to 1955, by J. Kistemaker from 1956 to 1984, and by P. van Nieuwenhuizen from 1985 to 1990. After that the Chair was held not by physicists but by historians of science: R. P. W. Visser from 1997 to 2007, and F. H. van Lunteren from 2007. In 2013 a second chair was added, on behalf of the Theological Society, which is held by E. Jorink. A number of PhD dissertations have resulted from this collaboration with Leiden University in recent years: Weiss 2013a (published in 2019a), Sliggers 2017, Streefland 2017, Boom (work in progress), and Trijp (work in progress).

FIGURE 3.19 The Spaarne façade of Teyler's Museum, by Christian Ulrich (1885); the frieze bears the inscription '1778 TEYLER'S STICHTING 1878'. Photo 2011.

developed into the most visible part of the Foundation. Due to factors both scientific and economic, however, the tide turned in the twentieth century: having formed a unit with the Foundation for two hundred years, the Museum acquired a relatively independent status in 1981, enabling both partners to continue their missions according to the demands of the times. Today, in cooperation, they still cover a field of undiminished importance: the natural sciences, the arts and the humanities, and their mutual relationships (figure 3.19).

PART 2

Teyler's as a Case in a Re-Reading of the History of Science

∵

CHAPTER 4

'The World We Have Lost': In Praise of a Comprehensive Concept of Science and Scholarship

Wijnand W. Mijnhardt

Our present-day notions of what constitutes reliable science and scholarship differ considerably from the ideas of people around 1500. At the onset of the early modern age in Europe knowledge was still a multifaceted amalgam of disciplines, arts, skills and beliefs. That situation persisted for longer than is generally assumed, which has consequences for our assessment of the Teyler Foundation. The purpose of this essay is to re-evaluate the scientific-historical position of this institution since its creation in 1778. With this in mind a provisional outline is presented of the development of the concepts of science, art, and technical expertise that diverges quite radically from the standard textbook interpretations of the advance of science. The key is a historization of these notions, as it has been undertaken in recent years by various researchers with regard to the sixteenth and seventeenth centuries. The history and historiography of the late eighteenth-century Teyler's Foundation also perfectly illustrate the changing views of the meaning of these concepts. On the basis of such arguments the author comes to the defence of the tenets of the original, comprehensive, concept of science and knowledge. He believes it is time for a fundamental revaluation of the sharp distinction between nomothetic and ideographic, between exact science and value-based disciplines, between trying to formulate generalizations and focusing on the unique, between hard and soft science. After all, the division between these models and ideas does not proceed logically from the nature of knowledge, but is strictly historical.

•••

In 1762, a few years after Pieter Teyler van der Hulst had drafted his will, Jean-Jacques Rousseau published *Émile*, his famous tract on the overriding importance of education. Here he claimed that children are accomplished imitators by nature. That is how we can explain their fondness for drawing at a very early age. Rousseau urged tutors to cultivate that affection, though never intending to make them into accomplished artists. He proposed to train the eye and the hand in order to improve children's mental agility, their tactile capacities, and the coordination between the two.

© KONINKLIJKE BRILL NV, LEIDEN, 2021 | DOI:10.1163/9789004441446_005

FIGURE 4.1 Jacob Ernst Marcus, *Interior of the Drawing Academy in the Amsterdam Town Hall, during a session of drawing after a male nude model*, between c. 1790 and 1822, pen and brush in brown and grey, 94 x 120 mm (sheet).
AMSTERDAM CITY ARCHIVES, M, K 165–22

Rousseau was no exception. A couple of years later Johann Bernhard Mérian (1723–1807), a Swiss philosopher in the service of the Prussian Academy of Sciences in Berlin, came up with an even more radical idea. He proposed an experiment to blindfold children from the day of their birth until they had reached the age of reason. He expected that this procedure would immensely improve their other senses: 'their fingers would turn into microscopes'. The extraordinary development of their tactile capacities would make these youngsters into highly talented practitioners of the arts and crafts.[1]

Mérian's scheme was never put into practice, but in the eighteenth century, especially in its second half, drawing became an essential part of the educational regime of the elites. Many cities boasted a college where well-to-do citizens and their offspring were taught the art of drawing (figure 4.1). Originally these

---

1 Rousseau 1762, II, 134; Mérian 1984. My thanks to Dr Marieke Hendriksen for these references.

FIGURE 4.2 Dutch engraver, *Animals and plants*, second half of the eighteenth century, print published by the Maatschappij tot Nut van 't Algemeen (Society for the Promotion of Public Welfare), 330 x 410 mm. This type of print was intended to popularize knowledge of natural history.
RIJKSMUSEUM, AMSTERDAM, RP-P-OB-84.335

academies had catered for professional artists, but after a while they began to accept prosperous youngsters as well. The Maatschappij tot Nut van 't Algemeen (Society for the Promotion of Public Welfare) even advocated drawing as useful in the schooling of the lower classes (figure 4.2).[2]

The close connection between hand and head advocated by people of that time might surprise us. We have been taught that since the Scientific Revolution of the seventeenth century theory took precedence over practice. The Enlightenment would reinforce that differentiation. *Philosophes* made conversation and theorized: they did not practice. They were in the business of knowing, not of doing. And one of the central tasks of knowing, especially in the natural sciences, was to show that religion, if not superfluous, was marginal. 'Écrasez l'infame', after all, was the battle cry for many.

---

2 Mijnhardt 2004a. For this Society see also Chapter 2.

In this essay I will first trace the historiographic fortune of contrasts such as science and religion and head and hand.[3] I will show how in surveys published so far received ideas about the character and timetable of the Scientific Revolution have led us down the garden path, preventing us from fully understanding the fundamental fluidity of ideas and concepts such as science, knowledge, art and scholarship in the modern age.[4] Secondly, I will provisionally outline the stages of the development of these concepts from the 1500s onward. At that time knowledge was still a multifaceted amalgam of disciplines, arts, skills and beliefs. Scholarly explorations, artisanal expertise, religious insight and ethical concepts contributed equally to an inclusive culture of knowledge and wisdom, with its own epistemological traditions.[5] Part of my story is still speculative. We do not know enough yet, but it is always wise to have a theory that can be disproved. Last but not least, I will come to the defence of some of the tenets of the original early modern comprehensive concept of science and knowledge. I believe it is time for a fundamental revaluation of the sharp division between hard science and soft scholarship. After all, the distinction between these models does not proceed logically from the nature of knowledge itself, but is, as I hope to show, strictly historical. In my story the early history of Teyler's Foundation takes centre stage.

1   The 'Classical' View

Right from its beginning in 1778 Teyler's Foundation cherished the equivalence of head and hand, of knowing and doing, of art and science, and of knowledge and religion. On the one hand its activities were inspired by a comprehensive concept of culture and scholarship, in which religion, collecting, aesthetics and artisanal excellence could all play a part. On the other, it cherished the

---

3   Cf. the research of Ann-Sophie Lehmann: https://rug.academia.edu/AnnSophieLehmann.

4   Even recent surveys such as Peter Burke's *What is the History of Knowledge* (2016) use these ideas only in a teleological and ahistorical manner. Remarkably, though, there is a sizeable industry for the history of concepts (http://www.historyofconcepts.org/node/17394; for a Dutch approach cf. Hampsher-Monk/Tilmans/Vree 1998 and Tilmans/Velema s.d.). For the Dutch eighteenth century there is no research available on concepts such as science and knowledge. For a fascinating new perspective, see Dijksterhuis 2017. Cf. also Smith 2004; Smith/Schmidt 2007; Harkness 2008; and Long 2011 (p. 76 below).

5   Dixhoorn/Munck 2015; recently, as part of the research project *Creating a knowledge society in a globalizing world, 1450–1800* and supported by the ARTECHNE – Technique in the Arts, 1500–1950, a working group, chaired by Dr Marieke Hendriksen and myself, was launched to produce a comparative history of the concepts of knowledge, science and scholarship.

THE WORLD WE HAVE LOST

new natural sciences and the culture of the mind. In many other Dutch scholarly societies a similar double orientation could be found.[6]

For a long time historians have explained this survival of the encyclopaedic humanist idea, of the equivalence of mind and hand and of religion and science, by the peculiarities of the Dutch Republic in its period of intellectual decline.[7] While in the seventeenth and early eighteenth centuries the Republic was at the forefront of the Scientific Revolution and the Enlightenment, boasting intellectual giants such as Beekman and 's-Gravesande, Spinoza and Descartes, in the second half of the eighteenth century it could not claim scientists or *philosophes* of European stature. Not until the end of the nineteenth century did the Netherlands return to high level science and scholarship, with Nobel Prize-winning scientists such as Kamerlingh Onnes, Zeeman, Lorentz and Van der Waals.

A central element in this traditional explanation of the Dutch intellectual falling behind was the fundamentally different organization of scholarly and scientific life.[8] Before 1808, it is argued, the Dutch Republic did not have any national institution concerned with promoting academic endeavour. In Great Britain, the German-speaking territories and France central authorities had created national academies, to the greater honour and glory of absolute monarchies. Indeed, the Republic lacked a political centre, and policy on science was shaped by a mixture of private initiative, urban commercial interests, and provincial competition. For more than 150 years this republican division of power was effective. After 1750, though, several provinces, especially those on the western seaboard faced with severe economic difficulties, began to question the traditional strategies. Inspired by the European examples, they founded their own academies of the arts and sciences: the first of these was the Holland Society in Haarlem, in 1752 (cf. Chapters 2 and 8 of this volume).

The new academies were still all private foundations. They drafted their own statutes and derived their income from the voluntary contributions of their director-patrons, mostly members of the old families who had ruled the cities before 1795. As a result, funding for research was limited. Private sponsorship imposed further limitations. There was a tacit understanding that the science

---

6 For instance the Zeeuwsch Genootschap der Wetenschappen in Vlissingen (Zeeland Society of Sciences, Flushing; since 1769), the Provinciaal Utrechtsch Genootschap van Kunsten en Wetenschappen (Utrecht Provincial Society of Arts and Sciences; since 1773) in Utrecht, and the Hollandsche Maatschappij der Wetenschappen in Haarlem (Holland Society of Sciences; since 1752).

7 Some forty years ago I was the first to advance that now flawed interpretation: cf. Mijnhardt 1978.

8 Mijnhardt 1987, 78–123.

and scholarship funded by this erudite burgher elite should not become divorced from their culture. Civic elites valued science and scholarship chiefly in terms of the degree to which these could contribute to individual development, to the cultivation of 'taste and learning'. They held the natural sciences in high regard because of their practical usefulness. Even more important was the moral significance with which the natural sciences were credited: they provided insight into the 'Wisdom, Omnipotence and Benevolence of the Creator'. In short, they affirmed the meaning of life.

Again according to the traditional view, in the revolutionary era cracks started to appear in the unanimous front. From then on, the philosophies of learned societies showed two different trends. On the one hand, the sponsoring elite continued to promote the pursuit of science, scholarship and the arts in the traditional, undivided way. On the other hand, there was growing support for the view that science and scholarship could provide concrete solutions to the many economic and social problems facing the Dutch Republic. The French example and its involvement in Dutch affairs after 1795 reinforced this trend. This conflict between science as a social and economic imperative and science as the prerogative of an elite with talent, interest, capital, and free time raged most severely in scholarly institutions in Haarlem, such as Teyler's Foundation and the Holland Society.[9]

As Teyler's Foundation commanded huge sums that could be devoted to either policy, a lengthy conflict was played out between the Foundation's governors, who were very much in favour of the encyclopaedic idea of scholarship and artisanal excellence combined, and the Director of Teyler's Museum, Martinus van Marum, the most capable Dutch scientist of the time (figure 1.3). Van Marum was a staunch disciple of the French utilitarian concept of science. He denounced – though mostly indoors, for fear of infuriating his superiors – major parts of the encyclopaedic idea as 'sciences de parlage', empty words that should be replaced by the exact and thus more reliable sciences.

This interpretation of Dutch intellectual history, as exemplified by Teyler's Foundation, was a logical corollary of a vision of the history of science that we have come to call whiggish, a history, usually practiced in surveys, that follows a path of inevitable progress and improvement.[10] The central stages of that vision

---

9   Mijnhardt 1996.

10 Since the 1980s several studies have been published which challenge this vision, such as Yale 2016 and Shapin/Schaffer 1985. However, in general they focus on specific themes in the sixteenth and seventeenth centuries. Their insights have not been applied to learned culture in the Dutch eighteenth century, or to research on Dutch learned societies in particular.

THE WORLD WE HAVE LOST   75

are well known. In the seventeenth century a fresh generation of philosophers such as Bacon, Descartes and Locke introduced new epistemological principles, doing away with outdated truths. The fresh doctrines not only changed scientific practice, but, most importantly, they transformed the nature of knowledge itself. Mathematics began to play a determining role in what could be considered as true knowledge, and consequently the standing of the natural sciences and mathematics increased dramatically. Where Teyler's Foundation is concerned, the inevitable conclusion was that the fierce debates in its boardrooms around 1800 reflected that development, though very much delayed by intellectual decline.

The end of the nineteenth century would see the final victory of the mathematics-based natural sciences. It resulted in a fundamental methodological compartmentalization of the academic field and the division of learning into well-defined disciplines. Even before the German philosopher Heinrich Rickert supplied its epistemological justification[11] many scholars had become used to drawing a sharp distinction between the natural sciences and the humanities, the umbrella term for the leftovers of the former comprehensive idea. The natural sciences were concerned with generalizations: they sought to formulate universal laws and formulas, and studied the physical reality. The humanities, in contrast, were concerned with individualization: they focused on the unique, and studied the reality in which *values* were central.

It is important to stress that humanities scholars were very much responsible for their 'Alleingang' – the fact that the humanities went their separate ways. They championed the new dichotomy, as they had been searching for their own identity, and they imagined a brilliant future for their disciplines. Anyone cherishing such hopes was to be utterly disillusioned. Compared to the natural sciences, the humanities had hardly any economic significance. A Calimero complex[12] gradually became part of the standard mental make-up in the field. It is hardly surprising that the concept of a 'Scientific Revolution', virtually unknown until the beginning of the twentieth century, was coined precisely in this period of the clamorous parting of the ways between the cultural disciplines and the natural sciences. With this concept, the triumphant natural sciences acquired a glorious history and a golden future, especially in universities, the strongholds of modern learning. For the humanities a more subservient position was designed.[13]

---

11   Rickert 1899.
12   This term refers to the main character in an Italian/Japanese cartoon about a charming but hapless little chicken. It is used to denote people who are staunchly convinced that their position as an underdog is due to their smaller size, either literally or symbolically.
13   Cohen 1994.

2 Towards a Conceptual History of Science and Knowledge

For almost a century this view of the development of science and scholarship as stepping stones towards an inevitable modernity, with universities, laboratories, libraries and qualified scholars and scientists, has blurred our view of what really happened. If we want to understand the issues at Teyler's or the projects of Rousseau and Mérian, we need to see the history of science as an open, possibilistic enterprise that does not simply trace the origins of today's practices but takes the issues of contemporaries as its lead.[14] In such a view the debate at Teyler's Foundation around 1800 is not a long overdue clash between the past and the future, but a captivating phase in a process in which ideas of knowledge and science were gradually transformed (cf. Chapter 2 of this volume).

For a series of explanatory previews of that transformation, I want to focus on three interlocking phenomena: on the locations of knowledge, on the various types of people active in those locations, and finally on the concepts and methods contemporaries employed to organize knowledge. In the sixteenth and seventeenth centuries universities and monasteries were only minor centres of knowledge production and distribution. In the urban and courtly worlds of Western Europe the critical production centres were artisanal workshops, guilds, cabinets and collections of curiosities, bookshops, and chambers of rhetoric and comparable sociable institutions. In these knowledge communities artisanal and scholarly practices were intertwined with work in the 'proto-natural sciences'.

Pamela Smith, for instance, has shown how in the workshops of the sixteenth- and seventeenth-century Low Countries artisans – painters, potters and goldsmiths – amalgamated their experiments with new materials with alchemy, naturalism, and a new materialist and often vernacular epistemology. Deborah Harkness has taught us that in Elizabethan London members of a great variety of professions – merchants, teachers, barber-surgeons, engineers, alchemists, and other experimenters – set the stage for an early variety of a scientific community, serving as a source of inspiration for Francis Bacon.[15] Underlying much of this activity was the interdependency of art and knowledge, recently analysed by Eric Jorink and Bart Ramakers. Students of nature could not do without art and serious drawing skills. Artists could not dispense with books and artefacts. As Willem Goeree in his book of 1668 (published in English in 1674 as *Introduction to the General Art of Drawing*) made abundantly clear, artists did not only need to have a full command of the various aspects of

---

14   Skinner 1969.
15   Smith 2004; Smith/Schmidt 2007; Harkness 2008; Long 2011.

THE WORLD WE HAVE LOST 77

their trade: they needed to be familiar with all branches of knowledge, including the Bible and the advances in the natural sciences. The firm combination would produce new knowledge, techniques and materials.[16]

Just as illustrative is the case of the St Luke's Guild in Antwerp, analysed by Arjan van Dixhoorn. The guild, an 'untraditional' community of making, practicing, knowing and learning, was instrumental in the shaping of a new discourse of knowledge in the Dutch-speaking Low Countries. One of the crucial characteristics of its epistemology was the redefinition of the disciplines, reducing the complexity of the liberal arts, the sciences and the mechanical arts to the single notion of the *consten*, making them perfectly suitable for vernacular distribution. Chambers of rhetoric and other societies would absorb these ideas and preach them until well into the eighteenth century. They were assisted by bookshops catering for this clientele, such as Thomas van der Noot in Brussels, Plantijn in Antwerp, and an ever expanding number of publishers specializing in books for a Dutch language audience in the Northern Republic.[17]

Some people are still used to seeing early modern collections of *naturalia* and *artificialia* as no more than the predecessors of the modern museum, but their role as centres of knowledge production was immensely more important. Their character was often encyclopaedic: they were theatres of knowledge and wisdom, frequently intended to provide a visual addition to a library or a collection of books, especially with minerals, plants and animals. Owners of such cabinets came from all over the social spectrum: not just kings, dukes and bishops, but town and government officials, merchants, artists, artisans, and other *liefhebbers* – informed lovers of the arts. In the Low Countries artefacts and botanical specimens from all over the world were on sale, and information from people who had actually visited the uncharted territories could be easily obtained.[18]

In number, scope and size these cabinets dwarfed the collections in what we used to call the real sites of learning, such as universities. Libraries tell a similar story. Private collectors often owned many more books, in the vernacular as well as in Latin, than the institutional reading rooms of any educational establishment. The learned universities and libraries played a much lesser role in the 'Grand Tours' of aristocrats than the cabinets of private individuals. And the pursuit of knowledge was not at all limited to those we regard as professional scholars: it involved much more varied segments of the population. *Liefhebbers* and amateurs came from a wide variety of professions.

---

16   Jorink/Ramakers 2011, 6–33. Roemer 2011, 184–207.

17   Dixhoorn 2014; Dixhoorn 2015.

18   Impey/MacGregor 2017 (1st edn 1985); Bergvelt/Kistemaker 1992a and 1992b; Bergvelt/
      Meijers/Rijnders 1993, 2005 and 2013.

I have been using the terms 'science' and 'knowledge' up to now without further distinction. It is one of the great problems of modern scholarship that we do not yet have a clear idea of the precise evolution of those concepts and all that is related to them. For the Low Countries systematic research has only just begun. A few examples might clarify the issue. For a modern audience, for instance, belief and religion, magic and superstition are intellectually separate and well defined categories. In the early modern era they were still closely connected. People had serious difficulties in ordering the bewildering religious reality that they discovered in an ever growing number of travel books from all over the globe. Most were used to carving up the world into the four traditional categories of rather unequal size and stature: Jews, Christians, Muslims, and the rest that could be called superstitious heathens or idolatrous peoples. How should one deal with this appalling new religious diversity?

The most influential work on the topic, demonstrating an inclusive concept of religion, was produced between 1723 and 1743, typically not by trained scholars but by what today we would call amateurs: a successful artist, Bernard Picart, and a gifted publisher, Jean Frederic Bernard, both based in Amsterdam. As Huguenots with an extensive experience of religious persecution, they shared an interest in the problem of the authenticity of religious doctrines and practices. Their *Cérémonies et coutumes religieuses de tous les peuples du monde* (*Ceremonies and Religious Customs of the Various Nations of the Known World*) of 1723–43, a blockbuster of seven heavily illustrated folio volumes, in a beautifully balanced blend of words and images hammered home the message that all religions could be compared on equal terms, all were equally worthy of respect, and all might be criticized (figure 4.3). Fundamentally, they turned the traditional belief in one unique, absolute, and God-given truth into 'religion' – discrete ceremonies and customs that reflected the truths relative to each people and each culture.[19]

The results of research in natural philosophy also threatened the dominance of this traditional belief and promoted the introduction of clearly separate intellectual categories. According to the Cartesians, God's creation was no complicated system of symbolic references and religious meanings that needed deciphering, but just a beautiful piece of engineering, at best reflecting the ingenuity of a divine architect. They thus prepared the way for a clear separation of religion and modern science. However, Newtonian views helped to defuse the radical implications of the Cartesian world picture. They inspired an extensive

---

19   Miles 2015, 23–27; Hunt/Jacob/Mijnhardt 2010. Also in Teyler's Theological Society there was a special interest in religions that had not known Revelation; for related prize contests, see Chapter 2 above.

FIGURE 4.3 Bernard Picart (workshop), *La Dédicace de la Synagogue des Juifs Portugais, à Amsterdam,* 1675 (The dedication of the Synagogue of the Portuguese [Sephardic] Jews in Amsterdam in 1675), from J. F. Bernard and B. Picart, *Cérémonies et coutumes religieuses de tous les peuples du monde* (Amsterdam 1723–43), etching and engraving, 340 x 417 mm.
RIJKSMUSEUM, AMSTERDAM, RP-P-OB-51.219

literature and a growing number of informal scientific societies committed to demonstrating the omnipotence and very often interventionist capacities of the Creator, facts that could only be established by the study of nature.[20]

The narrow bond between art and science, mind and hand, and religion and science also resulted in an important series of industrial innovations in the period, especially since philosophers such as Samuel Clarke had begun to stress the economic significance of religiously inspired natural research. For the Protestant Loosdrecht minister Johannes de Mol, for instance, the creation of a new type of porcelain was not simply a remarkable technological experiment but proof of God's benevolent creation (figures 4.4, 4.5). His workshop equally

20   Jorink 2010.

FIGURE 4.4
Pieter Oets, *Portrait of Joannes de Mol* (1726–1782), pastel, 460 x 355 mm (oval).
CASTLE-MUSEUM SYPESTEYN, NIEUW-LOOSDRECHT, Q079

FIGURE 4.5 Cup and saucer, multi-coloured painted porcelain, Oud-Loosdrecht Manufacture, 1774–84, cup h. 4.1 cm, d 7.4 cm; saucer h. 2.4 cm, d 12.1 cm.
CASTLE-MUSEUM SYPESTEYN, NIEUW-LOOSDRECHT, 8931

fulfilled God's plan by providing schooling and jobs for the uneducated, thus fighting the social consequences of economic decline. De Mol's philosophy served as an example for many followers all over the Republic.[21]

21   Zappey 1988; Wegen 2019.

THE WORLD WE HAVE LOST

Thus, boundaries between religion and natural philosophy, between art and science and between mind and hand remained fluid for a very long time. As a consequence, the research methods employed were only rarely those praised in the usual modern histories of science. Textual analysis of what Classical authors had written about the human body, the earth, the stars, etc., prevailed, but occasionally joined hands with experimental practices and mathematical techniques. Eclecticism ruled. Remarkably, after 1750 distrust of empirical philosophy even increased. For the Marquis de Sade, for instance, empiricism would result in a materialist determinism that would destroy the only moral compass humankind possessed. His novels (still read for completely different reasons) demonstrate his despair.[22]

It will be clear by now that Teyler's Foundation with its societies devoted to religion and many other branches of knowledge, its Museum, its Library and collections and its painter-custodian, was not a relic of a past characterized by outdated concepts of the arts, science and scholarship. It was perfectly in tune with the times. The same may be said of the other Dutch scientific societies.[23] It might even be argued that their organizational structure was perfectly adjusted to the leading knowledge concepts (figures 4.6, 4.7).

But if we accept this, how do we explain the conflict between the Directors of Teyler's Foundation and the Director of the Museum, Martinus van Marum? Is it conceivable that both were right? I am convinced that this was the case. Van Marum was an unwavering disciple of the French utilitarian innovations in science and scholarship. In a very short time-span the French abolished the Ancien Régime's world of knowledge without boundaries. They 'purged' the medical profession by separating doctors from surgeons, for instance, elevating the doctors who excelled in theoretical knowledge and downgrading the surgeons who relied on their manual skills. In the Institut de France in 1795 the letters and the arts were first relegated to separate sections and then excluded, leaving only the physical sciences undisturbed.[24] Van Marum's denunciation of the 'sciences de parlage' at Teyler's and elsewhere was following a powerful example.

It is not far-fetched to link the introduction of a modern distinction between knowledge and science to these events. The French scientific reforms would have been inconceivable without the changing appreciation of art, literature, and manual practices that was taking shape in the preceding decades. Slowly they would develop into separate domains with their own rules, techniques and evaluative discourses. Until far into the eighteenth century the Platonic idea of beauty

---

22   Meeker 2006.
23   See above, n. 6.
24   Fox 2012; Dhombres 1989.

FIGURE 4.6   Reinier Vinkeles, after a drawing by Jacques Kuyper and Pieter Barbiers, *A Public Presentation by the Amsterdam Professor Jan van Swinden for the Felix Meritis Society in Amsterdam ('Physica')*, 1801, etching and engraving, 376 x 514 mm.
AMSTERDAM CITY ARCHIVES, 010097015579

was the rule by which to judge art as well as writing. Towards the end of the age, social autonomy became the central prerogative of the artist in every domain.[25] Even personal expression gradually received a special place.[26] Rousseau's plea for the 'inner voice' as the only moral compass in a materialist world, triggered by the same issues as the novels of De Sade, was instrumental in these changes.

As a result, Dutch seventeenth-century painting came to be dismissed as 'boringly descriptive', and the style of the German painter Caspar David Friedrich to been seen as the guide to the future. Novalis in Germany and even Rhijnvis Feith in the Dutch Republic performed similar services for literature. From now on the artist was not required (as contemporary critics put it) simply to describe what he observed but also what he saw in himself, in order to

---

25   Cf. the contribution of Heumakers to this volume, also for the changing understanding of the term 'art'.
26   Hendriksen 2017.

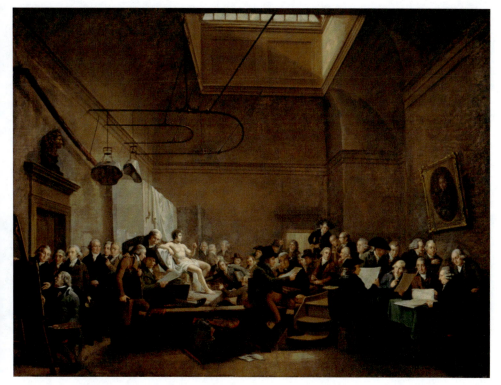

FIGURE 4.7 Adriaan de Lelie, *The Drawing Gallery of the Felix Meritis Society*, 1801, oil on canvas, 100 x 131 cm.
RIJKSMUSEUM, AMSTERDAM, SK-C-53

inspire the world around. The worst victim of the separation of the head and the hand was the craftsman. The author and the painter could make up for their losses in the world of science and could even applaud their subjective autonomy. But the artisan not only lost his position as a worthy occupant of the scientific domain: he was reduced to the status of a simple manual labourer. On top of that, he lost his prestige as a political burgher. After all, in early modern times urban politics had been the domain of the craft guilds.[27]

In the context of these radical transformations around 1800 it is very likely that the decision in the early nineteenth century of the governors of Teyler's Foundation to collect contemporary paintings, after having finally outmanoeuvered Van Marum, was as much inspired by a longing for the original encyclopaedic idea as by this new variety of art.[28] It would seem

27   Munck 2017.
28   Cf. the contribution of Van Druten to this volume.

logical to link the disappearance of literature and art from the realm of science to the methodological revolution that began to occur soon afterwards. Textual analysis, mathematization and eclectic empiricism had joined hands for centuries and together had accomplished great results. They now separated definitively, each improving its specific techniques, philology for the one and mathematics for the other. In the universities they were gradually assigned separate faculties, preparing the way for the fundamental methodological compartmentalization and the discipline formation that went with it later in the century. The key element in the parting process was the professionalization of scholarship that took place in scientific societies from the 1840s onwards. The Utrecht Provincial Society of Arts and Sciences is a case in point. It renounced the comprehensive idea of science and scholarship dating from its earliest days, transformed itself into a conglomerate of four subsections defined by academic background, and expelled laymen and amateurs. The Holland Society in Haarlem lagged behind, clinging to the governing model established in 1752, to the detriment of its reputation. Teyler's Foundation, on the contrary, once again shrewdly adapted itself to the times. The appointment of Hendrik Lorentz as Director of a new science laboratory in 1909 signified the full conversion of the governors to the new successful model of science (figure 4.8).[29]

3   Renewing the Bond between the Sciences and the Humanities

In 1965 the English historian Peter Laslett published *The World we have Lost. England before the Industrial Age*, still one of the best guides to social change in the field. Laslett was not afraid to ask difficult questions. Wasn't the pre-industrial world that we have lost, after all, a better place to live in? To recognize the urgency of such questions is not simply an uncritical yearning for a past long gone. It helps us to change our view of what we should be trying to do in the present. And we can only get into this position if we are to admit that all historical knowledge is after all knowledge about ourselves.[30]

Accordingly, it need not surprise us that soon after the seemingly definitive parting of the natural sciences and the humanities, scholars have been trying to restore their unity. The efforts of the Vienna Circle, active between the two world wars, that sought to achieve 'a renewed union of all fields of academic endeavour', failed, as the humanities were basically required to accept the

---

29   Mijnhardt 2004b.
30   Laslett 1965.

FIGURE 4.8
Hendrik Antoon Lorentz (1853–1928).
Photo *c.* 1925.
RIJKSMUSEUM BOERHAAVE, LEIDEN

methods of the natural sciences. Maybe today we are in a better position to appreciate the purely historical nature of the separation. After all, we now have realized that both the humanities and the sciences make models of reality, the one mostly with textual and the other with mathematical means. Arguably the chief difference is that the models of the sciences often last longer than those of the humanities; but – and this is absolutely crucial – none of them can claim eternal life. If the Amsterdam physicist Eric Verlinden is proved right, we will have to revise even Newton's law of gravity.

If we really want to solve the big scientific and social issues of today, we need to discard the naïve notion that mathematical measuring is the only key to knowledge. The solution of present-day problems requires a broad range of methods and techniques. I do not plead for a restoration of the amalgam of disciplines, arts, skills and beliefs that existed five centuries ago. However, in today's knowledge society, populated by almost countless numbers of scientists with brilliant analytical but often highly specialized minds, we cannot do without scholars, artists and accomplished artisans with a synthetic perspective that brings together the fragmented disciplines and knowledge domains in novel and surprising ways.[31]

Fortunately, the history of science in recent decades has exploded the notion of a universal scientific method that could easily divide good data sets from bad ones, that could immediately and effectively expose useless theories, and that would be infallible in identifying valuable scientific ideas. We know that behind the gleaming façade of the laboratories the real world of science looks a lot more chaotic than people used to think. Scientists themselves, it turns out, frequently have sharp differences of opinion about problems and options, and may indeed belong to different 'camps' or 'schools'. In a nutshell, biomedical researchers and physicists are not high priests who supply us with pure scientific knowledge. On the other hand, historians, artists and literary scholars are not methodological amateurs who mess about on the fringes of academia. Regardless of how much techniques and methodologies may differ, what all researchers, artisans and artists ultimately share is confidence in their trained intuition and in their imagination, in their learned – but fundamentally fallible – ability to seek solutions, honed by experience and acquired skills. When we put it like this, all scientific and scholarly research can be equated to a productive but by its nature never-ending debate, a declaration that should inspire humility first of all.

If what I have been discussing has some merit, wouldn't it then be commendable if Teyler's Foundation, that was perfectly adjusted to the times throughout its history, took the lead once again? It began its life as an unfaltering defender of the unity of knowledge. Around 1800 it supported the new conceptions of art and science, and in 1900 it embraced the ostensibly definitive victory of the sciences. Shouldn't it now devote its immense energies and prestige to the promotion of debates on the novel but crucial relations between the sciences, the arts and the humanities? Wouldn't that be the true spirit of Pieter Teyler's will?

---

31   In 2014, based on the same idea, a Society of Arts was established within the Royal Netherlands Academy of Sciences.

CHAPTER 5

The First Museum in the Netherlands? The Establishment of Teyler's Oval Room in Historical Perspective (*c.* 1600– 1800)

Eric Jorink

Visitors to Teyler's Museum will probably notice a metal plaque to the left of the entrance stating that this is the oldest museum in the Netherlands. Installed on the monumental façade in the 1980s, this is only one of many statements on the pedigree of this wonderful institution, including its core, the famous Oval Room, created in 1784.[1] However, presenting Teyler's Museum as the *oldest* museum in the Netherlands suggests that it was also the *first one*, which is problematic. As we shall see, historically speaking 'museum' is a fluid concept, not as now 'a building in which objects of historical, artistic, scientific and cultural interest are stored and exhibited'.[2] Consequently it is difficult to identify Teyler's Museum as a milestone. Rather than being a timeless institution for conservation, display and education, open to the public, a 'museum' evolved since the sixteenth century from being a private space for discussion, contemplation and scientific investigation.

• • •

1 Introduction

What became known as Teyler's Museum is now the best known and the most tangible manifestation of the organization that commissioned it: Teyler's Foundation. However in 1778, as explained in Chapter 2, the Foundation had established other institutions as well, including two famous learned societies,

---

1 See also Sliggers 2006, 17; https://www.teylersmuseum.nl/en (accessed 24 March 2019): 'Teylers Museum is the first and oldest museum in the Netherlands'. The gallery of Stadholder Willem V in The Hague, opened in 1774, also claims this status. Due to the confiscation of the Stadholder's collections by the French in 1795 it only existed for twenty years, but with its reconstruction in the 1970s that gallery (now part of the Mauritshuis) still claims the title.

2 https://en.oxforddictionaries.com/definition/museum (accessed 2 Sept. 2018). See also the definition by ICOM, https://icom.museum/en/activities/standards-guidelines/museum-definition/ (accessed 28 Feb. 2019): 'A museum is a non-profit, permanent institution in the service of society and its development, open to the public, which acquires, conserves, researches,

all bearing the name of its founder, Pieter Teyler van der Hulst (1702–1778). Thus, in the 1880s, a century after the completion of the Oval Room, newspapers reporting on Teyler's extension and new entrance facing the Spaarne River (figure 1.4) spoke in more general terms of 'the building that Teyler's Foundation has constructed' or 'the new house of Teyler's Foundation'. Besides mentioning the collections, the newspapers also explicitly referred to the scientific lectures and demonstrations held in the *gehoorzaal* (auditorium) and the annual prize essay competitions by the two scientific societies.[3] In other words, the Museum was – and to a certain extent still is – part of a larger organization.

The Foundation, the two societies, and what came to be known as Teyler's Museum had their origin in the will of Pieter Teyler, drawn up in 1756. A wealthy man, in true Enlightenment spirit, Teyler had had a strong interest in religion, art, science and the improvement of society. He had stipulated that his immense fortune, as well as his house and his cabinet of coins and medals and other (rather modest) collections of books, art and *naturalia* would be expanded and used for the benefit of the community. When he died twenty-two years later, on 8 April 1778, the Foundation bearing his name was established and the five trustees, called Directors, acted according to the more specific details of Teyler's will. His house, and the collections, passed to the Foundation (since then it was known as the Fundatiehuis or Foundation House, recently renamed the 'Pieter Teyler House'). Teyler had stipulated the maintaining of an almshouse and the institution of the two learned societies discussed in Chapter 2 of this book. They were to have six members each and were to meet weekly on different days.[4] The first society was devoted to Theology (the *Godgeleerd Genootschap*); the other, simply called the Second Society (*Tweede Genootschap*), would be concerned with science, poetry, history, art and numismatics. Each society would announce an annual competition on a subject relevant to science and society, which had to be answered in the form of a substantial paper. The winner was to be granted a gold or silver medal and the publication of the essay in the periodical *Verhandelingen* (Transactions) published by both societies. The Foundation, the two societies, and the almshouse are all still active institutions; even the tradition of essay competitions is still very much alive.[5]

---

communicates and exhibits the tangible and intangible heritage of humanity and its environment for the purposes of education, study and enjoyment'. ICOM is currently reconsidering the present definition – a fact that underlines the historical character of the term 'museum'.

3   *Algemeen Handelsblad*, 1 March 1881; ibid., 22 Jan. 1885; https://www.delpher.nl/nl/platform/results?query=teylers&coll=platform (accessed 25 Sept. 2018).

4   For a transcription of Teyler's will see Sliggers 2006, 192–206, especially 198–99.

5   https://www.teylersmuseum.nl/en/about-the-museum/organisation/who-we-are/the-ideals-of-pieter-teyler.

THE FIRST MUSEUM IN THE NETHERLANDS?   89

However, no mention was made in Teyler's will of the establishment of a museum. The document only instructed the executors (the Directors) to maintain and enlarge his library and other collections, in order to serve the needs of the members of both societies. As we have seen in Chapters 1 and 2, it was by a rather liberal interpretation of this document that the Foundation in 1779 initiated the establishment of an extension to the Foundation House which came to be known as the Oval Room. Intriguingly, initially it was not referred to as a 'museum' but as the 'Book and Art Room', and in more general terms as 'the intended building'.[6] Although nominally open to visitors, this space was intended as a fairly exclusive site for knowledge. Books, *naturalia*, cutting-edge scientific instruments such as the world's largest electrostatic generator, and prints and drawings were viewed, handled and discussed by a happy few. The intention was not to attract as many visitors as possible, but to foster and communicate scientific, historical, artistic and religious knowledge.

The 1784 establishment of the Oval Room was much in line with the rather fluid contemporary notion of the setting for scholarship, collecting and the pursuit of knowledge.[7] In the Dutch Republic as well as in the rest of Europe the word 'museum' only gained wider currency around 1770.[8] The Latin concept of *musaeum*, as a rather loosely defined space for contemplation, was of course known, but in Dutch dictionaries such as that of David van Hoogstraten (1723) it is not mentioned.[9] The *Encyclopédie* of Diderot and d'Alembert (1751–72) notices it more or less in passing.[10]

But whereas the settings of earlier collections had been referred to as 'bibliotheca', 'studiolo', 'scrittoio', 'templum', 'cabinet', and other similar and sometimes interchangeable words, by 1800 'museum' had become the dominant term. Tellingly, whereas around 1780 Van Marum in his negotiations with the board of Teyler's Foundation had used a variety of terms, chiefly 'library'; in the 'Instruction for the Director of Teyler's Musaeum' drawn up by himself in 1785 he already speaks of a *Musaeum*. Looking back on his achievements half a century later, he wrote a statement unequivocally called 'On my activities for Teyler's Museum'.[11] However, scholarship and the interplay between texts

---

6   Bouman/Broers 1988; Weiss 2013a, 63–64. As will become clear from the following notes, I elaborate on Weiss's dissertation, published in an abbreviated form as Weiss 2019a. See also Jorink 2015.

7   See e.g. Meijers 2013; MacGregor 2010.

8   See the seminal article by Findlen 1989; also Lee 1997; Jorink 2015.

9   Hoogstraten 1723.

10   'Musée' in Diderot/d'Alembert 1751–72, X, 893–94; see Lee 1997.

11   Board minutes, 25 Sept. 1784 (ATS 5, 118–21), and M. van Marum, 'De Geschiedenis van de oprigting van Teijler's Museum', 1823–33 (NHA 529-9).

and objects remained an important feature of the culture of collecting, as in the case of Van Marum's fascination for geology and the emerging debate on the chronology of the Bible, one of his key interests. How did the giant creature found near Maastricht – later known as the mosasaur, and still one of the iconic objects in Teyler's Museum – relate to the account in Genesis? How had mountains come into being? Had the Flood covered the whole of the Earth? Was the fossil found in 1726, now in Teyler's Museum and known as *Homo diluvii testis*, really a human witness of the Great Flood?[12]

Behind the issue of the semantics of the word 'museum' there are some related topics. First, hand in hand with the increasing currency of the word 'museum' new aims and audiences for collections of objects were defined. During the eighteenth century some important collections gained a more educational, public role rather than what they had traditionally been, a fairly private, scholarly enterprise. The establishment of the British Museum in 1753, based on the collection of the late Sir Hans Sloane (1660–1753), is the best-known example of this.[13] Secondly, before the eighteenth century the name and function of collections were only loosely linked with the space in which they were housed and studied. Early examples include the Ashmolean Museum in Oxford (opened in 1683) and the *Gallerij* built in the Leiden Botanical Garden (1610) where it was intended to keep books, maps and all kinds of *naturalia* as well as plants.[14] Collections were not physically limited by the walls of a room or building: their borders were rather of a metaphysical nature. The first significant collection in the Republic, that of Bernardus Paludanus (1550–1633), was referred to in 1609 in a poem by his friend Hugo Grotius as 'Treasury and compendium of the whole world; Ark of the universe, sacred storehouse of nature'.[15] Thirdly, in all these collections art, science and religion overlapped to a degree that is now somewhat hard to understand. Works of art would include not only drawings, paintings and sculptures but also *naturalia* skillfully 'crafted' by the Divine Creator. And *naturalia* were increasingly presented in an orderly, often aesthetically pleasing way, underlining the structure and beauty of the works of God. Present-day conceptions of art history, the history of science and theology, and the disciplinary boundaries between them, obscure the fact that until far into the eighteenth century these

---

12 Remarkably, there are no signs that the Theological Society was concerned with this theme (see Chapter 2 of the present book).

13 Lee 1997; Meijers 2003 and 2013; MacGregor 2010; Delbourgo 2017.

14 Jong 2000; Jorink 2010.

15 Grotius 1639, 276, as quoted in Jorink 2010, 267. For further information on Paludanus and his collection see Sliggers in Chapter 6 below, especially p. 117, n. 20.

THE FIRST MUSEUM IN THE NETHERLANDS? 91

realms overlapped. As I will argue, the Oval Room to a certain extent fits into this older pattern. What if we considered the establishment of what became known as Teyler's Museum from the perspective of a longer tradition, also strongly rooted in Haarlem, rather than seeing it as the first museum in the Netherlands?

2 Museums and the History of Collecting

The notion that both the word and the concept of 'museum' have a historical dimension was implicitly put on the academic agenda in 1983, when the Ashmolean Museum hosted a conference entitled 'The Cabinet of Curiosities'.[16] It became clear that early modern cabinets of curiosities – a hitherto rather neglected subject – were highly relevant for understanding both the history of art and the history of science.[17] Collections were not fixed in content, place or meaning.[18] Until well into the seventeenth century these were mostly private spaces, including books and objects, open only by invitation. The *studiolo* of Francesco de' Medici (1541–1587) in the Palazzo Pitti and the collection of Ulysse Aldrovandi (1522–1605) in the University of Bologna are well-known examples. These collections were closely linked with the Renaissance concept of knowledge (in the sense of both science and scholarship), in which the Bible and the writings of the ancients were seen as the keys to an encyclopaedic, all-encompassing understanding of the world. Most collections started with the library. By collecting objects described in texts – ancient coins and statues, shells and insects, precious stones, giant bones, and objects relating to biblical history – one could have the comforting idea of viewing the whole of God's creation. *Orbis in domo*, the world at home, was a current term (figure 5.1).

This point was also demonstrated by research on Dutch collections. A seminal exhibition, *De wereld binnen handbereik* (Distant worlds made tangible), accompanied by a two-volume publication, was held in 1992 in the Amsterdam Historical Museum.[19] In the early modern period the Republic witnessed a

---

16 The conference resulted in the publication of a seminal collection of essays: *The Origins of Museums. The Cabinet of Curiosities in Sixteenth and Seventeenth-Century Europe* (Impey/ MacGregor 1985). The title of the book is somewhat paradoxical and 'whiggish', projecting back in time present-day notions of the museum.

17 See, for example, Findlen 1989; Findlen 1994; Findlen 2006. Julius von Schlosser, with his *Kunst-und Wunderkammern der Spätrenaissance* of 1908, can be seen as a pioneer in this regard.

18 Findlen 1989; Findlen 1994.

19 Bergvelt/Kistemaker 1992a and 1992b.

FIGURE 5.1　'The Museum of Ferrante Imperato', from Ferrante Imperato, *Dell' historia naturale di Ferrante Imperato Napolitano libri XXVIII* (Naples 1599). This shows the interplay between books and objects, and the collection as a relatively closed space, intended for wonder, discussion and contemplation.
ROYAL LIBRARY, THE HAGUE

vigorous culture of collecting, not least on account of the emergence of a global network of trade.[20] When Leiden University was founded in 1575 the curators copied examples in Renaissance Italy and supported academic instruction with a botanical garden and an anatomical theatre, adorned with collections of objects.[21] The ever-expanding collections – the objects were either purchases or gifts – were also accessible to a more general audience. In the following centuries this went hand in hand with increasing scientific knowledge and the emergence of new academic disciplines – including, for example, geology and Egyptology – resulting in the establishment of specialized museums in the course of the nineteenth century. Objects from what was once a single academic collection can be found today in Leiden in the Rijksmuseum voor

20　See also Bergvelt/Meijers/Rijnders 1993, 2005 and 2013.
21　Huisman 2009; Jorink 2010.

THE FIRST MUSEUM IN THE NETHERLANDS?

Oudheden (National Museum of Antiquities), the Museum Naturalis (Naturalis Biodiversity Center) and the Rijksmuseum Boerhaave.

In the Dutch Republic these institutional and national museums had their roots in the collections of private citizens, who by the end of the seventeenth century often granted public access.[22] Their motives frequently overlapped: wonder, curiosity, practical use, financial considerations, and self-promotion. Relevant here are four collections established between *c.* 1670 and 1720: those of Frederik Ruysch (1638–1731), Nicolaes Witsen (1641–1717), Albertus Seba (1665–1736) and Levinus Vincent (1658–1727).[23] Interestingly, Ruysch, Seba and Vincent tried to sell their collections to Sir Hans Sloane, President of the Royal Society in London and by far the most important private collector of the first half of the eighteenth century.[24] Frederik Ruysch was a pioneer in anatomical material. His collection of specimens was sold to Tsar Peter the Great in 1717, as the cabinet of the pharmacist Albert Seba had been a year earlier.[25] In both collections we see the unity of order, beauty and practical utility. We have already noted the importance of the Bible with regard to collections: it provided the background to the collection of the Amsterdam burgomaster and VOC-director Nicolaes Witsen, who was intrigued by the biblical account of the Flood and took a great interest in the remains of animals found high on mountaintops or deep in the earth. This is one of the issues that later fascinated Van Marum, and it is significant that some of the *fossilia* auctioned by Witsen's heirs in 1753 are now in Teyler's Museum.[26] But where Witsen focused on a literal reading of Genesis, Van Marum found the biblical account of the Flood problematic.

This continuity in the culture of collecting, on a local level as well, is evident in the important case of Levinus Vincent (figures 5.2–5.4). Vincent, coming from a Mennonite background, was a dealer in printed textiles. His collection consisted of *naturalia*, ordered and displayed in an aesthetically pleasing way, including intricate compositions of beautifully arranged butterflies. In both

---

22 Berkel 2013. There were also cabinets with living rarities, such as the Menagerie of Blaauw Jan in Amsterdam (with exotic animals and occasionally also people, such as native Americans and people from Greenland): see Bergvelt/Kistemaker 1992a, 16, 18, 20, figs 5, 6 (R. van Gelder), and Bergvelt/Kistemaker 1992b, 138–42, cat. nos 284, 285 (W. de Bell). These cabinets will not be discussed here.

23 On those four in general see e.g. Bergvelt/Kistemaker 1992a and 1992b *passim*; Roemer 2004; Jorink 2010; Margócsy 2014; Roemer 2017. For the individual collectors see Peters 2009 (Witsen); Roemer 2008 (Ruysch); Kooijmans 2010 (Ruysch); and Sliggers in Chapter 6 below.

24 Jorink 2012. On Sloane see Delbourgo 2017.

25 Driessen-van het Reve 2006, 138–139 and 111–112; Driessen-van het Reve/Bleker 2017.

26 Sliggers 2017.

texture and structure the fluid boundaries between art and science, the creative power of God and that of men, were stressed.[27] In collections like these the underlying order and sheer beauty of nature was made visible, even tangible. Vincent opened his collection – or, as he called it, his *Wondertooneel der Nature* – 'wonder-theatre of nature' – to visitors in Amsterdam around 1690. He kept a visitors' book, showing the names of many visitors from all over Europe – including princes and surprisingly many women. Like Ruysch he had fixed times of entry, as well as an admission fee. He made his collection known through flyers and he published a splendid illustrated book on his collections in 1706, followed by a sequel in 1715 (figures 5.2, 5.3).[28] It can be seen as a catalogue, where each item was linked to relevant scientific literature. His work is a good illustration of the increasingly more public nature of collections, and of their more scientific nature. However collections like these, reflecting debates on the foundations and aims of knowledge, remained encyclopaedic in nature. Around 1750 the interplay between texts and objects – works of nature or works of men – remained key to the practice of collecting.

Around 1710 Vincent moved from Amsterdam to nearby Haarlem, where he registered as a member of the Guild of St Luke, and besides showing his collection he continued to trade in exquisitely printed textiles.[29] Within the community of the city, he must have been a well-known and trustworthy man.[30]

3 Scientific Culture in Haarlem

Relatively little is known of the context in which Vincent's collection in Haarlem was on display until his death in 1727.[31] The *Wondertooneel* seems to

---

27 Roemer 2017.

28 Vincent 1706 and 1715. His visitors' book was discovered in Dublin by Roelof van Gelder (Chester Beatty Library, Ms W 170), Gelder 1992.

29 The Guild of St Luke was open to (master) painters in the broad sense of the word and to designers of patterns for textiles. In most accounts of his life Vincent's move to Haarlem is dated around 1705; however, as late as 1708 he was receiving visitors in Amsterdam. The entries in his visitors' book (see the previous note) indicate a move to Haarlem around 1709–10. I would like to thank David van der Linden for providing me with photographs of the visitors' book. In earlier accounts on Vincent a move to The Hague is mentioned. I have found no evidence of this. After his death in 1727 his widow continued to trade in printed textiles from the Groote Markt in Haarlem: see *Oprechte Haerlemsche Courant*, 24 June 1728 (accessed via Delpher, 4 Feb. 2019).

30 This is indicated by the fact that he sometimes acted as an assistant to notaries: see *Oprechte Haerlemsche Courant*, 22 Nov. 1722 (accessed via Delpher, 4 Feb. 2019).

31 Evidence for where Vincent settled in Haarlem is somewhat confusing. Sliggers 2017, 91 and n. 82, says that he lived at the Rozenprieel near the city gate. The advertisements

THE FIRST MUSEUM IN THE NETHERLANDS?

FIGURE 5.2 Illustration from Levinus Vincent, *Wondertooneel der Nature* (Amsterdam 1706). In this idealized scene the *naturalia* are ordered by type. ALLARD PIERSON, AMSTERDAM, OTM OG 63-7032

FIGURE 5.3 Drawers of a wooden cabinet, from Levinus Vincent, *Wondertooneel der Nature* (Amsterdam 1706).
ALLARD PIERSON, AMSTERDAM, OTM OG 63-7032

have provided an important link in a longer tradition of studying and contemplating nature for the love of God, of which also the establishment of Teyler's Oval Room in 1784 could be seen as a result.

It is worth setting out some local conditions. First, fuelled by the Dutch Revolt, Haarlem had a long scholarly and artistic tradition. Moreover, in the course of the eighteenth century all kinds of informal scientific societies, where

---

quoted in the preceding notes give his address as 'De Groote Markt', i.e. in the heart of the city. Perhaps Vincent had, like so many wealthy citizens in Haarlem including Teyler, a second luxury home. Additional archival research could reveal more details.

THE FIRST MUSEUM IN THE NETHERLANDS?

sociability, the honour of God, and interest in the commonwealth overlapped, were established, almost all on a local level. These often rather small associations of scientific and artistic amateurs met regularly, doing experiments, discussing topics of mutual interest, and sometimes organizing public lectures.[32]

Secondly, in Haarlem an influential Mennonite community developed in the course of the seventeenth and eighteenth centuries. As discussed in Chapter 2, this was a relatively small but influential group, on account of their wealth and involvement in the textile industry and in printing, publishing and dealing in books (Levinus Vincent, Cornelis Loosjes and Pieter Teyler are only a few examples).[33] Initially barred from public institutions, they focused on a private life of piety and charity, but in the eighteenth century they became an economic and social factor of importance. Many of them also devoted themselves to the study of nature, and played a role in the societies mentioned above. Physico-theology – studying nature in order to honour God – was a characteristic eighteenth-century phenomenon to which Mennonites greatly contributed. Collecting shells, making observations with telescopes, and publishing lengthy poems or scientific books became extremely popular. With the advance of a new mechanistic concept of nature, attention was increasingly focused on the underlying order, beauty and utility of nature – the great work of the Divine Architect, so miraculously constructed that even the most stubborn atheist would be convinced of His existence.[34]

We see this reflected in Vincent's collection. It is shown in a room in classical style, with several cabinets – themselves geometrical works of art – containing the works of nature (figures 5.2–5.4). A *Simpliciakast*, a wooden cabinet in the Rijksmuseum in Amsterdam containing *naturalia*, many of them ingredients for drugs or pigments, dating from the same decades displays a highly complex structure and content, with many overlapping layers of meaning – including utility, order and wonder (figures 5.5, 5.6).[35] The complex geometrical shapes of the drawer linings can be read as references both to the skill of the craftsman and to the blueprint of God's creation. We could find a similar order in Vincent's collections.[36] Interestingly, the room housing Vincent's collection is depicted as having an oval plan and a domed ceiling (figure 5.4) – characteristic features of Teyler's 'Musaeum', established some seventy years later.[37]

---

32   Mijnhardt 1988; Zuidervaart 1999.
33   Sliggers 1987; Hamm 2011.
34   Vermij 1991; Jorink 2010; Jorink/Maas 2012.
35   Duin 2017.
36   Roemer 2005 and 2017.
37   First noted in Gelder 1992.

FIGURE 5.4 Gerrit Rademaker, *The Cabinet of Levinus Vincent in Amsterdam*, c. 1680–1709, pencil, pen and ink and chalk, 233 x 186 mm. Note the domed ceiling.
RIJKSMUSEUM, AMSTERDAM, RP-T-1980-7

FIGURE 5.5 Collector's cabinet with a miniature pharmacy, c. 1720, oak and pine, veneered with olivewood and other woods, tortoiseshell, ivory, gilt brass and other materials, h 206.8 x w 96.5 x d 74.0 cm.
RIJKSMUSEUM, AMSTERDAM, BK-1956-44

4 The Legacy of Pieter Teyler

As we have seen, Teyler's Foundation was established in 1778. Our knowledge of its founder, Pieter Teyler, remains somewhat scant.[38] Of relevance here are the following facts. Pieter Teyler was born in Haarlem in 1702, and, like his father,

---

38 See mainly Sliggers 2006, but also Weiss 2013a and https://www.teylersmuseum.nl/en/about-the-museum/organisation/who-we-are/the-ideals-of-pieter-teyler/the-ideals-of-pieter-teyler (accessed 17 Jan. 2019). Also Chapter 2 of the present book.

FIGURE 5.6   One of the drawers of the collector's cabinet (figure 5.5), containing minerals and petrified materials. The geometrical pattern could be interpreted as a reference to the order of nature, and to God, the Divine Architect.
RIJKSMUSEUM, AMSTERDAM, BK-1956-44

amassed a fortune with the production of and trade in silk fabrics. A member of the Mennonite community in his native town, he showed a strong interest in religion, art, science and public benefit. Although his name does not appear in Levinus Vincent's visitors' book, young Pieter Teyler may have been aware of that collection, his father being a close colleague of Vincent and belonging to the same religious community. In 1728 Teyler married Helena Wijnands Verschaave; the marriage remained childless. Teyler had a modest collection of books, coins, scientific instruments, paintings, prints and drawings and *naturalia*, but no written reports of visitors are known, and except for the Teekenakademie (Drawing Academy) he seems to have played no role in the many informal

THE FIRST MUSEUM IN THE NETHERLANDS? 101

scientific societies in Haarlem.[39] Much in the spirit of the Royal Society in London, the Hollandsche Maatschappij der Wetenschappen (Holland Society of Sciences) was established in Haarlem in 1752, with a library and a collection of *naturalia*.[40] In 1753 Sir Hans Sloane died and the British Museum, based on his immense collections, was established with an explicit reference to its benefit to the general public.[41] Teyler may have been aware of that. Be this as it may, some years later, in 1756, he drew up his will, stating that his immense fortune (an estimated two million guilders, roughly the equivalent of 20 million euros in 2018) should go to a foundation bearing his name, to be administered by five executors, or Directors, preferably members of his family and Mennonites. In addition, two societies were to be established, and an almshouse was to continue to be maintained.

When Teyler died in 1778 the regulatory six members for each of the two societies were appointed, and both societies started their weekly meetings, each announcing its first essay competition in 1778. The competitions drew attention from all over Europe, and made Haarlem as visible within the scholarly community as the Hollandsche Maatschappij had already done. Subjects to be treated included a comparison between revealed and natural religions (1778) and the national character of the Dutch School in drawings and paintings (1781).[42]

Of relevance here is the appointment of Van Marum (figure 1.3) as a member of Teyler's Second Society. A versatile man, he had obtained his MD in Groningen in 1776.[43] After being bypassed for a chair at his *alma mater* he moved to Haarlem, attracted by the city's lively scientific culture. He established himself as a physician; was appointed town lecturer in natural philosophy (an unpaid position); and was appointed keeper of the collection of *naturalia* of

---

39   On societies in Haarlem, Hamm 2011; on Teyler's role in the first Drawing Academy in Haarlem (1772–95) Sliggers 2006; on all these aspects also Chapter 2 of the present book.

40   Sliggers/Besselink 2002. Chapter 2 of the present book mentions Teyler's membership of the Oeconomische Tak (Economic Branch, a division of the Hollandsche Maatschappij) in 1778, the year of his death.

41   MacGregor 2010; Delbourgo 2017.

42   Bruijn 1971. Knolle in Chapter 8 below discusses the competitions of 1781 (published in 1787) and 1806 (published in 1809). With regard to the 1781 competition see also Reynaerts 2001. For the 1806/1809 competition see also Bergvelt 1976, 44–46, and for one of the unpublished entries for the 1811 competition Bergvelt 2007, 277–80. See also Chapter 2 in the present book.

43   On Van Marum see Wiechmann/Palm 1987; Weiss 2013a; Sliggers 2017; and Chapters 1–4, 6 and 10 in the present book.

the Hollandsche Maatschappij. Taking advantage of the dense intellectual network in the city, Van Marum responded to the first essay competition issued by the Second Society (on the properties of gases) – and won. By then he had been appointed a member of that Society, and he would dominate it for nearly half a century. Due to his efforts the Foundation's library and collections expanded enormously, and became famous in the world of learning. Moreover, Van Marum was instrumental in the establishment of the Oval Room.

As early as 1779 forces within the institution succeeded in giving a rather liberal interpretation to the will. Where the document had stipulated the preservation of the collections, the Directors soon started selling off the *naturalia* and most of the books and works of art. Only Teyler's numismatic collection was kept intact.[44] Things took a more constructive turn when in the same year, 1779, plans were discussed to construct 'a room for the library' behind the Foundation House.[45] Instrumental in this scheme were one of the Directors, Jacobus Barnaart Jr (1726–1780), and then Van Marum. Barnaart, a Mennonite trader with a strong interest in astronomy, seems to have had the idea. Interestingly, his father had seen Levinus Vincent's collection and might have retained memories of that event.[46] Later, Van Marum would recall how Barnaart 'acquired the consent of his fellow trustees for the construction of a spacious room, designed for the collection of scientific instruments and of *naturalia*, for the housing of drawings and prints, and, especially for the benefit of the natural sciences [i.e. the Second Society], a choice library'.[47] Note the vagueness in terminology, and the stated aim for the construction of a room especially for the benefit of the natural sciences, including a library.[48]

Back to 1779: a young architect, Leendert Viervant (1752–1801) (figure 2.1), was commissioned to make a design for 'the proposed building'. At the explicit request of Barnaart, there was to be an astronomical observatory on the roof of the new 'Book and Art Room'.[49] Within months the plans were agreed on. The surviving drawings include a rather undetermined sketch for the ground floor (where Van Marum would later install the minerals, rocks and fossils and the electrostatic generator) and a much more detailed design showing a library

---

44 Weiss 2013a, 41.

45 ibid., 63, n. 117: 'op dat men zoude kunnen vorderen om een Besluit te nemen wegens het Timmeren eener Zaal tot de Boekerij'.

46 Barnaart senior's signature is in Vincent's visitors' book: Chester Beatty Library, Dublin, Ms W 170, f. 20.

47 Weiss 2013a, 62.

48 ibid., 66. Pieter Teyler himself, as a collector, had only a superficial interest in the natural sciences, but in his will he mentions them as the first task of the Second Society.

49 Weiss 2013a, 64: 'Boek- en Konst Zael', 'het voorgenomen gebouw'.

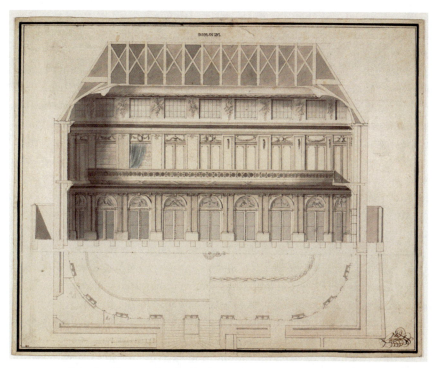

FIGURE 5.7   Leendert Viervant, *Longitudinal section and ground plan of the Oval Room*: final design, signed 'Viervant' lower right, undated (1779?), pencil, pen in brown, brush in grey, pink, ochre and blue, 480 x 600 mm. Note the details of the Library on the first floor, including shelves and a curtain.
TEYLER'S MUSEUM, ATS_339-009

on the first floor (figure 5.7). Building work began, and was completed in the summer of 1784.

Three points are of relevance here. First, as we have seen, the highly ambitious plans for what came to be known as the Oval Room were not anticipated by Pieter Teyler. Secondly, the new building was only occasionally referred to as the 'museum': it was intended as a place for research and contemplation, specifically for the use of the Directors and members of both societies and their guests. Notions of 'the general public' were secondary, if there were any at all.[50] Thirdly, it is worth looking a little more at Viervant's splendid design. The Oval Room has always aroused strong feelings of amazement and piety: its classical design, including the oval roof admitting daylight, can be experienced as a temple of art and science, prompting metaphysical reflections (figure 1.2).

---

50   ibid., 70–89.

In discussions of the Oval Room its design is usually seen as unique in the Netherlands, although as early as 1992 Roelof van Gelder had signalled the similar shape of Vincent's own 'wonder theatre' as depicted in the surviving visual material (figure 5.4).[51] I would strongly support this line of thought: the memory of Vincent (who died in 1727) and his collection must have been very much alive in the Mennonite community in Haarlem. Conclusive evidence for its influence on Viervant's design is lacking, but my basic point here is: might it not be worth thinking about the Oval Room more in terms of continuity than as a start from scratch? It is worth noting that the Oval Room was intended as a site of knowledge – bringing together books, various collections of objects, and scientific instruments in a space that was intended for establishing, discussing and diffusing knowledge. Much in the spirit of the late eighteenth century, it was intended as a *musaeum* in the Classical and Renaissance sense.

When construction started in 1780 this was a rather abstract idea. The projected building was far too big for Teyler's rather modest and soon reduced collections. This is where the ambitious Van Marum took his advantage. With his mixture of erudition and power-play he managed to get the attention of the Directors of the Foundation to expand the collections.[52] As is said elsewhere in this book, two of Van Marum's most spectacular purchases were made slightly before the Oval Room was completed in June 1784: the world's biggest electrostatic generator (figures 3.2, 7.6) and the mysterious remains of a huge aquatic animal, found in a quarry near Maastricht in 1760 – the extinct mosasaur, as would become clear in the nineteenth century (figure 7.5).[53] Both were bought for large sums, around 3,500 guilders each, and both were intended as objects for research. The 'Maastricht Creature' became the subject of learned discussion and was instrumental in shaping the context for new ideas on the true age of the world and the extinction of animals. Whereas electricity was a new branch of the natural sciences, Van Marum's fascination with geology and fossils is a vivid manifestation of the practice of linking objects with texts – including the Word of God. In 1783 the competition question of Teyler's Second Society, on the value of fossils for discussions of the true age of the world, was written (by Van Marum himself) specifically with the 'Maastricht Creature' in mind. Was it a fish, a whale, a crocodile? How did its unusually big bones end up deep in Mount St Pieter, more than 90 miles from the Dutch coast? What could scientists learn from the increasing number of highly problematic remains of animals and plants

---

51   Gelder 1992.

52   On Van Marum's acquisitions see for example Sliggers 2017 and Chapter 6 below; Meijers 2017 and Chapter 2 above.

53   Wiesenfeldt 2002; Sliggers 2006; Weiss 2013a; Sliggers 2017.

THE FIRST MUSEUM IN THE NETHERLANDS?

that were excavated from deep in the earth or found on top of mountains? The winning essay by François-Xavier Burtin considered the problems of the extinction of animals and the unstable geological shapes of the earth.[54] It opened the possibility of thinking of change and contingency in God's creation, fuelling the tendency not to take the biblical account literally in scientific matters. Tellingly, one of the deeply religious Directors of Teyler's Foundation, Adriaan van Zeebergh, a member of the official Dutch Reformed Church, took offence at Burtin receiving the gold medal. The relation between science and religion was not as unproblematic as many Enlightenment physico-theologists would believe it was. Objections from the (Mennonite) members of the Theological Society, however, have not come down to us.[55] Discussions of the 'Maastricht Creature' were instrumental in prompting new ideas on the true age of the world and the creation of men and animals – leading to Lyell's *Principles of Geology* (1830–33) and Darwin's *On the Origin of Species* (1859).

5   Texts, Images, Objects, Models

Van Marum kept a diplomatic silence on the issue of science and religion. He had, however, an open mind on the relation between books, visual culture and the pursuit of knowledge. Combining his membership of Teyler's Second Society (from 1804 as its chairman) with the newly created position of Director of Teyler's Museum and keeper of the Foundation's library from 1784, he managed to expand Teyler's original collection beyond recognition – mostly with instruments, minerals, and fossils.[56] The Oval Room was mostly a place for research of a more private character. Compared with Vincent's collection sixty years earlier, there were few visitors.[57] The collection of minerals and fossils,

---

54   Sliggers 2017 and the forthcoming dissertation by Mathijs Boom. For Burtin see also Chapter 2 above, p. 40, n. 69 and p. 41, n. 72.

55   For the assessment procedure of the competition entries, see Chapter 2.

56   In the early modern sense of the term, 'fossils' (Latin *fossilia*) referred to everything that was dug up from the ground, even coins and antique statues. Remains of dead creatures also counted as 'fossils'. See Rudwick 1985 and 2014. Van Marum, however, didn't use such an inclusive concept of 'fossil', and already made a clear distinction between minerals and fossils.

57   We lack detailed information on the number of visitors between 1784 and 1788, but visitors' books since 1789 survive, and are available online: see http://beeld.teylersmuseum. nl/digital_ library/Webs-Gastenboek/Gastenboeken/Gastenboeken.htm. The first years mark a rather irregular, low number of visitors, usually not more than ten a week. From the surviving evidence it can be deduced that Vincent had an average of twenty to thirty. See also Weiss 2013a.

however, was displayed in harmony with the building's design, in the tradition of stressing scientific order and utility as well as beauty. With the support of the Directors, Van Marum made many other acquisitions.[58]

Two points have hitherto received little attention: the expansion of the Library, and the collection of scale models of, for example, pumps and mills and also of Mont Blanc. First the library.[59] In the early designs what became the Oval Room was often referred to as the *Leeszaal* or *Boekerij*, the Library. The purchase of books, including the most recent publications in all fields of Van Marum's many interests, was at the centre of his attention. As in other Enlightenment sites of knowledge, such as the Museum Fridericianum in Kassel and the British Museum, books formed the heart of the collection – physically as well as intellectually. Van Marum kept a sharp eye on the scientific output of his peers, both in the Dutch Republic and abroad, and, in a way that needs further investigation, managed to persuade the Directors to acquire even the most expensive books.[60] Teyler's Foundation subscribed to all the leading scientific journals, including the *Philosophical Transactions of the Royal Society*, the oldest publication in the genre (first published in 1665). It also became the owner of such works as William Hamilton's books on the archeological findings (1766–67) and the eruption of Vesuvius (1776; with handcoloured illustrations), Diderot's and d'Alembert's *Encyclopédie* (a rare, complete set), and Audubon's *Birds of America* (1827–38), now one of the most expensive books. In order to satisfy the needs of the Theological Society, precious editions of the church fathers of the first four centuries AD were bought. In size the library soon surpassed Teyler's original collection (from which most had subsequently been sold off). Van Marum published a catalogue in 1826.[61] The introduction provides an interesting insight into his motives. He wrote that he had proposed to the Foundation's Directors and to his fellow-members of the Second Society 'to collect any work that, on account of its illustrations of objects, might be deemed too expensive to be purchased by its individual

---

58   Weiss 2013a; Sliggers 2017. In addition to the 'Maastricht Creature' the collection included another problematic item, given the name *Homo diluvii testis* (the man who witnessed the Great Flood), found in 1726 and purchased by Van Marum in 1790. See also above, p. 90, and Vos in Chapter 9 below, p. 139, n. 18.

59   Unfortunately Teyler's library is not yet catalogued in a user-friendly way. It is not accessible, for example, via WorldCat and only partly via STCN. Targeted searches can be performed via https://www.teylersmuseum.nl/nl/collectie/boeken-overzicht.

60   Cf. Sliggers 2017.

61   Marum 1826. For the catalogue online, with additional manuscript notes, see http://beeld. teylersmuseum.nl/Digital_Library/Emags/34d_61/ (accessed 4 Feb. 2019). Cf. Sliggers 2006, 227–30.

THE FIRST MUSEUM IN THE NETHERLANDS? 107

users'.[62] Illustrated travel accounts were to be collected, as well as works on exotic peoples, flora and fauna. But not only those books had to be purchased: 'also less expensive, in which the best or latest systematic illustrations of this kind can be found'.[63] Sharing, viewing, and discussing knowledge, including illustrations, with one's peers was an important aspect of eighteenth-century scientific societies.

Interesting is the great emphasis that Van Marum put on the visual. Texts, images and objects clearly had overlapping epistemological values – as they already had in the scholarly and scientific culture of the seventeenth century. Elsewhere in this volume, Koenraad Vos explores the way in which Van Marum relied on Wybrandt Hendriks' artistic skills to provide illustrations of scientific objects. The great importance given to images is also clear in article 11 of the Instruction of the Directors of Teyler's Foundation to the Director of Teyler's Museum (drawn up by Van Marum himself) of 25 September 1784:

> The Director is bound to have the [aforementioned] Fossils depicted and described in a way appropriate to communicate with the Public. Among other items, the Maastricht Fish-head is deemed most worthy to be depicted and described as an appendix to the publication of the prize-winning essay answering the question issued [in 1783] by the Second Foundation.[64]

Texts, objects, and images of objects were all instrumental in the establishment and communication of knowledge. Wybrand Hendriks was also commissioned to provide images of the electrostatic generator. However, it took several experienced craftsmen before the drawings were successfully converted into prints (figure 7.6). When the sixteen engravings were at last published in Van Marum's treatise on the generator, the total cost of the images was a stunning 6,594 guilders – 3,344 more than the machine had cost![65]

Finally there is another group of collectibles that has received too little attention. In addition to objects (books, instruments and minerals) and images, the Directors of Teyler's Foundation instructed Van Marum to acquire all kinds of scale models. In the eleven articles of the Instruction to the Director of Teyler's Museum, models are mentioned five times, which suggests the importance attached to them. Models of windmills, crystals (figure 6.7) and

---

62   Marum 1826, ii.
63   ibid., iv.
64   See Weiss 2013a, 304.
65   Wiesenfeldt 2002, 222.

Mont Blanc – all still present at the Museum – were of heuristic value: they could be instrumental in viewing and understanding specific processes or shapes. But they seem to be more than scale models of the creations of God and men at the same time. Could they give the viewer an idea of seeing the world at a single glance like the Almighty Architect – as the cabinet, the *orbis in domo*, once did?

6   Conclusion

When the Oval Room was opened in 1784 it did not mark the beginning of something totally new, but was chiefly the continuation of a powerful long tradition, local, national and European. Under what was still an uncertain concept of the 'museum' lay an early modern epistemological basis: the establishment of knowledge was a joint enterprise, based on experiment, observation, examination and discussion of texts and objects, and their presentation in images, words and models. Knowledge could serve overlapping purposes, ranging from sheer wonder to practical utility. The library, as both a physical space and a heuristic instrument, was at the core of this, as it had been in the Renaissance and in ancient Alexandria – or so Enlightenment scholars were happy to believe. The collection of books, instruments, fossils, coins and medals and works of art, bequeathed by Pieter Teyler and subsequently adapted and expanded by Teyler's Foundation, was mainly intended as a tool for the scholarly and scientific research of the two learned Societies and their guests, and not simply as a collection in itself, or for the benefit of the general public. Collections open to a wider audience had a longer pedigree, such as those of Frederik Ruysch and Levinus Vincent, both of which had opened their doors to visitors a century earlier, the latter in Haarlem *c.* 1710. Nor was the Oval Room the first building explicitly commissioned for the purpose: the *Gallerij* built in the Leiden Botanical Garden in 1610 had had a similar function. What made the Teyler project unique in Europe was that it was the result of a private initiative, establishing a well-endowed Foundation and two learned societies that, by means of meetings, lectures, competitions and, last but not least, a soon famous collection, made Haarlem a key point in the rapidly changing European landscape of art, science and religion.

CHAPTER 6

How to Collect Minerals, Rocks and Fossils for a Museum: The International Networks of Martinus van Marum (1750– 1837)

Bert Sliggers

This chapter shows the ways in which Martinus van Marum built up the geological collections of Teyler's Museum, especially with regard to minerals and rocks (solid aggregates of one or more minerals), and to a lesser extent fossils. We look at his successful efforts as director of scientific collections to convince those in charge of the purse-strings to make major investments in those areas. We see how he built up an extraordinarily large and important network through his travels, correspondents and trading partners, and how he made acquisitions from professional dealers as well as private collectors, by engaging in exchanges and through auctions. The international trade in fossils, rocks and minerals underwent a transformation in the final quarter of the eighteenth century, reflected in the collections of Teyler's Museum. Rocks and fossils in particular were at the heart of a growing debate in the scientific community. This also applied to Van Marum: his acquisitions played an important role in his lectures, in which he used the collections to explain the history of the earth, a topical issue in late eighteenth-century Europe.

● ● ●

1   The World behind the Geological Collections in the Oval Room[1]

The central cabinet in the Oval Room contains the nucleus of the mineral collection of Teyler's Museum (figure 6.1). Part of the interior of the cabinet still dates from the days of Martinus van Marum (1750–1837), the first Director of the Museum, appointed in 1784 (figure 1.3).[2] Another 10,000 minerals and rocks in storage can be attributed to his activity as a collector.[3] Combined with

---

1   This article is based on my PhD dissertation, Sliggers 2017.

2   For Van Marum see Forbes/Lefebvre/Bruijn 1969–76; Snelders 1980; Wiechmann/Palm 1987; Palm 1999. For information about the history of Teyler's Foundation, its two learned societies and museum, see Chapter 2.

3   At present the collection of Teyler's Museum contains 12,000 minerals and rocks and 75,000 fossils. The fossils were collected mainly by Van Marum's successors in the department,

FIGURE 6.1 The Oval Room of Teyler's Museum, opened in 1784. In the centre is the 1802 display case, with rocks and minerals. Photo 2011.

thousands of handwritten labels that have been detached from the objects but luckily preserved, they are silent witnesses to a largely forgotten world of collecting practices, classifications, academic networks, commercial habits, debates on the nature of fossils and the formation of the earth's crust, and much more besides. My research has been an attempt to reveal the world behind these particular objects, all of which were collected for Teyler's Museum by Martinus van Marum. It seeks to give the collection back its voice. Combining the financial records of Teyler's Foundation with the minutes of meetings held by the Directors and Teyler's Second Society, as well as Van Marum's travel journals, written records of lectures, correspondence, and other manuscripts made it possible to reconstruct his purchases and to match labels to objects. In this article I will sketch the international networks that made it possible for Van Marum to assemble a scientific museum collection. I will also discuss the ways in which the objects were arranged after they had arrived in Haarlem.

---

especially Jacob Gijsbertus Samuël van Breda (1788–1867, keeper 1839–64), Tiberius Cornelis Winkler (1822–97, keeper 1864–97), and Eugène Dubois (1858–1940, keeper 1898–1940).

HOW TO COLLECT MINERALS, ROCKS AND FOSSILS FOR A MUSEUM

My studies of the geological collections of Teyler's Museum also shed fresh light on the acquisition and composition of collections of this kind in a more general sense. Recent years have witnessed a surge of interest among science historians in *naturalia* and other material objects related to scholarship, as well as in collection-building in this field. The potential of these objects has been overlooked for a long time, partly because the initial emphasis in the history of science was on the experimental and mathematical sciences. Today there is a greater awareness of the important role they play in the formation, dissemination, and circulation of knowledge. For instance, collections of fossils, minerals and rock samples played a key role in the emergence of new disciplines such as mineralogy and geology.

2 Archival Sources for a Reconstruction

Strikingly, Van Marum's geological collecting has never before been the subject of a separate study,[4] in contrast to his activities in the disciplines of physics, chemistry, botany and medicine. The thousands of objects with their accompanying labels,[5] the hundreds of letters,[6] and several travel journals[7] allow us to reconstruct his collecting policy very well, up to and including the arrangement of objects in the museum's exhibition rooms. These sources also provide insight into the complex networks that were essential to the development of scientific collections around the year 1800. Personal ties and mutual trust, built up partly by foreign travel, were key to this process. Van Marum undertook ten collecting journeys, to destinations including Brabant (1782), Paris (1785), Germany (Lower Saxony, Saxony and Brandenburg; 1786), London (1790), Weimar and Jena (1798), and Switzerland (1802). The journey to England focused largely on physics, while the others were used to acquire fossils, minerals, and rocks. Although the journals Van Marum kept of these trips were published in their entirety in 1970,[8] few wrote at the time about the relationship between these trips and the Museum's existing material collections. The journals, combined with the correspondence, the labels, and the financial accounts in the archives of Teyler's Foundation,[9] make it

---

4   Except for the article by Meijers 2017, focusing on Van Marum's Russian aspirations.
5   The labels date back to the previous owners of the items. They are kept in the Paleontological and Mineralogical Cabinet of Teyler's Museum, numbered with L for label, sometimes in combination with M for mineral.
6   NHA, Van Marum Archives 529–14 to 529–23.
7   NHA, Van Marum Archives 529–10.
8   Forbes/Lefebvre/Bruijn 1969–76, II (1970; R. Forbes).
9   ATS 547-548; 610-634.

possible to reconstruct the provenance of the collection accurately. Most of the acquisitions mentioned in Van Marum's journals still exist in the geological collections of the museum.

3 Acquisitions by Auctions, Correspondence and Exchange

Invaluable sources in this connection are the surviving letters exchanged between Van Marum and the scientists and collectors that he met on his travels. They often led to new acquisitions for Teyler's. The greatest mineralogists of the period may thus be regarded as the founding fathers of the collection: they are René-Just Haüy (1743–1822), professor of mineralogy at the Jardin des Plantes and the École des Mines in Paris, Johann Friedrich Wilhelm Toussaint von Charpentier (1779–1847) and Abraham Gottlob Werner (1749–1817), both active at the Freiberg Mining Academy,[10] and the Swiss statesman and geologist Hans Conrad Escher von der Lindt (1767–1823). The provenance of objects can sometimes be inferred from notes about previous owners on some of the original labels that came with the objects that Van Marum acquired (figures 6.2–6.4). Besides illuminating his collecting policy, the labels also reveal a great deal about older collections that he acquired for the Museum, by purchasing them from the owner or at auctions. Examples are Willem van der Meulen (1714–1808, auction in 1782), Johannes le Francq van Berkhey (1729–1812, auction in 1785), Johann David Hahn (1729–1784, auction in 1785), Wouter van Doeveren (1730–1783, auction in 1785), and Martinus Houttuyn (1720–1798, auction in 1789). Comparing handwriting has made it possible to identify labels from the collections of Jakob Samuel Wyttenbach (1748–1830), Johann Georg Lenz (1748–1832), Barthélemy Faujas de Saint-Fond (1741–1819), Horace-Bénédict de Saussure (1740–1799), Johann Wolfgang von Goethe (1749–1832) and sixty other private individuals.

Another interesting area of study is the flourishing trade in minerals, rocks and fossils. Van Marum built up good ties with merchants who visited Teyler's Museum and who in their turn welcomed him on his travels. In Holland the best suppliers were Georg Friedrich Danz, Johann Gottfried Voigt and Johann Christian Stock, all originating in Germany. In England Van Marum had good relations with Jacob Forster, John Mawe, White Watson and William Humphrey. Relatively recent publications, such as that of Michael P. Cooper,[11] show that Van Marum did business with the leading dealers of his day.

---

10 For mining academies see below. Freiberg was one of the first, founded in 1765. See also n. 27.

11 Cooper 2006.

4 Scientific, Religious and Decorative Aspects

In order to view Van Marum's approach to this collection area historically, we must go back in time. In the seventeenth century minerals, rocks and fossils were generally incorporated in the cabinet (or *simpliciakast*) of a physician or pharmacist.[12] In the eighteenth century, however, while such cabinets still existed (figure 5.5), their main focus was on non-specific raw materials with medicinal associations. The religious associations that had been so important in such collections faded into the background. Direct references to the Bible had vanished by the beginning of the eighteenth century. The objects were slowly but surely pried loose from a traditional textual framework, a process that went hand in hand with the rise of a new conceptual framework and the emergence of new disciplines, most notably geology. Nevertheless, rocks and fossils continued to be regarded as testimonies of Creation until the beginning of the nineteenth century, even though the biblical story had to be stretched considerably in time because of new discoveries. For the followers of physico-theology these observations confirmed all the more how almighty and ingenious the Creator was.[13]

At the same time, the decorative aspect remained immensely popular throughout the eighteenth century, for example in the form of cut agates, carnelians and opals, as well as marble, soapstone, and dendrite. The relationship between nature and art, and the encyclopaedic ideal in general, endured longer in eighteenth-century collections than is generally assumed.[14] However, it can be observed that in the last quarter of the eighteenth century collectors became less interested in the decorative qualities of handsome minerals and went in search of often inconspicuous rocks (solid aggregates of one or more minerals) that could help to explain the history of the earth's crust.

5 Early Mineral and Paleontological Collections in the Netherlands

The relative lack of modern scholarly interest in the earth sciences in natural history collections in the Netherlands of the seventeenth and eighteenth centuries is striking. A possible reason for this is that the other two realms of nature – fauna and flora – were generally well represented in such collections, whereas minerals, rocks and fossils tended to be rarer. One of the exceptions is

---

12   For a recent discussion of a *simpliciakast* see Duin 2017.
13   Grafton 2012; Jorink 2007, 311.
14   See chapter 6 in Roemer 2005: 'De geregelde natuur. Parallellen tussen kunst en natuur', esp. 167–68.

FIGURE 6.2 Label with the writing of Johannes le Francq van Berkhey (1729–1812) concerning a piece of malachite (figures 6.3, 6.4) that reached the Museum via the collection of Martinus Houttuyn (1720–1798).
TEYLER'S MUSEUM, L2751

the natural history collection of Pieter Valckenier (1641–1712), a diplomat and envoy to the cantons of Switzerland, who collected fossils both there and in southern Germany.[15] As we can see in the *Thesaurus* of the Amsterdam pharmacist Albertus Seba (1665–1736), he too possessed a large collection of fossils and minerals.[16] A third example is the Leiden physician Johannes Frederik Gronovius (1686–1762), a patron of Carl Linnaeus, who had a large collection of minerals and rocks acquired through an extensive international network, in addition to his other collections.[17] A special case is the collection of fossils

---

15   Lange/Schwinge 2004; Berkel 1992, 184, 189; Gelder 1992, 284; Bergvelt/Kistemaker 1992b, 40–41, cat. nos. 51 and 52; Engel 1986, no. 1554.
16   Bos 2015; Seba 2011; Driessen-van het Reve 2006; Bergvelt/Kistemaker 1992a, *passim*; Bergvelt/Kistemaker 1992b, 33–37, 57–58, cat. nos. 33–41, 85–88; Ahlrichs 1986; Boeseman 1970; Holthuis 1969; Engel 1961; Engel 1937. For Seba and his collections see also the contribution of Jorink to this volume, p. 93, especially the main text between n. 23 and n. 25.
17   Prak 1985, 388–89 (for his genealogy). For his mineralogical collection, Gronovius 1740 and 1750.

FIGURE 6.3 A piece of malachite acquired via Martinus Houttuyn (1720–1798), from the collection of Johannes le Francq van Berkhey (1729–1812).
TEYLER'S MUSEUM, M605

FIGURE 6.4 The same piece of malachite (see figure 6.3), illustrated as fig. 5 in Martinus Houttuyn, *Natuurlyke Historie of uitvoerige beschrijving der dieren, planten en mineralen volgens het samenstel van den Heer Linnaeus*, Amsterdam, vol. 33, 1783, p. 200, pl. xlvi.
TEYLER'S MUSEUM

and minerals of Petrus Camper (1722–1789), enlarged by his son Adriaan Gilles Camper (1759–1820). Unlike previous fossil collections, which were fairly randomly composed, it reflected a specific area of interest, namely mammals.[18] Other examples can be found: private collections that generally appear to have vanished from the earth after their owner's death. 'Appear' is an important *caveat* here, since research enables us to reconstruct numerous provenances. In the mid-eighteenth century a number of mineralogical collections started to be developed, the University of Leiden being a primary example, but there was no such thing as a systematic collecting policy.

Dutch interest in the earth sciences certainly increased as the eighteenth century wore on, but most scholars who wanted to study geology *in situ* and in collections were obliged to go abroad, to the places where most rocks and fossils were found. This changed from around 1782, when the governing board of Teyler's Foundation gave Martinus van Marum the opportunity to build up a large palaeontology and mineralogy collection for its new museum in Haarlem. Van Marum had already made some spectacular acquisitions before then – since 1778 in fact, as the Director of the natural sciences collection of the Holland Society of Sciences, also based in Haarlem. In 1783 it was agreed, in order to prevent possible conflicts of interest and competition, that Teyler's Museum would henceforth dedicate itself to fossils and minerals while the Holland Society would focus on animals and plants. Van Marum carried on making acquisitions until his death in 1837, building up a large – and for the Netherlands unique – palaeontology and mineralogy collection, most items being acquired between 1784 and 1803. In that year, the Teyler Directors put a brake on his expenses.[19]

---

18   Berkel/Ramakers 2015; Heiningen 2014; Schuller tot Peursum-Meijer/Koops 1989; Visser 1985.

19   It is possible that a clash of religious beliefs was at the basis of the Directors' prohibition to expand the collections, but there is no indication of that in the archives. For Van Marum's point of view see his 'Journaal van mijne verrichtingen ter verkrijging eener Verzameling van Fossilia in Teyler's Museum' and his 'Geschiedenis van de oprigting van Teijler's Museum' (NHA, Van Marum Archives 529–9). The first author who used these sources was Nieuwenkamp 1971. A second study of the history of the Palaeontological and Mineralogical Cabinet of Teyler's Museum is Wiechmann/Touret 1987. About Van Marum and mineralogy in relation to the crystal models that he bought for the museum (discussed below) see Hooykaas 1949, Saeys 2003, and Touret 2004; in relation to volcanism, Tex 2004, esp. 35–36. About palaeontology and fossils of the Cretaceous bought by Van Marum, Regteren Altena 1956 and Regteren Altena 1963. Van Marum also plays an important role in Rudwick 2005. For Van Marum and the natural history cabinet of the Holland Society of Sciences see Sliggers/Besselink 2002.

FIGURE 6.5
Label with the writing of Martinus van Marum concerning the fragment from the summit of Mont Blanc (figure 6.6) collected by Horace-Bénédict de Saussure (1740–1799) and acquired by Van Marum in 1802 from his son Théodore de Saussure (1767–1845).
TEYLER'S MUSEUM, M6052

FIGURE 6.6
Fragment chipped from the summit of Mont Blanc in 1787 by Horace-Bénédict de Saussure (1740–1799), acquired in 1802 from his son Théodore de Saussure (1767–1845).
TEYLER'S MUSEUM, M3353

6 Acquisition by Travelling

The largest collections in the Dutch Republic soon attracted interest from elsewhere. As a result, large parts of them sometimes ended up in other countries (for instance from the collections built up in the seventeenth and early eighteenth centuries by Bernardus Paludanus, Pieter Valckenier, and Albertus Seba).[20] Conversely, many of the objects in Dutch collections (those of Levinus Vincent and Nicolaes Witsen, for example) were acquired from foreign collections, through the collectors' international contacts. Major items from the fossil collection of the Swiss Johann Jakob Scheuchzer, for instance, ended up in the Netherlands. Meanwhile, auctions attracted a growing crowd of wealthy

---

20   For Paludanus see Gelder 1998; K. van Berkel, 'Paludanus als verzamelaar van naturalia', in Berkel 1992, 170–77; R. van Gelder, 'Het wonder van Enkhuizen', in Gelder 1992, 263–66; and Bergvelt/Kistemaker 1992b, 28–32, cat. nos. 23–32. For Paludanus and his collections see also the contribution of Jorink to this volume. For Valckenier see n. 15 above; for Seba n. 16 above.

enthusiasts as the eighteenth century wore on. Such sales provided opportunities to expand their collections without the need to travel, and the purchasers had the necessary means. The collectors' items circulated within what was ultimately a fairly small world.

For Van Marum too auctions provided a source of acquisitions. Many private collections appeared on the market (see above) during his time at Teyler's Museum, and he took full advantage of the opportunities these sales afforded him. But, as noted above, the main way in which he sought to expand the palaeontology and mineralogy collections of the museum was to undertake frequent journeys around Europe. On his travels he met with collectors, dealers, scholars, and mine supervisors from whom he purchased items directly for the Museum. He maintained this network of contacts after returning home, noting in correspondence which items he was eager to acquire. Van Marum also journeyed to mines and mountain peaks, where he collected specimens himself. In 1802 he did so in Switzerland near Mont Blanc with mineral dealers including Maria Deville, who collected for travellers and scientists. In Geneva, for instance, Van Marum met the son of Horace-Bénédict de Saussure and bought a fragment of the summit of Mont Blanc collected by de Saussure in 1787, and more than thirty other geological items, mostly well described on the labels (figures 6.5, 6.6).

7 How to Subdivide and Classify the Collection

In the early years of the museum, between 1783 and 1802, Van Marum divided the collection into four parts – a scientific mineral collection, a didactic mineral collection, a geological collection of rocks, and a fossil collection. The scientific mineral collection was classified systematically, according to four different systems in succession (see below), and stored in drawers, while the didactic mineral collection, similarly classified but with a more obvious visual appeal, was arranged behind glass on top of the central display case of the Oval Room from 1802 onwards (figure 6.1).[21] Then there was what Van Marum called the 'geological' section: he attached great importance to the collection of rocks, since 'the way in which they have been formed – which must have occurred

---

21   Already since its manufacture (1784–85) the central cabinet had storage space at both rounded ends, that could be opened by lifting and securing the top. In this way the 'most beautiful gold and silver ores, gems or other *fossilia* that are most beautiful to the eye' could be exhibited to the visitors. This construction came to light during the restoration of the cabinet in 2009–10 (see the report of preparatory research by Anne-Marie ten Cate, 8 June 2009, where Van Marum's *Journaal* of 1784 is quoted).

in very different eras – teaches us about the different upheavals or disruptions of rock layers that have taken place on the surface of the earth. It also teaches us the great age of our planet, for which these specimens provide the clearest evidence'.[22]

Rocks were at the heart of a growing debate in the scientific community. In this connection, Van Marum followed Abraham Gottlob Werner in referring to 'primary' and 'secondary' rocks – the former consisting of igneous and metamorphic rocks, and the latter of sedimentary rocks and fossils. This was one of the most didactic collections, which Van Marum did indeed use in his geology lectures.

The fourth collection was that of 'petrefacts', 'fossilized remains of creatures that have inhabited the earth, and plants that have grown on it, in earlier centuries'. This collection was placed in drawers, arranged geographically. The largest items were set behind glass in cabinets in the Oval Room. It is crucial to note that Van Marum kept the fossilized remains of animals and plants separate from the mineral and rock collection, which he saw as testimony to a remote past that could shed light on the history of the earth's crust.[23]

Within a fairly short space of time, the minerals and rocks were classified in accordance with four different mineralogical systems, based on physical or chemical characteristics. This reflects Van Marum's eager embrace of the new science of mineralogy and his close attention to its turbulent developments. He always tried to follow the latest trends. In 1783, a year before the Oval Room opened to the public, he began to classify the still small collection according to the system of the Swedish chemist and mineralogist Johann Gottschalk Wallerius (1709–1785), who was the first to base his classification on chemical research. In 1790 Van Marum switched to the system proposed by the Irish physicist Richard Kirwan (1733–1812), who in his *Elements of Mineralogy* (1784) perfected the chemical classification, to be followed in 1799 by that of Abraham Gottlob Werner, based on the handbook of Johann Georg Lenz (1748–1832). Finally, in 1802, he adopted the system proposed by René-Just Haüy, while retaining Werner's as well. Werner's classification was primarily based on the external appearance of rocks, while Haüy followed the modern science of crystal morphology, based on measurements of the angles between the faces of crystals. Van Marum was immediately interested in the system to recognize minerals by the use of crystal models, first made in terracotta by Jean-Baptiste Romé de l'Isle (1736–1790). In 1785 in Paris he bought a set of 448 models. Between 1802 and 1804 he ordered new sets in pearwood by Haüy, of 597 models. Most are still in Teyler's Museum,

---

22   NHA, Van Marum Archives 529–9, fol. 75; Gelder 1998.

23   Van Marum probably introduced this distinction in line with Werner, the first mineralogist who removed fossils from the mineralogical system (Werner 1774).

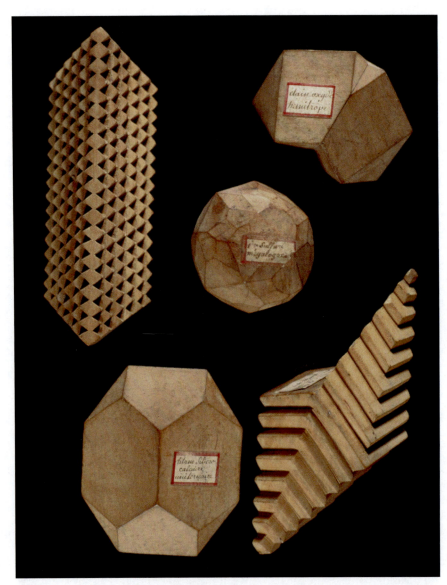

FIGURE 6.7 Five of a set of 597 models of crystals by René Just Haüy, pearwood, ordered between 1802 and 1804 by Martinus van Marum.
TEYLER'S MUSEUM, M11800

the most complete collection of Haüy crystal models that survives (figure 6.7).[24] That Van Marum was able to acquire such a unique collection was again due to his networking: he nominated Haüy for membership of the Holland Society of

---

24   For Haüy's models of crystals see also the contribution by Vos to this volume p. 144.

HOW TO COLLECT MINERALS, ROCKS AND FOSSILS FOR A MUSEUM

Sciences – a position to which Haüy attached great importance, judging by the fact that he mentioned it in all of his publications.

It is clear from the painstaking attention that Van Marum paid to these collections that he considered them of fundamental importance to the Museum, from the point of view of specialized scholarship as well as for their didactic and entertainment value for uninformed visitors. The fact that he adopted four different classification systems in just twenty years demonstrates his fierce determination to keep the collections up-to-date and to ensure that they were classified, preserved, and displayed in accordance with the latest scholarly views.

8   What Handwritten Labels Can Tell Us

What conclusions can we draw from the collections in Teyler's Museum that are – and this is truly unique – still *in situ*? As mentioned before, the Museum has preserved some 6,000 largely handwritten eighteenth-century labels that were once attached to its rocks, minerals, and fossils by their previous owners (figures 6.2, 6.5, 6.8, 6.9).[25] Most became detached over the years, but they have been retained, many serving as index cards. They give a description of the object together with its name, the place where it was found, and sometimes stratigraphic and bibliographical details and provenance – noted by the previous collectors, sometimes copied by Van Marum. Effectively, they constitute the Teyler collection's 'genealogy'. By using handwriting analysis and comparing the labels to receipts, auction catalogues, travel journals, and correspondence, much of the provenance or previous owners of the collection can be reconstructed. This procedure yielded the names of over seventy former owners, besides identifying the auctions at which Van Marum made purchases and the dealers with whom he corresponded. It also revealed that Teyler's Museum is possibly the one institution that still possesses remnants of collections that have otherwise long since been dispersed.[26] Teyler's label collection is probably the oldest, largest, and most diverse of its kind. Thanks to the labels the palaeontology and mineralogy collections reflect the dynamic way in which Van Marum made acquisitions, by travelling, trading, corresponding, buying at auctions, and arranging exchanges – at local, national, and international level.

---

25   For the labels in the Teyler collection see Touret 1985. For the English labels, Cooper 2006. For labels of collectors and traders in Vienna, Fitz 1993. Grundmann published the labels used by the Bergakademie in Freiberg (Grundmann 1986), and Fuchs did the same for Krantz's Mineralien Kontor (Fuchs 1983). For the labels used by Johann Friedrich Blumenbach see Reich/Böhme 2012.

26   Sliggers 2017, Appendix I, 360–97.

9 Economic Aspects of Geological Collections

In Van Marum's time geological research was booming everywhere in Europe and beyond. It was done for the exploration of minerals, ranging from silver, gold and precious stones to more everyday materials such as coal and lignite as fuels, and marble, sandstone and slate as building materials. Mines were dug and exploited, and raw materials were exported.

It is striking that trade and science were in general not separate areas, and even became more and more entwined in the period under review. Dealers were often experts in their field, and experts were sometimes dealers. This trend emerged around the beginning of the eighteenth century, when more and more quarries and mines were being opened up, also in the overseas trading areas, to serve the countries' economic interests (figure 6.10). Soil mapping produced images that added greatly to the stock of knowledge in the earth sciences, which was used for stratigraphic correlation, for instance. Invaluable here were rock and fossil collections, some of which were built up by enthusiastic private collectors. In the latter half of the eighteenth century it became increasingly common to publish these new findings, sometimes merely describing a new mineral, but often registering a specific profile or part of an area, frequently accompanied by maps. Dealers exploited this trend by offering 'the geology' of a specific area to collectors in convenient pieces. Some of these dealers were private retailers, but more and more often they were people with official positions at mines or quarries, or mineralogy lecturers at a university or mining academy (mining academies were technical universities, mostly founded in the eighteenth century, to study and teach all aspects of mining).[27]

Van Marum bought his first collection *Gebirgsarten* (species of rocks) from the mining engineer Johann Karl Wilhelm Voigt at Weimar, minerals from Saxony from Johann Friedrich Wilhelm Toussaint von Charpentier, and minerals from the Harz assembled by the engineer Georg Sigmund Otto Lasius.[28] Most of these collections are still complete in Teyler's Museum.

10 A New Trend: Rocks Instead of Minerals

The public's growing fascination with the earth's history gradually shifted interest away from crystals in favour of rocks and fossils. France had long been the

---

27   Two important examples are those in Chemnitz, founded in 1762 in what was then Hungary, and Freiberg in Saxony (1765): Vaccari 2009.

28   Toussaint von Charpentier 1778; Lasius 1789–90.

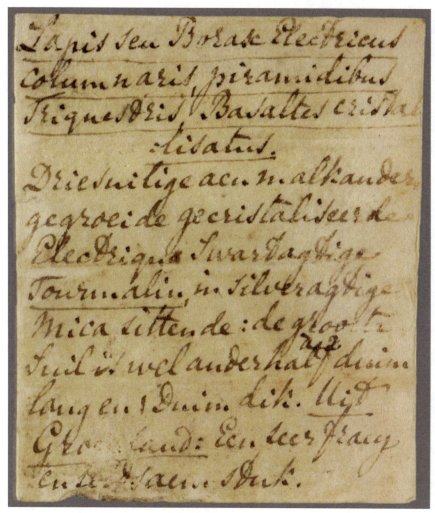

FIGURE 6.8 Label with the writing of Martinus van Marum (1750–1837).
TEYLER'S MUSEUM, L2593

centre of trade in beautiful crystals – stimulated by the classification systems of Romé de l'Isle and then Haüy – whereas the trade in rocks was concentrated in Germany, clearly because of the country's mining areas and the associated academies. The market could scarcely keep up with the new trends, as is clear from Van Marum's complaints that he was compelled to cancel his geology lectures for lack of particular rocks. Dealers could very easily offer all kinds of minerals, but had difficulties to find nice pieces of basalt and granite. Van Marum's purchases show that he was always pursuing two aims: first, to present visitors

FIGURE 6.9
Label with the writing of Barthélemy
Faujas de Saint-Fond (1741–1819).
TEYLER'S MUSEUM, L2067

FIGURE 6.10 Wooden box with tin ores from Malacca, a gift from Cornelis Matthieu
Radermacher to Martinus Houttuyn, acquired after Houttuyn's death in 1798 by
Martinus van Marum.
TEYLER'S MUSEUM, M10010

with a collection in the Oval Room that was clearly arranged and classified in accordance with the latest views; and second, to have the most comprehensive geological collection he could obtain, for educational purposes.[29] Mineralogical items, with their long tradition as beautiful and valuable collector's items,

---

29   Sliggers 2017, chapter 7, 152–80.

HOW TO COLLECT MINERALS, ROCKS AND FOSSILS FOR A MUSEUM

were often purchased at auctions from the collections of private individuals, while rock samples and profiles, sometimes insignificant in appearance, but increasingly sought after by those interested in the history of the earth's crust, were mainly obtained through trade.[30]

Teachers at mining academies took advantage of the fine samples they had of geological profiles. At the end of the eighteenth century it became increasingly common for them to take over from dealers, who had only sold separate pieces. The teachers were able to compile convenient sets of samples displaying a mountain's successive rock layers, which they offered for sale to collectors. The items would generally be numbered, the numbers corresponding to a handwritten or printed catalogue. The origins of these *Suitensammlungen* lay in Freiberg, where some mineralogists went so far as to set up a trading company to sell the rock formation sets. Some collections only contained the different types of rocks, while others came from a specific area and showed the entire succession of a geological profile. For Van Marum this was the best way of expanding the collection of Teyler's Museum. More than any other collector in Holland he plumbed every corner of the market, buying variously from private dealers, mine employees, and university and mining academy teachers. Because of this eclectic approach, numerous collections of this kind, which greatly illuminated the geological development of specific regions, ended up in Teyler's Museum not long after they had been compiled. This was the case in 1828 with 120 rocks and minerals from the Heidelberger Mineralien Comptoir, assembled in 1826 by Karl Cäsar von Leonhard, still present in the Museum (figure 6.11).

11 Promoting Knowledge by Lectures

From 1796 to 1803 Van Marum gave a series of winter lectures to the five Directors and their guests, and the members of the two learned societies of Teyler's Foundation, in which he presented his ideas about fossils and the formation of mountains, the creation of the earth, and the Great Flood.[31] The series give an excellent picture of how Van Marum approached his work in the Museum. In these lectures he could first demonstrate precisely why all the purchases from individuals, at auctions, and on his travels had been so necessary. He always

---

30 ibid., chapter 8, 182–219.

31 Only people related to Teyler's Foundation, societies and Museum were allowed to attend these lectures, so around twenty. The manuscripts are in NHA, Van Marum Archives 529–6.

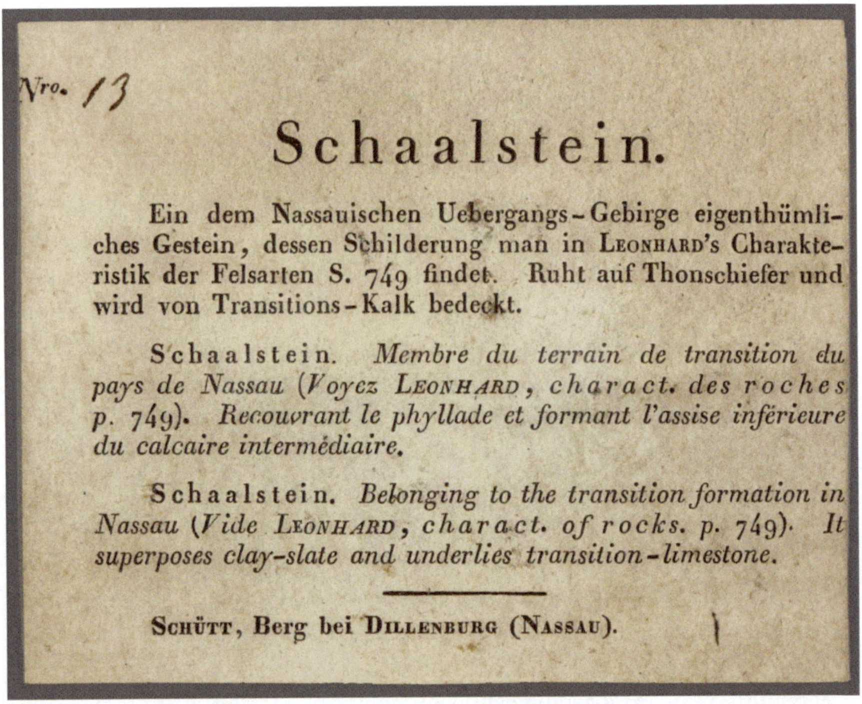

Schaalstein.

Ein dem Nassauischen Uebergangs-Gebirge eigenthümliches Gestein, dessen Schilderung man in LEONHARD's Charakteristik der Felsarten S. 749 findet. Ruht auf Thonschiefer und wird von Transitions-Kalk bedeckt.

Schaalstein. Membre du terrain de transition du pays de Nassau (*Voyez* LEONHARD, *charact. des roches p. 749*). Recouvrant le phyllade et formant l'assise inférieure du calcaire intermédiaire.

Schaalstein. Belonging to the transition formation in Nassau (*Vide* LEONHARD, *charact. of rocks. p. 749*). It superposes clay-slate and underlies transition-limestone.

SCHÜTT, Berg bei DILLENBURG (NASSAU).

FIGURE 6.11 Label of *Schaalstein*, no. 13 in the *Suitensammlung* of 120 rocks and minerals from the Heidelberger Mineralien Comptoir, assembled in 1826 by Karl Cäsar von Leonhard, bought by Van Marum in 1828. The objects have been dispersed throughout the collection.
TEYLER'S MUSEUM, L1113

promised that the objects he discussed would be placed in the Museum (if they were not already on display), with explanatory captions. All this preliminary work could help to produce a catalogue with arguments that were built up more coherently. Since his audience consisted mainly of colleagues and patrons, it was easy enough to show what was lacking, and even to cancel discussing certain topics if the material he needed was not available. In this way he hoped to encourage his patrons to enable him to purchase the missing items.

The objects were also intended to give curious visitors more insight into the origins of the earth and the way life on the planet had developed.[32] Since those visitors were not in the audience, his lectures may be seen as a kind of laboratory in which he worked out the ideas and theories that would eventually be

---

32 NHA, Van Marum Archives 529–6 (1797–98 season, lecture 9).

presented in the Museum. The collection became more and more educational in nature.

Van Marum always kept abreast of the latest theories of mountain formation, volcanism and the Great Flood, for which he had a fine library at his disposal that he had founded in the Museum. He followed the debates about volcanism and basalt formation, but took no active part in them. He did present visual references in the Museum, however, by purchasing a basalt column in 1796, delivered by the English mineral dealer William Humphrey, and volcanic products, as well as prints of the Giant's Causeway, 40,000 interlocking basalt columns in northern Ireland.

12 Religious Aspects of the Geological Collections

In his lectures Van Marum always emphasized the religious aspect of the collections, so as to 'give every philosophical viewer an opportunity to broaden his views of the works of Creation'.[33] In contrast to his physics and chemistry lectures, which tended to highlight the practical usefulness of scientific research, those on geological topics had a more religious flavour. It is not inconceivable that Van Marum saw this emphasis as a tactical way of stimulating the board of Directors to extend funds, and to continue to do so, since their interests and sympathies inclined more to physico-theology than to the more utilitarian aspects of science. Basing himself on the writings of Jean-André De Luc, Van Marum outlined the natural history of the world before the Creation as related in the Old Testament.[34] But he went a step further than that, by suggesting the possible existence of successive waves of creation, each with a more perfect form of humanity. He translated his belief in these successive advances into a suggestion of entirely new 'communities' of reasoning beings, each one surpassing its predecessor. Not until the time described in the Book of Genesis did the present human beings emerge on the scene. It was impossible to recognize a fossilized human being as such, since no one knew what such a creature had looked like. Presented in this way, his views did not appear incompatible with the Bible. However, he confined such philosophical reflections to the restricted audience that attended his lectures: his ideas about pre-Adamite man[35] were only uttered behind closed doors.

---

33   NHA, Van Marum Archives 529–6 (2 November 1798), p. 1 (*aan elken wijsgerigen beschouwer geleegenheid te geeven zijne inzichten in de werken der schepping uit te breiden*).

34   Luc 1779–80. For De Luc see Rudwick 2005.

35   Pre-Adamism is the theological belief that humans (or intelligent but non-human creatures) existed before the biblical character Adam. Van Marum took the idea from the

13   Conclusion

In conclusion, how should we assess the protagonist of this investigation? His greatest achievement was indisputably the creation of the collections themselves. It is important to note, in this connection, that Teyler's Museum soon became organized in a modern way, and that in most respects it came close to the ICOM criteria for professional museums: 'a non-profit, permanent institution in the service of society and its development, open to the public, which acquires, conserves, researches, communicates and exhibits the tangible and intangible heritage of humanity and its environment for the purposes of education, study and enjoyment'. Van Marum took the first steps in these respects.[36]

While as a physicist and a chemist Van Marum was an original thinker – see, for example, his experiments in the field of electricity and the composition of air[37] – as an anatomist and a geologist he was more of a follower. When he did present original ideas, as in the case of the elliptical tree trunks from the Carboniferous Period, they were usually wrong.[38] His classification of the marine reptile known as the mosasaur was flawed even by the standards of his own time.[39] It is not insignificant that the relationship between Van Marum and Georges Cuvier, the French naturalist and zoologist sometimes referred to as the 'founding father of paleontology', was less than cordial, and that Van Marum did not correspond at all with Werner. This was partly because of their respective fields, that of the large fossil mammals and of the stratigraphy of the earth's crust, but the essential difference was that he did not possess their erudition. In that sense, the Van Marum period marks the transition to a new phase in science: that of specialist disciplines separated by strict dividing lines. Van Marum remained throughout his career an encyclopaedic know-it-all, a generalist, whose work as a collector above all was of incalculable value.

---

seventeenth-century French scholar Isaac La Peyrère, who published this theory in his *Prae-Adamitae* in 1655.

36   However, compare the interpretations of Eric Jorink and Terry van Druten in this volume. Van Druten sees this professionalization as only taking place after *c.* 1880, on the way to the opening of the new wing of Teyler's Museum in 1885.

37   See Chapter 2 , p. 37, n. 59 and p. 40, n. 68, and Weiss 2013a and 2019a.

38   Marum 1817 (lecture of 12 May 1814).

39   Pieters 2009.

PART 3

Teyler's between the Natural Sciences and the Visual Arts

∴

CHAPTER 7

'Truth-to-Nature' in the Museum? Wybrand Hendriks, Martinus van Marum and the 'Reasoned Image'

Koenraad Vos

From 1785 until 1819 Teyler's Museum was both the studio of the *kasteleijn* (keeper) and artist Wybrand Hendriks (1744–1831) and the laboratory of its director, the naturalist Martinus van Marum (1750–1837). These important figures in the Museum's history collaborated regularly, as Hendriks made scientific drawings for Van Marum. The images depicted the physical instruments, fossils and minerals that Van Marum assembled in the Museum, and were used for the prints accompanying Van Marum's publications or sent to scientists and collectors with whom he corresponded. This study describes how scientific depiction was viewed and used by Hendriks and Van Marum, by looking at their collaboration and the drawings and prints that it produced. In the discourse surrounding these images, as well as in some of their formal and structural qualities, we can see affinities with what Daston and Galison call 'truth-to-nature' in their book *Objectivity* (2007).

According to that view, in the eighteenth century artists and naturalists did not strive for 'objectivity', a concept that was developed in the course of the nineteenth century, but produced 'reasoned images' that were the result of active interventions by their makers. These images strove to highlight aspects of the depicted object that were representative of their general type. The tension between this generalizing paradigm of the eighteenth century and an individualizing approach towards depicting objects of study, the cause of a conflict between Hendriks and Van Marum, is clearly reflected in the images born of the collaboration between them. In the end, however, it was mostly the generalizing outlook that won out.[1]

• • •

1 Introduction: an Unscientific Image

In 1819 the Dutch artist Wybrand Hendriks (figures 7.1, 9.5) sent an etching to the Hollandsche Maatschappij der Wetenschappen (Holland Society of

---

1 I would like to thank the editors of this volume for their help and their many important suggestions. My thanks also go out to those who helped me during my project at Teyler's Museum or while writing this text: Eric Jorink, Michiel Plomp, Terry van Druten, Celeste Langedijk, Trienke van der Spek, Herman Voogd, Bert Sliggers and Sietske Fransen.

© KONINKLIJKE BRILL NV, LEIDEN, 2021 | DOI:10.1163/9789004441446_008

FIGURE 7.1 Wybrand Hendriks, *Self portrait*, 1807, oil on panel, 30 x 22 cm.
RIJKSMUSEUM TWENTHE, ENSCHEDE (ON LOAN FROM FRANS HALS MUSEUM, HAARLEM), BR2874

'TRUTH-TO-NATURE' IN THE MUSEUM?

Sciences) in Haarlem for inclusion in their periodical, the *Natuurkundige Verhandelingen* (Natural Philosophical Transactions). The etching, by Jacob Elias van Varelen (1757–1840), was based on a drawing by Hendriks featuring a curious tree in the Haarlemmerhout, a wood near the city (figures 7.2, 7.3). The print was received by a person well known to him, Martinus van Marum, who was not only the Maatschappij's secretary but also Director of Teyler's Museum, where Hendriks was *kasteleijn* and curator of the art collection.[2] There was, however, a problem with the etching: Van Marum considered it unfit for publication in a scientific context.

What made the tree of potential interest to science, according to a note accompanying the drawing, was the fact that its trunk had split in two and that from this split a root shot down straight into the ground. The same note records the rejection of the image by Van Marum.[3] It suggests that the tree was considered for publication because it was a curiosity, a singular case of an extraordinary specimen. However it was not the post-Enlightenment rejection of wonder as a scientific category that made Van Marum disapprove of it:[4] it was specifically the way the theme was represented that did not fit his idea of science. The note says that Van Marum disliked the image of the tree because 'the figures added to it' were 'according to his judgment not fit to be included in a scientific work'. This was an unscientific image because of the picturesque addition of human figures in the background. Perhaps it reminded Van Marum too much of Hendriks' country scenes (figure 7.4). But Hendriks had

---

2   Hendriks is relatively understudied compared to Van Marum, especially his works that fall outside traditional art history. The principal catalogue of Hendriks' work is Regteren Altena/ Borssum Buisman/Bruyn Kops 1972; it only contains a selection of his œuvre, including land-scapes, portraits, genre scenes, and some zoological and botanical works.

3   The note in full reads: *Teekening eener boom die zich in de Spanjaardslaan bevindt; uit het midden der gespletene stam schiet van boven naar beneden eene wortel, die zich in den grond vast hecht. Naar deze teekening heeft E. van Varelen, de hierbijgaande etsen gemaakt, en waren bestemd voor de werken der Hollandsche Maatschappij van Wetenschappen te Haarlem, doch derzelver secretaris M. van Marum, keurde die af, om de beeldjes die daarbij gevoegd waren, volgens zijn oordeel ongepast om aldus in wetenschappelijk werk geplaatst te worden, hetwelk echter noodig was, om evenredigheid der groote van dien stam aan te duiden.* (Drawing of a tree in the Spanjaardslaan; from the middle of the split trunk a root shoots straight down and attaches itself to the ground. After this drawing E. van Varelen made the accompanying etchings, intended for the works of the Hollandsche Maatschappij van Wetenschappen of Haarlem, but the selfsame's secretary M. van Marum rejected them, because of the figures added to it – according to his judgment not fit to be included in a scientific work, but need-ed to indicate the relative size of the trunk.) It is not entirely clear who wrote the note, but because it tries to defend the artist's decision we can assume it was Hendriks. The note is catalogued with the drawing: Noord-Holland Archief, Haarlem, NL-HlmNHA_53002867_M.

4   On the place of wonder in Enlightenment science see Daston/Park 2001, 329–63.

FIGURE 7.2
Wybrand Hendriks, *The Wonder Tree on the Spanjaardslaan in the Haarlemmerhout, Haarlem*, 1819, black chalk with watercolour wash, 395 x 251 mm.
NOORD-HOLLANDS ARCHIEF, HAARLEM, NL-HLMNHA_53002867_M (APP. 27a)

FIGURE 7.3
Wybrand Hendriks and Elias van Varelen, *The Wonder Tree on the Spanjaardslaan in the Haarlemmerhout, Haarlem*, 1819, etching, 188 x 122 mm.
NOORD-HOLLANDS ARCHIEF, HAARLEM, NL-HLMNHA_53002631_K (APP. 27b)

'TRUTH-TO-NATURE' IN THE MUSEUM?   135

FIGURE 7.4   Wybrand Hendriks, *Path through the Village of Manen near Ede*, 1783, pen, black chalk and colour wash, 258 x 383 mm.
RIJKSMUSEUM, AMSTERDAM, RP-T-1894-A-2873

good reason for his addition: the figures showed the relative size of the tree. This divergence of ideas is interesting not only because it gives us an insight into what was considered an appropriate scientific image, but also because it came after artist and scientist had collaborated for decades.

It is this collaboration between Hendriks and Van Marum from 1785 until 1819 that is at the centre of this study. What can we reconstruct of the working relation between these two pivotal figures in the history of Teyler's Museum when it comes to the making of scientific images? And what does their combined story tell us about the use of imagery in a scientific context in that time and place? After looking at the historical details of Hendriks' involvement with Teyler's Museum, we will explore these images and the wider context of the use of images in Enlightenment natural philosophy, a paradigm that Daston and Galison have called 'truth-to-nature'.[5] This will

---

5   Daston/Galison 2007, 55–113.

lead us to a discussion of the reconstructed scientific œuvre of Hendriks, mostly in the service of Van Marum, and what it tells us about the way art and science came together around ideas about the depiction of nature that were current in Teyler's Museum at the time. An Appendix listing works by Hendriks and prints based on drawings by his hand can be found at the end.

2 Hendriks, Van Marum and Teyler's Museum

Wybrand Hendriks was born in Amsterdam in 1744, the son of a sculptor.[6] He attended the Amsterdam drawing academy from 1765 to 1774, where he won third, second, and first prizes in 1772, 1773, and 1774. He moved to Haarlem in 1776 and was involved in the city's drawing academy between 1777 and 1782 and between 1785 and 1795, having spent the years 1782–85 in Ede and Amsterdam.[7] He became one of the founders of its successor, the Haarlem Teekencollegie Kunstmin en Vlijt (Drawing Society Love of art and diligence), in 1796.[8] Hendriks' œuvre is extensive and varied, and he worked in almost every genre: individual and group portraits, landscapes and city views, church interiors, flower pieces and still lifes of animals, genre interiors, hunting scenes, allegories, depictions of current events, overdoor and overmantel pieces and painted wallpaper. He became *kasteleijn* at Teyler's Museum in 1785 and stayed in that position until his retirement in 1819, twelve years before his death in 1831.

Wybrand Hendriks and Martinus van Marum were of the same generation. Van Marum, born in Delft in 1750, was one of the most important scientists of his time in the Netherlands, recognized for his achievements by membership of several learned societies and academies all over Europe (figure 1.3).[9] In 1776 he too came to Haarlem, at the time an important centre for the sciences in the Netherlands, especially because of the prominent Hollandsche Maatschappij der Wetenschappen. In that year he was appointed to give lectures in natural philosophy and mathematics to the city. After that his career quickly took off. In 1777 he became Director of the Cabinet of Natural Curiosities of

---

6   The biographical information on Hendriks is based on Regteren Altena/Borssum Buisman/ Bruyn Kops 1972, 5–20. See also the RKD's entry on Hendriks: https://rkd.nl/explore/artists/ 37479.

7   Hendriks' time in the country town of Ede has not been fully accounted for, but it has been suggested that he took on some work in that town after the death there of the painter Anthony Elliger (1701–1781): see Regteren Altena/Borssum Buisman/Bruyn Kops 1972, 8.

8   Hendriks painted a group portrait of its members in 1799: see figure 9.5 in the contribution of Van Druten to this volume. See also Tuyll 1988.

9   The biographical information on Van Marum here is based on Theunissen 1987.

'TRUTH-TO-NATURE' IN THE MUSEUM?

the Hollandsche Maatschappij, and in 1784 he was also appointed Director of the newly founded Teyler's Museum (originally conceived as a Boek- en Konstzael – Book and Art Room – in the service of the two learned Teyler societies). As Director Van Marum was largely responsible for the Museum's collecting policy concerning the natural sciences, assembling an impressive assortment of scientific instruments (most prominently the big electrostatic generator that he had built especially for the Museum) and also of minerals and fossils.[10]

The relationship between Hendriks and Van Marum is partly framed by the institution where they worked. The position of *kasteleijn* was not necessarily subordinate to that of Director in the Museum's hierarchy. This position was already mentioned in Teyler's will of 1756, and the *kasteleijn* was appointed by the Directors of the Teyler Foundation, not by the Museum's Director.[11] A document outlining Hendriks' duties shows that he was responsible for the day-to-day running of the Museum, and also suggests that he was mostly left to his own devices without any official oversight by the Director.[12] The Oval Room dedicated to displaying the collections had opened behind Teyler's former town house in 1784, and Hendriks was responsible for giving visitors access to the Museum and showing them around. He had to live in the house, which meant that he had the responsibility of keeping the whole complex, where he also had his studio, in good order.[13] As an artist – and this quality is specifically mentioned in the instructions for the position of *kasteleijn* (or *Castelein*) – he was also in charge of the art collection, its arrangement, keeping lists and catalogues, ensuring that the works were well kept, going to auctions to acquire drawings and prints, putting these in albums, and even restoring them to some extent.[14]

---

10   For the collection of minerals and fossils see the contribution of Sliggers to this volume.

11   Teyler's will is published in Sliggers 2006, 191–206; for this passage see 199.

12   The only references to the Museum's Director in this document are in relation to the collection of instruments and the library, and to the admissions policy: see *Instructie voor den Castelein*, ATS 5, 143–44.

13   On the Museum as studio see Druten 2010.

14   *Instructie voor den Castelein*, ATS 5, 143. There are many mentions of new acquisitions by Hendriks in the financial records (*kasbewijzen*) of Teyler's Foundation: ATS 618–35. These came directly from his contemporaries or from auctions of other collections. For a short overview of this see Regteren Altena/Borssum Buisman/Bruyn Kops 1972, 12. For the restorations specifically see the *kasbewijs* dated 15 February 1793, ATS 624-002-01, which mentions that he had 'plugged' holes and retouched parts of the Italian drawings (*aan de Italiaansche Teekeningen gaaten gestopt en bijgeteekend*); the catalogues of the Museum's collection of work on paper document these alterations extensively: see Plomp 1997 and Tuyll 2000.

3   Hendriks' Scientific Œuvre: an Overview

In the description of his rights and duties as *kasteleijn* Hendriks was not officially tasked with making images of the Museum's collections.[15] The financial records of Teyler's Foundation do however show that Van Marum asked him to draw fossils and instruments in the collection, or to correct prints of them; he was paid separately for this on top of his salary as *kasteleijn*. The vast majority of works contained in the Appendix (nos 1–18) are related to Van Marum's published work in the *Verhandelingen van Teylers Tweede Genootschap* (Transactions of Teyler's Second Society). When the works are not related to the *Verhandelingen*, they are still connected to the dissemination of part of the Museum's collections through correspondence or other publications.[16] The only exceptions to this are connected to the Hollandsche Maatschappij der Wetenschappen of which Van Marum became secretary in 1794 (Appendix, nos 20–21 and 26–27).

Prints are our most important pictorial sources for studying Hendriks' scientific œuvre. The only scientific *drawings* by Hendriks that survive are those related to Van Marum's correspondence. This might suggest that, at least in Haarlem where the objects were at hand, the documentary value of the drawings themselves was not highly regarded, and in any case the prints made the preparatory drawings obsolete on most accounts. The surviving drawings were perhaps considered to contain additional useful information. The tracing sent to the 'Prince de Lambertini' (Appendix, no. 10c) is an illustrated letter explaining the principles of a new design for the electrostatic generator.[17] The drawings that formed part of an exchange between Van Marum and the naturalist Georges Cuvier were valuable to the latter's research, as demonstrated by the fact that he discussed the fossils they show in his published work.[18]

---

15   It was among the Director's responsibilities to have prints made of discoveries and experiments: see ATS 5, 118–21.

16   Appendix, nos 10c and 23–25 (related to correspondence) and 7–8 (related to other publications).

17   I have been unable to discover who 'M. le Prince de Lambertini' (addressed thus in French) was, but he was probably a member of the Lambertini family from Bologna, possibly Giovanni Lambertini (1739–1806): see *ww-Person, A data base of the titled nobility in Europe*, http://ww-person.com/. For the drawing see also Dibner 1957, 46.

18   On the relations between Van Marum and Cuvier, see Touret 1983, and Wiechmann/Touret 1987, 130–35. The large bone and the drawing sent by Van Marum (Appendix, no. 23) are discussed in Cuvier 1823, 393–96. The specimen is reproduced as fig. 16 in pl. XXVII of that volume, where it is credited as 'Laurillard del'. and 'Coutant sculp'. and its orientation is reversed. The draughtsman is C. L. Laurillard (1783–1853), Cuvier's assistant,

As part of this overview, it is helpful to look at some of the formal and structural aspects of the images in this corpus. As Bredekamp, Schneider and Dünkel have argued, the way objects are depicted is of as much consequence in shaping knowledge as what is depicted.[19] It is important to note that we are dealing with different classes of images (drawings and prints) and different classes of objects depicted (*naturalia* and instruments). This is significant, because some of the drawings were steps in the process towards reproduction in print. We also need to take into account the challenges involved in depicting different classes of objects, for example a fossil versus an electrostatic generator.

First, there is the issue of line. The medium of engraving, in which almost all of the published images were made, lends itself well to a clear line that gives the impression of being very precise. In contrast, the etching of the mosasaur (figure 7.5) and extant preparatory drawings, with watercolour (figure 7.2 and Appendix, no. 20a), feature outlines that are at times much less tidy, especially when one looks closely at some areas. This focus on line in the engravings is taken to an extreme in some cases, where instruments are reduced to their outline (a series of geometric shapes). The focus of these images is on the general form of the objects.

Second, there is the issue of shading and colour, which also serves this focus on form. Shading is particularly pronounced in the case of the mosasaur fossil (figure 7.5).[20] The increased contrast makes its forms much more visible. Significant parts of the print are simply the blank sheet of paper, while the teeth and the darkest shadows are rendered almost completely black by a dense mass of lines and cross-hatching. Shading is also used to suggest the materiality of what is depicted. With the instruments, highlights are used to represent shine on glass and metal. In the fossil, rougher areas are darker, as are the teeth. But at times the material of the objects is still difficult to make out.

---

who also accompanied him on his visit to Haarlem, and the engraver is probably J. L. D. Coutant (1776–after 1831). The text states that the image is also based on a drawing by the naturalist Robert de Lamanon (1752–1787). The mosasaur is discussed in Cuvier 1823, 310–38; only a detail of the Teyler specimen is reproduced as fig. 8 of pl. XVIII in that volume. The so-called *Homo diluvii testis* is discussed in Cuvier 1823, 431–44. Two states of the fossil are reproduced (fig. 2 in pl. XXV and fig. 2 in pl. XXVI), neither of them based on the drawing by Hendriks. The images reproduced in Cuvier can be considered different enough for them not to feature in the list in the Appendix. For the *Homo diluvii testis* see also Jorink's contribution to this volume (p. 90 and p. 106, n. 58).

19   Bredekamp/Schneider/Dünkel 2012 (2008), 8; see Bredekamp/Schneider/Dünkel 2015 for the English edition. The following analysis owes much to Meijers 2018.

20   Cf. the images of the other mosasaur fossil discovered at the time, in Pieters 2009.

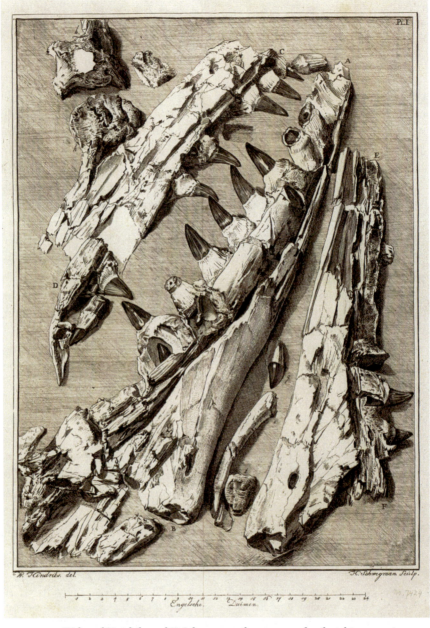

FIGURE 7.5 Wybrand Hendriks and H. Schwegman, the mosasaur fossil, etching, 1790, in *Verhandelingen van Teyler's Tweede Genootschap* 8 (1790) (App. 3).
TEYLER'S MUSEUM, HAARLEM

The use of similar techniques to depict glass and metal makes them virtually indistinguishable (cf. the metal of the conductors and the glass of the supporting columns of the electrostatic generator, figure 7.6), though the difference in materials is significant: metal conducts electric currents and glass is an insulator. The decision to leave these images uncoloured, in contrast to the preparatory watercolours or zoological prints (e.g. Appendix, no. 21 or 26), therefore has consequences. The focus on form through the use of line and shading is in the end at the expense of the depiction of material.

The third issue to be considered is the setting of the objects depicted, which in general is not indicated. The instruments in Van Marum's publications mostly float in nothingness. There are, however, aspects that suggest external factors. The instruments throw shadows on the ground beneath them, and on their surface they show effects of light and shadow that result from some external light source, supposedly the skylight of the museum's Oval Room (figure 7.6). The example of a spark made by Van Marum's electrostatic generator is similarly shown in a nondescript environment (figure 7.8).[21] The only exceptions to the lack of setting are the 'wonder tree' (figures 7.2, 7.3) and the big electrostatic generator in the Oval Room (figure 7.6), where a decorative continuity is shown between the machine and the architecture of the room. The prints tend to show not simply instruments but working experimental set-ups (without people operating them): examples are the spark flying off the conductor of the electrostatic generator, and the appearance of bubbles in some of the vessels of chemical apparatuses (figures 7.6, 7.7).

In addition there is the fact that some prints give the dimensions of objects in precise measurements. For instance, Van Marum's first description of the electrostatic generator (1785, fig. 2 in pl. 11) shows a schematic outline of the conductor with the size of its various parts in inches (*Engelsche duimen*). In the mosasaur print a scale, also in inches, is given under the fossil itself (figure 7.5).

Finally, there is the issue of perspective. There are several instances of minor perspectival distortions in which details do not completely line up, e.g. in the complex three-dimensional shapes of the carved feet of the conductor of the electrostatic generator (figure 7.6). Another example is in the print of the mosasaur (figure 7.5), where the end of the broken tooth and the two empty sockets have been flattened relative to the picture plane, resulting in a better view of the inside.

Taking these aspects together will help us to answer the question of how Hendriks and Van Marum conceived of scientific depiction, especially in terms of individualization vs. generalization. First, however, we need to look at this

---

21   As far as we know, Hendriks was not involved with this image.

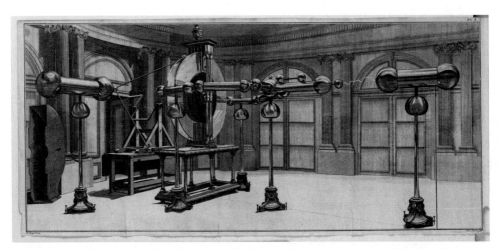

FIGURE 7.6 Wybrand Hendriks and Barent de Bakker, *Large electrostatic generator: situational view of the Oval Room* (without the long cabinet, seen in figure 3.2), 1787, engraving, 257 x 579 mm.
TEYLER'S MUSEUM, KG 07577A (APP. 1b)

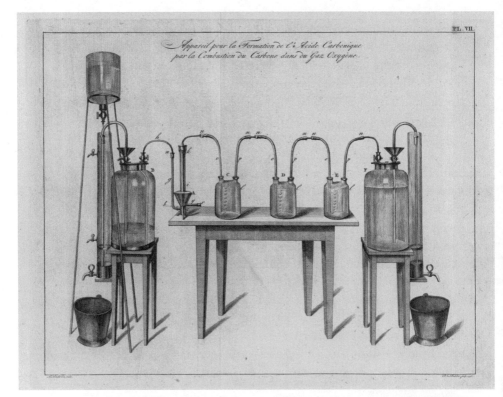

FIGURE 7.7 Wybrand Hendriks and Barent de Bakker, *Apparatus for the production of carbon dioxide*, 1798, engraving, in *Verhandelingen van Teyler's Tweede Genootschap* 10 (1798) (App. 13b).
TEYLER'S MUSEUM, HAARLEM

FIGURE 7.8 C. H. Koning, *Large electric spark*, 1787, etching, in
Verhandelingen van Teyler's Tweede Genootschap
8 (1790).
TEYLER'S MUSEUM, HAARLEM

question in the international perspective of eighteenth-century theory of (visual) representation.

4   The 'Reasoned Image'

Throughout the early modern era images were used as a means for the production and dissemination of knowledge. As such, they were an important part of what we would now call scientific practice.[22] That is not to say that the formal characteristics of these images and the way they functioned within that practice remained unchanged across time. Whereas from the early to mid-nineteenth

---

22   See for example Dackerman 2011.

century more and more people started to expect that scientific practice and its images would be objective in order to produce valid knowledge, eighteenth-century Europe had different criteria by which to judge whether something was an accurate depiction of the world: a paradigm that the historians of science Daston and Galison have called 'truth-to-nature'.[23]

Truth-to-nature revolved around 'taming nature's variability'.[24] In that sense it was a response to the age-old question of how to make sense of the myriad specimens, events, and sensations that people experienced when studying the world. The answer to this question changed during the eighteenth century. Things were put together into classes and categories to reveal the underlying order of the natural world. Building on earlier work by others (after a number of preliminary stages by yet others), this paradigm was shaped by the work of Carl Linnaeus (1707–1778), who changed the field of natural history with his binomial method of classifying natural specimens. The Linnaean system, as part of wider developments, was supposed to allow naturalists to focus on the essential and constant features of species, instead of being dazzled by individuality and accidental traits.[25]

This meant that every class, genus, or species had to be represented by a type, whose characteristics were not necessarily found in any single specimen. This presented a problem to researchers, such as the mineralogist René-Just Haüy: 'Among crystals the varieties of the same kind often appear at first glance to have no relation to each other and sometimes even those [kinds] one detects become a new source of difficulties'.[26] That is why Haüy developed a system for classifying minerals according to their crystalline shapes. It is apparently difficult even for a trained person to discern common characteristics within the idiosyncrasies of nature, but that is exactly what the naturalist's job is within the paradigm of truth-to-nature. In order to come to a system of mineralogy like Haüy's, one had to judge what were variations and what were the underlying forms. Van Marum was convinced by Haüy's system and ordered a set of wooden models of his crystallographic system for Teyler's Museum (figure 6.7).[27] These ideal or characteristic models of crystals did not correspond to any particular mineral specimen, but they were present in every mineral of a particular type. Capable natural philosophers or natural

---

23 Daston/Galison 2007, 34–35.
24 ibid., 63–68.
25 ibid., 57–59.
26 Haüy 1784, 3, as quoted in Daston/Galison 2007, 63. See for Haüy's models of crystals also Sliggers' contribution to this volume (pp. 119–21) and figure 6.7.
27 Wiechmann/Touret 1987, 129.

'TRUTH-TO-NATURE' IN THE MUSEUM? 145

historians would be able to use their mental faculties and their knowledge of a wide range of specimens or events to see more than the untrained eye could.

In a similar way, artists were trained in drawing academies to learn a wide range of human and artistic shapes, drawing from models such as plaster casts of revered antique statues and the works of great modern masters before being introduced, bit by bit, to raw nature. What 'after nature' meant then is generally not the designation of a certain kind of naturalism, but a means of indicating something that was not drawn from models or copied.[28] In fact, even when drawn from nature the ideal image was still a synthesis of the most perfect parts of a diversity of specimens according to the dominant classicist art theory in Europe at the time. Joshua Reynolds (1723–1792), for example, drew explicit parallels between the naturalist's method and what an artist should do in his third letter *To the Idler* of 1759.[29]

In art as in science, during the eighteenth century active intervention by the maker was part of what made an ideal image. This is in direct contrast to the later ideal of mechanical objectivity, which was supposed to involve as little intervention as possible.[30] Within the paradigm of truth-to-nature images were supposed to reflect something that surpassed the individual specimen or subject matter. Instead they were to show an ideal that could be taken to stand for something larger. Artists, like scientists, were supposed to use their active judgment and mental faculties to bring out something that the non-expert would not be able to see: the characteristic aspects in the specimen they were drawing. Ideas about the accurate depiction of nature in the eighteenth century operated at the intersection of the activities of artists and naturalists, resulting in something that Daston and Galison call the 'reasoned image'.[31] This is an image that transcends the peculiarities of the individual thing that it depicts – as well as the variety that exists among different specimina of a certain species of plant, type of crystal, etc. – and thus shows a more truthful version of that thing through the trained eye and good judgment of its author(s).

---

28 Daston/Galison 2007, 98. See also Swan 1995.

29 Reynolds/Zimmern 1887, 280, as quoted in Daston/Galison 2007, 81: 'Thus among the blades of grass or leaves of the same tree, though no two can be found exactly alike, the general form is invariable: a Naturalist, before he chose one as a sample, would examine many; since if he took the first that occurred, it might have been an accident or otherwise such a form as that it would scarce be known to belong to that species; he selects as a painter does the most beautiful, the most general form of nature'. Cf. Knolle in this volume, on classicist art theory in the Netherlands.

30 On mechanical objectivity see Daston/Galison 2007, 115–19.

31 ibid., 60.

146 VOS

5 'Truth-to-Nature' in the Museum?

The question whether the most truthful image of nature is a simple impression or a 'reasoned image' comes down to a decision to individualize or generalize. Thus in order to gauge how nature is represented in Hendriks' scientific œuvre, we have to relate the formal and structural aspects discussed above to this issue.

There are several elements in Hendriks' scientific œuvre that work towards individualizing the objects depicted. The etching of the mosasaur fossil is full of attention to particular details, such as the textured rendering of fragments and cracks (figure 7.5). In addition, the engraving of the electrostatic generator in the Oval Room situates it in a particular time (given the light striking the machine from above) and place (the Museum) (figure 7.6). It also explicitly links the machine to that place by showing the correspondence between the decoration of the machine and the woodwork of the room. Likewise, the scale provided with the mosasaur fossil turns it into an image of this particular specimen with certain observable traits. In the third publication on the electrostatic generator Van Marum even refers back to the scale and measurements of the drawings in the first description, revealing a consistency and precision over several publications spanning a period of ten years.[32]

Nevertheless there are also many elements that show the generalizing tendency of 'reasoned images'. The clarity of line in the engravings and the use of shading lead to an emphasis on the general geometry of things analogous with Haüy's focus on form in determining minerals. Even in cases where there is attention to particular details, as in the mosasaur print, an attempt is still made to emphasize certain forms by augmenting the contrast between light and dark and by presenting the remains of the animal as lying on top of the matrix. Furthermore, the perspectival distortion of the broken tooth and the empty sockets enhances Van Marum's argument about the nature of the fossil, which depended in part on the fact that these teeth were largely hollow, a general characteristic of the order of *pisces cetacea*.[33] This suggests that while an individual specimen is depicted, an attempt has been made to emphasize certain general and typical aspects. Reference to any particular scale or dimension is also not necessarily a sign of individualization. Van Marum remarks that the image of a spark accompanying his first publication on the

---

32 Marum 1795, 27.

33 Marum 1790, 385.

electrostatic generator depicts a phenomenon at its true size, but that it also shows the spark 'as it would generally appear' (figure 7.8).[34] This indicates that we are looking at a visual synthesis, an idealized type that is, however, still true to scale.

The fact too that in most images the setting is only implicit points to their universality. Instruments floating in nothingness are not localized, so they refer to times and places beyond their immediate context. And even when an instrument appears to be situated in a particular context, such as the museum's Oval Room, this does not necessarily mean that its staging is not unmediated.[35] For instance, Van Marum requested an imaginary, more ideal setting for a print of the electrostatic generator: in one of his journals he records that he gave instructions to the architect Viervant for a drawing to be made of the machine from a point of view precisely in the centre of the room, together with a battery of Leyden jars – that he had only ordered the day before, so they were not yet there.[36] While it is clear that there is sometimes a tension between the individual and the general in these images, the balance tips to the side of the general in most cases.

6 'To Imitate Nature in Art Precisely'

One final aspect that we can look at to situate the collaboration between Hendriks and Van Marum is the presentation and reception of the images.

It seems clear that Van Marum considered illustrations to be an important part of his publications. He was quite specific about the images published with his works, and he went through at least four engravers before he finally decided that the prints engraved by Barent de Bakker would do for his first description of the large electrostatic generator. He also had a specific example in mind, namely the print of Benjamin Wilson's electrical

---

34   Marum 1785, 37.

35   Wiesenfeldt 2002 accounts for the difference between the presence of a setting for the generator in the Oval Room in Marum 1785 and the lack of setting in Marum 1795 by pointing to the changing relationship between Van Marum and his collaborators.

36   See the entry for 25 February 1785 in his 'Journaal van mijne Verrichtingen ter verkrijging eener Verzameling van Physische Instrumenten & Modellen van nuttige Werktuigen in Teylers Museum' (Journal of my Transactions to obtain a Collection of Physical Instruments & Models of useful Utensils in Teyler's Museum), 1783–90, Noord-Hollands Archief, Haarlem, 529 (Archief van Marum), no. 11d, fols 1–23; this is probably the view featured in pl. VI of Marum 1785, though that print by Barent de Bakker (no mention is made of Viervant) does not show the machine in the Oval Room.

experiments in the Pantheon in London (figure 7.9).[37] Van Marum mentions two details about that image: first the fact that it shows an experiment in a specific setting, and second the manner of the drawing. That he was inspired to imitate Wilson's print to a certain extent in the print of his own machine is shown by the fact that it is situated in an architectural setting (figure 7.6). Wilson's print incidentally also includes several people operating the machine, which turns it into the record of a specific event more than the depiction of a type of machine or experimental set-up. As we have seen, the print by Hendriks and De Bakker explicitly avoids giving this much contextual information.

Van Marum also expresses the importance of images in his published articles. Because it took him some time to find a suitable engraver, some of the images intended to accompany his first publication on the generator were not ready in time to be included, and he apologizes for their absence (figure 7.6 is one of them). He adds that his description of the apparatus is still comprehensible if one looks at the included plates II and VI.[38] Apparently substitute images were required, and the text alone was not enough to convey what he wanted to say.

In certain instances making an image was even central to Van Marum's experimental setup. In the second publication on the electrostatic generator he conducted electricity through wires composed of various metals over a sheet of paper, leaving a residue that recorded the chemical reaction. These 'drawings', as Van Marum calls them, subsequently formed the basis for the prints that accompanied the volume and carried meaning as the end result of an experiment.[39] In other cases, too, he considered the image itself as a means to support a particular argument. In an article on the pelvis of a young whale (1801, 201) he explicitly equates observing the object to observing the image: 'every perceptive beholder of this piece or its image' should be able to see certain elements.

A consideration for beauty and aesthetic experience in the broader sense can be found in Van Marum's writing on his experiments and the images that accompanied them, as well as in the design of his instruments. This is

---

37   This is an engraving by J. Basire (1730–1802) after Michael Angelo Rooker (1742/43–1801) in Boddington 1778; Van Marum specifically comments on this print in the entries for 24 December 1784 and 27 January 1785 in one of his journals. Part of the process of commissioning the prints is also described there, although the involvement of Hendriks is not mentioned. Van Marum does not say why he eventually settled on De Bakker as engraver for most of the images: the precise outcome of the situation is not recorded, as Van Marum does not mention the images after June 1785, and made very few entries in 1786. See 'Journaal van mijne Verrichtingen', cited in the previous note.

38   Marum 1785, 205.

39   Marum 1787, 81.

FIGURE 7.9 J. Basire and Michael Angelo Rooker, *A View of the Apparatus and part of the Great Cylinder in the Pantheon*, 1778, engraving, in *Philosophical Transactions of the Royal Society of London* 68 (1778).
TEYLER'S MUSEUM, HAARLEM

particularly true of the large electrostatic generator, which was decorated with designs by Viervant so that it would suit the Oval Room.[40] His preference for the image of Wilson's experiment in the splendid London Pantheon as an example is probably also an expression of his desire to present the machine in its aestheticizing architectural setting. In another instance, when he describes how an iron wire connected to the conductor lights up, he writes that it is a curious phenomenon and that is why he thought it worthy to be depicted. However, he claims that in reality it is much more beautiful than the image is able to show.[41] Also when describing one of the experiments on the electrification of metal wires Van Marum admits that aesthetics play a role: he writes that he found that using a smaller battery would result in a 'more beautiful drawing'.[42]

---

40 Wiechmann/Touret 1987, 118.
41 Marum 1785, 41–42.
42 Marum 1787, 85.

Parallels between images Hendriks was involved with and the concept of truth-to-nature can also be found in the reception of his work as a painter. Contemporaries regularly praised him for the accurate depiction of the sitters in his portraits.[43] The most relevant source in this case is the 1790 dedication to Hendriks (in the form of a short poem by J. van Walré) of the Dutch translation of Johann Jakob Engel's *Ideen zu einer Mimik* of 1785, *De kunst van nabootzing door gebaarden*.[44] Though this is a treatise on the use of gesture in the theatre, it shows certain affinities with the paradigm of the 'reasoned image'. According to Engel, actors and rhetoricians alike should evoke typical emotions through the use of gestures and postures. Their goal was to depict a kind of ideal archetype of the same kind that made scientific images truthful or artistic images beautiful. In the dedicatory poem Hendriks is praised precisely for his ability to capture the essential elements of these character types in his art. Moreover, the Dutch preface to the second edition of 1807 says that the treatise teaches us 'to imitate nature in art precisely'.[45] What is important here is not the fact that Hendriks' portraiture was praised: it is a different genre from scientific images. What is most interesting about this dedication to Hendriks is that it shows that these ideas about the accuracy of images – ideas that fit the paradigm of truth-to-nature – circulated in Hendriks' circle at the time and that he was judged to be working within them.

7 Conclusion

Drawing mostly on the Teyler Foundation's archival records and Van Marum's publications it is possible to paint a good picture of the kind of activities Hendriks was involved in as a maker of scientific images. He regularly drew and corrected prints for the Director during the latter's period of most intensive involvement with Teyler's Museum. While most of the time the images that resulted from the collaboration between Hendriks and Van Marum tend more towards the general than the specific, in certain instances they

---

43 Regteren Altena/Borssum Buisman/Bruyn Kops 1972, 15–16.

44 Engel 1790, n.p. Part of the poem reads: *Het werk eens wijsgeers, die in 't menschelijk harte leest,/ Moet eenen schilder, die als HENDRIKS denkt, behaagen:/ Hij leert; hij schildert ons de werking van den geest,/ En ENGEL zou zijn boek zeer gaarne uw' naam zien draagen* (The work of a philosopher, who reads the human heart,/ Must please a painter who thinks like HENDRIKS:/ He teaches; he paints for us the workings of the human mind,/ And ENGEL would be very pleased to see his book bear your name.) A slightly modified English version was published in 1822 as *Practical Illustrations of Rhetorical Gesture and Action*.

45 Engel 1807, 3.

'TRUTH-TO-NATURE' IN THE MUSEUM?

incorporate aspects that point to an individual situation or specimen: the inclusion of specific measurements or a scale, and the use of a specific setting (the Oval Room, the Haarlemmerhout), or at least the implicit reference to a context (shadows, shading, working experiments). In the case of the electrostatic generator in the Oval Room we may compare the result to Wilson's example and speculate that aesthetic consideration played a role in the choice of a contextual representation. In the case of the 'wonder tree' in the Haarlemmerhout it becomes clear that it was precisely its setting that was a step too far for Van Marum in a scientific context. As his request to Viervant for an imaginary setting of the machine (see p. 147) shows, even in the situations where a setting is provided the idea of a mode of representation that points beyond the individual object is never far off. This is also why in most cases references to context are only implicit, and why in cases where the dimensions are given attempts are also made at using other formal elements – highlighting form through line and shading, subtle perspective distortion – to construct a more generalized representation. Even though history is messy here, as perhaps in most cases, we see a pattern emerge. Hendriks and Van Marum tended to produce scientific images that were firmly embedded in widely held ideas about what we could now describe as the 'reasoned image'.

'TRUTH-TO-NATURE' IN THE MUSEUM?

Appendix: Wybrand Hendriks' Scientific Images

This list comprises extant images and those mentioned in the archival records (*kasbewijzen*) of Teyler's Foundation, as far as I have been able to find them. In some cases Van Marum's articles contain images that are compositionally identical pairs, but of which one only shows an apparatus in outline (i.e. without shading, etc.; e.g. 9a). The list excludes these duplicates, except when they can be explicitly linked to Hendriks in other ways, either by naming him as artist on the plate or via the archival records (with the exception of 10b).

All references to publications are to texts by Van Marum, unless otherwise indicated.

Where possible, this list shows whether and where drawings or prints are mentioned in the financial records. However there are mentions of payments that could not be traced to any extant print or drawing, and conversely there are prints and drawings on the list that could not with certainty be traced to the financial records.

All in all, the list postulates that Hendriks made 23 drawings on scientific subjects in the period 1786–1819, 22 of them between 1786 and 1804.[46] The extant material consists mostly of prints, of which 21 were published and one remained unpublished. These were made by several different printmakers: Barent de Bakker (*c.* 1762–1805; 16 prints), Jacob Elias van Varelen (1757–1840; 1 print), Isaak de Wit Jansz (1744–1809; 3 prints), Jan Christiaan Sepp (1739–1811; 1 print), and Hendrik Schwegman (1761–1816; 1 print). Some of these prints were later hand-coloured (21 and 26, the former possibly coloured by Hendriks himself).

Three copies of 21 are in the archive of the Hollandsche Maatschappij der Wetenschappen as part of a set of material concerning the publication of its *Verhandelingen* (Transactions).[47] Five drawings of scientific subjects by Hendriks are to be found in international collections (10c, 23–25, 27a). Except for the drawing of the 'wonder tree' (27), which could be considered a picturesque landscape in its own right, the only drawings that survive are in Van Marum's correspondence (10c, 23–25).

Abbreviations

n.a.	not applicable
Nat. Verh. HMW	*Natuurkundige Verhandelingen van de Hollandsche Maatschappij der Wetenschappen* (Natural Philosophical Transactions of the Holland Society of Sciences)
Verh. TTG	*Verhandelingen van Teyler's Tweede Genootschap* (Transactions of Teyler's Second Society)

---

46   Cf. the 33 paintings and roughly 36 drawings in Regteren Altena/Borssum Buisman/Bruyn Kops 1972 for the period 1786–1804.

47   I was able to find three coloured copies (proofs?) of the print giving a side view of the platypus (21), but not the detail of its bill (20a), although that was mentioned in the inventory; Sliggers/Besselink 2002, 118 has an image of Hendriks' drawing of the platypus bill that I was unable to locate.

TABLE 7.1   List of Wybrand Hendriks' Scientific Images

No.	Description	Maker(s)	Date	Publication/ function or use otherwise
1a	Drawing of the large electrostatic generator: situational view of the Oval Room	Wybrand Hendriks	29 May 1786	Preparatory drawing for 1b
1b (fig. 7.6)	Print of the large electrostatic generator: situational view of the Oval Room	*W. Hendriks del., B. de Bakker sculp.*	Proof corrected by Hendriks 17/21 October 1786. Published with *Verh. TTG* 4 (1787)	'Description d'une très grande machine électrique', *Verh. TTG* 3 (1785)
2a	Drawing of a detail of an electrometer attached to the large electrostatic generator	Wybrand Hendriks	29 May 1786. Changes made 21 October 1786	'Description d'une très grande machine électrique' in *Verh. TTG* 3 (1785)
2b	Print of a detail of an electrometer attached to the large electrostatic generator	[*W. Hendriks del., B. de Bakker sculp.*]	Proof corrected by Hendriks 2 February 1787. Published with *Verh. TTG* 4 (1787)	'Description d'une très grande machine électrique', *Verh. TTG* 3 (1785)
3 (fig. 7.5)	Print of the mosasaur fossil	*W. Hendriks del., H. Schwegman sculp.*	Proof corrected by Hendriks 30 April 1790	'Beschryving der beenderen van den Kop van eenen Visch', *Verh. TTG* 8 (1790)
4a	Drawing of the head of a crocodile	Wybrand Hendriks	Drawn by Hendriks at Van Marum's home, 28 May 1790	'Beschryving der beenderen van den Kop van eenen Visch', *Verh. TTG* 8 (1790)
4b	Print of the head of a crocodile	[*Wybrand Hendriks del.*]	*c.* 30 April 1790	'Beschryving der beenderen van den Kop van eenen Visch', *Verh. TTG* 8 (1790)
5a	Drawing of a new battery and the electrostatic generator	Wybrand Hendriks	28 May 1790. Possibly alterations made 20 April 1792	'Seconde continuation', *Verh. TTG* 9 (1795)

'TRUTH-TO-NATURE' IN THE MUSEUM? 155

nique	Teylers Foundation financial records (*kasbewijzen*)	Collection	Notes
drawing	ATS 618-007-01	Not found	Tentative: only mentioned in the financial records. There is a drawing of the generator in the Oval Room in the Teyler's Museum collection that is quite similar to the view of 1b and so might be the preparatory drawing. It is currently attributed to the architect Viervant (e.g. by Wiesenfeldt 2002). Theunissen/Wiechmann/Palm 1987 attribute it to Hendriks in the caption on p. 110.
aving	ATS 618-008-01	n.a. (published print)	Published with *Verh. TTG* 4 (1787), with accompanying text and instructions to bind with *Verh. TTG* 3 (1785).
drawing	ATS 618-007-01; ATS 618-008-01	Not found	Tentative: only mentioned in the financial records. Probably preparatory drawing for 2b.
aving	ATS 619-002-01	n.a. (published print)	Published with *Verh. TTG* 4 (1787) as supplement, with accompanying text and instructions to bind with *Verh. TTG* 3 (1785).
ng	ATS 622-011-01	n.a. (published print)	It is remarked in Sliggers 2017, 236 that this image seems to have been copied as plate V in Barthélemy Faujas de Saint-Fond's *Histoire Naturelle de la Montagne de Saint-Pierre de Maestricht* (1798) without the proper attributions. See 19 for a possible connection to this.
drawing	ATS 622-011-01	Not found	Tentative: only mentioned in the financial records. Probably preparatory drawing for 4b.
aving	not found	n.a. (published print)	Ascribed to Hendriks based on the existence of 4a in the financial records; no mention of the artist on the print.
drawing	ATS 622-011-01; ATS 624-016-01	Not found	Tentative: only mentioned in the financial records. Possibly preparatory drawing for 5b. The financial records (ATS 624-016-01) mention that Hendriks drew alterations (*verteekend*) to the large battery and several spheres. It is not clear whether that refers to the earlier drawing of 28 May 1790. Note that a proof of a print of the battery existed by 3 October 1792 (5b), which indicates further work on the topic.

TABLE 7.1 List of Wybrand Hendriks' scientific images (*cont.*)

No.	Description	Maker(s)	Date	Publication/ function or use otherwise
5b	Print of the big battery with the big electrostatic generator in the background	*H: Henderiks delin.* [Wybrand Hendriks] *B: de Bakker fecit*	Little hand pulling a rope added to proof 3 October 1792	'Seconde continuation', *Verh. TTG* 9 (1795)
6a	Drawing of the large electrostatic generator	Wybrand Hendriks	10 September 1791	'Seconde continuation', *Verh. TTG* 9 (1795)
6b	Drawing of the outline of the large electrostatic generator	Wybrand Hendriks	10 September 1791	'Seconde continuation', *Verh. TTG* 9 (1795)
7	Print of a new design for an electrostatic generator	*W. Hendriks delin., B. de Bakker fecit* (in 1791 edn); *W. Hendriks delin. B. de Bakker sculp.* (in *Verh. TTG* 9 (1795))	First published accompanying a letter dated 30 April 1791	*Lettre à Jean Ingenhousz*, Haarlem 1791. Republished as supplement to 'Seconde continuation', *Verh. TTG* 9 (1795)
8a	Drawing of a setup for experiments using a gasometer (1)	Wybrand Hendriks	22 October 1791	*Lettre à Berthollet*, Haarlem 1791
8b	Drawing of a schematic outline of setup for experiments using a gasometer (1)	Wybrand Hendriks	22 October 1791	*Lettre à Berthollet*, Haarlem 1791
8c	Print of a setup for experiments using a gasometer (1)	*H. Henderik* [Wybrand Hendriks] *delin., B. de Bakker fecit* (in 1791 edn). *H. Henderiks* [Wybrand Hendriks] *delin., B. de Bakker sculp.* (in *Verh. TTG* 10 (1798))	Between 22 October 1791 (date of 8a) and 31 December 1791 (date of letter)	*Lettre à Berthollet*, Haarlem 1791. Republished in 'Description de quelques appareils chimiques', *Verh. TTG* 10 (1798)

nique	Teylers Foundation financial records (*kasbewijzen*)	Collection	Notes
aving	ATS 624-005-01	n.a. (published print)	Hendriks' name is misspelt (Dutch spelling was not standardized at this time), but attributing this to him is supported by the presence of other prints with the correct spelling in the same volume (and elsewhere) and the mention of alterations to the proof in the financial records, as well as by his involvement in the Museum in general.
lrawing	ATS 623-034-01	not found	Tentative: only mentioned in the financial records. Possibly preparatory drawing for 10a and 10c.
lrawing	ATS 623-034-01	not found	Tentative: only mentioned in the financial records. Based on 6a according to the financial record. Possibly preparatory drawing for 10b.
aving	not found	n.a. (published print)	The fact that the *Lettre à Jean Ingenhousz* was first published separately from *Verh.* TTG might explain the absence of it or its preparatory drawing from the financial record, despite its republication in *Verh.* TTG in 1795.
lrawing	ATS 623-034-01	not found	Tentative: only mentioned in the financial records. Probably preparatory drawing for 8c.
lrawing	ATS 623-034-01	not found	Tentative: only mentioned in the financial records. Probably preparatory drawing for 8d.
aving	not found	n.a. (published print)	Pl. I in *Verh.* TTG 10 1798.

158 VOS

TABLE 7.1   List of Wybrand Hendriks' scientific images (*cont.*)

No.	Description	Maker(s)	Date	Publication/ function or use otherwise
8d	Print of a schematic outline of setup for experiments using a gasometer (1)		Between 22 October 1791 (date of 8a) and 31 December 1791 (date of letter)	*Lettre à Berthollet*, Haarlem 1791. Republished in 'Description de quelques appareils chimiques', *Verh.* TTG 10 (1798)
9a	Print of a schematic outline of a setup for experiments using a gasometer (2)	Unattributed (in *Annales de chimie* 14 (1792)) [*Wybrand Hendriks del.*]	First published accompanying a letter dated 20 May 1792	*Seconde lettre à Berthollet*, Haarlem 1792. Republished in 'Description de quelques appareils chimiques', *Verh.* TTG 10 (1798)
9b	Print of a setup for experiments using a gasometer (2)	*H. Henderiks* [Wybrand Hendriks] *delin. B. de Bakker sculp. 1798* (in *Verh.* TTG 10 (1798))	Published 1798	'Description de quelques appareils chimiques' in *Verh.* TTG 10 (1798)
10a	Print of the updated design of the large electrostatic generator	*W. Hendriks del. Is. de Wit, Jansz. sculp.*	Between 10 September 1791 and 8 October 1792 (see 6b). Published in 1795	'Seconde continuation', *Verh.* TTG 9 (1795)
10b	Print of a schematic outline of the updated design of the large electrostatic generator	[*W. Hendriks del. Is. de Wit, Jansz. sculp.*]	Between 10 September 1791 and 8 October 1792 (see 6b). Published in 1795	'Seconde continuation',*Verh.* TTG 9 (1795)
10c	Traced drawing of a schematic outline of the updated design of the large electrostatic generator	Wybrand Hendriks; Isaak de Wit Jansz; Martinus van Marum	8 October 1792	A letter to the *Prince de Lambertini*

'TRUTH-TO-NATURE' IN THE MUSEUM? 159

nique	Teylers Foundation financial records (*kasbewijzen*)	Collection	Notes
aving	not found	n.a. (published print)	Pl. II in *Verh.* TTG 10 1798.
aving	not found	n.a. (published print)	First published with *Seconde Lettre à Berthollet*, Haarlem 1791, but not present in copies seen; also published in *Annales de chimie* 14 (1792), and elsewhere. The fact that the *Seconde lettre à Berthollet* was first published independently of *Verh.* TTG might explain the absence of it or its preparatory drawing from the financial record, despite its republication in *Verh.* TTG in 1798. Probably based on the same drawing as 9b, hence the attribution to Hendriks.
aving	not found	n.a. (published print)	Hendriks' name is misspelt, but this work is attributable to him (see comment on 5b).
aving	not found	n.a. (published print)	Pl. I in *Verh.* TTG 9 1795.
aving	not found	n.a. (published print)	Based possibly on 6b and on 10a, hence the attribution to Hendriks and De Wit.
drawing	not found	Smithsonian Libraries, Washington, D.C., Dibner Library Manuscripts, Ms 000911 B folio	Annotated copy of 6a, as mentioned in Van Marum's marginal notes: *Le dessein de cet appareil, dont celui ci est la copie (qui en donne seulement le contours) sera gravée et publiée* [*sic*] [...] *l'année prochaine*. Marginal notes addressed to the *Prince de Lambertini* explain the design and are signed by Van Marum, 8 October 1792.

160 VOS

TABLE 7.1 List of Wybrand Hendriks' scientific images (*cont.*)

No.	Description	Maker(s)	Date	Publication/ function or use otherwise
11a	Drawing of an apparatus for experiments on the composition of water and the decomposition of carbonated hydrogen gas	Wybrand Hendriks	Between 20 August 1797 and 22 February 1798	'Description de quelques appareils chimiques' in *Verh.* *TTG* 10 1798
11b	Print of an apparatus for experiments on the composition of water and the decomposition of carbonated hydrogen gas	*H. Henderiks* [Wybrand Hendriks] *delin., B. de Bakker. sculp.*	Signed 1798	'Description de quelques appareils chimiques' in *Verh.* *TTG* 10 (1798)
12a	Drawing of an apparatus for producing phosphoric acid	Wybrand Hendriks	Between 20 August 1797 and 22 February 1798	'Description de quelques appareils chimiques' in *Verh.* *TTG* 10 1798
12b	Print of an apparatus for producing phosphoric acid	*H. Henderiks delin.* [Wybrand Hendriks], *B. de Bakker. sculp.* 1798	Signed 1798	'Description de quelques appareils chimiques', *Verh.* *TTG* 10 (1798)
13a	Drawing of an apparatus for producing carbon dioxide	Wybrand Hendriks	Between 20 August 1797 and 22 February 1798	'Description de quelques appareils chimiques' in *Verh.* *TTG* 10 1798
13b (fig. 7.7)	Print of an apparatus for producing carbon dioxide	*H. Henderiks* [Wybrand Hendriks] *delin. B. de Bakker. sculp. 1798*	Signed 1798	'Description de quelques appareils chimiques', *Verh.* *TTG* 10 (1798)
14a	Drawing of an apparatus for studying the products of the combustion of oils	Wybrand Hendriks	Between 20 August 1797 and 22 February 1798	'Description de quelques appareils chimiques', *Verh.* *TTG* 10 (1798)

nique	Teylers Foundation financial records (*kasbewijzen*)	Collection	Notes
drawing?	ATS 629-022-01; ATS 630-021-01	not found	Tentative: only mentioned in the financial records. Probably preparatory drawing for 11b. The financial records mention several apparatuses drawn between these dates, but the descriptions are not clear enough to connect dates to specific prints.
aving	not found	n.a. (published print)	Hendriks' name is misspelt, but this work is attributable to him (see comment on 5b).
drawing?	ATS 629-022-01; ATS 630-021-01	not found	Tentative: only mentioned in the financial records. Probably preparatory drawing for 12b. The financial records mention several apparatuses drawn between these dates, but the descriptions are not clear enough to connect dates to specific prints.
aving	not found	n.a. (published print)	Hendriks' name is misspelt, but this work is attributable to him (see comment on 5b).
drawing?	ATS 629-022-01; ATS 630-021-01	not found	Tentative: only mentioned in the financial records. Probably preparatory drawing for 13b. The financial records mention several apparatuses drawn between these dates, but the descriptions are not clear enough to connect dates to specific prints.
aving	not found	n.a. (published print)	Hendriks' name is misspelt, but this work is attributable to him (see comment on 5b).
drawing?	ATS 629-022-01; ATS 630-021-01	not found	Tentative: only mentioned in the financial records. Probably preparatory drawing for 14b. The financial records mention several apparatuses drawn between these dates, but the descriptions are not clear enough to connect dates to specific prints.

162 VOS

TABLE 7.1   List of Wybrand Hendriks' scientific images (*cont.*)

No.	Description	Maker(s)	Date	Publication/function or use otherwise
14b	Print of an apparatus for studying the products of the combustion of oils	*H. Hendriks. delin.* [Wybrand Hendriks] *B. de Bakker. sculp. 1798*	Signed 1798	'Description de quelques appareils chimiques', *Verh. TTG* 10 (1798)
15a	Drawing of a schematic outline of part of an apparatus for studying the products of the combustion of oils (1)	Wybrand Hendriks	Between 20 August 1797 and 22 February 1798	'Description de quelques appareils chimiques', *Verh. TTG* 10 (1798)
15b	Print of a schematic outline of part of an apparatus for studying the products of the combustion of oils (1)	*H. Hendriks. delin.* [Wybrand Hendriks] *B. de Bakker. sculp. 1798*	Signed 1798	'Description de quelques appareils chimiques', *Verh. TTG* 10 (1798)
16a	Drawing of a schematic outline of part of an apparatus for studying the products of the combustion of oils (2)	Wybrand Hendriks	Between 20 August 1797 and 22 February 1798	'Description de quelques appareils chimiques', *Verh. TTG* 10 (1798)
16b	Print of a schematic outline of part of an apparatus for studying the products of the combustion of oils (2)	*H. Henderiks. delin.* [Wybrand Hendriks] *B. de Bakker. sculp. 1798*	Signed 1798	'Description de quelques appareils chimiques', *Verh. TTG* 10 (1798)
17a	Drawing of an apparatus for experiments on the oxidation of mercury	Wybrand Hendriks	Between 20 August 1797 and 22 February 1798	'Description de quelques appareils chimiques', *Verh. TTG* 10 (1798)
17b	Print of an apparatus for experiments on the oxidation of mercury	*H. Henderiks. delin.* [Wybrand Hendriks] *B. de Bakker. sculp. 1798*	Signed 1798	'Description de quelques appareils chimiques', *Verh. TTG* 10 (1798)

nique	Teylers Foundation financial records (*kasbewijzen*)	Collection	Notes
aving	not found	n.a. (published print)	Hendriks' name is misspelt, but this work is attributable to him (see comment on 5b).
drawing?	ATS 629-022-01; ATS 630-021-01	not found	Tentative: only mentioned in the financial records. Probably preparatory drawing for 15b. The financial records mention several apparatuses drawn between these dates, but the descriptions are not clear enough to connect dates to specific prints.
aving	not found	n.a. (published print)	Hendriks' name is misspelt, but this work is attributable to him (see comment on 5b).
drawing?	ATS 629-022-01; ATS 630-021-01	not found	Tentative: only mentioned in the financial records. Probably preparatory drawing for 16b. The financial records mention several apparatuses drawn between these dates, but the descriptions are not clear enough to connect dates to specific prints.
aving	not found	n.a. (published print)	Hendriks' name is misspelt, but this work is attributable to him (see comment on 5b).
drawing?	ATS 629-022-01; ATS 630-021-01	not found	Tentative: only mentioned in the financial records. Probably preparatory drawing for 17b. The financial records mention several apparatuses drawn between these dates, but the descriptions are not clear enough to connect dates to specific prints.
aving	not found	n.a. (published print)	Hendriks' name is misspelt, but this work is attributable to him (see comment on 5b).

TABLE 7.1   List of Wybrand Hendriks' scientific images (*cont.*)

No.	Description	Maker(s)	Date	Publication/ function or use otherwise
18a	Drawing of a design for an air pump	Wybrand Hendriks	20 november 1797	'Description de quelques appareils chimiques', *Verh.* *TTG* 10 (1798)
18b	Print of a design for an air pump	*H. Henderiks.* *delin.* [Wybrand Hendriks] *B. de Bakker.* *sculp. 1798*	Signed 1798	'Description de quelques appareils chimiques', *Verh.* *TTG* 10 1798
19	Two drawings of minerals (12 pieces)	Wybrand Hendriks	15 September 1797	Possibly Barthélemy Faujas de Saint-Fond, *Histoire Naturelle de la Montagne de Saint-Pierre de Maestricht*, Paris 1798
20a	Drawing of the bill of a platypus (top and bottom)	W. Hendriks	Published 1803	J. Calkoen, 'Beschrijving' van den Ornithorhynchus paradoxus of Zonderbaar Zoogend Vogel-bek-dier van Nieuwe Hollandia', *Nat.Verh. HMW* (1803), p. 177
20b	Print of the bill of a platypus	*W. Hendriks (del.),* *B. de Bakker (fec.)*	Published 1803	J. Calkoen, 'Beschrijving' van den Ornithorhynchus paradoxus of Zonderbaar Zoogend Vogel-bek-dier van Nieuwe Hollandia', *Nat.Verh. HMW*, 2/1 (1803), 177

'TRUTH-TO-NATURE' IN THE MUSEUM? 165

nique	Teylers Foundation financial records (*kasbewijzen*)	Collection	Notes
drawing?	ATS 629-022-01	not found	Tentative: only mentioned in the financial records. Probably preparatory drawing for 18b. The financial records mention several apparatuses drawn between these dates, but the descriptions are not clear enough to connect dates to specific prints.
aving	not found	n.a. (published print)	Hendriks' name is misspelt, but this work is attributable to him (see comment on 5b).
drawing	ATS 630-020-01	not found	The connection between this entry in the financial records and Faujas' publication is tenuous. Sliggers 2017, 235–236 traces the correspondence between Van Marum and Faujas, wherein reference is made to two drawings of minerals/fossils sent to Faujas by Van Marum, received in early 1799. Sliggers (without reference to this entry in the financial records) raises the possibility these were made by Hendriks. He then links plate XLI in Faujas 1798 to 6 fossils in the Museum collection, suggesting that the print was based on one of those drawings sent by Van Marum. An argument against identifying the drawings received by Faujas with this entry in the financial records is the gap in the dates between the payment to Hendriks and the moment Faujas received them. See 3 for a further connection to Faujas.
rcolour	n.a. (not produced as part of the Foundation's activities)	missing	Drawn after a taxidermy specimen in the cabinet of the Hollandsche Maatschappij der Wetenschappen
aving d ured)	n.a. (not produced as part of the Foundation's activities)	n.a. (published print)	Drawn after a taxidermy specimen in the cabinet of the Hollandsche Maatschappij der Wetenschappen. Proofs lost (formerly in the archive of the Hollandsche Maatschappij der Wetenschappen, stored in Teyler's Museum, Haarlem). Copies were also distributed as part of the normal print run of the *Nat. Verh. HMW*.

166 VOS

TABLE 7.1   List of Wybrand Hendriks' scientific images (*cont.*)

No.	Description	Maker(s)	Date	Publication/ function or use otherwise
21	Print of a side view of a platypus	*W. Hendriks del.*, *B. de Bakker fec.*	Published 1803	J. Calkoen, 'Beschrijving den Ornithorhynchus paradoxus of Zonderba Zoogend Vogel-bek-die Nieuw Hollandia', *Nat.* *HMW* 2/1 (1803), 177
22	Drawing of the mosasaur fossil	Wybrand Hendriks	9 February 1801	unknown
23	Drawing of a large bone	Wybrand Hendriks	2 July 1803	Sent to Cuvier in Paris by Van Marum
24	Drawing of the fossil known as *Homo diluvii testis*	Wybrand Hendriks	2 July 1803	Sent to Cuvier in Paris by Van Marum
25	Drawing of the mosasaur fossil	Wybrand Hendriks	10 October 1804	Sent to Cuvier in Paris by Van Marum
26	Print of *Ardea purpurea/ Purpere reiger*	*Wybrand Hendriks del.*, *C. Sepp sculp.*	1809	C. Nozeman and M. Houttuyn, *Nederlandsche Vogelen*, IV, Amsterdam 1809
27a (fig. 7.2)	Drawing of the wonder tree on the Spanjaardslaan in the Haarlemmerhout, Haarlem	Wybrand Hendriks	1819	Intended for publication in *Nat. Verh. HMW*, but rejected by Van Marum
27b (fig. 7.3)	Print of the wonder tree on the Spanjaardslaan in the Haarlemmerhout, Haarlem	*Wybrand Hendriks del.*, *E. van Varelen sculp.*	1819	Intended for publication in *Nat. Verh. HMW*, but rejected by Van Marum

'TRUTH-TO-NATURE' IN THE MUSEUM?

nique	Teylers Foundation financial records (*kasbewijzen*)	Collection	Notes
aving d ured)	n.a. (not produced as part of the Foundation's activities)	n.a. (published print)	Drawn after a taxidermy specimen in the cabinet of the Hollandsche Maatschappij der Wetenschappen. Three hand-coloured proofs in part of the archive of the Hollandsche Maatschappij der Wetenschappen, stored in Teyler's Museum, Haarlem. Copies were also distributed as part of the normal print run of the *Nat. Verh. HMW.*
drawing	ATS 633-057-01	not found	Tentative: only mentioned in the financial records
drawing	ATS 633-057-01	Bibliothèque du Muséum national d'histoire naturelle, Jardin des plantes, Paris	
drawing	ATS 633-057-01	Bibliothèque du Muséum national d'histoire naturelle, Jardin des plantes, Paris	
drawing	ATS 634-062-01	Bibliothèque du Muséum national d'histoire naturelle, Jardin des plantes, Paris	
aving d ured)	n.a. (not produced as part of the Foundation's activities)	n.a. (published print)	Drawn after a taxidermy specimen in the cabinet of the Hollandsche Maatschappij der Wetenschappen. According to the accompanying text, *den beroemden tekenaar* (the famous artist) Hendriks was asked by Van Marum to supply the drawing.
and rcolour	n.a. (not produced as part of the Foundation's activities)	Noord-Hollands Archief, Haarlem, NL-HlmNHA_53002867_M	
ing	n.a. (not produced as part of the Foundation's activities)	Noord-Hollands Archief, Haarlem (3 states): NL-HlmNHA_1477_53012163; NL-HlmNHA_1477_53012164; NL-HlmNHA_1477_53012165	

CHAPTER 8

An Asset to Art. The Purchase of Italian Drawings by Teyler's Foundation in 1790 and the Context of Art Theory in the Netherlands

Paul Knolle

In 1790, on the recommendation of Willem Anne Lestevenon, Teyler's Foundation purchased a collection of some 1,700 drawings in Rome, the majority of which were by great Italian masters such as Michelangelo, Raphael, Parmigianino and Guercino. Also included in the purchase were Dutch and French drawings, by Goltzius and Claude Lorrain among others. The acquisition of the Italian works has often surprised later researchers. For a long time the prevailing assumption was that Dutch collectors in the eighteenth and nineteenth centuries were primarily interested in their own cultural and artistic heritage. It was assumed that the Italian drawings lay dormant after their acquisition until they were discovered by art historians around 1900. In this contribution the author will examine the validity of that interpretation with the help of hitherto neglected source material, and take an important step in research into the motivation, function, and context of art theory regarding that acquisition. The role of Lestevenon, the hitherto neglected key figure in this transaction, will be emphasized.

•••

The secretary's account of the meeting of Teyler's Foundation on 13 March 1789 sounds surprisingly dry, at least to us in retrospect. After all, a document was discussed that would prove to be of considerable importance for the future of the institution. Willem Anne Lestevenon (1750–1830), a member of Teyler's Second Society, had sent a letter from Rome to the Director, Adriaan van Zeebergh (1746–1824), offering to acquire a number of unspecified 'Italian drawings' for the Foundation, as well as rarities in the field of natural history, and several books and prints on the subject of ancient history.[1] According to the writer

---

1 ATS 5, 193 (13 March 1789). Lestevenon had been elected to Teyler's Second Society on 29 December 1780; on 5 January 1781 his membership was confirmed. See ATS 5, 72–73. Until recently 1803 was given as the year in which Lestevenon died, but it was 1830. See http://mapage.noos.fr/xgen/roglo/ga.lestevenon.jpg (accessed 7 Sept. 2019). The correspondence with Van Zeebergh has unfortunately not survived. Van Zeebergh was a member of the board

© KONINKLIJKE BRILL NV, LEIDEN, 2021 | DOI:10.1163/9789004441446_009

AN ASSET TO ART   169

prices were far lower than 'in our country'. The Director agreed and requested
that Lestevenon take steps to secure the purchase, making *f* 8,000 available.
There is implicit faith in Lestevenon's knowledge of fine art with regard to the
drawings; however, the advice of the Director of the Museum, Martinus van
Marum (1750–1837; figure 1.3), was sought regarding the other items offered
for sale. At the same time, the decision was taken to award David Humbert de
Superville (1770–1849), a young The Hague artist then living in Rome, a yearly
stipend of *f* 100.[2] We will come back to this stipend later.

On 29 May 1789, the proposed acquisition was again on the agenda.
Lestevenon wrote to Van Zeebergh informing him that the collection of Italian
drawings 'excelling in their Beauty and Authenticity' had been assembled by
Queen Christina of Sweden; it was being offered for sale at 6,000 *scudi*, but
he intended to pay only 4,000 *scudi* or less.[3] The drawings had been bought
by Don Livio Odescalchi in 1692 after the death of Queen Christina in Rome
in 1689; he added further works on paper, and subsequently bequeathed the
collection to his heirs, who were now selling it. After consultation with
the Teyler's Foundation *kasteleijn* (keeper) Wybrand Hendriks (1744–1831;
figure 7.1) 'over the suitability of such a collection for the museum', the board
of Directors instructed Lestevenon to secure the purchase for as low a price
as possible.[4] On 11 December 1790 Lestevenon sent an invoice from Rome for
f 10,000 (the budget had been exceeded), and informed the board that the
items were in his possession. On 31 December 1790 the invoice was paid in full
by the board.[5]

---

of Teyler's Foundation; his tenure lasted from 1780 until 1824, and although he was only officially appointed as president of the board in 1807, he had been acting as such since 1788/89.
Mijnhardt 1988, 312; see also Chapter 2 in this volume.

2 ATS 5, 193, 13 March 1789. See also Tuyll 2000, 523, app. 2:13. For the stipend paid to Humbert
de Superville, and for Lestevenon as his patron, see also Bolten 1997, 13–14.

3 It appears that the 4,000 *scudi* covered the purchase of nine albums containing sketches, two
containing landscapes, three containing drawings not otherwise specified, and four containing prints; see Tuyll 2000, 524, app. 2:15. For the contracts drawn up in Rome, see ibid., 15–16,
and the corresponding appendix.

4 ibid., 196 (29 May, not 29 April as in Tuyll 2000, 523, app. 2:13). The wording, consultation
'over the suitability of such a collection for the museum', could lead to the supposition that a
specification existed.

5 For Lestevenon's invoice, see ATS 622 ('Invoices and receipts, 1790–1791'), no. 622–607–01. See
also Tuyll 2000, 524, app. 2:14. The invoice was, according to the *Grootboek* or general ledger,
paid in full on 31 December 1790: ATS 520 (*Grootboek*), 184. See also Tuyll 2000, 525, app. 2:16.
According to the calculation tool of the International Institute of Social History in Amsterdam,
the equivalent of 10,000 florins in 1790 is €95,579 in 2020: https://iisg.amsterdam/en/re-
search/projects/hpw/calculate.php?back-link=1 (Nov. 2020). However, this concerns purchasing power for everyday consumer goods and not for Old Master Drawings.

FIGURE 8.1   Claude Lorrain (c. 1600–1682), *View in Rome*, c. 1630–35, pencil, pen in brown ink, brush in brown wash, 116 x 185 mm. Acquired in 1790 in Rome from the Odescalchi heirs.
TEYLER'S MUSEUM, L 021

Thus the acquisition became a fact: at least 1,700 Italian drawings, 80 drawings by Claude Lorrain (figure 8.1) and 90 prints and drawings by Hendrick Goltzius (figure 8.2) from the collection of the Roman nobleman Don Livio Odescalchi (1655–1713; figure 8.3).[6] There was however considerable delay in its arrival at Haarlem, and in the meantime Lestevenon housed it in his property in Rome, where, according to him, many artists and amateurs came to view and admire the works before they were shipped from Civitavecchia to Haarlem.[7]

---

6   When Queen Christina died her drawings passed to Cardinal Decio Azzolino (1623–1689); his nephew and heir, Marchese Pompeo Azzolino (1654–1705), sold her albums in 1692 to Don Livio Odescalchi. The works were sold by Don Livio Odescalchi's heirs. Tuyll 2000, 22. For Goltzius, see Bleyerveld/Veldman 2016, 71–189, cat. nos. 54–182.

7   See Lestevenon's undated letter to Van Marum of Spring 1791 (Tuyll 2000, 525, app. 2:17 and Forbes/Lefebvre/Bruijn 1969–76, vol. 6 (1976), 218–19). In a curious aside, Lestevenon states that he was still of the opinion that the purchase would not live up to expectations. In this he was playing his hand cautiously. Many will, understandably, have had high hopes of the quality of the works. Possibly he feared that 'they' (probably the board and members of Teyler's and the artists involved) would expect complete drawings rather than the sketches of which the collection was mainly composed. For the treatment of the collection by Wybrand Hendriks after its arrival in Haarlem, see Tuyll 2000, 16–17.

FIGURE 8.2
Hendrick Goltzius, *Portrait of Giovanni da Bologna*, 1591, black, red and white chalk, brush in brown and brown-grey, brush in white bodycolour, 371 x 300 mm. Acquired in 1790 in Rome from the Odescalchi heirs.
TEYLER'S MUSEUM, N 072

FIGURE 8.3
Jakob-Ferdinand Voet (1639–c. 1700), *Portrait of Livio Odescalchi*, 1676–77, oil on canvas, 75 x 60.5 cm.
THE WALTERS ART MUSEUM, BALTIMORE, MARYLAND, 37.371 (ACQUIRED BY HENRY WALTERS WITH THE MASSARENTI COLLECTION, 1902)

Today, those who appreciate the significance of the drawings can barely contain their excitement. The collection, still a vital component of the renowned collection of drawings and prints in Teyler's Museum, contains not only twenty-five studies by Michelangelo (figure 8.4) and twelve by Raphael (figure 8.5), but also fine specimens from the hand of other famous masters including Guido Reni and Parmigianino. Other drawings entered the collection under famous names, but they later turned out to be made by less well known masters, such as Giovanni Battista Franco, called Il Semolei (figure 8.6), Giovanni Bandini, and Bernardino Campi.

This spectacular collection has been the subject of several studies.[8] There are, however, a number of interesting aspects that have remained under-explored. So far, the figure of Willem Anne Lestevenon – the initiator and executor of the purchase – has not come into his own as an art connoisseur and a committed member of Teyler's Second Society. His multi-faceted and turbulent life, which was to a large degree dedicated to art, should, I hope to prove, be worthy of a study in itself.

Moreover, the preference for valuable Italian drawings can be placed in a broader context. In the following text I hope to demonstrate that this acquisition was understandable with regard to the practice, theory and didactics of art at the time, and simultaneously to prove that Teyler's Foundation chose to follow a new direction, and with this grand gesture to help Dutch art out of its reputed decline.

But first, Lestevenon.

1 Willem Anne Lestevenon

Willem Anne Lestevenon was a versatile and colourful character. Born in Paris in 1750 as the son of Mattheus Lestevenon, an alderman of Amsterdam and ambassador to France, Willem Anne trained as a solicitor. He chose politics, and the side of the Patriots. The only known likeness of Lestevenon, in a drawing by Wybrand Hendriks, confirms his political alliance (figure 8.7). He appears in 'The chamber of the former Burgher Society in the Golden Lion, depicted on the morning of 19 Jan. 1795, at dawn on the day when the citizens departed for the market, each of them armed according to his own judgment, after the

---

8 The most recent is Tuyll 2000. Earlier publications concerning the purchase and history of this collection are Regteren Altena 1966; Meijer 1984; Plomp 2001, 128, 129 (n. 18) and 156; for the Netherlandish part of the acquisition see Bleyerveld/Veldman 2016, 10–17.

FIGURE 8.4 Michelangelo Buonarroti (1475–1564), *Figure study of a walking man*, between c. 1527 and 1560, black chalk and pencil, 404 x 258 mm. Acquired in 1790 in Rome from the Odescalchi heirs.
TEYLER'S MUSEUM, A 019

FIGURE 8.5
Raphael (Raffaello Sanzio, 1483–1520), *Putto holding the Medici ring*, c. 1513–14, black chalk, heightened with white chalk on dark beige paper, 338 x 193 mm. Acquired in 1790 in Rome from the Odescalchi heirs.
TEYLER'S MUSEUM, A 57

revolution had already been accomplished. Drawn by W. Hendriks from life'. Lestevenon stands at the front in the centre.[9]

---

9 *De kamer der geweesen burger sociteit [sic] in de Gouden Leeuw, verbeeld op de morgen van den 19. Jan. 1795, bij 't aanbreeken van den dag daar de burgers ieder na zijn welgevallen gewapent na de markt trekken toen de omwenteling reeds bewerkt was. Getekent door W. Hendriks na 't leven, 1795.* Steur 1970. The situation depicted refers to the 'Velvet Revolution' of 18 January 1795, which was followed the next day by the proclamation of the Batavian Republic. While patriotic rebellions in the 1780s had resulted in power being restored to the house of Orange in 1787 with the help of the Prussian army, the revolution of 1795 led to the flight of Stadholder Willem V to England on the same night. Lestevenon played a central role in the preparation of this revolution in Haarlem and beyond. Several others associated with Teyler's Foundation and its institutions were active in the Patriot movement, among them the *kasteleijn* Hendriks. But Orangists were also represented in Teyler's, for example by Gerrit Willem van Oosten de Bruyn, and, in a more hidden way, by Martinus van Marum. Mijnhardt 1988, 320; Daalder 1975, 47–48 and *passim*. See also Chapter 2 in this volume.

FIGURE 8.6 Giovanni Battista Franco, called Il Semolei (1498–1561), *Discovery of Achilles among the daughters of Lycomedes*, c. 1545–50, pen and brown ink, brown wash, on beige paper, 466 x 390 mm. Acquired in 1790 in Rome from the Odescalchi heirs as a Raphael.
TEYLER'S MUSEUM, K 27

In addition to several positions on the Haarlem city council, Lestevenon was a member of the States General. After the Dutch Orangist Revolution of 1787 he was dismissed from his positions and travelled through France and Italy. Only after the Batavian Revolution of 1795 did he return to the council in Haarlem, the States of Holland and the States General, after which he was elected to the First National Assembly in 1796. In addition to those positions, he was a member

FIGURE 8.7   Wybrand Hendriks, 'The chamber of the former Burgher-Society in the Golden Lion', 1795, drawing, 230 x 350 mm. According to the explanation accompanying the drawing two members of Teyler's Second Society were present: Willem Anne Lestevenon is standing in front of the table with his back turned, and Johannes Enschedé is fourth from the left, seen from the back.
NOORD-HOLLANDS ARCHIEF, HAARLEM, NL-HLMNHA_53001222_M

of the Board of Trustees of the University of Leiden. Besides his membership of Teyler's Second Society from 1781, he was Director of the Holland Society of Sciences from 1778 onwards, and from 1792 also a member of the Freemasons' Lodge, both in Haarlem. An experienced and highly accomplished diplomat, he played a significant role in the peace negotiations with France on behalf of the Batavian Republic in 1795. But his eventful life took another turn. In 1797 he was accused not only of involvement in extortion but of sodomy: no longer welcome in the Republic, he based himself in France.[10] Years earlier, in 1779, he had married Johanna Hodshon, who died in 1780.

---

10   Molhuysen/Kossmann 1933, 600–601; https://www.parlement.com/id/vgo9llviinui/w_a_lestevenon; see also https://www.parlement.com/id/vigfgov2wpxl/staten_generaal_1588_1795; Bolten 1997, 13–14; Tuyll 2000, 15 and n. 7; and Plomp 2001, 129, n. 18 and the literature referred to in that note.

AN ASSET TO ART

Lestevenon's love of art was reflected in a formidable collection of drawings, including many Italian ones. These works disappeared with him to France. Roeland van Eynden and Adriaan van der Willigen noted with regret in their *Geschiedenis der vaderlandsche schilderkunst* of 1820: 'a few years earlier, art there [in Haarlem] suffered a great loss due to the removal to Paris of the collection of the gentleman Lestevenon, rich in Italian drawings and mostly assembled by himself, exploiting his knowledge and taste. There these art treasures were subsequently sold'.[11] In this context it is also interesting that Lestevenon owned plaster copies of antique sculptures: in 1806 the City Drawing Academy and the Felix Meritis Society, both in Amsterdam, purchased from Wybrand Hendriks a number that came from Lestevenon's collection.[12]

Lestevenon was not only a collector: during his travels through France and Italy in the 1780s and 1790s he frequently dealt in works of art and, as was the case with the Italian drawings for Teyler's, brokered deals for other collectors.[13] He was also active in organizations concerned with fine art. On 18 November 1778, after the death of Pieter Teyler van der Hulst (1702–1778), Lestevenon was elected to succeed him as chief Director of the Haarlem Drawing Academy, founded in 1772.[14] It was a time when almost every Dutch city that wished to be taken seriously in the field of fine arts founded a drawing society, as a municipal or private initiative. This was a new type of organization, intended not only to inspire local artists by offering them practice and education in the visual arts, but also to teach better design to artisans, in order to stimulate the economy. Connoisseurs could apply for special membership.[15] Having a chief Director with a high social status was considered important: Lestevenon is explicitly referred to in Academy minutes as 'Alderman to the Council and Municipal Offices of this city'. In 1788, when many had cancelled their membership due to dwindling financial means, he loaned the destitute Academy *f* 600.[16] On 30 April that same year, because the Patriot Lestevenon was out of favour (see

---

11   Eynden/Willigen 1820, 438–39, n. 3. For Lestevenon as collector and dealer, see Bacou 1962.

12   Offerhaus 1979, 53 and 71, n. 47.

13   For a few examples, see Plomp 2001, 129, n. 18, 156, 157, n. 120. The main purpose of Lestevenon's frequent correspondence with Van Marum was to discuss possible purchases of fossils, anatomical models and other scientific objects. See Forbes/Lefebvre/Bruijn 1969–76, vol. 6, 1976, 197–219.

14   'Tekenacademie: register van notulen van bestuursvergaderingen, 1775–1795': Archive Tekencollege Kunst Zij Ons Doel and predecessors, 1772–1972, NHA, acc. no. 3496, no. 1, 30. For the history of the drawing societies in Haarlem, see Sliggers 1990a and Sliggers 1990b.

15   For the origins and function of Dutch drawing academies, see among others Knolle 1979, 1983, 1984c and 1989b.

16   Sliggers 1990a, 18.

p. 175) and planned a long journey through France and Italy, the board decided to appoint Gerrit Willem van Oosten de Bruyn as his successor. On 14 June 1792, however, Lestevenon appeared again as chief Director. Although his attendance at board meetings was sporadic, he retained his position until the closure of the Academy in 1795. Judging by the following incident, he also resumed his role as a mediator. The year 1792 ended with a dispute with the board of Teyler's Foundation about their subsidy: the Academy had not submitted the required application for a contribution, which was assessed each year. In a meeting at the Foundation Lestevenon attempted to smooth things over, but it would be some time before the Foundation invested in art education again.[17]

That the board of Teyler's Foundation trusted Lestevenon where his taste in the visual arts was concerned is understandable. As a judicious and remarkably diplomatic connoisseur with an exquisite collection of Italian drawings, in addition to his contribution as Director of the Drawing Academy in Haarlem, he could be trusted for the purchase of works of art. That the board valued his opinion in such matters is also demonstrated by the fact that he devised the competition of 1781 (to be considered below), from which the winning submission, that of Roeland van Eynden, is so frequently connected with the Odescalchi purchase.[18] At the time, 1783, Lestevenon was living in Paris, so he expressed his opinion in a letter. That letter survives, and will be discussed later.

Lestevenon was a presence in Teyler's Second Society for sixteen years. On 22 September 1797 Van Marum informed the board that Lestevenon was stepping down.[19] Whether his departure was related to the aforementioned sex scandal is not recorded; the timing, however, is revealing.

2   Motives for the Purchase of the Drawings

The Directorate unfortunately did not record the motives for the purchase, but these can be deduced from circumstantial evidence. It would stimulate artists for whom a trip to Italy was too expensive, and encourage competition

---

17   See the same archive (see n. 14), no. 1, 95, and unpaginated minutes. See also ATS 5, 247ff. Mijnhardt 1988, 316, refers to a change in the financial priorities of the Foundation. Sliggers 1990a, 18, states that Lestevenon was chief Director only until 1788, which is incorrect.

18   As mentioned earlier in this volume, both Teyler societies were expected to hold a prize competition every year. See also Chapter 2. For Lestevenon as the instigator of the competition of 1781, see Velden 1995, 11.

19   ATS 5, 312.

AN ASSET TO ART

179

and develop their artistic insights and skills to a higher level; at the same time, connoisseurs could study fine examples of the Italian School, which unquestionably displayed the highest standards.[20] The exceptional quality of the collection was undoubtedly a decisive factor. It enabled the Foundation to stimulate contemporary art, in accordance with the aims and ideals stated in the testament of Pieter Teyler van der Hulst, where draughtsmanship played an explicit role in the activities envisioned for the Second Society. The Foundation's collection was presented as a serious resource for study.[21]

The purchase was in line with a series of costly acquisitions of exceptional quality from Dutch auctions, for each of which the *kasteleijn* was allocated a maximum, often considerable, amount. A number of purchases were made by Vincent van der Vinne (1736–1811; Hendriks' predecessor as *kasteleijn*), or, when he was ill, by his brother Jan van der Vinne (1734–1805), for example at the auction of Jan Tak in 1780.[22] From 1785 Wybrand Hendriks made purchases at the sales of Jonas Witsen (1790),[23] Jan van Dijk (1791),[24] Aert Schouman (1792; Hendriks received f1,000, to be spent specially on bird drawings by the master),[25] Cornelis Ploos van Amstel (1800) and Jan Gildemeester (1800).[26] Considering the strict style of management at Teyler's, it is remarkable that Hendriks was given such a free hand. In addition to Dutch seventeenth- and eighteenth-century drawings, he also acquired smaller collections of Flemish, French and German drawings.[27] It is also remarkable that the board was prepared to spend considerably more money on the purchase of the Italian drawings in 1790, in which Hendriks was indirectly involved, than on purchases from important sales of Dutch drawings.

3　Interest in the Acquisition

As is evident from several issues of the *Algemeene Konst- en Letter-bode*, the acquisition in 1790 did not go unnoticed, although a few years later. The issue of 19 April 1793 reported the arrival of the Italian drawings (the rest of the

---

20　E. Ebbinge in Tuyll 2000, 9. For possible motives for the purchase see also ibid., 20–21.
21　Meijer 1984, 78.
22　ATS 5, 68 (6 October 1780).
23　ATS 5, 214 (13 August 1790). On 13 March 1789, Wybrand Hendriks had already received f3,000 to spend at an unspecified auction of drawings and prints in Rotterdam. ATS 5, 193.
24　ibid., 224 (11 March 1791).
25　ibid., 246 (7 December 1792). For Schouman's watercolours of birds, see Knolle/Vlek 2017.
26　ATS 5, respectively 356 (21 February 1800) and 372 (30 October 1800).
27　For Hendriks' policies see Plomp 1997, 5–15.

purchase was not mentioned).[28] The anonymous author reported that Teyler's department of drawings had recently been 'in a notable manner augmented and enriched with more than seventeen hundred drawings by distinguished Italian Masters, of which many are incomparably beautiful'. The notable provenance of a number of the drawings was emphasized, as was the fact that the collection was 'purchased at some considerable cost'. The article went on to say that in order to encourage art in the homeland and to 'embellish and expand the cabinet even more', from time to time the Directors commissioned two or more drawings from the best Dutch artists and added them to the collection.

The *Algemeene Konst- en Letter-bode* promised to publish regular updates regarding the expansion of the department of drawings, but this was realized only in the first few years. In September 1793 interest in the purchase was still evident.[29] When one considers the presence of works by great names in the collection, it is notable that in this article the accent was placed on a number of (at the time) lesser-known Italian masters born before Raphael and Michelangelo, such as Francesco Squarcione and Andrea Mantegna. The works mentioned (no longer attributed to the masters) had a special value because of their age, the author notes: it was clear to see how 'remarkably' art began to develop at that time. The identity of the writer is unfortunately unknown; in any case the article reflects the developing interest in the 1790s in the 'primitives'.[30]

In the next article, of 17 January 1794, Michelangelo was finally discussed.[31] His drawings provided 'the most significant proof of the splendid artistry of the most famous of the Old Masters'. Examples demonstrated 'what a rare talent he possesses, to express what his imagination experiences, or his soul feels, through his art'. One would like to know who the author of this romantic interpretation was.

The reports regarding the acquisition were also attracting international attention. The historian Johann Georg Meusel published 'Zeichnungen von Michael Angelo' in his *Neues Museum für Künstler und Kunstliebhaber* of 1794.[32] According to Van Tuyll, this was the last publication on the Italian drawings in Haarlem for almost a century,[33] but that is not entirely accurate. In 1820 Van Eynden and Van

---

28   *Algemeene Konst- en Letter-bode* 251 (19 April 1793), 121–22. See also Tuyll 2000, 19–20, and the contribution by Van Druten to this volume, pp. 193–194.This weekly, published in Haarlem, was founded in 1788. The last year of publication was 1861. It was one of the first important arts magazines in the Netherlands. See also Chapter 2 in this volume, p. 31, n. 40.

29   *Algemeene Konst- en Letter-bode* 271 (6 September 1793), 78–79.

30   Previtali 1964 and 1994.

31   *Algemeene Konst- en Letter-bode*, 3 (17 January 1794), 21–22.

32   Meusel 1794. This article is also noted in Tuyll 2000, 20.

33   Tuyll 2000, 21. According to him, serious scholarly attention to the collection was not paid until four German art historians, attending the 5th congress of Art Historians of

der Willigen raised the subject of the collection of Teyler's Foundation in the third volume of their *Geschiedenis der vaderlandsche schilderkunst,* and considered the Italian component to be worth mentioning: 'In addition to these drawings from the Dutch School, there are also a number of Italian works, originating from the collection of Queen Christina of Sweden, who resided mostly in Rome'. In a note they refer to the *Algemeene Konst- en Letter-bode.*[34]

The question now is how the drawings were received in Haarlem itself. Is there any evidence that artists and art lovers did benefit from their presence? Researchers have so far doubted this. In his catalogue of the early Italian drawings in Teyler's Museum, Van Tuyll considers that if the Odescalchi drawings had been purchased to stimulate contemporary art, that aim had been unfulfilled due to a lack of public interest. As a reason for this he cites the fact that the works were not always readily available for viewing, but he considers that a far greater cause was the gradual shift away from interest in foreign schools of art to an almost exclusive preoccupation with 'national' art.[35]

There are several things that can be said against this assumption. First, a lack of accessibility does not necessarily mean that the collection lay dormant. Admittedly, the Museum visitors' books do not seem to indicate an increase in attendance. However there are at least indications that in the drawing societies established in Haarlem in the eighteenth and nineteenth centuries after the first public drawing academy (1772–95) there was interest in the works: these societies were Kunstmin en Vlijt (1796–1826; figure 9.5) and the society that stemmed from it, Kunst zij ons Doel (established in 1821 and still in existence today).[36] Whether this interest led to an improvement in the quality of art is difficult to trace, but one can expect that the discussions of art held in these societies had at least some impact on fine-tuning the tastes of the attendees, both professionals and honorary members.

Two examples are interesting in relation to this. On 24 November 1796, during a general meeting of members of Kunstmin en Vlijt, a viewing was held with 'beautiful English prints' and Italian drawings.[37] Since Kunstmin en Vlijt did

---

1898 in Amsterdam, visited Haarlem and 'discovered' Michelangelo's drawings; August Schmarsow (University of Leipzig) and Adolf Bayersdorfer (German Institute in Florence) published them. See Marcuard 1901. See also Chapter 3, p. 55, n. 13.

34   Eynden/Willigen 1820, 485.

35   Tuyll 2000, 21.

36   Kunst zij ons Doel in Haarlem is not related to the Amsterdam drawing society of the same name. For entries in the visitors' books, see the contribution by Terry van Druten in this volume.

37   Archive Tekencollege Kunst Zij Ons Doel 1772–1972 (see n. 14), 3496, no. 4 (minute book of the Drawing Academy, established on 14 September 1796), 14–15.

not own any Italian art, it must be assumed that Wybrand Hendriks, Director of the drawing academy and *kasteleijn* at Teyler's, had brought drawings from the Museum. This is the only occasion when the use of the drawings is explicitly recorded, but Hendriks had probably made drawings from the Teyler's collection available to Kunstmin en Vlijt on other occasions (figure 9.5).[38] Though the other records of *kunstbeschouwingen* (gatherings for art appreciation) are very vague, it is quite possible that more frequent use was made of the Odescalchi Collection. Such gatherings were organized not only in the Haarlem art society but also in Teyler's Museum itself. Van Eynden and Van der Willigen recorded that 'the rich collection of drawings and prints [belonging to Teyler's Museum] serves well for art appreciation gatherings on autumn and winter evenings, when not only art lovers and accomplished painters but also young artists are invited by the Directors, so the acquisition has a valuable purpose'.[39] Since the 'rich collection' referred to here included the Italian drawings acquired in 1790, it would be incorrect to state categorically that they had received little attention before the collection was 'rediscovered' by art historians around 1900.[40]

4 Interest in Italian Art in the Netherlands

Although, after 1770, a true lobby for 'Dutch' art developed for a variety of patriotic reasons – hoping for a revival of the successful and profitable art of the Golden Age – the acquisition of this extensive collection of Italian drawings was neither an unexpected nor an isolated development. Teyler's Directors shared the prevailing attitudes in the country on collection policy, art education, travel patterns of young artists, and contemporary art theory.

Though Dutch collectors in the second half of the eighteenth century often preferred Dutch drawings, several among them owned large numbers of notable Italian ones. Plomp quotes their names, adding the number of their Italian drawings: Gosuinus Uilenbroek (died 1740; 740), Isaac Walraven (sale in 1765; 489), Antoni Rutgers (sale in 1778; 537), Cornelis Ploos van Amstel (sale in 1800; 420), and Dirk Versteegh (sale in 1823; at least 1,020).[41] An advocate of Dutch

---

38 In 1820, Hendriks was reprimanded by the board for supplying works – what works is not clear – for an art appreciation gathering outside Teyler's Foundation, without the prior knowledge of the Directors. This was after his departure as *kasteleijn*. The incident could imply that Hendriks made a habit of this. See also Van Druten in Chapter 9 below, p. 199, n. 25.

39 See n. 34. This quote is put into a different perspective by Van Druten in Chapter 9 below, p. 201, n. 30.

40 See n. 33.

41 Plomp 2001, 26–34, 125–26 and 291–92. The number of Italian sheets usually exceeded the number of drawings by other foreign artists; ibid., 142–43.

AN ASSET TO ART

iconography such as Ploos van Amstel was not altogether blind to the beauty of foreign masters. Cornelis Apostool, appointed as the first Director of the Rijksmuseum in Amsterdam in 1808, had a passionate interest in Italian art; he was keen for the museum to expand its collection of Italian and French art, but this was primarily hampered by financial limitations, especially where paintings were concerned.[42] When Italian paintings were collected in the Netherlands it was primarily by private individuals, such as Josephus Augustinus Brentano.[43] All in all, the purchase of the Odescalchi Collection would have seemed appropriate to many Dutch collectors.

Of the two Italian giants in the Odescalchi Collection Raphael was pre-eminent. Dutch aficionados clearly preferred his refined elegance, and found the contours and muscles of Michelangelo too emphatic. This preference is also demonstrated in the prices: only drawings by Raphael, Annibale Carracci and Parmigianino commanded anything like the sums that were paid for Dutch drawings.[44] (There is of course a difference between these Dutch watercolours, seen as independent works of art, and the 'unfinished' studies by the Italian masters.) At any rate, the purchase by Teyler's Museum in 1790 – to which only a handful of Italian sheets would later be added[45] – was the first significant collection of studies by Michelangelo and Raphael to be brought to Holland.[46]

If the Directors of Teyler's Foundation wished to help young artists by giving them access to stimulating visual material with this acquisition, that wish was fully in line with the educational ideals in the Netherlands at the time. As mentioned earlier, drawing academies were established after 1765 in almost every large town in the Netherlands, and there a curriculum was followed that was based on classical ideals of beauty. Students might eventually specialize not in historical works but in landscapes, genre pieces or still lifes, but a classical education in art was a *sine qua non* until the late nineteenth century. Students learned to draw (and later to paint) from casts of antique statues and from nude models, according to the parameters of ideal beauty. In this context we should also remember that in 1806 the City Drawing Academy

---

42 Jonker 1977, 105. For purchases for the Rijksmuseum and Mauritshuis and the interest in Italian art at the time of King Willem I, see Bergvelt 1992 and Bergvelt 1998, 92–96.

43 See Bionda 1986.

44 Plomp 2001, 147–48.

45 Hendriks bought a *Capriccio met ruïnes* with pendant by Giovanni Paolo Panini in 1802. See Berge-Gerbaud/Menalda/Plomp/Tuyll 2000, 53–54, no. 12.

46 ibid., 51. It might be added that some decades later another famous drawings collection was assembled by King Willem II (r. 1840–49). That collection also included drawings by Michelangelo, Raphael and Leonardo. Most of these drawings are now in the British Museum or the Louvre. See Paarlberg/Slechte 2014, 278–91, cat. nos. 176–88.

and the Felix Meritis Society, both in Amsterdam, purchased from Wybrand Hendriks a number of plaster casts that came from Lestevenon's collection (see above, p. 177).

These 'antique' ideals of beauty were also evident in Italian art of the Renaissance. Studying good examples helped young draughtsmen. That is why the Director Cornelis Ploos van Amstel donated seven splendid Italian drawings, including a Guercino, to the Amsterdam City Drawing Academy in 1767.[47] In 1810 Jan Konijnenburg gave a lecture to the Kunst zij ons Doel drawing society in Amsterdam entitled 'Over het kunst-schoone in Raphaël, als voorbeeld ter navolging' ('On the artistic beauty in Raphael as an example for imitation').[48]

After decades of economic recession, when artists could not afford a trip to the south, many wished to see the beauty of antique art in Italy for themselves. From about 1780, a study tour became a realistic ambition for young artists, supported by institutions or individuals. Jean Grandjean set out for Rome in 1779 with a scholarship from the Amsterdam City Drawing Academy. In 1783 Daniel Dupré travelled south with the support of the Holland Society of Sciences. Hendrik Voogd followed in 1788, thanks to the collector Dirk Versteegh. In 1789, and on the recommendation of Lestevenon, the Directorate of Teyler's Foundation awarded a yearly stipend of ƒ100 to David Humbert de Superville, who had arrived in Rome that year; as we have seen, the decision was taken in the same meeting of 13 March 1789 in which the purchase of the Italian drawings was decided. Jan Kamphuijsen (1792) and Alexander Liernur (1794) also went to Italy. During the reign of Louis Napoleon as King of Holland (1806–10), a number of *élèves* or *pensionnaires* went south after being awarded the Prix de Rome.[49] Some artists never returned to the Netherlands, so the intended effect of their travels – improvement of the visual arts in the Netherlands – failed to be realized.[50] But it is clear that the acquisition can be linked to the renewed interest in Italian art, which was in line with the renewed appreciation of antique art on an international level.[51]

---

47 Ploos van Amstel 1980, 109, n. 21.

48 Konijnenburg 1810, 45–88.

49 For an overview, *Reizen* 1984, 10. See further Bergvelt 1984; Dekkers 1984; Bolten 1997, 14; and Tuyll 2000, 20–21, n. 24.

50 Grandjean died in Rome in 1781; Hendrik Voogd stayed in Rome all his life. Of the *élèves*, to mention two examples, Abraham Teerlink remained in Rome, while Antonie Sminck Pitloo founded the 'School of Posillipo' in Naples. See for the biographies of the *élèves* Bergvelt 1984, unpaginated.

51 Aymonino/Lauder 2015.

AN ASSET TO ART   185

5   Van Eynden (1787) and Kikkert (1809)

The purchase of the Odescalchi Collection, combined with other activities at Teyler's Foundation, fitted into a broader framework of concepts of art, so it is imperative to consider it in the realm of art theory. Important sources for this are the competitions at Teyler's Second Society in 1781 and, to a lesser extent, in 1806.[52]

Dutch art was in decline, as many in the Netherlands also believed. How to turn the tide was widely discussed after 1770.[53] The return to the themes and the style of painting of the Dutch seventeenth century was one possibility, but it was not the only option. The fact that the Directorate at Teyler's was aware of the debate, and wished to contribute to its solution, is evident in the competition concerning national taste that the Second Society, at the suggestion of Lestevenon, instigated in 1781. It was won in 1783 by Roeland van Eynden, who was both author and painter.[54] His winning essay was finally published in 1787, three years before the purchase of the Odescalchi Collection.

The final, most relevant part of the prize question reads: how can Dutch taste in art be improved 'by the study of antiquity and the works of artists from other schools'? The answer is implied: Classical art, frequently considered to include Italian art of the Renaissance, could assist in developing the taste of Dutch painters and help Dutch art out of its decline. Van Eynden endorsed this view, but his solution is interesting. The Dutch School was, according to him (and in line with contemporary international opinion), famous for 'its faithful imitation and artistic depiction of fair nature, in so far as that can be achieved from observable objects'. It exceeded all other schools in the choice and harmony of colour, the natural expression of emotions, and 'extraordinarily beautiful and fluid brushwork, applied to depictions of subject matter that is neither elevated nor ideal'. Van Eynden concluded – undoubtedly to his regret – that 'the artistic character of our painting nation cannot be defined by history painting'.[55]

This proved to be the Achilles heel of the Dutch School that foreign critics had focused upon for almost a century. They wrote that it was full of artists

---

52   See for both Velden 1995.

53   Discussions concerning national or international orientation have been considered at length by e.g. Koolhaas-Grosfeld 1982; Knolle 1984a; Knolle 1984b; Koolhaas-Grosfeld 1986; Knolle 1989a; Knolle 1992; and Grijzenhout/Veen 1992.

54   The manuscripts of the four submissions to the competition of 1781 can be found in ATS 1408–1411. The publication was delayed because Van Eynden was required to correct errors of style in his essay. See also the adjudications in ATS 1412. For Van Eynden see also Koolhaas-Grosfeld 1982, 615–16.

55   Eynden 1787, 95–96. For his definition of Dutch national taste, see also 175–76.

who 'only imitated the least worthy and contemptible pursuits of the lowest class of people'. Van Eynden could refute this view, however, by pointing out that Gerard de Lairesse, Adriaen van der Werff and Jacob de Wit through their choice of historical and mythological subject matter proved the opposite. But he was forced to admit when drawing an 'impartial comparison' that the art of the Dutch School fell short in essential elements such as invention, composition, drawing, and – shockingly – colour and chiaroscuro.[56]

In genres other than history painting he also did not count the Dutch among the international best, except – albeit not without reservation – in 'modern representations of the lives of important people'.[57] Dou, Van Mieris, Metsu, Ter Borch, Netscher, etc., often produced nothing beyond images of the everyday life of common people. If only they had exercised more care in their choice of subject matter –

> not only to please the eye but also the heart and the moral sense, which is evident in numerous works by the Frenchman Greuse [sic] and the Englishman West. Had they chosen grand and beautiful subjects, in which the history of the Fatherland is rich, their accomplishment as artists would have produced strikingly artistic scenes, no less beautiful or grand than the death of Wolf by West, Calas by Chodowiecky, or Abelard and Heloïse by Angelica Kaufman.[58]

Regardless of how patriotic Van Eynden was, he gave his preference to Italian art, 'the most perfect, [...] the most consistent with the highest aims of the arts'.[59] And he came to a somewhat forced Dutch 'polder model', a compromise that matched the apparently inescapable national taste and the internationally recognized quality of painters of 'contemporary scenes'. This last group should encourage further development of the quality of Dutch art if they

> managed to combine the noble simplicity and the beauty of the delineation of the Ancients in their statues, and their reasonable selection,[60]

---

56 Lairesse: Eynden 1787, 110–11; Van der Werff: ibid., 113–14; De Wit and criticism of the Dutch history painters: ibid., 164–72.

57 Eynden 1787, 136–43, distinguished between three types in what we now call genre: 'modern representations of the lives of important people' (for example Frans van Mieris de Oude), 'subjects that imitate daily life', and the burlesque and the bambocciades (where he placed Jan Steen).

58 Eynden 1787, 172.

59 ibid., 24.

60 For this concept see the contribution of Koenraad Vos to this publication.

omitting the insignificant; the greatness of Michelangelo; the expertise [*weetenschap*], truthfulness and expression of Raphael; the gracefulness of Correggio; the colour of Titian; the composition of the French School; and the unification of these perfections, following the example of Mengs; if they managed to combine all these elements judiciously with the execution and truthful imitation, qualities in which the Dutch School excels.[61]

Van Eynden advocated historical paintings in a cabinet format, like Mengs and Greuze, adapted to Dutch circumstances. With a combination of international choice of subject and national implementation, he opted for a happy medium.

It is notable that sixteen years after the acquisition, the winner of the Teyler's prize of 1806, the draughtsman and engraver Pieter Kikkert, offered comparable advice. This time the issue under debate was why the Dutch School had produced so few masters of history painting, and what methods could be employed to expand the development of high quality history painters.[62] Kikkert also believed that the solution lay in stimulating a revival of Dutch art by combining traditional Dutch values in art with the study of Antiquity and of the Renaissance. In a passage that is reminiscent of Van Eynden, he writes that if history painters combined the noble drawing of the Romans, the gracefulness of the Florentines, the truth of the Venetians, and the 'invention' of the French School, and enriched 'the handsome brush, excellent use of colour and the true nature of the Dutch School, by a reasoned and astute theory', the taste of art lovers would improve as a consequence.[63]

If we may assume that the Directorate at Teyler's were in agreement with Van Eynden's essay, then the purchase of Italian drawings of such high quality and value can certainly be viewed as a serious attempt to encourage the improvement of Dutch art by making works of this school available. Lestevenon played a crucial role in both initiatives: as instigator and adjudicator of the competition of 1781, and as central figure in the acquisition of 1790.

---

61 Eynden 1787, 179–80. Van Eynden recognized that the drawing academies and magazines could play a crucial role in the achievement of these improvements: 180–83.

62 His piece was published in 1809: Kikkert 1809, 12. (There are three other submissions in that volume; eleven are preserved in manuscript form.) See also Bergvelt 1976; Koolhaas-Grosfeld 1982, 617; and Dam 2002.

63 Kikkert 1809, 241–42.

6   Lestevenon and Van Eynden's Prize Essay

Lestevenon was not only the instigator of the competition in 1781, but also one of the adjudicators. On 5 October 1783 he sent a four-page letter from Paris to Haarlem with his comments on the four submissions.[64] To my knowledge, this interesting letter has never been the subject of attention or research. In the present context I will only discuss Lestevenon's judgment on Van Eynden's submission, which was, according to him, the best of the four. The (to him) anonymous author demonstrates particular merits: he shows evidence of his years as a connoisseur, demonstrating his 'acuity and taste'. He is lauded for his summary of the best Dutch painters and his 'exceedingly accomplished description of their different manners of execution'. This was, says Lestevenon, the most proficient section of the submission. If he was to select a winner of the competition, then this submission would receive his recommendation, but in fact he did not want to award the prize to this paper, because of its style and the poor elaboration of the subject.

As the other three submissions had even less to recommend them, Lestevenon suggests that none of the four be awarded the prize, but that three of the applicants be invited to work on the style and content of their text. The money for the prize would then be spent on implementing one of the methods suggested in the best submission, to stimulate the improvement of the taste of the Dutch School, and as a financial incentive to the artists. Lestevenon proposes that either a medal or a comparable financial remuneration be awarded to the creator of the best painting or drawing of a prescribed historical and preferably patriotic subject. A donation could also be made to a student living abroad 'and in particular in Italy', or a student who was to travel to Italy to continue his studies in art or architecture. He also wishes that a similar sum should be given to the Holland Society of Sciences, and that a similar amount should be spent on the translation of 'a prominent and useful work related to the arts of painting and drawing, such as the letters of Winckelman and Mengs'. These are interesting suggestions. As we saw, a few years later the Directorate presented the funds to the young Humbert de Superville, at the suggestion of Lestevenon. And the fact that Lestevenon championed the works of Winckelmann and Mengs, those two heroes of the Neoclassic style, shows where his heart lay.

---

64   ATS 1412.

7 Conclusion

The acquisition of a remarkable collection of Italian drawings in 1790 echoed, to a certain degree, the spirit and legacy of Pieter Teyler van der Hulst, but above all it fitted in particularly well with the contemporary developments in the Dutch art world in the field of art education, art theory and collecting. With its decision, the board made a choice in the debate over the improvement of Dutch art. It was intended to give Dutch artists, and particularly artists in Haarlem, a substantial financial and artistic boost, although it is difficult to establish whether it had the desired effect. The board was advised by Willem Anne Lestevenon, who possessed a broad knowledge of the art concerned, and skills that he was very keen to put into action. In the acquisition everything came together: his preference for Italian art, his diplomatic skills, his efforts to improve society and patriotic culture, and his devotion to Teyler's Foundation. Thanks to his dedication, the Foundation was able to make an acquisition that still gives art lovers the opportunity to view superb exhibitions of works of Michelangelo and Raphael at Teyler's Museum that go back to the year 1790.

Acknowledgement

I would like to thank Nicola Knox for her initial translation of the text.

CHAPTER 9

Collecting and Displaying Art in Teyler's Museum, 1778–1885: The Usefulness of Drawings, Prints and Contemporary Paintings, and the Development of Public Access

Terry van Druten

Since 1780, based on Pieter Teyler's will, Teyler's Foundation collected drawings and prints with the aim of offering models to living artists and stimulating the artistic climate in the Netherlands. The private societal nature of the Foundation, however, hindered the use of the collection by artists. When contemporary paintings began to be acquired in the 1820s, and the collection was opened to the public from 1830, part of the art collection became more easily accessible. It was an important step in a development that culminated in 1885 for all the Teyler's collections with the opening of a monumental new wing. By then the Foundation's focus had shifted from that of an institution for a specialized audience – scientists, philologists and artists, and informed amateurs in those areas – to a museum aimed at a more general public.

•••

On 23 November 1885 – shortly after the opening of Teyler's Museum's new wing on the Spaarne – the artist Hendrik Jacobus Scholten (1824–1907) wrote a letter to his friend and protégé, the artist Jacobus van Looy (1855–1930). In his letter Scholten, keeper of the Teyler art collections from 1863 to 1907, gave a rare insight into the inner workings of Teyler's Museum. He described a recent visit to an exhibition of works by living masters held at the art society Arti et Amicitiae in Amsterdam, and discussed the possible acquisition of works for the Museum: 'I fancied I'd found something for Teyler's collection, but a townscape by Maris, which every connoisseur and I find very beautiful, did not meet with the Directors' approval'.[1] He concludes with a remark that is as acerbic as it is telling:

---

1 Letter from H. J. Scholten to J. van Looy, 23 November 1885, Jacobus van Looy Foundation (Frans Hals Museum, Haarlem), letter no. 1122: *Ik dacht er nog iets voor Teyler's verzameling te vinden, maar een Stadgezicht van Maris, dat ieder kenner en ik zeer mooi vind, kon niet de goedkeuring van Directeuren. verwerven.* I wish to thank Esme de Goede for drawing my attention

---

© KONINKLIJKE BRILL NV, LEIDEN, 2021 | DOI:10.1163/9789004441446_010

COLLECTING AND DISPLAYING ART IN TEYLER'S MUSEUM, 1778–1885   191

> I'm curious to see what happens when they see your studies; no doubt
> they'll say 'So this is what they call beautiful nowadays?' [...] They never
> understand what makes true art – and these are the people who are
> expected to decide at the highest level which works are acquired for
> Teyler's Collection. 'Tis a sorry affair![2]

This paragraph is of particular interest for several reasons. First of all, it sets
out the division of roles and the hierarchy that were in place when collecting
for Teyler's Museum. The keeper is a connoisseur who looks out for possible
additions, and the Foundation's five Directors have the final say on which
works are acquired, in accordance with the instructions Scholten had received
when he started as keeper.[3]

More intriguing, therefore, is the difference in critical perspective reflected
in this quote. Scholten's idea of what constituted 'true art' apparently went
too far for the more conservative Directors. Their imputed comment, 'So this
is what they call beautiful nowadays?', shows that he believed they had a
flawed understanding of the art of their time. Similar to statements like 'my
three-year-old sister could make that too', such hackneyed judgments fail to
recognize the artist's aim – in this case to present a sensual impression of the
visual world.

Above all, the quote emphasizes that for both parties – the more
progressive keeper and the conservative Directors – the primary factor
determining whether a work should be added to the collection was its
artistic quality, regardless of their precise understanding of what makes
something 'beautiful'. As the quote shows, these ideas can differ and do of
course evolve over time. The changing of such ideas lies at the basis of many
misunderstandings about Teyler's Museum. From today's standpoint, it is

---

 to this letter. The painting must have been cat. no. 126, a 'Stadsgezicht' by Jacob Maris (1837–
 1899): *Arti* 1885, 16. For Arti et Amicitiae see Heij 1989.

2 ibid.: *Ik ben nieuwsgierig als ze je studien zien; dan vragen ze ook zeker heet dat nu mooi? [...]
 Wat ware kunst is snappen ze nooit en zulke lui moeten in het hoogste ressort beslissen wat voor
 Teyler's Verzameling zal worden aangekocht, T'is treurig!*

3 See board minutes, 9 October 1863, ATS 9, 331: *Art 8. Bij voorkomende gelegenheid zal hij
 aan HH. Directeuren voorstellen wat tot aanvulling en uitbreiding der Kunstverzamelingen
 dienstig is, en toestemming tot aankoop verkregen hebbende zulks met getrouwe inachtne-
 ming der belangen van de Stichting ten uitvoer brengen, zoowel hier ter stede als elders, en
 zulks tegen vergoeding alleen van reis- en verblijfkosten.* All the keepers of the art collection
 received the same instructions throughout the nineteenth century, basically unchanged
 since the instructions given to Wybrand Hendriks in 1785: board minutes, 20 June 1785, ATS
 5, 143–47.

often hard to see what rationale connects a collection of master drawings and paintings with scientific instruments, natural history books, fossils and minerals.

In this paper I will present the comments of a number of contemporaries from within and around the Foundation to help us understand the position of the art collection from its beginning in the late eighteenth century to the opening of the new wing in 1885. Unfortunately only a few statements like those in Scholten's letter survive from Teyler's Museum's long history that shed light on the motives and ideas that informed the institution's collecting activities. But from them we can trace the development from a closed private foundation collecting art with a utilitarian idea aimed at artists into a public museum addressing a more general audience.

1 Art as a Useful Element

As with everything at Teyler's Museum, the collecting of art originated in the will of Pieter Teyler van der Hulst (1702–1778) and his stipulation to do everything 'by which the Testator's intention – being [...] the advancement of Religion, the encouragement of the Arts and Sciences and the public benefit – can be promoted and achieved to the greatest extent'.[4] Most relevant to this paper is that 'the encouragement of the Arts' was pursued in a variety of ways. To begin with, one of the Foundation's key tasks was the organization of annual competitions by its two learned societies (the Theological Society, and the Second Society, that focused on the Arts and Sciences) with carefully selected questions on the five fields set out by Pieter Teyler. Every five years one of these questions would be related to the art of drawing.[5] Although many of these questions would remain unrewarded, and often even unanswered, this resulted in published articles on national taste and on history painting in the early years of the Foundation.[6]

The Foundation also decided to support the local drawing school, and every now and then it supported an individual artist.

---

4 'Resolutien en Schikkingen van Heeren Executeurs van het Testament van de Heer Pieter Teyler van der Hulst, Directeuren van deszelfs Nalatenschap' 1778, ATS 1, 14–15: everything *waardoor des Testateurs intentie, zijnde* [...] *de bevordering van Godsdienst, aanmoediging van Kunsten en Weetenschappen, en het nut van het Algemeen allermeest bevorderd en bereikt worden kan.*

5 The other subjects were theology, natural history, poetry, and history and numismatics. For the two learned societies, see Mijnhardt 1987, 339–66 and Chapter 2 in this volume.

6 For an overview of the questions up to 1978 see *'Teyler'* 1978, 37–55.

COLLECTING AND DISPLAYING ART IN TEYLER'S MUSEUM, 1778–1885   193

Finally there was the Foundation's 'collection of Medals, Prints and Drawings', which according to the will could be 'added to, expanded and completed [...] for use by the aforementioned Societies'.[7] This recalls a fact that many people today are not aware of: the Museum collection was originally set up first and foremost for the benefit of the learned societies – to help the six members of each society to pursue their research.

At this point we should bear in mind that for contemporary readers of Pieter Teyler's will the term *kunst* (art) would have had far more practical associations than it has today – something closer to our understanding of the Dutch terms *kunde* or *vaardigheid* (skill).[8] Drawing performed an essential role, as a tool for visualization. This practical aspect must have been what Pieter Teyler had in mind when composing his will. The encouragement of the arts advocated in his bequest was not a goal in its own right. Rather, like the encouragement of science, it was for the public good.

It is difficult to determine how this primacy of utility shaped the Foundation's policy with regard to its art collections. Hardly anything can be found on the subject in the minutes of the board meetings – not even in connection with an exceptional transaction like the 1790 acquisition of a large collection of drawings by Italian artists including Michelangelo and Raphael and by the Haarlem artist Hendrick Goltzius. One could be excused for concluding that these drawings were acquired solely for aesthetic reasons, since the only relevant detail recorded is that the collection 'excels in Beauty and Authenticity' and that it would be 'suitable' for the Museum.[9] However, an article in the Haarlem periodical *Algemeene Konst- en Letterbode* shows that more considerations were at play when determining whether a drawing was 'suitable'. The article starts by setting out just how extraordinary the recently acquired Italian drawings are:

---

7   'Resolutien en Schikkingen van Heeren Executeurs van het Testament van de Heer Pieter Teyler van der Hulst, Directeurs van deszelfs Nalatenschap' 1778, ATS 1, 8: *De* [...] *verzameling van medailjes, Prent, en Tekenkonsten tot gebruik van de gemelde Collegien* [...] *vermeerderd, uitgebreid en tot volkomenheid zal mogen gebracht worden*. Works on paper owned by Pieter Teyler provided only a small basis for the collection: see Plomp 1997, 2–3. And a large part of Teyler's art collection was sold in the early years of the Foundation: see Sliggers 2006, 82.

8   See the definition of *kunst* in the *Woordenboek der Nederlandsche Taal* on http://gtb.inl.nl (accessed April 2017). For the concept *kunst* see also the contributions by Mijnhardt (p. 76) and Heumakers (*passim*) in this volume.

9   Board minutes, 29 April 1789, ATS 5, 196: *eene Verzameling van Italiaansche Tekeningen bijéén-gebracht door Koningin Christina van Zweeden, welke in Schoonheid en Echtheid uitmunt* [...]; *na den Heer Hendriks geraadpleegt te hebben over de geschiktheid van zodanige verzamelinge voor het Musaeum besluiten HHDD. om den Heere Lestevenon te verzoeken dien koop op de voordeeligste wijze aan te gaan*. For more about this acquisition see Tuyll 2000, 13–29; Plomp 2001, 151–52; and Knolle in this volume.

194 DRUTEN

> The Cabinet of Drawings at Teyler's Foundation [...] was recently enlarged and enriched in a considerable way by over 1,700 drawings by distinguished Italian Masters, among which many are uncommonly fine, and all of which belonged to the collection of Drawings left by the late Swedish Queen Christina [...].[10]

We now know that some drawings did not come from Christina's famous collection. But what is relevant here is that what seems to be an aesthetic judgment – the drawings are called 'uncommonly fine' – is given primary importance. In the following paragraph, however, the writer puts that qualification in a different light:

> Furthermore, new domestic Works of Art are constantly being added, in accordance with the Directors' plan – aimed both at promoting the arts in our Fatherland and at further enhancing and expanding the Cabinet – regularly to commission two or more Drawings from the ablest of our contemporary Dutch Artists and to add them to the general collection.[11]

Beauty did indeed have a utilitarian connotation. 'Further enhancing and expanding' the collection was intended to 'promote the arts in our Fatherland'. This is consistent with the perception, widely held at that time, that Dutch art had deteriorated in quality since its prime in the seventeenth century and needed to be stimulated.[12] This patriotic aspect is expressed even more clearly in another paragraph written a few years later, in 1801, in the first sequel to Wagenaar's history of the Dutch Republic.[13] There Petrus Adriaanszoon

---

10 *Algemeene Konst- en Letterbode* 251 (19 April 1793), 121–22: *Het Kabinet van Tekeningen, by Teyler's Stichting* [...] *is onlangs, op ene aanzienlijke wyze vermeerderd en verrykt geworden, met ruim 17 honderd tekeningen van onderscheidene Italiaansche Meesters, waar onder velen die ongemeen schoon zyn en die allen behoord hebben tot de verzameling van Tekeningen, door de overledene Zweedsche Koningin Christina, nagelaten* [...]. For another discussion of this quote (and that in the following note) see the contribution of Knolle to this volume, 179–182.

11 ibid.: *Wyders komen 'er, telkens, nieuwe inlandsche Konststukken by, in gevolge het by Direkteuren gemaakt plan, om, zo wel ter aanmoediging der konst in ons Vaderland, als tot meerdere vervraaying en uitbreiding van het Kabinet, twee of meer Tekeningen door de bekwaamsten van onze thans levende Nederlandsche Konstenaars, van tyd tot tyd, te doen vervaardigen, en aan de algemene verzameling toe te voegen.*

12 See for instance Koolhaas-Grosfeld 1982 and Koolhaas-Grosfeld 1986. See also Bergvelt 1998, 130–37.

13 Loosjes 1801.

Loosjes (1735–1813), a Mennonite minister and one of the six members of Teyler's Theological Society, describes the general collection and the Foundation's acquisition of the Italian drawings in virtually the same words as the *Konst- en Letterbode*.[14] He then continues:

> In addition, [this Foundation] has spared no cost in acquiring Drawings by old Dutch Masters, which would otherwise be likely to fall into the hands of Foreigners, and storing them in its Art Collection. We make a special mention of this matter since it serves as a most telling refutation of the assumption that the Dutchman has no Love of Art and that he torpidly allows all the most splendid examples of our old Masters to leave the country for more art-loving Regions, and that he denies living Practitioners of Art any kind of encouragement.[15]

The Foundation's collecting of works by both old and contemporary masters continued unabated. This was done it seems with the very practical purpose of encouraging 'living practitioners of art': to provide models for living artists, in line with general tendencies of the period.[16]

2 Limited Accessibility of the Drawings Collection

In practice, however, it seems that the private societal structure that Pieter Teyler had adopted for his legacy did not encourage its usefulness for living artists in the first decades of the Foundation. Just as with other collections at the time, access was limited. It had been decided that first and foremost the Foundation's collections had to be accessible at all times to the members of the two learned societies and the Foundation's Directors – seventeen people in all. This would allow them to fulfil the task assigned to them in Pieter Teyler's will. As a

---

14   This journal was published in Haarlem by Petrus's son Adriaan Loosjes (1761–1818). See also Chapter 2 in this volume, p. 31, n. 40.

15   Loosjes 1801, 252–53: *Terwyl [deeze Stichting] ook geen geld spaarde om Tekeningen van oude Vaderlandsche Meesters, die anders veelligt in de handen van Buitenlanderen vielen, zich eigen te maaken, en in hunne Kunstverzameling op te leggen. Wy vermeldden deeze byzonderheden eenigzins uitvoerig: dewyl het ter spreekendste wederlegging dient, dat by den Nederlander geen Kunstmin zou plaats hebben, en dat deeze verdoofd, alles wat 'er van oude Meesters heerlyk was, uit den Lande laat verhuizen, naar kunstlievender Gewesten, en het den nog leevenden Kunstbeoefenaaren aan alle aanmoediging laat ontbreeken.*

16   Bergvelt/Hörster 2010; Bergvelt 1998, 31, 56–59; for later in the nineteenth century, ibid., 86, 99, 166–67. See also Bergvelt 2005b, 330–32.

secondary consideration, the collections were open to the public for a limited number of hours per week. Shortly after the opening of the Oval Room in 1784, the instructions for the keeper mention two hours on Tuesday for residents of Haarlem, and one hour a day – except Sundays – for out-of-town visitors.[17] This would remain more or less unchanged until the late nineteenth century, when in 1874 it was decided that the Museum would open for four hours between 11 a.m. and 3 p.m. on weekdays.[18]

There were no special visiting hours for artists, unlike the Rijksmuseum in Amsterdam's Trippenhuis and the Royal Cabinet of Paintings at the Mauritshuis in The Hague.[19] Indeed, the Teyler visitors' books hardly mention any artists at all in the first decades of the Foundation (see the Appendix). Before 1830 only twenty artists can be identified with certainty, members of the Andriessen family, Cornelis Kruseman and Jan Willem Pieneman the most prominent among them.[20] No doubt the keeper's artist friends visited the Museum by personal appointment, without having to sign their name. But it is impossible to say how many artists were involved, and how many used the collection for study purposes. There are few traces of such activities, and the art collection's limited general accessibility, especially compared to the other collections, is also reflected in the paucity of references to drawings and prints in visitors' accounts of the period.[21]

The clearest and most telling example of the use of the collection by an artist is a few sheets by Wybrand Hendriks (1744–1831), keeper of the art collection between 1785 and 1819. In one drawing, for instance, he combined themes from three seventeenth-century drawings in the Foundation's collection by Pieter van Bloemen, Nicolaes Berchem, and Herman Saftleven into one new work of his own (figures 9.1–9.4).[22] If the Foundation's aim was to have the collection used as a source for emulation, Hendriks' rather cut-and-paste dealing with the

---

17   *Instructie voor den Bewooner of Castelein van het Fundatiehuis van wylen de Heer Pieter Teyler van der Hulst*, board minutes, 20 June 1785, ATS 5, 143–47. For examples of what Wybrand Hendriks did as keeper (he was keeper 1785–1819) see the contribution of Knolle to this volume; somewhat outside the regular activities of the keeper are the drawings Hendriks made for Martinus van Marum, the subject of Vos's contribution.

18   Board minutes, 29 May 1874, ATS 10, 133.

19   Bergvelt 1998, 99; Bergvelt 2005a, 356–57; for an international comparison see Bergvelt 2005b, 330–32.

20   Visitors' books 1789–1851, ATS 148–51. Cf. Janse 2010 and Weiss 2010. See Appendix.

21   Cf. Weiss 2013a, 149–52. Later examples of drawings viewed by (non-artist) visitors are recorded in Dethmar 1839, 159, and Kneppelhout/Bilders 2009, 251 (letter K 35).

22   See Plomp 1997, 14–15. A very comparable way of working, be it with his own drawings made in different places in Italy, can be seen in the painted compositions by Josephus Augustus Knip (1777–1847): see Bergvelt 1976, where this method is placed in the context

FIGURE 9.1   Wybrand Hendriks (1744–1831) after Pieter van Bloemen (1657–1720), Nicolaes Berchem (1620–1683) and Herman Saftleven (1609–1685), *Dune Landscape with Ruins*, n.d., pen and brown ink and brown wash over graphite or black chalk, 273 x 256 mm.
LEIDEN UNIVERSITY LIBRARY, PK-T-168

FIGURE 9.2   Pieter van Bloemen (1657–1720), *Two Horses and an Open Carriage*, n.d., brush in black and grey ink, pen in brown ink, 197 x 237 mm.
TEYLER'S MUSEUM, R+ 084

FIGURE 9.3 Nicolaes Berchem (1620–1683), *Landscape with Shepherds near a Ruin (Brederode?)*, c. 1670–83, pen and brush in light and dark brown ink and brown wash over traces of graphite, 247 x 351 mm.
TEYLER'S MUSEUM, Q 015

FIGURE 9.4 Herman Saftleven (1609–1685), *Ruins*, 1649, black chalk and brown wash, 185 x 245 mm.
TEYLER'S MUSEUM, P 043

COLLECTING AND DISPLAYING ART IN TEYLER'S MUSEUM, 1778–1885   199

drawings is somewhat disappointing, even if we take into account that it was not unusual to make use of earlier sources in such a way. Moreover, it is telling that this drawing was made by an artist who as keeper had direct and easy access to the collection. Not many other examples are known.[23]

Altogether therefore it seems that the Foundation's role as a stimulus for contemporary art was limited. It was chiefly useful thanks to the financial support that it offered artists, via the acquisition of their work. After entering the collection a work of art might be taken as an example by a limited number of artists. The best occasion for this may well have been *kunstbeschouwingen* (literally, viewings of art). These were special social gatherings that originated in the Netherlands in the eighteenth century, when collectors presented a selection of drawings and prints to a number of invitees: with the guests seated around a table, the sheets passed from hand to hand and were viewed and discussed. This formed an important platform for connoisseurship.[24] Teyler's Foundation also organized art appreciation gatherings on a regular basis, but once again it is difficult to estimate how many meetings there were, and what effect they had. Details of the number and nature of such gatherings at the Museum only begin to be recorded in the late nineteenth century.[25] Just one – negative – mention of such an occasion occurs in the board minutes of the first decades of the Foundation, in 1820, when Bartel Willem van der Vlugt, one of the Directors, informed his colleagues that he

> heard from aside that Art from this Foundation had been viewed in the Concert Hall, without permission from Messrs the Directors, and that His Grace [the speaker] had seriously called Mr [Wybrand] Hendriks to account for this and judged that henceforth no Art should be passed to whoever it might be without the knowledge of Messrs the Directors.[26]

Hendriks had just retired in November 1819 as keeper of the Teyler art collections. The negative reaction of the board of Directors to this art appreciation

---

of the Neoclassical art theory of the time in the Netherlands and France. For more about Neoclassical art theory in the Netherlands see the contribution of Knolle to this volume.

23   See Tuyll 2000, 20–21, for an example of a copy after Michelangelo by Jacobus van Looy.

24   Plomp 2001, 101–3. See also Knolle in this volume, p. 182.

25   *Notitie van kunstbeschouwingen* 1873–96, ATS 147b. See also Druten 2015, 72–74, 82–83. For art appreciation gatherings at the Koninklijk Nederlandsch Instituut (Royal Netherlands Institute) in the early nineteenth century see Bergvelt 1998, 131–33.

26   Board minutes, 28 January 1820, ATS 7, 123–24: *De Heer B:W: van der Vlugt geeft kennis dat ZijnEd. van ter zijde had vernomen dat er Kunst van deze Stichting in de Concert zaal bezigtigd is, zonder toestemming van Hr. Directeuren en dat ZijnEd: den Heer Hendriks daar*

FIGURE 9.5 Wybrand Hendriks, *Directors and Members of the Haarlem Drawing College Kunstmin en Vlijt*, 1799, oil on panel, 63 x 81 cm. At the far right with a top hat is the painter himself.
TEYLER'S MUSEUM, KS 1987 002

gathering in 1820 seems to imply that until his retirement Hendriks could handle the collection more freely, outside the Museum as well.[27] A glimpse of this may possibly be given in a painting by Hendriks of 1799 (figure 9.5): there a group of artists gather at Haarlem's drawing college, of which Hendriks was an influential Director and where he organized an art appreciation gathering at least once.[28]

---

      om ernstig heeft onderhouden en geënjuugeerd om voortaan aan wien het ook zoude mogen zijn, geen Kunst aftegeeven dan met voorkennis van Heeren Directeuren.

27   Hendriks retired in November 1819 but stayed in position until the arrival of his successor G. J. Michaëlis in May 1820, see board minutes 19 May 1820, ATS 7, 130. Apparently he had less freedom to handle the collection during this intermediate period.

28   Board meeting minutes, Kunstmin en Vlijt, 9 November 1801, later Kunst Zij Ons Doel Archive (NHA, Haarlem), no. 3496–4. For the painting see Aymonino/Lauder 2015, 215–17. For the drawing college see Sliggers 1990a , 16–27, and Knolle in the present volume.

COLLECTING AND DISPLAYING ART IN TEYLER'S MUSEUM, 1778–1885

However, before we think that such art appreciation gatherings were frequent, it is useful to see the Foundation's board minutes of August 1837: there the Directors answer a request for a gathering by the department of drawing of the Felix Meritis Society in Amsterdam, saying that 'the nature of the Foundation forbids the satisfaction of this request'.[29] It does give some nuance to the positive description of the Foundation's art appreciation gatherings by Adriaan van der Willigen (1766–1841), a connoisseur and member of Teyler's Second Society. In 1840 he writes in his *Geschiedenis der vaderlandsche schilderkunst* (History of national painting), initially published together with Roeland van Eynden: 'the rich Collection of Drawings and Prints [of Teyler's Foundation], [is used] on Autumn and Winter evenings for Art Appreciation Gatherings [...]; to which Messrs. the Directors not only invite Art-lovers and experienced Painters, but also young Artists, making these occasions very useful'.[30] The great usefulness of these private gatherings was limited by nature to a small number of invitees. Not until the later nineteenth century would special exhibition spaces for works on paper make such collections in general more easily accessible to a larger audience, for example in the Rijksmuseum after the opening of the new building by Cuypers in 1885.[31] This was also the case in Teyler's Museum with the opening of a 'new room for the exhibition and conservation of Drawings belonging to Teyler's Cabinet' in 1886.[32]

3   Paintings Begin to Be Collected

By the time that a special gallery for prints and drawings opened in 1886 (figure 3.7, no. 7), the Foundation had already been on the way to wider public

---

29   Board minutes, 11 August 1837, ATS 8, 222: *Gelezen eene missive van HH. Bestuurderen der Afdeeling Teekenkunde van de Maatschappij Felix Meritis te Amsterdam, dd. 4 dezer, houdende eene uitnodiging tot het geven van eene Kunstbeschouwing aldaar in den aanstaanden Winter. Wordt goedgevonden die Heeren te berigten, dat de aard der Stichting verbiedt aan dit verzoek te voldoen.* Later in the century Scholten kept track of the art appreciation gatherings that he organized with the collection, and would also present the collection outside the museum: see Druten 2015, 82.

30   Eynden/Willigen 1840, 310: *de rijke Verzameling van Teekeningen en Prenten [van Teylers stichting], [dient] bij Herfst- en Winteravonden, tot Kunstbeschouwingen [...]; waarbij niet alleen Kunstminnaars en geoefende Schilders, maar ook jeugdige Kunstenaars, door Heeren Directeuren genodigd worden, zoodat dezelve met der duur van veel nut is.* This quote is put into a different perspective by Knolle in this volume, p. 182, n. 39.

31   Bergvelt 1998, 239–40.

32   Druten 2015, 87: *nieuwe zaal voor het tentoonstellen en bewaren der tot Teylers Kabinet behoorende Teekeningen.*

202 DRUTEN

accessibility for a while. From the late 1820s on, it started to modernize the management of its collection. For some time already it had been criticized by outside parties for being too insular. 'Complaints about a certain degree of inutility of so many of the resources offered by this Foundation for the advancement of Science and the Arts'[33] (as the Foundation's Directors put it in a letter to the society members in 1828), combined with a positive experience in granting public access to the Library in 1825,[34] gave rise to the idea to use the space below the new Reading Room as an Auditorium for lectures by society members (figure 3.3, no. 7).[35]

However, this idea was poorly received by the members themselves, and was therefore abandoned. Adriaan van der Willigen, who was himself a member of one of the societies, wrote about the plan in his diary in the 1830s. Like Scholten's letter later in the century, Van der Willigen's account gives us a rare look behind the scenes of the institution as well as a view of the beginning of the collecting of paintings – possibly the most significant decision for the future of Teyler's Museum since the opening of the Oval Room:

> Meanwhile, there was this new room [under the Reading Room], which had to be put to some use or other. Well, one of our almighty Messrs the Directors, having developed some fondness for paintings and drawings, came up with the idea of hanging paintings in this unused space, no matter how low its ceiling and how poorly lit [...] In addition, it was decided to concentrate on the work of well-known [contemporary] Dutch masters, as the members of the societies learned indirectly, and this decision should not be viewed with disapproval. However, having embarked on this chosen course, they should have continued to purchase the best works of these masters, as honourable examples of their artistic talent. But did they do so? The general feeling among those competent to judge is No; and unfortunately many people hold the members [of the societies] accountable for this state of affairs – particularly those members who specialize in the discipline of painting.[36] For surely exhibitions at Teyler's Foundation would not be organized without consulting these members? Nevertheless that is the case, and the decisions are chiefly, if not exclusively, taken by the director, Mr W. van der Vlugt, who is the

---

33 Board minutes, 13 June 1828, ATS 8, 1–7: *klagten over zekere mate van werkeloosheid bij zoo vele hulpmiddelen, als die Stichting ter bevordering van Wetenschappen en Kunsten aanbiedt.*
34 Board minutes, 20 May 1825, ATS 5, 248–54.
35 For this and the following, see also Kersten 1986 and Weiss 2013a, 160–63.
36 Undoubtedly a reference to Van der Willigen himself.

COLLECTING AND DISPLAYING ART IN TEYLER'S MUSEUM, 1778–1885 203

responsible party in this matter and who relies on the services of the keeper and caretaker of paintings, drawings and prints, Michaëlis, when he, the director, sees fit.[37]

This text, similar to the comments by Scholten quoted earlier, shows the hierarchical distinction between the supporting role of the keeper – at that time Gerrit Jan Michaëlis (1775–1857), who held this position from 1820 to 1856 – and Willem van der Vlugt (1787–1849), one of the five Directors of the Foundation from 1817 until his death.[38] Indeed, Van der Vlugt can be recognized as a driving force behind the Foundation's new collection of paintings. For instance, he was the person delegated by the other Directors to buy paintings – in consultation with Michaëlis – at the exhibition of works by living masters in Amsterdam in 1826.[39] And, more telling, it was Van der Vlugt who was given responsibility for the art collection when in April 1829 it was decided to assign the care of the various parts of the Foundation to specific Directors in order to make operations run more effectively.[40]

What we can clearly sense in the passage by Van der Willigen is that in these developments he felt passed over as a recognized connoisseur and member of Teyler's Second Society. The paintings were acquired for the collection without him being consulted, and thus without the advice of the societies. Nor were Van der Willigen and the other society members consulted on the decision to

---

37 Sliggers 1991, 8: *Intusschen stond er de kamer en moest toch tot het een of ander gebruik dienen. Wel nu, een der oppermachtige heeren directeuren, min of meer liefhebberij hebbende in schilderijen en teekeningen, viel het in om in deze ongebruikte kamer, hoe zeer laag genoeg van verdieping en slechts verlicht, schilderijen te plaatsen [...]. Het besluit was tevens om zich alleen te bepalen tot het werk van bekende Nederl. meesters, naar de leden der genootschappen van ter zijde vernamen en dit besluit moge dan ook niet te misprijzen zijn. Doch men had dan ook het aanvankelijk betreden spoor volgende, van de beste stukken dezer meesters als vereerende proeven van hun kunsttalent moeten blijven aankoopen – heeft men dit gedaan? – het algemeen gevoelen van bevoegde beoordelaars zegt neen; en ongelukkig dat deze handelswijze ook bij velen voor rekening komt van de leden [van de genootschappen], in zonderheid van dezulken welke het vak der schilderkunst inzonderheid voor hunne rekening hebben, dewijl men toch wel niet aan tentoonstellingen bij Teylers Stichting geheel buiten deze leden zou omgaan, nogthans is dit zoo en het is hoofdzakelijk zoo niet alleen de heer directeur W. van der Vlugt, die in dit opzigt handelt, zich bedienende van den concierge en opzigter der schilderijen, teekeningen en prenten, Michaelis, wanneer hij directeur zulks goedvint.* The wish to start a paintings collection had been put forward at least as early as 1786: see board minutes, 16 June 1786, ATS 5, 161.

38 A division of roles that is confirmed in a number of documents, including the following board minutes: 29 September 1826, ATS 7, 316; 17 November 1826, ATS 7, 324; 12 October 1827, ATS 7, 347.

39 Board minutes, 29 September 1826, ATS 7, 316. See also 3 October 1828, ATS 8, 20.

40 Board minutes, 27 March 1829, ATS 8, 41–45. Van der Vlugt was also treasurer.

FIGURE 9.6   Johan Conrad Greive (1837–1891), *The First Paintings Gallery of Teyler's Museum*, 1862, black chalk and brush in grey ink, 647 x 802 mm.
TEYLER'S MUSEUM, DD 042d

open the collection to the public. This began in 1830 in the empty room under the Reading Room, now the gallery of prints and drawings.[41] A few years later, this initiative culminated in the realization of the first Paintings Gallery, which opened in 1839, specifically created for the display of contemporary painting (figure 3.3, no. 9; figure 9.6; see also figures 11.4–11.6).[42]

The development that we have just seen in the art collection also took place in other parts of the institution. Teyler's Foundation started to change course towards what we recognize today as museum activities. It gradually turned away from the eighteenth-century world of private learned societies that had given birth to the Oval Room towards the publicly accessible institution, represented by the new Museum wing opened in 1885. This offered ample

---

41   Board minutes, 10 July 1829, ATS 8, 47; 13 August 1830, ATS 8, 81.
42   Board minutes, 20 October 1837, ATS 8, 224; 20 September 1839, ATS 8, 276. A year earlier, in 1838, a presentation of contemporary paintings from the national collection had opened in Paviljoen Welgelegen, not far from Teyler's Museum; see Bergvelt 1998, 98.

COLLECTING AND DISPLAYING ART IN TEYLER'S MUSEUM, 1778–1885   205

exhibition space for the collections of fossils and instruments, an extension
for the Library, and – after refurbishment of the space below the old Reading
Room – for the first time an exhibition space specifically devoted to works on
paper, as well as an exhibition space for the numismatic collection and a large
auditorium (figures 3.6, 3.7, nos 8 and 11–14; figures 3.8, 3.9).[43] Ironically, one
could argue that the societies themselves played a decisive role in putting the
Foundation on this path by their very unwillingness to give public lectures.

4   From Secretiveness to Accessibility

Despite his criticisms, Van der Willigen applauded the decision to purchase
works only from living Dutch painters for the new collection. This was of
course in keeping with the Foundation's policy from the outset – to support
and stimulate contemporary artists through the acquisition of their work.
But did artists actually benefit more from the collection and its new, more
accessible presentation after the opening of the Paintings Gallery? The documentary evidence is not very heartening. Between 1830 and 1880 the number
of artists recognizably registered in the visitors' books hovers between fifteen
and twenty-five per decade (see the Appendix).[44] Only once is there a specific
mention in the board minutes of 'these or other artists' asking permission to
copy works in the collection, and it was decided that that was *not* allowed,
'in view of the numerous objections that can be raised against this'.[45] The
Museum clearly was not an attraction for artists in the same way as the Municipal Museum of Haarlem was for its Frans Hals paintings (now the Frans Hals
Museum): after its opening in 1862 the visitors' books of that museum were
often signed by more than twenty artists a year.[46] Still, writing for the periodical *Eigen Haard* in 1875, Jeronimo de Vries (1838–1915), a Mennonite clergyman
and a future member of Teyler's Second Society, presented Teyler's Museum
as a source of inspiration for artists: 'Paintings are exhibited in an adjoining
hall [adjoining to the Oval Room]. While it is a modest collection, many of

---

43   The numismatic cabinet opened in 1887: board minutes, 28 October 1887, ATS 11, 120.
44   Visitors' books 1828–84, ATS 151–56. Teyler's Museum does not have a record of copyists,
      as many other nineteenth-century museums have.
45   Board minutes, 30 July 1852, ATS 9, 120: *Komt ter sprake de vraag, of aan deze of gene schil-
      ders vergund zou kunnen worden om stukken van het Museum dezer Stichting te kopiëren.
      Uit hoofde van de vele bezwaren, die daaraan verbonden zijn, wordt besloten, zoodanige ver-
      gunning niet* [underlined] *te verleenen.* See also Weiss 2010, 277.
46   Chu 1987, appendix 2, 132–41.

the works will warm the artist's heart, and he will not moan, as he would in the Trippenhuis, but will rather praise the heater set up in the centre of the room'.[47] Further on in De Vries's account, it becomes clear what audience the collections were mainly intended for then. They are no longer aimed exclusively at the learned societies or at specialists such as artists. Rather, they are geared to a more general public:

> Father Teyler would be pleased with this scene! And as long as we need societies to devise and organize programmes that are too expensive and too large-scale to be borne by private citizens; burdens and enterprises that are too heavy and long-term for the wealthiest, bravest and oldest among us; I hope Teyler's Foundation will continue to open its doors wide to everyone who wants to browse through its treasures and who is able to appreciate its riches.[48]

This development towards accessibility for 'everyone' reached a new stage in 1885 with the opening of the institution's new wing on the Spaarne, with a façade 'that at once shows unmistakably that it belongs to a museum', as *Eigen Haard* wrote a few years later when the magazine again paid attention to the Museum in its columns (figure 9.7).[49] General visitor numbers grew, and the number of visiting artists jumped to more than fifty per decade (see the Appendix).[50] By then the Foundation had clearly shifted from an organization set up by societies for a specialized audience including scientists, philologists and artists, as well as informed amateurs in those areas, to a museum institution aimed at a more

---

47   Vries 1875, 204: *In een nevenzaal zijn schilderijen ten toon gesteld. De verzameling is klein, maar de kunstenaar kan er zijn hart aan menig kunstwerk ophalen en zal hier geene Trippenhuis-verzuchtingen slaken, maar het verwarmingstoestel prijzen, dat in het midden der schilderijzaal is aangebracht.* Compare Bergvelt 1998, 165.

48   Vries 1875, 207: *Vader Teyler zou tevreden zijn, als hij het zag! En zoo lang er genootschappen nodig zijn om te bedenken en uit te voeren, wat voor particulieren te duur, te omvangrijk zou zijn om het op hunne schouders te tillen, lasten en ondernemingen, te zwaar en te langdurig voor den rijkste, den moedigste, den oudste onzer, zoolange moge Teyler's stichting zijn deur wijd blijven openzetten voor ieder, die in hare schatten wenscht te grasduinen en hare rijkdommen op prijs weet te stellen.*

49   Craandijk 1885, 118: *die geeft het terstond onmiskenbaar te zien, dat hij aan een museum, of althans aan een inrichting van dien aard behoort.* In that same year the Rijksmuseum opened its new building and the national collection of contemporary paintings moved back from Paviljoen Welgelegen in Haarlem to Amsterdam.

50   Visitors' books 1878–1902, ATS 156–61.

general public. Around the same time as Scholten was sharing his progressive views on art in his letter to Van Looy, the 'secretiveness' of the old private societies had made way for the wider public accessibility of the Museum:

> Whereas in the past there were occasional complaints about Teyler's 'secretiveness', this accusation could in no way be levied against the current Directors, who do everything they can to let as many people as possible share in the ample pleasures and benefits yielded by this wonderful foundation that has been put in their care.[51]

FIGURE 9.7 Postcard showing the façade of Teyler's Museum (1885), c. 1925.
GEERT-JAN JANSE COLLECTION

---

51   ibid., 122: *Werd er vroeger wel eens geklaagd over Teyler's 'geheimzinnigheid', dat verwijt is wel geenzins toepasselijk op de tegenwoordige directeuren, die alles doen, om zoo velen als hun mogelijk is te doen deelen in het genot en het nut, dat de schoone stichting, aan hun zorgen toevertrouwd, zoo ruimschoots kan opleveren.*

208 DRUTEN

TABLE 9.1 Artists who signed Teyler's Visitors' Books from 1789 to 1900.

Compiled by Frouckje van Hijum, Geert- Jan Janse and Terry van Druten.
Note: This chronological list includes visitors who specifically signed the books (which began in 1789) as artists and those who could be identified as such beyond reasonable doubt.

ATS 148 (1789–1802)

Name	Date
Cornelis Struyk (?–?)	1 June 1789
Adriaan van der Willigen (1766–1841)	25 May 1791
Jurriaan Andriessen (1742–1819)	5 June 1791
Anthonie Andriessen (1746–1813)	5 June 1791
Rhijnvis Feith (1753–1824)	28 June 1797
Adriaan van der Willigen (1766–1841)	30 March 1798
Christiaan Andriessen (1775–1846)	3 September 1799
Warnaar Horstink (1756–1815)	14 January 1800
Hendrik Rochussen (1779–1852)	1 June 1801
Richard Smirke (1778–1815)	27 July 1801
Robert Smirke (1780–1867)	27 July 1801

ATS 149 (1803–16)

Name	Date
Friedrich Johann Gottlieb Lieder (1780–1859)	7 April 1804
Charles Spruyt (1769–1851)	May 1808
J. Dhont (?–?)	1811
G. Michielsen (?–?)	1811
J. A. Visser Bender (active 1800–1849)	1811
Friedrich Georg Weitsch (1758–1828)	26 July 1811
Petrus van den Eynde (1787–1840)	1813
Willem Bilderdijk (1756–1831)	1813
Ferdinand Bauer (1760–1826)	14 September 1814

ATS 150 (1816–27)

Name	Date
Wessel Lubbers (1755–1834)	8 May 1817
Job Augustus Bakker (1796–1876)	August 1817

COLLECTING AND DISPLAYING ART IN TEYLER'S MUSEUM, 1778–1885

Cornelis Kruseman (1797–1857)	8 May 1818
Charles Baumann (?–?)	22 May 1819
Jean. Sannack (?–?)	22 May 1819
Jan Willem Pieneman (1779–1853)	March 1820
Johannes Boshamer (1800–1852)	1822

ATS 151 (1827–36)

Name	Date
Nicolaas Beets (1814–1903)	8 August 1829
Willem de Klerk (1800–1876)	21 September 1829
L. Kloos (?–?)	October 1829
Johannes Reekers (1790–1858)	1833
Willem Gruyter (1817–1880)	1833
Hendrik Reekers (1815–1854)	1833
Johannes Gijsb.zn. van Ravenzwaay (1815–1849)	1834
Antonie Waldorp (1803–1866)	1834
Nicolaas Pieneman (1809–1860)	1834
Cornelis Lieste (1817–1861)	1835
James de Rijk (1806–1882)	1835
Christiaan Julius Lodewijk Portman (1799–1868)	16 April 1836
Johannes Gijsb.zn. van Ravenzwaay (1815–1849)	1836

ATS 152 (1836–43)

Name	Date
Raden Sarief Bastaman Saleh (1811–1880)	1837
Frederik Marinus Kruseman (1816–1882)	1837
Christiaan Immerzeel (1808–1886)	1838
Johan Coenraad Hamburger (1809–1871/91)	1838
Pieter Ernst Henk Praetorius (1791–1876)	1838
J. Dekker (?–?)	1838
W. B. Stoop (?–?)	1840
François Adriaan Molijn (1805–1890)	1840
Joseph Moerenhout (1801–1875)	1840
Nicolaas Johannes Roosenboom (1805–1880)	1840
Augustus Knip (1819–1859)	1840

210 DRUTEN

Nicolaas Johannes Wilhelmus de Roode (1814–84)	1840
Login Frikke (1820/21–1893)	1841
Johannes Immerzeel (1776–1841)	1841
François Adriaan Molijn (1805–1890)	1841

ATS 153 (1848–54)

Name	Date
Joseph Moerenhout (1801–1875)	1844
Andreas Danekes (1788–1855)	1845
Alexander Hugo Bakker Korff (1824–1882)	1845
Albertus Brondgeest (1786–1849)	1846
Pieter Frederik van Os (1808–1892)	1848
Nicolaas Hopman (1794–1870)	1848
Paul Joseph Constantin Gabriël (1828–1903)	1848
Coenraad Ritsema (1834–1916)	1848
Jan Willem Pieneman (1779–1853)	23 August 1849
Adriana Haanen (1814–1895)	1849
Willem George Frederik Heijmans (1799–1867)	1850
Gerrit Pieter Verschuur (1830–1891)	16 March 1852
Hendrik Willem Mesdag (1831–1915)	24 June 1852
Taco Mesdag (1829–1902)	24 June 1852
Hendrik Dirk Kruseman van Elten (1829–1904)	1852
Gerrit Pieter Verschuur (1830–1891)	1852
David Oyens (1842–1902)	31 May 1853
Pieter Ernst Hendrik Praetorius (1791–1876)	10 September 1853
Jacobus Ludovicus Cornet (1815–1882)	1854
Eugène Pirou, Louvain (?–?)	1854
Jacob Hofstra (1805–1875)	1854

ATS 154 (1854–71)

Name	Date
Johannes Warnardus Bilders (1811–1890)	1854
August Allebé (1838–1927)	19 September 1854
Anthelme Trimolet (1798–1866)	28 September 1855
L. Richard (?–?)	1856

COLLECTING AND DISPLAYING ART IN TEYLER'S MUSEUM, 1778–1885   211

Jan David Geerling Grootveld (1821–1890)	1856
E. J. de Vries (?–?)	1856
Carl Rensing (1826–1898)	1856
Anton Mauve (1838–1888)	22 January 1857
Jan Theodoor Kruseman (1835–1895)	June 1857
Jacob Joseph Eeckhout (1793–1861)	1858
Johannes Andries Martinus Haak (1831–1903)	9 November 1858
Edouard Daliphard (1833–1877)	April 1859
John Leighton (1822–1912)	1861
Moritz Calisch (1819–1870)	1862
Anton Mauve (1838–1888)	24 February 1862
W.F. Berneman (?–?)	1862
P. v.d. Meer Cz. (?–?)	1862
P. W. M. Wap (?–?)	1863
Maurits Lodewijk Christiaan Staring (1840–1914)	1864
Dirk Weeshoff (1825–1887)	1864
Jan Gerard Smits (1823–1910)	August 1865
Jozef Israëls (1824–1911)	1866
Petrus Antonius Balmakers (1831–1903)	1867
Cornelis Johannes de Vogel (1824–1879)	1868
Jacob Maris (1837–1899)	1869

ATS 155 (1871–78)

Name	Date
Jacob Maris (1837–1899)	26 October 1871
H. J. J. Bunck (?–?)	22 July 1872
Carl Schuch (1846–1903)	1873
Karl Hagemeister (1848–1933)	1873
H. H. Schaeken (?–?)	1874
Gerard Portielje (1856–1929)	1874
Pieter van der Burg (1840–1890)	March 1875
W. Heyboer (?–?)	March 1875
P. van Hemert (?–?)	March 1875
August Malmström (1829–1901)	1875
Gustaf Fredrik Rydberg (1835–1933)	1875

Johannes Stortenbeker (1821–1899)	August 1875
Willem Stortenbeker (1789–1882)	August 1875
Tina Blau-Lang (1845–1916)	1875
Emil Jacob Schindler (1842–92)	1875
August Xaver Karl Ritter von Pettenkofen (1822–1889)	1875
Jan Hendrik Heijmans (1806–1888)	1875
Herman Frederik Carel ten Kate (1822–1891)	15 October 1875
Ernst Josephson (1851–1906)	1876
Gerard Portielje (1856–1929)	1876
Gijsbertus Pieterse (1847–78)	August 1877

ats 156 (1878–85)

Name	Date
Jozef Israëls (1824–1911)	May 1879
Hendrik Hartman (active 1875–1914)	1879
Willem Roelofs (1822–1897)	February 1880
Adrien-Louis Demont (1851–1928)	February 1880
Virginie-Elodie Demont-Breton (1859–1935)	February 1880
Johannes Graadt van Roggen (1867–1959)	August 1880
Joseph Thors (active c. 1835–1920)	August 1880
Henricus Joannes Melis (1845–1923)	November 1880
Pieter Frederik van Os (1808–1892)	1881
Johannes Reekers (1824–1895)	August 1881
Theo van Hoytema (1863–1917)	August 1881
Victor Meirelles de Lima (1832–1903)	1881
Willem Johannes Oppenoorth (1847–1905)	February 1882
Louis Robin (b. 1845)	June 1882
Jan Toorop (1858–1928)	August 1882
Johann Eduard Karsen (1860–1941)	September 1882
Thérèse Schwartze (1851–1918)	September 1882
Carel Vosmaer (1826–1888)	5 October 1882
Vladimir Stasov (1824–1906)	18 May 1883
Ilja Repin (1844–1930)	18 May 1883
Marie Louise Catherine Breslau (1856–1927)	July 1883
Léon Bonnat (1833–1922)	July 1883

COLLECTING AND DISPLAYING ART IN TEYLER'S MUSEUM, 1778–1885

M. de Munck (?–?)	July 1883
José Serra y Porson (1824–1910)	August 1883
Felix Borchardt (1857–1936)	September 1883
Carel Vosmaer (1826–1888)	September 1883
Hubert Vos (1855–1935)	September 1883
Guillaume Romen (?–?)	September 1883
Marinus van Regteren Altena (1866–1908)	April 1884
Henri Rochussen (1812–1889)	May 1884
Johannes Graadt van Roggen (1867–1959)	September 1884
Jacques Delanoy (1820–1890)	September 1884

ATS 157 (1885–88)

Name	Date
Willem Vaarzon Morel (1868–1955)	June 1885
Johannes Stortenbeker (1821–1899)	1885
Anton Erik Christian Thorenfeld (1839–1907)	August 1885
Jan van Mastenbroek (1827–1909)	28 August 1885
Carel Vosmaer (1826–1888)	September 1885
Johannes Reekers Jr (1824–1895)	September 1885
Hendrik Adriaan Christiaan Dekker (1836–1905)	September 1885
Joseph Mendes da Costa (1863–1939)	16 October 1885
Jacob Willem Gruijter (1856–1908)	15 February 1886
Nicolas van den Eeden (1856–1918)	March 1886
Frantz Charlet (1862–1928)	May 1886
Émile François Michel (1818–1909)	June 1886
A. W. Stortenbeker (?–?)	1886
A. C. Hazen (?–?)	1886
W. Hoogbruin (?–?)	15 September 1886
Willem Vaarzon Morel (1868–1955)	December 1886
Petrus Theodorus van Wijngaerdt (1816–1893)	23 July 1887
Eduard Schalbroeck (1853–1935)	August 1887
Johannes Bosboom (1817–1891)	19 August 1887
Philip Sadée (1837–1904)	31 August 1887
Otto Eerelman (1839–1926)	September 1887
Jan Toorop (1858–1928)	1888

| J. C. Wieringa (?–?) | May 1888 |
| Carolus Lambertus Waning (1844–1928) | May 1888 |

ATS 158 (1888–92)

Name	Date
Hendrik Willem Mesdag (1831–1915)	10 September 1888
Marius Bauer (1867–1932)	11 June 1889
Johannes Graadt van Roggen (1867–1959)	28 March 1890
David de la Mar (1832–1898)	17 July 1890
H. Hartman (?–?)	18 July 1890
Alphonse Stengelin (1852–1938)	28 July 1890
Johannes Graadt van Roggen (1867–1959)	26 February 1891
Johannes Graadt van Roggen (1867–1959)	9 March 1891
Nicolaas Beets (1814–1903)	9 April 1891
H. J. Hunck (?–?)	11 August 1891

ATS 159 (1892–94)

Name	Date
H. Bottelier (?–?)	25 April 1892
A. Brouwers (?–?)	2 May 1892
Aug. B. Kaufman (?–?)	13 May 1892
Paul Joseph Constantin Gabriël (1828–1903)	19 May 1892
Anton Lodewijk Koster (1859–1937)	3 June 1892
Nicolaas Bastert (1854–1939)	3 June 1892
Theodor Renkewitz (1833–1913)	July 1892
Edmund Louyot (1861–1920)	29 July 1892
Frederik Carel de Graaff (1819–1897)	3 August 1892
Arend Hijner (1866–1916)	9 February 1893
Johannes Graadt van Roggen (1867–1959)	11 April 1893
Johannes Carolus Roodenburg (1852–1928)	4 July 1893
Ludwig Noster (1859–1910)	5 July 1893
Reinhold Bressler (1868–1945)	5 July 1893
Ernst Christian Pfannschmidt (1868–1949)	13 October 1893
'Company of 8 persons. Artists of all continents'	8 January 1894
Albertine Mesdag (1859–1936)	16 Februay 1894

COLLECTING AND DISPLAYING ART IN TEYLER'S MUSEUM, 1778–1885

Louis Apol (1850–1936)	8 May 1894

ATS 160 (1894–98)

Name	Date
Sergei Diaghilev (1872–1929)	10 June 1895
Jan Veth (1864–1925)	21 August 1895
Pelagia Petrowna Couriard (1848–1898)	3 October 1895
Sergei Alexandrovich Scherbatov (1875–1962)	13 April 1896
Johann Victor Krämer (1861–1949)	6 July 1896
Carel Adolph Lion Cachet (1864–1945)	1 July 1897
Théodore Jacques Ralli (1852–1909)	20 August 1897
Hendrik Dirk Kruseman van Elten (1829–1904)	1 September 1897
Lodewijk Schelfhout (1881–1943)	8 September 1897
Willem Maris Jbzn. (1872–1929)	8 November 1897
Johannes Graadt van Roggen (1867–1959)	1 February 1898
Lodewijk Schelfhout (1881–1943)	7 June 1898
Lodewijk Schelfhout (1881–1943)	5 July 1898

ATS 161 (1898–1902)

Name	Date
Jacob Coenraad Ritsema (1869–1943)	4 August 1898
Aimée Rapin (1869–1956)	19 October 1898
Hendrik Petrus Berlage (1856–1934)	28 December 1898
Willem Witsen (1860–1923)	14 April 1899
Lodewijk Schelfhout (1881–1943)	20 October 1899
Lodewijk Schelfhout (1881–1943)	5 February 1900
Lodewijk Schelfhout (1881–1943)	27 February 1900
Isidore Bourgeois (?–?)	2 April 1900
Frederik van Eeden (1860–1932)	16 August 1900
René Janssens (1870–1936)	23 August 1900
Lodewijk Schelfhout (1881–1943)	11 October 1900
Arthur R. Freedlander (1875–1940)	24 October 1900
W. O. Smith (?–?)	24 October 1900
Ethelbert W. Brown (1870–1946)	24 October 1900

PART 4

Teyler's in an International Perspective

∴

CHAPTER 10

Visiting Haarlem: August Hermann Niemeyer, the Cabinet of Artefacts and Natural Curiosities at the Halle Orphanage, and Teyler's Museum

Holger Zaunstöck

In 1823/24 August Hermann Niemeyer, theologian and educationalist at Halle in Germany, published an account of his journey through the Netherlands, undertaken nearly twenty years earlier, in 1806. He was one of the German writers around 1800 who had a considerable influence on Dutch intellectual life. As co-director of the Franckesche Stiftungen, an institution with an important collection of its own, Niemeyer visited Teyler's Museum and its director, Martinus van Marum, who in turn had been to Halle in the 1780s. This essay explores Niemeyer's experiences and observations concerning Teyler's Museum and the people he met in Haarlem. And it addresses a wider question – the problem of writing about collections. Niemeyer was one of the protagonists who created a shift in the way collections were seen in the early nineteenth century by visiting and writing about them.

• • •

In 1806 August Hermann Niemeyer (1754–1828), professor of theology at the Fridrichsuniversität and co-director and central figure of the Franckesche Stiftungen (Francke Foundations) in Halle, travelled extensively through the Netherlands (figure 10.1). One of the most respected educational theorists in Prussia,[1] he can be counted among the group of 'the most influential German writers to affect Dutch intellectual life' at that time.[2] He arrived in Haarlem on 26 September and left the city for Leiden on the afternoon of 28 September.[3] The tight touristic programme that Niemeyer followed during his stay can be considered as typical for an educated bourgeois scholar. Through his introduction to learned men and their families in Haarlem he had the chance of a personal visit to Martinus van Marum (1750–1837), as well as a viewing

---

1 Cf. Klosterberg 2004a, Soboth 2007.
2 Eijnatten 2012, 132–33. Niemeyer's works were widely received in the Netherlands.
3 His travel route is given in Kuby 2007, 54–55.

© KONINKLIJKE BRILL NV, LEIDEN, 2021 | DOI:10.1163/9789004441446_011

FIGURE 10.1
Franz Gareis, *Portrait of August Hermann Niemeyer (1754–1828)*, 1800, oil on canvas, 72 x 60.5 cm.
FRANCKESCHE STIFTUNGEN, HALLE, AFST/B G 0118

FIGURE 10.2
Franz Gareis, *Portrait of Agnes Wilhelmine Christiane Niemeyer, née von Köpken (1769–1847)*, 1800, oil on canvas, 72 x 60.5 cm.
FRANCKESCHE STIFTUNGEN, HALLE, AFST/B G 0119

VISITING HAARLEM

of Teyler's Museum. Niemeyer published his memories and observations, including his remarks on Haarlem, under the title *Beobachtungen auf einer Reise durch einen Theil von Westphalen und Holland* (Observations on a Journey through a Part of Westphalia and Holland) in 1823, followed by a reprint a year later.[4] In this visit two worlds of collecting met. This essay explores the meeting in five steps, concentrating on the question of what Niemeyer saw (and Van Marum did not, when he visited Halle in the 1780s) and why he described his impressions as he did. Using the example of Niemeyer, the article further aims to show a shift in the way collections could be interpreted in the early nineteenth century.

1   The Diversity of the Collections in the Francke Foundations: 'to Make the Visitors Familiar with the School Institutions and Aware of God's Work'

In 1695, just outside the city gates of the town of Halle in Brandenburg-Prussia, the Pietist theologian and educationalist August Hermann Francke (1663–1727) founded an orphanage and an educational establishment for boys and girls from all classes of society (figure 10.4). For this comprehensive system of education and social welfare, Francke and his successors created an entire 'school town' during the decades from 1698 to 1748, known from 1792 as the Franckesche Stiftungen, the Francke Foundations. From the outset, collections were considered to be one pillar of this pedagogical and institutional vision. In addition to a Cabinet of Natural Curiosities (*Naturalien-Cammer*), set up to give the young a thorough education, as Francke wrote in 1698 to Friedrich III, Elector of Brandenburg, the collections included a botanical garden, a Cabinet of Anatomy, mathematical, optical, and physical instruments, a 'Mechanical Cabinet', an astronomical observatory, a laboratory, a library, and even a *camera obscura*. Thus in the early eighteenth century the school town already had a complex of collections with a range of purposes (figure 10.3).[5]

First of all, the collections had a physico-theological application. The objects were used in 'recreational lessons' (*Rekreationsstunden, Realienunterricht, Anschauungsunterricht*) at the Royal Pädagogium for children of the nobility and well-to-do citizens,[6] and the collections were also open at times to orphans

---

4 Niemeyer 1824a, 147–59. (This edition is identical with the first, Halle 1823.) His *Beobachtungen* were also published in Dutch: 1824b.
5 Müller-Bahlke 2012, 15–19; Hornemann/Veltmann 2013.
6 Müller-Bahlke 1999, Whitmer 2015.

FIGURE 10.3 Johann Georg Mauritius, *Das Hällische Waysenhaus* (The orphanage in Halle), 1740, engraving, 265 x 410 mm.
FRANCKESCHE STIFTUNGEN, HALLE, AFSt/B sd 0091

and children of the poor.[7] Secondly, the steadily growing Cabinet of Natural Curiosities, founded in 1698, was a key element in the Foundations' campaign to establish the Orphanage as a household name (as *Marke Waisenhaus*).[8] As we know from the records, from the early eighteenth century on visitors were shown around Francke's school town and the collections by staff trained for the purpose, called *Herumführer*.[9] In 1713, for example, the growing Pietistic site and its components were shown to Friedrich Wilhelm I, King of Prussia.[10] The Cabinet of Natural Curiosities and the Mechanical Cabinet served importantly to display the school town's prosperity and its educational approach. By 1727, the year when Francke died, the collections were frequently viewed by more than sixty people a day.[11] There is also a third point here. At that time, too,

---

7   For an example of this see the advice concerning astronomy and physics issued by Gotthilf August Francke in October 1732: AFSt/W VII/1/20: *Instruction für den Herumführer* (Instruction for the guide), October 1732, here Instruction no. 7.
8   On the *Marke Waisenhaus* see Zaunstöck 2013.
9   Cf. Müller-Bahlke 2012, 20; Stelter 2014, 53–59 and *passim*; Dolezel 2019, 191–93.
10 *Pietist und Preussenkönig* 2005, 11–12.
11 Directorium 1863, 222.

VISITING HAARLEM 223

we find the Cabinet of Natural Curiosities being used to publicize the Danish-Halle mission in Tranquebar (Tharangambadi) in southern India, initiated in 1706. The objects sent from India to Halle were specifically used to promote the missionary work there. For example, in 1712 Francke was concerned that natural history specimens sent from India via Copenhagen had failed to arrive in Halle. He was worried about the loss not so much of the objects themselves as of their symbolic value: in a letter to the minister of state Johann Georg von Holstein (1662–1730) he says that foreign visitors arriving every day to view the natural history collection could be counted on to contribute not insignificant sums to the Danish-Halle mission.[12]

From the 1730s, under Gotthilf August Francke (1696–1769), the son and one of two successors of August Hermann Francke as Director, the Cabinet of Natural Curiosities was professionally arranged according to the macrocosm-in-microcosm model. The figure entrusted with this task was Gottfried August Gründler (1710–1775), an artist and natural scientist, who was deeply involved in the first translation of Carl von Linné's *Systema Naturae* into German. The combination of the macrocosm-in-microcosm model with Linnaeus's system (orderings principles that are usually considered to be contradictory) emphatically demonstrates the changeable character of the collection at the Orphanage in Halle on the one hand, and, on the other hand, reminds us that we should not see the changing patterns of collecting during the eighteenth century as progressing in a straight line.[13] From 1736 to 1741, in an approach that combined religion, natural history and art, Gründler laid out the cabinet on the Orphanage's attic floor under the mansard roof, where it can still be seen today (figures 10.4, 10.5).[14] It comprised artefacts from the beginning, but now the naming of the cabinet began to change.[15] From 1741 onwards it was known as the Cabinet of Artefacts and Natural Curiosities, signalling the shift in emphasis.

In the wake of Gründler's new display, the structure and order of the collection were given a new profile. Even in 1732, when the collection's re-structuring was in the planning phase at best, Gotthilf August Francke was already emphasizing the need to ensure 'that when guiding visitors around the

---

12 August Hermann Francke to Johann Georg von Holstein, 16 December 1712 (Royal Library, Copenhagen, Ledreborg 389 2° a). My thanks to K. Hommel (Leipzig) for this reference. Cf. further Hommel 2006.

13 AFSt/W VII/I/20, *Instruction für den Der das Herumführen der Fremden in den Anstalten des Waysenhauses hat. Zusammen getragen 1741 in Augusto* (Instruction for him who has to Guide Foreigners through the Orphanage Buildings, drawn up in August 1741), Sect. III, §18. The Francke Foundations are currently working on an edition of this source. For the broader context see Dolezel 2019.

14 Ruhland 2018; Müller-Bahlke 2012, 38–54; for a broader context see Dietz 2010.

15 Müller-Bahlke 2012, 15; AFSt/W VII/I/20, Sect. II, §5 and Sect. III, §18.

FIGURE 10.4　Front view of the main building of the Orphanage, *c.* 1750, coloured engraving, 321 x 411 mm.
FRANCKESCHE STIFTUNGEN, HALLE, AFSt/A 04/ 01/ 03

curiosa should not be shown alone, but efforts should also be made to acquaint the visitors with the school's institutions and with the work of God'.[16] From 1741, the Cabinet of Artefacts and Natural Curiosities was chiefly used to publicize the idea of divine providence and to disseminate the Foundations' history and missionary activities – a goal specifically listed as the purpose (*Der Zweck*) under paragraph 1 in the instructions for the guides of that year.[17] Educational purposes and its function within the schools were by contrast remarkably downplayed.[18] The Cabinet, supplemented by a collection of portraits of the Foundations' Directors on the wall directly opposite the entrance door,[19] was

16　AFSt/W VII/1/20: *daß beym herumführen nicht allein die curiosa zu zeigen denn auch zu suchen daß den Leuten die Schul Anstalten bekannt werden, und sie auf Gottes werck gewiesen werden.*
17　ibid.; cf. Rieke-Müller 2006, 73.
18　Müller-Bahlke 2012, 21.
19　Schulze/Knapp/Niemeyer 1799, 166.

FIGURE 10.5   View into the 'Kunst- und Naturalienkammer' (Room for art and *naturalia*) of the Francke Foundations with the geocentric world system according to Tycho Brahe. Photo 2015.

FIGURE 10.6   Johann August Gottlob Eberhardt, *View from the City Wall of Halle to the West*, c. 1800, oil on hardboard, 21 x 30 cm. On the left is the complex of the Francke Foundations; we are looking from near the Leipziger Tor, more or less Van Marum's spot in 1786.
FRANCKESCHE STIFTUNGEN, HALLE, AFST/B M 4086

226 ZAUNSTÖCK

used as a Pietistic showroom, open to the public on a daily basis at 10 a.m. and at 3 p.m.,[20] until the nineteenth century.

Concurrently, the collections of school materials were expanded. In 1736 expensive devices to conduct experiments in physics were being set up specifically for the *Latina* grammar school, which catered primarily for children from urban middle-class families; for this the students and their families contributed a certain sum.[21] In 1764, the plan was mooted to acquire for the Royal Pädagogium a costly astronomical instrument not yet available anywhere in Halle.[22] And in 1774 the Royal Pädagogium advertised an *auserlesenes* (exquisite) cabinet of minerals as well as 'good' instruments for mathematics and physics.[23]

To summarize: by the mid-eighteenth century two worlds of collections had become defined in Francke's school town. The first was the popular and popularizing Cabinet of Artefacts and Natural Curiosities, which also provided an insight into Pietism. The second was the different collections assembled for instruction.

2   Van Marum in Halle: 'Bad Architecture and Untidiness'

It is against this background that we should see Martinus van Marum's brief and not very successful visit to Halle on 15 July 1786 while travelling through Germany. Van Marum, who had been Director of Teyler's Museum for two years, undertook this journey to assemble a series of up-to-date cabinets for fossils, minerals and physical instruments, as well as a library, through contacts with important German collectors and scientists. On entering the city he had a very bad impression, noting: 'because of its bad architecture and untidiness [the town] pleased us less than we had expected'. On the same day he visited Johann Reinhold Forster (1729–1798), famed as the naturalist who accompanied Captain Cook 'on his second voyage around the world'. Forster showed Van Marum fossils (by which the latter was not impressed), sketches of unfamiliar animals made on his voyage, and an extensive collection of travellers' accounts (that he praised). Van Marum had also planned

---

20   AFSt/W VII/I/20, Sect. II, §8.

21   Freylinghausen 1736, 41.

22   Niemeyer 1764, 35: *Ein Quadrante, der im halben Durchmesser noch etwas über vier Fuß beträgt, und also schon von einer seltenen Grösse ist* (A quadrant that measures something over four feet in half its diameter, and is thus unquestionably of a rare size).

23   *Kurzer Bericht* 1774, 8–9.

to see Wenceslaus Johann Gustav Karsten (1732–1787), professor of mathematics and physics, a foreign member of the Hollandsche Maatschappij der Wetenschappen (Holland Society of Sciences) in Haarlem, renowned for his mathematics instruction books, but that did not happen. The final dinner, held with students from Halle, was also less than a pleasure. Van Marum noted that they 'seemed to be living very roughly there and to imitate the military in their mode of living'. To cap it all, Van Marum was incensed at the treatment he received when he came to leave Halle: 'On entering the town a few hours earlier we had twice written down not only our names, but also exactly where we were going, how long we were going to stay, what was our purpose, etc. On leaving we had to repeat and write down exactly all these data again, not only once, but three times'.[24]

It seems that Van Marum visited Halle without knowing of the Cabinet of Artefacts and Natural Curiosities in the Orphanage (and without Forster mentioning it to him). However, he could certainly have known that it was there. Gottlob Friedrich Krebel (1729–1793), for instance, had written in his *Vornehmsten Europaeischen Reisen*, published in 1775:

> In the suburb of Glaucha, the world-famous Halle Orphanage and Pedagogium merit the admiration of all travellers for their excellent regulation and management. Here one can find a stately Cabinet of Artefacts and Natural Curiosities, a pharmacy, the laboratory of the famous Halle medicines, a bookstore, a printing press, the Canstein Bible Institute, a sizeable library, facilities for silk cultivation, etc.[25]

As he passed through the Leipziger Tor, harassed by the Prussian city guard, Van Marum could not have failed to glimpse the architecturally ground-breaking and impressive school town nearby (figure 10.6). But he did not visit the Orphanage, so he did not see its Cabinet of Artefacts and Natural Curiosities.

Van Marum returned to central Germany again in 1798. During his stays in Gotha, Weimar, Jena and Erfurt he visited collections, gardens, observatories, laboratories, and more. His descriptions tend to highlight new, thematically

---

24 Forbes/Lefebvre/Bruijn 1969–76, vol. 2 (1970), 249.

25 Krebel 1775, 78: *In der Vorstadt Glaucha verdienen das weltberühmte hallische Waysenhaus und das Pädagogium, wegen ihrer vortrefflichen Einrichtungen, aller Reisenden Bewunderung. Man findet da eine ansehnliche Kunst- und Naturalien-Cammer, eine Apotheke, das Laboratorium der berühmten hallischen Arzeneyen, eine Buchhandlung, eine Buchdruckerey, die Cansteinische Bibelanstalt, eine ansehnliche Bibliothek, Anstalten zum Seidenbau etc.* My thanks to Holger Trauzettel (Halle) for this reference.

specialized collections rather than universalist older ones.[26] In Erfurt he did see the collection of curiosities in the Lutheran orphanage. It had been established in 1735, probably on the Halle model, to attract financial support for the orphanage.[27] But Van Marum, focused as he was on material for physical, mineralogical and paleontological research, commented that the collection was not very valuable.[28] He did not visit Halle again, so he never saw Francke's Orphanage or its Cabinet of Artefacts and Natural Curiosities.

3   Niemeyer in Haarlem: 'Enough Here to Captivate the Traveller'[29]

Niemeyer's visit to Haarlem in 1806 was very different. Through Josué Teissèdre l'Ange (1771–1853), a clergyman, school reformer and member of Teyler's Second Society, who translated Niemeyer's *Grundsätze der Erziehung* (Principles of Education) into Dutch, he had an introduction to the society of the town.[30] It is thus not surprising that he visited Teyler's Museum. As we have seen, he left an account of that visit in his *Beobachtungen auf einer Reise durch einen Theil von Westphalen und Holland* (Observations on a journey through part of Westphalia and Holland) (figure 10.7). In that work, published seventeen years after his visit to Haarlem, Niemeyer characterizes Pieter Teyler (1702–1778) as a stingy person, repeating a rumour claiming that two dairymaids were posted at the front and back doors of his house to acquire not one but two spoons as a free gift.[31] He then goes on to mention the *Hofje*, a housing complex for ladies over seventy, endowed by Pieter Teyler, which he thought too grand.[32] Remarkably, he does not mention the role of the patron's Mennonite beliefs in founding that and his other institutions, as one might have expected, since the Orphanage and schools in Halle were founded on the strong Pietistic beliefs of August Hermann Francke, who was Niemeyer's great-grandfather. He describes the Museum in particular, listing such details as the magnificent building (*prächtiges Gebäude*), the Oval Room,[33]

---

26   Forbes/Lefebvre/Bruijn 1969–76, vol. 2 (1970), 301–11; cf. in this context Meijers 2017.

27   See Schloms 2017, 175–76; Laube 2018.

28   Forbes/ Lefebvre/Bruijn 1969–76, vol. 2 (1970), 311.

29   Niemeyer 1824, 148: *genug in sich, was den Reisenden fesseln kann.*

30   Niemeyer 1824, 148; cf. on Teissèdre l'Ange http://www.biografischportaal.nl/persoon/11607802; Niemeyer 1799–1810. His first guide in Haarlem was the German Lutheran minister J. W. Statius Müller.

31   Niemeyer 1824, 150; cf. Weiss 2013a, 34–35.

32   Niemeyer 1824, 151.

33   Schmidt 2006, 109–43; Weiss 2013a, 63–67.

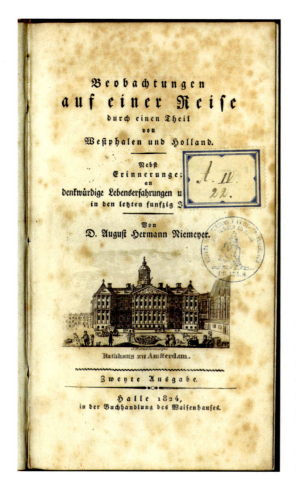

FIGURE 10.7
Title page of August Hermann Niemeyer, *Beobachtungen auf einer Reise durch einen Theil von Westphalen und Holland* (Observations on a journey through part of Westphalia and Holland), Halle 1824.
FRANCKESCHE STIFTUNGEN LIBRARY, HALLE, BFST S/FS.2:662

and the world-famous electricity machine (*weltberühmte Electrisirmaschine*), the display of minerals in glass-topped cases, the Library with its excellent collection of books, the prize competitions, and the scientific instruments. 'Given the immense financial effort involved', Niemeyer calls the entire institute a *Prachtstück*, a magnificent place, rather than just a research collection of common usefulness.[34] Admittedly, he adds, one should also take into account the winter lectures on natural science, the publications, and the opportunity for frequent visits to such a rare collection; Haarlem in addition offered the possibility of visiting the collections of the Hollandsche

---

34 Niemeyer 1824, 151–52: *im Verhältnis des ungeheuren Aufwands den es gekostet hat und fortdauernd kostet.*

Maatschappij der Wetenschappen, including a zoological cabinet. He notes that in 'sensitive spirits this variety of collections had already generated a multitude of ideas'; moreover, it had allowed people to view with their own eyes what they otherwise would have known only from descriptions.[35] In this presumably Niemeyer was acknowledging the value of Teyler's Museum and the remarkable standard of scientific society in Haarlem, as well as the stimulating atmosphere of thematically diverse but connected collections and the scientific activities surrounding them.

Niemeyer met Van Marum on his country estate, 'Plantlust', but the only detail of this encounter that he chose to record for posterity was that the Museum Director had freed himself from 'the burdensome business of showing visitors around' – something for which Niemeyer, unlike other travellers, shows understanding. To underline his point, Niemeyer appealed to his readers with the rhetorical question: 'Who can expect a scholarly man to torment himself with every inquisitive person?'[36]

In addition to the description of the world of Teyler's Museum and other attractions in Haarlem, Niemeyer's account indicates that he was keen to become part of Haarlem society, gaining new contacts, 'friends' (Freunde).[37] His acquaintance with the school reformer and member of Teyler's Second Society Adriaan van den Ende (1768–1846), who gave him an insight into the state of the Dutch school system in 1806, left a lasting impression. Niemeyer characterized him as being 'at the forefront of all the national education in the Netherlands'.[38] This was also a major factor in Niemeyer's decision to visit Haarlem again in 1819 when he was on his way to England. His account of that journey, published in the following year, includes a description of his meeting again with Teissèdre l'Ange in Amsterdam and Van den Ende in Rotterdam.[39]

---

35   ibid.: *in empfänglichen Geistern schon eine Menge von Ideen geweckt*; Weiss 2013a, 154.

36   ibid., 152: *sich des lästigen Geschäfts des Herumführens überhebt* [*entzieht*] and *Wer kann dem wissenschaftlichen Manne anmuthen* [*zumuten*], *sich mit jedem Neugierigen abzuquälen?* Cf. Weiss 2013a, 83–85, 144–55.

37   ibid., 148, 158–59.

38   ibid., 158. Van den Ende was the designer of the Education Law of 1806, which made the Netherlands, from a European perspective, a very progressive country in this respect. This law generated great international interest. See also Chapter 1, p. 17, n. 30. On Van den Ende see Heiningen 2010, 327, and for further detailed biographical information http://www.biografischportaal.nl/persoon/44287831.

39   Niemeyer 1820, 65–68. The second edition appeared in 1821, without any significant alterations in the details of the visit to Haarlem, Teissèdre l'Ange and Van den Ende.

VISITING HAARLEM

4 Note, Remember, Borrow, Publish: Work on the Text

The published account of Niemeyer's journey in 1806 is based on extensive manuscript notes.[40] Some passages are nearly identical with the book, some are more detailed, and some differ significantly.[41] In the passage on Van Marum, Niemeyer wrote originally that he visited

> the famous Heer van Marum at his country house, where it is his custom to spend the summer. I found him more pleasant than I had been given to hope. As the Director and first administrator of Teyler's great legacy he is granted all rights and privileges. Everything was set up and will be maintained under his guidance. The Directors assigned to him are said to have little knowledge and little activity, and to enjoy their pension in comfortable repose.[42]

The manuscript notes have a specific emphasis here: paying tribute to how Van Marum deals with his considerable and responsible task in spite of the phlegmatic nature of the Directors of Teyler's Foundation appointed over him. But there is nothing of that in the printed version, possibly because Niemeyer sensed the difficult relationship between Van Marum and his superiors and did not want to aggravate the situation. Instead, the focus there is on the matter of withdrawing from the public relations activity of showing visitors around. There are also some differences in the descriptions of the collections in the Oval Room. In his notes, for example, Niemeyer observes that prints and drawings are kept below the glazed mahogany display cases for minerals. He praises the order as well as the quality of the mineral collection, and mentions the

---

40   AFSt/N: A. H. Niemeyer 2:8, fols 359–67.

41   See in this context Klosterberg 2004b.

42   AFSt/N: A. H. Niemeyer 2:8, fols 360–61: *den berühmten H. van Marum auf seinem Landhause, wo er den Sommer gewöhnl[ich] zubringt. Ich fand ihn gefaelliger als man mir Hofnung gemacht hatte. Als Aufseher und ersten Ausführer des grossen Teylerschen Vermaechtnisses laesst man ihm alle Gerechtigkeit wiederfahren. Unter seiner Leitung ist alles entstanden und wird alles fortgesetzt. Die ihm zugesellten Directoren sollen wenig Kenntniss und wenig Thaetigkeit haben, und in behaglicher Ruhe ihre Pension geniessen.* The state of affairs portrayed here (possibly by Van Marum himself?) does not entirely correspond to reality. Van Marum was, to his dissatisfaction, subordinated to the five Directors of Teyler's Foundation, which increasingly led to conflicts. See also Mijnhardt (p. 81) and Sliggers (p. 116) in this volume. Directors received a remuneration of 1000 guilders per year (nowadays roughly 10,000 euros). See Sliggers 2006, Appendix 2, 194. https://iisg.amsterdam/en/research/projects/hpw/calculate.php?back-link=1 (accessed 9 Nov. 2020).

prize contests, but adds that 'little is to be gained for scholarship' from the theological competitions carried out by Teyler's First Society – in contrast to those in the physical sciences by Teyler's Second Society, of which both his new friends Van den Ende and Teissèdre l'Ange were members.[43] His notes also mention the natural science lectures, given by the excellent Adriaan van den Ende during the winter season.[44] In a long passage of the manuscript Van den Ende's staunch support for higher elementary and village schools is emphasized (Niemeyer also refers to that, more briefly, in his book). A great deal has been done here, Niemeyer continues, in which the greatest achievements are due to the Maatschappij tot Nut van 't Algemeen (Society for the Promotion of Public Welfare, founded 1784), whose patrons were also 'inspired' (*begeistert*) by the example of Halle's August Hermann Francke.[45]

In addition to these notes, the Francke Foundations Archive includes other documents related to Niemeyer's journey to Holland in 1806. One of them, part of a letter, also deals with the visit to Teyler's Museum, and was written on the journey itself. Although the author is not named, it seems from the style and the overall context that it is Niemeyer's wife, Agnes Wilhelmine Christiane (figure 10.2). In the letter she reports on the activities of the couple in Haarlem, referring to her husband as 'der Vater', from which we can deduce that she was addressing her children in Halle. Agnes Wilhelmine accompanied Niemeyer on his journey through the Netherlands as an attentive and interested traveller and observer.[46] A gifted woman, widely educated in music, poetry and literature, she held a famous, very popular salon on Wednesdays in their home in Halle, and was the heart of those cultural events.[47] She also passed on her knowledge and experiences to her children, for example by reporting her impressions of Haarlem. Agnes Wilhelmine's letter includes a description of a visit to the natural and zoological collection 'in Van Marum's house' on the last day of their stay.[48] On the tour of this large, famous cabinet, as she called it, they were shown around by

---

43   ibid., fols 361–62: *bey denen wenig für die Wissenschaft gewonnen wird*. Though Niemeyer mentions the prize essays in his printed travel report he left out these judgments: Niemeyer 1824, 151–52.

44   AFSt/N: A. H. Niemeyer 2:8, fols 361, 365. Cf. Roberts 1999, 381–82.

45   ibid., fols 365–66, Niemeyer 1824, 158 (on Van den Ende). In Halle in 1799 Niemeyer had also founded a patriotic society for the common good called the Gesellschaft freiwilliger Armenfreunde (Society of Voluntary Friends of the Poor). On this see Veltmann/Zaunstöck 2006.

46   AFSt/N: A. H. Niemeyer 1:131, 275, 276, 279, 280, 282; and Kuby 2007, 48.

47   See Piechocki/Soboth 2004.

48   Besides Teyler's natural history collections Van Marum curated the zoological collection of the Hollandsche Maatschappij der Wetenschappen, where he also held the position of secretary. Because he lived in the Society's house in Grote Houtstraat, it could seem that

VISITING HAARLEM 233

Van den Ende. Among other things, she says that the collection of great apes was first-rate and complete – but the apes were an abomination (*Gräuel*) to her, so she didn't care to stay with them for long. Afterwards, she continues, they went straight to Teyler's Museum. Here she lists the sights as her husband did, and then writes: 'There was still more to see and discover, but I really can't remember everything'. Then she recalls, with emphasis, the enjoyable concluding luncheon with their new friends in Haarlem. Niemeyer himself briefly noted the visit to the zoological collection (describing it as excellent) and also reported briefly on the last 'delightful' luncheon in Haarlem.[49]

Assuming that Agnes Wilhelmine is not mistaken, her notes indicate that the visit to Teyler's Museum must have taken place at the very last minute, as the final part of the programme during their stay at the Spaarne. In fact she stresses that the visits to the zoological collection and Teyler's Museum were only made when their hosts in Haarlem emphasized their importance as 'must see' attractions in the town. This would suggest that for Niemeyer the Museum did not have primary importance.

Yet one gets the impression that Niemeyer worked with his wife, or at least used her observations, in compiling his travel report. This becomes apparent for example by comparing the manuscript and printed passages on Teyler's Museum itself and on the visits to gardens and garden owners in Haarlem, such as the botanist George Voorhelm Schneevoogt.

When compiling the text for his book Niemeyer may also have resorted to other authors. In 1804 Caspar Heinrich von Sierstorpff (1750–1842) published the second volume of his *Bemerkungen auf einer Reise durch die Niederlande nach Paris* (Remarks on a Journey through the Netherlands to Paris), which includes a description of his visit to Teyler's Museum.[50] Niemeyer was probably familiar with the book, since there is a copy in the library of the Francke Foundations in Halle which originates from the library of the Royal Pädagogium (figure 10.8). In this context, two passages are particularly interesting.[51]

---

the collection was his own. Niemeyer himself noted the collection correctly as the *zoologische Cabinet der Gesellschaft der Wissenschaften*, AFst/N: A. H. Niemeyer 2:8, fol. 367.

49   Agnes Wilhelmine: ibid., 1: 344l: *Es gab noch mehreres zu sehen u[nd] kennen zu lernen, aber ich kann mich wahrlich nicht mehr an alles erinnern*; Niemeyer: ibid., 2:8, fol. 367.

50   What Niemeyer apparently did not borrow from Sierstorpff is the term 'Museum' (Sierstorpff 1804, 551: 'Taylorschen Museums', 555: 'Museo', 557 and 562: 'Museum'). In contrast, both Niemeyers always refer to Teyler's as an 'Institut' (AFst/N: A. H. Niemeyer 2:8, fol. 361; AFst/N: A. H. Niemeyer 2:8, fol. 571; AFst/N: A. H. Niemeyer 1: 344l). See for the term 'Museum' also Weiss 2013a, 64–66, 86 and Eric Jorink's contribution to this volume.

51   For further similarities see Weiss 2013a, 149–50 (e.g. the magnificent building, the exquisite minerals). For the system of press-marks (as seen in figure 10.8) in the Library of the Royal Pädagogium see Sturm 2017.

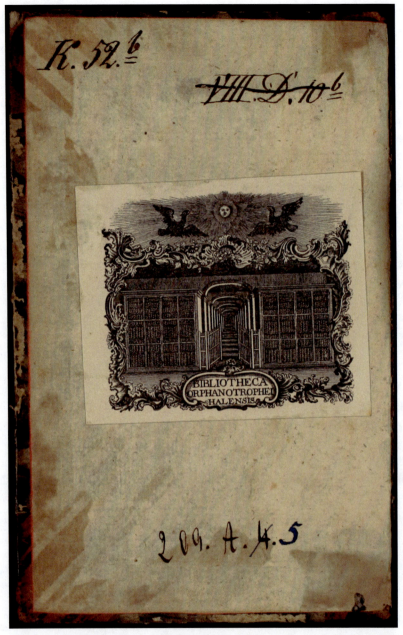

FIGURE 10.8 *Ex libris* of the library of the Franckeschen Stiftungen, pasted in Caspar Heinrich von Sierstorpff, *Bemerkungen auf einer Reise durch die Niederlande nach Paris im eilften Jahre der grossen Republik* (Remarks on a journey through the Netherlands to Paris in the eighteenth year of the Great Republic), vol. 2, Hamburg 1804. The crossed out press-mark shows that this copy belonged to the library of the Royal Pädagogium at the time. Niemeyer may have used it.
FRANCKESCHE STIFTUNGEN LIBRARY, HALLE, BFST 209 A 5

VISITING HAARLEM 235

In one of them Sierstorpff recalls visiting Van Marum, noting that he met him as 'A director of such an institution, who is tired of always showing visitors around'.[52] As we have seen, Niemeyer also emphasized this point in his book. It is certainly conceivable that Van Marum complained about his situation at Teyler's Museum and his withdrawal from the public affairs of the Museum after 1802 during brief meetings with both Directors,[53] and Niemeyer may simply have remembered it. But this important observation cannot be found in Niemeyer's handwritten notes, suggesting that he did indeed borrow it from Sierstorpff. He might have intended it as a concealed message – that directors in general (hence Niemeyer as well) should not be expected to take on such tasks.

A second passage lends further weight to the idea of Niemeyer borrowing a comment. The passage in question in Sierstorpff 's writings (as pointed out by Martin Weiss)[54] states that some day the entire collection will be capable of serving only as an example of the history of physics: 'Mahogany display cupboards are set all around, full of the most exquisite instruments for physics which one day, in the ever-advancing perfection of the sciences, will be able to serve as examples of the history of physics'.[55] One searches in vain in Niemeyer's notes for this key assessment of the collection. Niemeyer has borrowed Sierstorpff's text almost word for word, but he has again given it a positive twist, by omitting the adverb 'only'. In Sierstorpff, the 'only' emphasized that Teyler's Museum with all its valuable instruments was something to look at, but had no particular use any more.[56] By omitting 'only', Niemeyer highlights the collection's value for the history of science even at that time.

The route from a direct observation made on site at the moment to a printed published travel report is marked by different stages of work. In this process Niemeyer wove together personal impressions with descriptions by others, underlining his vision of himself as an eclectic person.[57] His printed report is created from different sources – his own notes and memories, the letters of his wife sent home to their children during the journey, and borrowings from other

---

52 Sierstorpff 1804, 551: *Ein Aufseher eines solchen Instituts, der das ewige Fremdenherumführen müde geworden ist.* See Weiss 2013a, 146.
53 My thanks to Martin Weiss for this reference. See Weiss 2013a, 125–28.
54 ibid., 199.
55 Sierstorpff 1804, 559: *diese ganze Sammlung wird dermaleinst nur als Belag* [sic] *zur Geschichte der Physik dienen können.* This is how it reads in Niemeyer: *Rings umher laufen Mahagonyschränke voll der kostbarsten physikalischen Instrumente aller Art, die einst, bei der stets fortschreitenden Vervollkommnung, als Belege zu einer Geschichte der Physik werden dienen können;* Niemeyer 1824, 151; Weiss 2013a, 153; Weiss 2013b, 199.
56 See the description in Sierstorpff 1804, 556–59; cf. Weiss 2013a, 153.
57 Schmid 2004, 186.

published travel reports.[58] The selection and treatment of themes was presumably also influenced by cultural and political changes in the period between 1806 and the year of publication in 1823;[59] and in some cases the confidential, even possibly offensive, character of his observations led Niemeyer to adjust the text (for example regarding Van Marum's conflicts with the Directors of Teyler's Foundation, especially in 1803, and his tendency to give broad evidence of these conflicts[60]). The splendour of Teyler's institution may have become a sort of commonplace in the public sphere all over Europe by the years around 1820, and Niemeyer probably responded to that as well.[61]

Niemeyer visited Haarlem for a second time on his trip to England, on 9 June 1819, but his brief handwritten notes only give some hints of what he was doing on that early summer day by the river Spaarne, and add no further details. Among other places and people he visited the Cabinet of Natural History and Teyler's institution, and the wife of Adriaan van den Ende.[62]

5 Conclusions and Further Areas of Research

To sum up: When Niemeyer visited Haarlem and Teyler's institution in September 1806 it was with a vision of collections shaped by those of the Francke Foundations, where they formed a complex with their different elements fulfilling different functions, from education to the promotion of the Foundations' image and propagating the idea of divine providence. He emphasized the significance of collections for educational purposes in general: 'Wherever possible, one ought to present the products of nature to the children's senses, and lead them to cabinets wherever the opportunity arises'.[63] From this perspective, he pays tribute to the magnificence of Teyler's Museum and its value to the history of science, yet tends to view it as a museum of physical items and not as a laboratory for physical experiments, as it was for Van Marum.[64] At the same time, he highlights how fruitfully Teyler's Museum is placed in the variety of collections and how it

---

58 In this context see Rees/Siebers 2005, 24–27, and Youngs 2014.

59 See Klosterberg 2004b; Jost 2012.

60 See for the conflict between Van Marum and the Teyler's Directors also the contributions to this volume of Mijnhardt (p. 81) and Sliggers (p. 116).

61 Cf. Jost 2012, 165; Weiss 2013a, 149; and Meijers 2015, 142.

62 AFSt/N: A. H. Niemeyer 2:8, fol. 571.

63 Niemeyer 1796, 525: *Wo es irgend möglich ist, bringe man die Naturproducte vor die Sinne der Kinder, führe sie in Cabinette, wo nur irgend Gelegenheit dazu ist.*

64 Cf. Weiss 2013a, 15–17, 85–89; Weiss 2013b, 199, 214. For the wider context, Bergvelt/ Meijers/Rijnders 2013[3].

VISITING HAARLEM   237

furthered sociability in Haarlem. In addition, he uses the person of Van Marum
to consider the problems of having collections regularly open to the public. That
raises the fundamental question of the social profile of visitors, and how the composition of the public changes depending on specific local conditions as well as
within wider networks.[65] The Cabinet at the Orphanage in Halle, for example,
was open to the public on a daily basis, was well attended during the local fairs,
and was shown to noble visitors from abroad.[66]

These observations give rise to further areas of research. The connections
between Niemeyer, Teissèdre l'Ange and Van den Ende seem to be valuable
for further in-depth research on educational concepts and school systems in
Prussia and the Netherlands, considering intellectual exchange and cultural
transfer. We also need to ask what active role the wives of those men played in
creating a stimulating intellectual social world. As a whole, these observations
point to the need for a further transnational comparative perspective in the
field of the history of collections and museums.[67] Likewise there is a need for
micro-historical analyses of individual and institutional intentions, specific
urban contexts, perceptions, and handwritten as well as printed descriptions.
The study of travel reports and the related manuscripts seems especially
fruitful.[68]

It seems essential to take a wider look at the variety of collections, considering
institutional, urban and regional contexts in the long eighteenth century, in con-
junction with the social contacts that accompanied it. Travellers like Niemeyer
were aware of and interested in the various types of collections, and in those that
formed a complex within an institution and fulfilled different functions there.[69]
They observed, described, compared and assessed the diversity of collections.
Current studies have started to look at these wider contexts of the cultures of

---

65 Cf. Linnebach 2014; *National Museums and National Identity* 2012, 20–26; Savoy 2006.

66 Directorium 1863, 222; Müller-Bahlke 2012, 20. In comparison, Teyler's Museum had limited
  opening hours: in 1785 it was open for only two hours on Tuesday for residents of Haarlem,
  and one hour a day – except Sundays – for out-of-town visitors. Terry van Druten's article in this volume refers to *Instructie voor den Bewooner of Castelein van het Fundatiehuis*
  van wylen de Heer Pieter Teyler van der Hulst (Instruction for the Resident or Castellan of
  the Foundation House of the late Mr Pieter Teyler van der Hulst), 20 June 1785 (Teyler's
  Foundation Archive ATS 5, 144–45). For later (also limited) opening hours see Weiss 2013a.

67 Cf. *National Museums and National Identity* 2012; Meyer/Savoy 2014.

68 Cf. Savoy 2006, 9–26 and 359–553: *Zeitgenössische Stimmen*. See also B. van de Roemer,
  'Von Uffenbach's visits. Disclosing the cultural industries of Amsterdam in the early eighteenth century' (forthcoming).

69 Van Marum, however, prefered single, scientific cabinets owned by renowned individuals. His interest was primarily in expanding and completing his collections in Teyler's
  Museum. See Bert Sliggers' contribution to this volume.

collecting in eighteenth-century Europe.[70] For the study of the specific features of this diversity of collections, showing different patterns in different cities and regions, the phrase 'topographies of collections' is suggested here. Such topographies of collections could be drawn up by examining the typology of collections in specific areas, the connections between those collections and their protagonists, and the specific intentions that individual collectors had with their collections in the spheres of religion, science, education and art.

It is within the world of the complex patterns of collections around 1800 that learned men like Niemeyer started to separate utilitarian cabinets, regularly used for education and research, from collections that unintentionally or intentionally illustrated the history of sciences. By accentuating this differentiation process in the early nineteenth century, as Niemeyer did in the case of Teyler's Museum, published travel reports seem to contribute to the transition to the modern museum.

The main question that arises from the material presented here, regarding the visit of August Hermann and Agnes Wilhelmine Niemeyer to Haarlem in 1806 and the literary processing of it seventeen years later, is: In what way, and to what extent, did the practices of speaking and writing about collections influence their modification in the early nineteenth century, and in so doing affect the emergence of the modern museum?

---

70 Cf. Mencfel 2010, Zuidervaart 2013, Wyka 2013, Hommel 2016, Brückner 2017, and Veen 1992.

CHAPTER 11

The Rise of the Modern Romantic Concept of Art and the Art Museum

Arnold Heumakers

In the course of the eighteenth century an aesthetic revolution took place, from which a new concept of art emerged that expressed itself fully for the first time in early German Romanticism. What was the connection of this new Romantic concept of art and its main characteristics, such as aesthetic autonomy and aesthetic education, to the modern art museum that developed in the early nineteenth century alongside the older 'encyclopae-dic' museum? Since the modern aesthetic theory was chiefly invented by poets, writers and philosophers, an answer to this question is not simple to find. But by consulting a committed enemy of the new museums a surprising, negative, connection can be found that might clarify the relations between the art museum and the new concept of art.

•••

In 1782 Karl Philipp Moritz (1756–1793), a young German writer, visited the British Museum (figure 11.1). In his account of his travels he tells how glad he was to have obtained an admission ticket from an English friend with connections to the museum: instead of having to wait for several weeks or possibly months, he could go there at once. But the visit turned out to be a disappointment. It was a guided tour, and the tour members, among whom Moritz noticed people 'of the lower classes and of both sexes', were rushed through 'in little more than an hour'. As a result he was 'stunned when going from room to room and stared in wonder at all these stupendous treasures of natural curiosities, antiquities, and scholarship, which one needs at least a year to observe closely and a lifetime to study'. Moritz found some compensation in the fact that, equipped as he was with a German guidebook to the museum, at one point the other members of the tour gathered around him to listen to his explanations, with the British tour guide watching in 'mocking amazement'.[1]

The British Museum is a good example of the 'encyclopaedic' museum, exhibiting a vast miscellany of objects, including *naturalia*, antiquities, and

---

1   *Reisen eines Deutschen in England im Jahr 1782*, in Moritz 1997–99, II, 286–87.

© KONINKLIJKE BRILL NV, LEIDEN, 2021 | DOI:10.1163/9789004441446_012

manuscripts. Works of art were only a small subsection of the collection. In the decades after its official opening to the public on 15 January 1759, however, another kind of museum emerged that did specialize in works of art. What was the connection of this art museum to the new concept of art? To answer that question I started with Moritz, for he is one of the thinkers and writers who were involved in what I call the 'aesthetic revolution' of the eighteenth century. In the course of this revolution the classical concept of art changed into the modern or Romantic concept of art. The aesthetic revolution was the necessary precondition of the rise of the art museum: without that modern concept there would have been no art museum at all. The developments that led to the art museum – for instance the opening to the public of princely art collections in several European countries, and the fact that a general public had emerged eager to visit them – were part of the aesthetic revolution itself. Here, as so often in changes of ideas on this scale, theory and practice are closely interwoven.

I shall first concentrate on theory, and then consider its relationship to the new art museum, including the situation in the Netherlands. Because it is impossible to do justice to every theoretical aspect of the aesthetic revolution, I shall mention just three important stages that shaped the modern, Romantic concept of art – modern, because it is still largely *our* concept of art; Romantic, because it only fully unfolded with the aesthetic programme of the first German Romantics, among whom we may count Moritz at the end of the eighteenth century.[2]

1   The Aesthetic Revolution

The aesthetic revolution had already begun a century earlier with the famous *querelle des Anciens et des Modernes*, that ended the almost undisputed authority of the Ancients. The crucial question for a work of art, Abbé Du Bos concluded in 1719, is no longer whether it was created in accordance with the correct ancient rules, but whether we are *moved* by it.[3] Subjective feelings and

---

2 For a more generous treatment, including chapters on the aesthetics of Moritz and Schiller and an extensive bibliography, see my *De esthetische revolutie. Hoe Verlichting en Romantiek de Kunst uitvonden*, Amsterdam 2015.

3 See his *Réflexions critiques sur la poésie et sur la peinture*, repr. Geneva 1967. Paradoxically, in the *querelle* Du Bos belonged to the Ancients. The Moderns defended the superiority of the modern poets with the argument that they had better rules. For Du Bos the superiority of the ancient poets was proved by the fact that they had touched the feelings of their readers for many centuries, something about which their modern colleagues were of course still uncertain.

genius became more important than objective rules. This shift from objectivism to subjectivism opened the Enlightenment debate on aesthetics to which my three important stages belong.

The first stage is the establishment of the fine arts as a coherent whole by Abbé Batteux in his *Les beaux-arts réduits à un même principe* (The Fine Arts reduced to a Single Principle) of 1746. Painting, sculpture, poetry, music and dance (and peripherally rhetoric and architecture), the arts that first and foremost give 'pleasure', were distinguished from the 'mechanical arts focused on their usefulness'. This distinction did not exist in the old system of the *artes*, in which the dissimilarity between the liberal and mechanical arts was based on completely different criteria. Logic, astronomy and mathematics were also considered to be liberal arts, for instance.[4] Thanks to Batteux a new classification of the arts developed.

At the same time, a whole new concept of art emerged as a singular noun (as opposed to the plural) – 'art-as-such', as M. H. Abrams called it.[5] It expressed an almost sacred exaltation beyond simple pleasure, as well as the distinction between art and its opposite, plain entertainment. Only since the aesthetic revolution of the eighteenth century can we ask whether a painting or a novel is *art* (or not) and be understood by everyone, however much the answers may differ. Before the eighteenth century the question would have been baffling.

This distinctive, exalted concept of 'art' as a singular noun could be developed thanks to the second stage: the rise of *aesthetics* as a separate branch of philosophy – a philosophy of art, given its name by the young German philosopher Alexander Baumgarten in 1735. His main work, *Aesthetica*, written in scholarly Latin, came out in two volumes in 1750–58.

Closely related to this second stage is the third stage: the invention of 'aesthetic autonomy' as a theoretical development within the new discipline of aesthetics, a discipline which rapidly gained considerable popularity among the educated and scholarly classes, in particular in Germany. The term 'autonomy' was introduced into aesthetics by Immanuel Kant in his *Kritik der Urteilskraft* (Critique of Judgment) of 1790. However Kant used this notion only in relation to the judgment of taste, which had to be disinterested as well as autonomous, to become simultaneously subjective and universal. About the autonomy of a specific genre of art or of a work of art Kant did not have much to say.

---

4   See Kristeller 1965.
5   Abrams 1989.

2 Moritz

For this we have to turn again to Moritz. In 1785, three years after his visit to the British Museum, he published an article in the *Berlinische Monatsschrift* entitled 'Versuch einer Vereinigung aller schönen Künste und Wissenschaften unter dem Begriff des In sich selbst Vollendeten' (An Attempt to unify all the Fine Arts and Sciences under the Concept of That which is Complete in Itself). One can hear the echo of Batteux's title (*Les beaux-arts réduits à un même principe*), but the leading principle of the two men was different. Batteux's principle is the imitation of beautiful nature, whereas Moritz's principle is centred on the autonomy of every beautiful or perfect work of art. Moritz does not use the word 'autonomy', alas, but his 'concept of that which is complete in itself' means more or less the same thing: a work of art that is 'complete in itself' obeys no rules but its own, it is a law unto itself – the literal, originally Greek, meaning of the word 'autonomy'.

Moritz illustrates his theory by comparing a beautiful work of art to a useful object, such as a knife. A knife always has its perfection or its purpose outside itself: it is perfect when you can cut your bread or steak with it. But what is the perfection or purpose of a beautiful work of art? It finds both in itself, Moritz claims, thereby turning beauty and practical usefulness into opposites.

> So when an object lacks an external use or purpose, purpose must be sought in the object itself if it is to awaken pleasure in me. Put another way, I must find so much purposiveness (*Zweckmäßigkeit*) in its individual parts that I forget to ask what actually is the point of the whole thing. In other words, I must find pleasure in a beautiful object only for its own sake; to this end, the lack of external purposiveness must be compensated for by inner purposiveness; the object must be complete in itself.[6]

In his article Moritz never writes about any moral, political or religious use or purpose of works of art. To be complete in itself means indeed to be autonomous. Here we have, one could say, the basis of the modern concept of art.

What is the connection to the art museum? Is there actually any connection? This is not immediately evident. The encyclopaedic museum claimed to be useful in many ways. The same applies to the French revolutionary museums, where a political purpose was never absent, even when the exhibits consisted exclusively of paintings and sculpture.[7] To clarify the connection

---

6 For the English translation see Moritz 2012, 99; for the German original Moritz 1785, also in Moritz 1997–99, II, 943–49.

7 See Meijers 2013 and McClellan 1994.

RISE OF MODERN ROMANTIC CONCEPT OF ART AND THE ART MUSEUM

between art and the art museum I propose to listen for a moment to one of the staunchest opponents of the museum in France. It is always rewarding to hear the arguments of one's adversary.

3 Quatremère de Quincy

The adversary here is the philosopher and archaeologist Antoine-Chrysostome Quatremère de Quincy (1755–1849; figure 11.2). In 1791 he successively argued against the museum as an ideal school for artists and as a replacement for the Academy. In 1796 he disagreed that the museum should be the chosen 'home' for the works of art that the French army had confiscated in Italy: according to him these belonged not in the Louvre but in Rome, which was a 'museum' in its own right.[8] Finally, he systematically formulated his arguments against the art museum in his *Considérations morales sur la destination des ouvrages de l'art* (Moral Considerations on the Destination of Works of Art) of 1815 (figure 11.3).

Quatremère's main objection is that to place a work of art in a museum is to rob it of its 'necessity' and its 'destination'. That is what happens when art is detached from its original surroundings and context (as the Italian works of art were by the French army under Napoleon): 'How better to proclaim the uselessness of works of Art than by announcing in the collections that have been made of them the nullity of their service? Divorcing them all indiscriminately from their social destination – what is this but to say that society has no need for them?' To defend the museum as the proper place to educate young artists is no solution, Quatremère argues, because it produces the bizarre 'vicious circle' of the museum educating artists who inevitably produce art fit only for the museum.[9]

In other words, art loses its purpose and function in a museum, and is handed over to commerce, to art history (in Quatremère's words the 'epitaph' of

---

8 For more on Quatremère see Schneider 1910, and Becq 1994, 500–504 and 799–810. On the French looting of art and its consequences see Bergvelt/Meijers/Tibbe/Wezel 2009.

9 Quatremère de Quincy 1815, 41: *Or, peut-on mieux proclamer l'inutilité des ouvrages de l'Art, qu'en annonçant dans les recueils qu'on en fait la nullité de leur emploi. Les enlever tous indistinctement à leur destination sociale, qu'est-ce autre chose, sinon dire que la société n'en a pas besoin?* Quatremère's notion of 'original' context remains rather unclear, especially regarding paintings: are they never to leave the studio of the artist? The notion seems more appropriate with regard to Greek and Roman antiquities; these indeed lose much if not all of their traditional function and meaning when removed from their 'native' surroundings. Though also sculptures often had left their original sites already long before the French confiscations.

FIGURE 11.1
Karl Franz Jacob Heinrich Schumann, *Portrait of Karl Philipp Moritz*, 1791, oil on canvas, 51.5 x 42.7 cm.
DAS GLEIMHAUS, HALBERSTADT, A 117

FIGURE 11.2
Julien-Léopold Bouilly, *Portrait of Antoine-Chrysostome Quatremère de Quincy. Chevalier de St Michel, de la Légion d'honneur, élu Secrétaire perpétuel de l'Académie des Beaux-Arts en 1816* [...], 1820, lithograph, 275 x 200 mm.
BIBLIOTHÈQUE NATIONALE DE FRANCE, PARIS, EST. QUATREMÈRE DE QUINCY A. C. 001

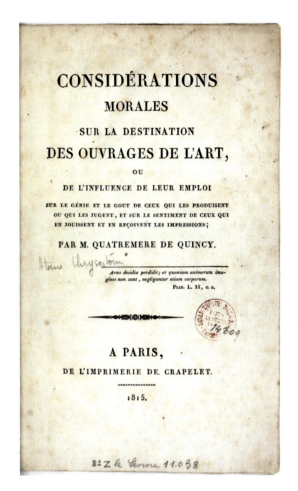

FIGURE 11.3
Title page of Quatremère de Quincy's *Considérations morales sur la destination des ouvrages de l'art* (Moral Considerations on the Destination of Works of Art), Paris 1815.
BIBLIOTHÈQUE NATIONALE DE FRANCE, PARIS, 8-Z LE SENNE-11038

all living art), and to sterile critical competition.[10] In this way Quatremère describes negatively some of the aspects of that which, in a positive sense, we call the *autonomy* of art.

There are indeed several similarities to Moritz's ideas. For instance, a work of art that is complete in itself, according to Moritz, demands the utmost

---

10   For a similar argument see Chateaubriand's *Génie du Christianisme* (1802). Of works of art in a museum he writes: 'Crowded into a narrow space, divided according to centuries, torn from their connection with the antiquity of the temples and of the Christian worship, subservient only to the history of the arts, and not to that of morals and religion, not retaining so much as their dust, they have ceased to speak either to the imagination or to the heart'. English translation in White 1871; original French text in *Génie du Christianisme*, Paris 1978, 936.

attention, not to say devotion, from the artist. He has to sacrifice himself to the perfection of his work and he should not pay attention to the demands of the public. Rewards or fame should not play any part in the making of pure art. Disinterestedness is no less demanded from the beholder, as Moritz makes perfectly clear:

> While the beautiful draws our contemplation entirely to itself, it draws our contemplation away from ourselves for a while and causes us to seem to lose ourselves in the beautiful object; and precisely this losing, this forgetting of ourselves is the highest degree of the pure and selfless pleasure that the beautiful affords us. In that instant, we sacrifice our individual, limited existence to a kind of higher existence.[11]

We lose ourselves in the work of art, we sacrifice our individuality. Art, in Moritz's view, is a severe mistress, standing all by herself, without context or setting, and in this respect similar to a confiscated work of art in a museum. There is no mention either in Moritz's essay of an external necessity or purpose for art. What is completely lacking is the *social* dimension: Moritz speaks only of the *individual* experience of art. Nonetheless, in his formulation we encounter a certain usefulness of art, or at least a reward for our undivided attention, in the shape of what Moritz calls rather enigmatically 'a kind of higher existence' (*eine Art von höheren Dasein*). The enigma disappears in a later essay where this kind of higher existence turns out to be a kind of redemption, a temporary deliverance from finiteness and mortality.[12]

It is not an accident that this sounds religious. Much secularized theology resonates in Moritz's theory of art: the 'selfless *love*' that true art requires is not so different from the loving devotion to God that Quietism, the mystical Christian sect in which Moritz was brought up, expects from its believers.[13] There is a direct line from Moritz's aesthetic principles to the typical Romantic conception of art as a substitute for religion. Art replaces God as the object of love and devotion. With this, we come close to the art museum as the ideal temple for this love and devotion. Listen to Moritz's student Wilhelm Heinrich Wackenroder in his *Herzensergießungen eines kunstliebenden Klosterbruders* (Outpourings from the Heart of an Art-Loving Monk) of 1797:

---

11 Moritz 1785, 98.

12 *Über die bildende Nachahmung des Schönen* (1788), in Moritz 1997–99, II, 958–91.

13 'The pleasure we take in the beautiful must thus increasingly approach selfless *love* if it is to be genuine': Moritz 1785, 98. German Quietism was particularly inspired by the seventeenth-century French mystic Madame Guyon.

> Picture galleries are thought of as fairs where people judge, praise, and despise works of art in passing, but they should be temples where in silent and inexpressible humility and in inspiring solitude one may admire artists as the highest among mortals, and where, in long and uninterrupted contemplation of their works, one may warm oneself in the sunshine of the most eminent thoughts and sentiments.

The 'joy of noble works of art' is like a 'prayer' according to Wackenroder, who, in his complaint about the 'fairs', joins Quatremère de Quincy in his aversion to the commercial side of art. But above all he joins Moritz in his quasi-religious approach to art. To Wackenroder, as to his close friend Ludwig Tieck (who after Wackenroder's early death in 1798 edited his writings) and to many other Romantics, museums were sacred places for individual aesthetic bliss.[14]

4   Schiller

The modern art museum, however, often pretends to be something more than that. The problem with making art autonomous – and here again Quatremère de Quincy proves to be of relevance – is that in the process art loses all traditional moorings. Aesthetic autonomy can be valued as a liberation and emancipation of art and the artist, but with it art sacrifices its social and political functions. That is why art, since it became autonomous, has to legitimize itself time and time again by inventing some social and political relevance for itself. In this respect autonomous art does not differ much from the art museum, something that underlines the intimate relationship between the two. The task is to find or invent a social and political function for art without giving up its autonomy.

Artists are still struggling with this rather paradoxical problem. Yet Friedrich Schiller (1759–1805), an admirer of Moritz, had already solved it in his famous *Letters on the Aesthetic Education of Man* of 1795. Focusing on the bloody aberrations of the French Revolution, Schiller presents a bleak view of the modern world. Modernity appears to cause many unforeseen evils, from the abstract 'barbarism' of the French elite to the murderous sensuality of the common people of France, and it causes estrangement, discord, and nihilism everywhere. To remedy this and to restore freedom and morality as well as harmony, Schiller offers his recipe for an aesthetic education for which the autonomy of

---

14   Wackenroder 1938/1967, 79.

FIGURE 11.4   Gerrit Jan Michaëlis, *Landscape at Vogelenzang*, 1824, oil on canvas, 77.5 x 100 cm.
TEYLER'S MUSEUM, KS 001

art is a necessary precondition. Art is a product of the present, but thanks to its autonomy it does not belong entirely to the present. As a result art is 'immune' (Schiller's word for autonomous in the *Ninth Letter*) to all modern ills and evils, and can be related to the art of older, healthier times, more specifically to the Classical art of ancient Greece.[15] Therefore an education by art, an education in true moral freedom, can serve as the great healer, able to purify modern culture and restore harmony between the senses and reason in the individual as well as in society. After all, a free, moral, and harmonious society is impossible without the presence of free, moral, and harmonious individuals.

Not only in spite of but also because of their autonomy, art and the art museum can have the social and political 'destination' that Quatremère de Quincy denied them. In many ways autonomous art and the art museum have a similar distant relationship to the present and to society, and together they can function so to speak as an Archimedean point, as a healing outsider. This constellation took material shape for the first time in the 1820s when Karl Friedrich Schinkel designed and built the first Berlin art museum, now called

---

15   *Über die ästhetische Erziehung des Menschen in eine Reihe von Briefe*, in Schiller 2004, V, 593.

the Altes Museum. In this Wackenroder's 'temple' was realized: it honoured Moritz's semi-sacred autonomy of the true work of art, and supported Schiller's aesthetic education with a social and political purpose.[16]

5   In Holland

How much of all this reached the Netherlands in the first decades of the nineteenth century? Here we can turn to Teyler's Museum, which opened its doors in 1784. Although there had been no mention of a museum in the 1756 will of its founder, Pieter Teyler van der Hulst, he had explicitly instructed the Foundation to collect natural and scientific artefacts, but *also* works of art. The latter initially consisted mostly of drawings and prints, but from the 1820s Teyler's Museum also collected and exhibited contemporary paintings. The fact that works of art were specifically mentioned is remarkable. Unfortunately we do not know much about the motives of the founder or of the Directors who introduced paintings to the collection, except that they hoped to raise the level of good taste in Holland. Their initial audience consisted of members of the two learned societies that the Museum was supposed to serve, but artists and the general public were later included.[17]

There had been many art lovers (*konst-beminders*) in the Dutch Republic since the seventeenth century – generally well-to-do men who collected works of art and who frequently met to enjoy and discuss them. A lively art market already existed in the late sixteenth century. *Kunst* or *konst* meant primarily the visual arts, but without the associations of the Romantic concept of art, such as aesthetic autonomy or Schiller's aesthetic education.[18] This is also true of the idea of Romanticism itself, with which these notions were associated in Germany and soon also in France.

There were however Dutchmen who showed some Romantic susceptibility early in the nineteenth century. In the 1820s a young Dutch scholar travelled through Germany. He arrived in Berlin too soon to visit Schinkel's museum (which opened in 1830), but in Dresden he visited the famous Gemäldegalerie. Overflowing with enthusiasm, he wrote in a letter to his parents in Zwolle:

---

16   See Sheehan 2000, 70–81; Wezel 2001; and Trempler 2012, 164.

17   See the contributions of Terry van Druten and Paul Knolle to this volume, as well as Ouwerkerk 2010.

18   See Vries 1992, 72–73; Leeuw/Reynaerts/Tempel 2005; and Bergvelt 2013, 361. For other discussions of the concept *kunst* (art) at that time see the contributions to this volume of Mijnhardt (p. 76) and Van Druten (p. 193, n. 8).

FIGURE 11.5 Johannes Christiaan Schotel, *Storm at Sea*, c. 1825, oil on canvas, 124.7 x 164.5 cm.
TEYLER'S MUSEUM, KS 004

FIGURE 11.6 Johannes Christiaan Schotel, *Calm Water*, 1829, oil on canvas, 125.5 x 165 cm.
TEYLER'S MUSEUM, KS 021

RISE OF MODERN ROMANTIC CONCEPT OF ART AND THE ART MUSEUM   251

A great past presents itself to the mind and lifts the mist that hindered the view of the height on which the genius of art gathers its high priests. Raphael, Correggio, Michelangelo open up to the young man a new world that he, just like Columbus, assumed to exist rather than knew about. One senses an indescribable desire not just to drink from this stream of pleasure but to jump right into it and go under.

Our susceptible young scholar from the Netherlands is none other than Johan Rudolf Thorbecke (1798–1872), later a very important liberal statesman, who was only twenty-three years old in October 1821. In the same letter to his increasingly anxious parents he described what the experience of art did for him. It could 'liberate me from all my doubts and unrest, and with mighty hand [it] puts the mind in the midst of the highest and the eternal and reconciles the divided heart with itself'.[19] Schiller's aesthetic education in action, one is tempted to conclude. This last quotation, though, does not reflect Thorbecke's experiences in the museum, but in the theatre, where he attended a performance of Mozart's *Don Giovanni*. In 1821, it seems, music was still a more appropriate key to the heart of a Romantic young Dutchman than an art gallery full of beautiful paintings and sculptures.

Although the word 'Romantic' was introduced in Dutch art criticism in the wake of the partial translation in 1810 of August Wilhelm Schlegel's *Vorlesungen über dramatische Kunst und Literatur* (Lectures on Dramatic Art and Literature) of 1809,[20] scholars are still debating whether a Romantic school existed in the Dutch visual arts of the early nineteenth century. In 2010 Ouwerkerk does indeed characterize quite a few earlier nineteenth-century paintings in the collection of Teyler's Museum as Romantic, albeit on the basis of their style and theme rather than on the theoretical convictions of their makers.[21] There is no evidence that the artists in question – Gerrit Jan Michaëlis (1775–1857; figure 11.4), Johannes Christiaan Schotel (1787–1838; figures 11.5, 11.6) and Cornelis Kruseman (1797–1857), to mention a few – shared the modern concept of art that is central to the present chapter. In the Netherlands Romantic art, associated with the modern concept of art and its attendant ideas, seems to have emerged only much later in the nineteenth century.[22]

---

19 Hooykaas 1991, 39–40. On Thorbecke's German trip see also Evers 2006, ch. 3.

20 *Geschiedenis der Tooneelkunst en Tooneelpoëzij, door A. W. Schlegel. Uit het Hoogduitsch vertaald door N. G. [Nicolaas Godfried] van Kampen*, I, Leiden 1810. No further parts were published.

21 Ouwerkerk 2010.

22 On the concept of 'Romantic/Romanticism' in the Netherlands see Berg 1973, Tilborgh 1984, and Leeuw/Reynaerts/Tempel 2005.

Bibliography

Manuscript Sources

Copenhagen
August Hermann Francke to Johann Georg von Holstein, 16 Dec. 1712. Royal Library, Ledreborg 389 2° a.

Dublin
Visitors' book of Levinus Vincent. Chester Beatty Library, Ms W 170.

Haarlem
Frans Hals Museum
Letter from H. J. Scholten to J. van Looy, 23 Nov. 1885. Jacobus van Looy Foundation, letter no. 1122.

Noord-Hollands Archief (NHA)
NL-HlmNHA_53002867_M; (3 states): NL-HlmNHA_1477_53012163; NL-HlmNHA_1477_53012164; NL-HlmNHA_1477_53012165.
Archive Martinus Van Marum NHA 529.
>529–6 Lectures.
>529–9 M. van Marum, 'De Geschiedenis van de oprigting van Teijler's Museum' 1823–33.
>529–10 Travel journals.
>529–11b M. van Marum, 'Journaal van mijne verrichtingen ter verkrijging eener Verzameling van Fossilia in Teyler's Museum'.
>529–11d M. van Marum, 'Journaal van mijne Verrichtingen ter verkrijging eener Verzameling van Physische Instrumenten & Modellen van nuttige Werktuigen in Teylers Museum', 1783–90.
>529–1423 Letters.

Archive Tekencollege Kunst Zij Ons Doel and predecessors, 1772–1972, 3496, no. 1 ('Tekenacademie: register van notulen van bestuursvergaderingen, 1775–1795'), 30.
Minutes 9 Nov. 1801, Kunstmin en Vlijt, later Kunst Zij Ons Doel, no. 3496–4.

Teyler's Foundation Archive, Teyler's Museum (ATS)
ATS 1: *Resolutien en Schikkingen van Heeren Executeurs van het Testament van de Heer Pieter Teyler van der Hulst, Directeurs van deszelfs Nalatenschap, 1778.*
ATS 5: *Registers van resoluties, naderhand notulen van de vergadering van het kollege van directeuren van de stichting, met indices, 1778–1945* (Registers of resolutions,

254 BIBLIOGRAPHY

subsequent meetings of the Board of Directors of the Foundation, with indexes, 1778–1945).

Board minutes (1778–1800): 6 Oct. 1780, 68; 5 Jan. 1781, 72–73; 25 Sept. 1784, 118–121 (*instructie voor den directeur*); 20 June 1785, 143–44 (*Instructie voor den Bewooner of Castelein van het Fundatiehuis van wylen de Heer Pieter Teyler van der Hulst*); 16 June 1786, 161; 13 March 1789, 193; 29 April 1789, 196; 13 Aug. 1790, 214; 11 March 1791, 224; 26 Oct. 1792, 243; 23 Nov. 1792, 245; 7 Dec. 1792, 246–247; 4 Jan. 1793, 247; 18 Jan. 1793, 248; 21 Feb. 1800, 356; 30 Oct. 1800, 372.

ATS 7: Board minutes (1816–28): 28 Jan. 1820, 123–24; 19 May 1820, 130; 20 May 1825, 248–54; 29 Sept. 1826, 316; 17 Nov. 1826, 324; 12 Oct. 1827, 347.

ATS 8: Board minutes (1828–1846): 13 June 1828, 1–7; 3 Oct. 1828, 20; 27 March 1829, 41–45; 10 July 1829, 47; 13 Aug. 1830, 81; 11 Aug. 1837, 222; 20 Oct. 1837, 224; 20 Sept. 1839, 276.

ATS 9: Board minutes (1846–67): 30 July 1852, 120.

ATS 11: Board minutes (1883–94): 28 Oct. 1887, 120.

ATS 147b: *Notitie van kunstbeschouwingen* (Note about art appreciation gatherings) 1873–96.

ATS 148–161: *Bezoekersregisters* (Visitors' books) 1789–1902.

ATS 148 (1789–1802); ATS 149 (1803–16); ATS 150 (1816–27); ATS 151 (1827–36); ATS 152 (1836–43); ATS 153 (1848–54); ATS 154 (1854–71); ATS 155 (1871–78); ATS 156 (1878–85); ATS 157 (1885–88); ATS 158 (1888–92); ATS 159 (1892–94); ATS 160 (1894–98); ATS 161 (1898–1902).

ATS 520: *Grootboek* (General Ledger), 184.

ATS 547–548 *Kasboeken* (Cash books).

ATS 610–634 *Kasbewijzen* (Receipts).

ATS 618-007-01; ATS 618-008-01; ATS 619-002-01.

ATS 622: (Invoices and receipts, 1790–1791), 622-607-01; ATS 622-011-01.

ATS 623-034-01.

ATS 624-002-01 (restorations); ATS 624-005-01; ATS 624-016-01.

ATS 629-022-01.

ATS 630-020-01; ATS 630-021-01; ATS 633-057-01; ATS 634-062-01.

ATS 1408–1411: (about the competition of 1781); see also the adjucations in no. 1412 (*Brieven en beoordelingen* [*van de prijsvraag van 1781*], *1783–1786*) (Letters and adjudications [of the 1781 competition], 1783–1786).

ATS 2283: A. Krantz to J. G. S. van Breda, 21 Feb. 1851.

Halle

Archiv der Franckeschen Stiftungen, AFSt/W VII/1/20: *Instruction für den Herumführer*.
Archiv der Franckeschen Stiftungen, AFSt/N: A. H. Niemeyer 1.
Archiv der Franckeschen Stiftungen, AFSt/N: A. H. Niemeyer 2.

BIBLIOGRAPHY   255

Washington, D.C.

Smithsonian Libraries, Dibner Library Manuscripts, Mss 000911 B folio, letter of Martinus van Marum to the 'Prince de Lambertini' with a drawing, 8 Oct. 1792.

Publications

Aa, A. J. van der, *Biographisch woordenboek der Nederlanden*, vol. 21 (1878).

Abrams, M. H., 'Art-As-Such: The Sociology of Modern Aesthetics', in M. H. Abrams, *Doing Things with Texts; Essays in Criticism and Critical Theory*, New York 1989, 135–58.

Ahlrichs., E., *Albertus Seba – zu seinem 250. Todestag. Monographie des berühmten Apothekers und Naturaliensammlers aus Ostfriesland*, Aurich 1986 (*Ostfriesische Familienkunde*, 6).

Algemeen Handelsblad, 1 March 1881, 22 Jan. 1885.

Algemeene Konst–en Letter-bode 251 (19 April 1793), 121–22; 271 (6 Sept. 1793), 78–79; 3 (17 Jan. 1794), 21–22.

Arti 1885: *Catalogus van de tentoonstelling van kunstwerken van levende meesters in de kunstzalen der Maatschappij Arti et Amicitiae*, Amsterdam 1885.

Aymonino, A., and A. Varrick Lauder, *Drawn from the Antique. Artists and the Classical Ideal*, London 2015.

Bacou, R., 'Le marquis de Lagoy, grand collectioneur du dix-huitième siècle', *L'Oeil* 91–92 (1962), 46–52.

Becq, A., *Genèse de l'esthétique française moderne 1680–1814*, Paris 1994 (1984[1]).

Beer, L. de, 'Voor iedere vriend van de wetenschap. Het publiek van het naturaliën-kabinet van de Hollandsche Maatschappij der Wetenschappen in de jaren 1772–1830', *Studium* 7/1 (2014), 19–35. DOI: http://doi.org/10.18352/studium.9428 (published online in 2014).

Bennett, J., and S. Talas (eds), *Cabinets of Experimental Philosophy in Eighteenth-Century Europe*, Leiden/Boston 2013 (*History of Science and Medicine Library*, 40).

Berg, W. van den, *De ontwikkeling van de term 'romantisch' en zijn varianten in Nederland*, Assen 1973.

Berg, W. van den, 'Literaire genootschapscultuur in Nederland', in Sliggers 1995, 11–15.

Berg, H. (ed.), *De gelykstaat der Joden. Inburgering van een minderheid*, Amsterdam/Zwolle 1996 [exh. Joods Historisch Museum, Amsterdam].

Berge-Gerbaud, M. van, M. Menalda, M. C. Plomp and C. van Tuyll van Serooskerken, *Hartstochtelijk verzameld. Beroemde tekeningen in 18de-eeuwse Hollandse collecties*, Paris/Bussum 2001 [exh. Teylers Museum, Haarlem/Institut Néerlandais, Paris 2001–2].

Bergvelt, E., 'J. A. Knip (1777–1847). De werkwijze van een 19de-eeuwse landschapschilder in relatie tot de kunsttheorie in Holland en Frankrijk omstreeks 1800', *Nederlands Kunsthistorisch Jaarboek* 27 (1976), 11–71.

Bergvelt, E., 'De élèves-pensionnaires van Koning Lodewijk Napoleon. Problemen bij de voltooiing van een Hollandse kunstopleiding in Parijs en Rome (1807–1813)'/'Gli élèves-pensionnaires di Re Luigi Napoleone. Problemi inerenti al perfezionamento a Parigi e a Roma di una formazione artistica conseguita in Olanda (1807–1813),' in *Reizen* 1984, 45–77.

Bergvelt, E., 'Koning Willem I als verzamelaar, opdrachtgever en weldoener van de Noordnederlandse musea', in C. Tamse and E. Witte (eds), *Staats- en natievorming in Willem I's koninkrijk*, Brussels 1992, 261–85.

Bergvelt, E., *Pantheon der Gouden Eeuw. Van Nationale Konst-Gallerij tot Rijksmuseum van Schilderijen (1798–1896)*, Zwolle 1998.

Bergvelt, E., 'Tussen geschiedenis en kunst. Nederlandse nationale kunstmusea in de negentiende eeuw', in Bergvelt/Meijers/Rijnders 2005a, 343–72.

Bergvelt, E., 'De Britse Parlementaire Enquête uit 1853. De "modernisering" van de National Gallery in Londen', in Bergvelt/Meijers/Rijnders 2005b, 319–42.

Bergvelt, E., 'Lodewijk Napoleon, de levende meesters en het Koninklijk Museum (1806–1810)', in *Lodewijk Napoleon en de kunsten in het Koninkrijk Holland*, Zwolle 2007 (*Nederlands Kunsthistorisch Jaarboek* 56/57 (2005–6)), 257–99.

Bergvelt, E., 'Tussen geschiedenis en kunst. Nederlandse nationale kunstmusea in de negentiende eeuw', in Bergvelt/Meijers/Rijnders 2013, 359–88.

Bergvelt, E., and C. Hörster, 'Kunst en publiek in de Nederlandse rijksmusea voor oude kunst (1800–1896). Een vergelijking met Bennetts *Birth of the Museum*', De Negentiende Eeuw 34 (2010), 232–48.

Bergvelt, E., and R. Kistemaker (eds), *De wereld binnen handbereik. Nederlandse kunsten rariteitenverzamelingen, 1585–1735*, 2 vols [1, essay vol. (1992a); 2, cat. (1992b)], Zwolle/Amsterdam 1992a,1992b.

Bergvelt, E., D. J. Meijers and M. Rijnders (eds), *Verzamelen. Van rariteitenkabinet tot kunstmuseum*, Heerlen 1993[1].

Bergvelt, E., D. J. Meijers and M. Rijnders (eds), *Kabinetten, galerijen en musea. Het verzamelen en presenteren van naturalia en kunst van 1500 tot heden*, Zwolle 2005[2].

Bergvelt, E., D. J. Meijers and M. Rijnders (eds), *Kabinetten, galerijen en musea. Het verzamelen en presenteren van naturalia en kunst van 1500 tot heden*, Zwolle 2013[3].

Bergvelt, E., D. J. Meijers, L. Tibbe and E. van Wezel (eds), *Napoleon's Legacy: The Rise of National Museums in Europe, 1794–1830*, Berlin 2009.

Berkel, K. van, 'Citaten uit het boek der natuur. Zeventiende-eeuwse Nederlandse naturaliënkabinetten en de ontwikkeling van de natuurwetenschap', in Bergvelt/Kistemaker 1992a, 169–91, 303–4.

Berkel, K. van, 'Institutionele verzamelingen in de tijd van de wetenschappelijke revolutie (1600–1750)', in Bergvelt/Meijers/Rijnders 2013, 145–68.

Berkel, K. van, and B. Ramakers (eds), *Petrus Camper in context. Science, the Arts, and Society in the Eighteenth-Century Dutch Republic*, Hilversum 2015.

BIBLIOGRAPHY

Bierens de Haan, J., *Van Oeconomische Tak tot Nederlandsche Maatschappij voor Handel en Techniek, 1777–1952*, Haarlem 1952.

Biografisch lexicon voor de geschiedenis van het Nederlands protestantisme, 6 vols, Kampen 1978–2006.

Bionda, R. W. A., 'De Amsterdamse verzamelaar J. A. Brentano (1753–1821) en de inrichting van zijn "zaal" voor Italiaanse kunst', *Bulletin van het Rijksmuseum* 34 (1986), 135–76.

Bleyerveld, Y., and I. M. Veldman, *The Netherlandish Drawings of the 16th Century in Teylers Museum*, Leiden 2016.

Bloemgarten, S., *Hartog de Hartog Lémon, 1755–1823. Joodse revolutionair in Franse Tijd*, Amsterdam 2007.

Boddington, J., E. Nickson, B. Wilson, J. Pringle, C. Frederick, C. Cocks *et al.*, 'Sundry Papers Relative to an Accident from Lightning at Purfleet, May 15, 1777', *Philosophical Transactions of the Royal Society of London* 68 (1778), 232–317.

Boeseman, M., 'The Vicissitudes and Dispersal of Albertus Seba's Zoological Specimens', *Zoologische Mededelingen* 44/13 (1970), 177–206.

Bolten, J. (ed.), *Miscellanea Humbert de Superville*, Leiden 1997.

Boom, M., Onvoorstelbare oudheid. Een revolutie in historisch denken rond 1800: https://www.shellsandpebbles.com/2018/05/05/onvoorstelbare-oudheid-een-revolutie-in-historisch-denken-rond-1800/.

Boom, M., Nature and Culture in the History of Time, 1760–1860, PhD dissertation (work in progress).

Bos, P., 'Rariteiten op Reis. De invloed van Albertus Seba's contacten met reizigers op de totstandkoming van zijn rariteitenkabinet', *Studium* 8/1 (2015), 1–17.

Bosch, R., 'Met wie las Pieter Teyler van der Hulst de *Vaderlandsche Letteroefeningen?*', *Tijdschrift voor tijdschriftstudies* 3/nos 5/6 (1999), 16–25. See also https://www.dbnl.org/tekst/_tst001199901_01/_tst001199901_01_0013.php.

Bouman, P., and P. Broers, *Teylers 'Boek – en Konstzael': de bouwgeschiedenis van het oudste museum van Nederland*, The Hague 1988 (*Kleine Monumenten Reeks*).

Bredekamp, H., B. Schneider and V. Dünkel (eds), *Das Technische Bild: Kompendium zu einer Stilgeschichte wissenschaftlicher Bilder*, Berlin 2012 (2008[1]); English transl. *The Technical Image: A History of Styles in Scientific Imagery*, Chicago 2015.

Brückner, J., ' "Ein vornehmer Herr hat ein Kabinett ..." Dresdner Sammler im 18. Jahrhundert', in U. C. Koch and C. Ruggero (eds), *Heinrich Graf von Brühl (1700–1763). Ein sächsischer Mäzen in Europa*, Dresden 2017, 194–211.

Bruijn, J. G. de, 'De prijsvragen van Teylers Genootschappen in de 18[e] eeuw', *Documentatieblad werkgroep Achttiende Eeuw* 3 (1971), 20–28.

Brunner, O., W. Conze and R. Koselleck, *Geschichtliche Grundbegriffe: Historisches Lexikon zur politisch-sozialen Sprache in Deutschland*, 8 vols, Stuttgart 1972–97.

Bunge, W. van, *et al.* (eds), 'Gerrit Willem van Oosten de Bruyn', in *The Dictionary of Seventeenth and Eighteenth-Century Dutch Philosophers*, London 2003, 752–54.

Burke, P., *What is the History of Knowledge*, Cambridge 2016.

Burtin, F.-X. (de), 'Réponse à la question physique [...] sur les révelations génerales, qu'a subies la surface de la terre, et sur l'ancienneté de notre globe', *Verhandelingen van Teyler's Tweede Genootschap* 8 (1790).

Burtin, F.-X (de), 'Verhandeling over de oorzaak van het gebrek aan uitmuntende historieschilders in ons land, en de middelen geschikt tot derzelver vorming', *Verhandelingen van Teyler's Tweede Genootschap* 17 (1809), 425–62.

Calkoen, J., 'Beschrijving van den Ornithorhynchus paradoxus of Zonderbaar Zoogend Vogel-bek-dier van Nieuwe Hollandia', *Natuurkundige Verhandelingen van de Hollandsche Maatschappij der Wetenschappen* 2/1 (1803), 177–87.

Chateaubriand, F. R. de, *Génie du Christianisme* (1802); English transl. by C. I. White: *The Genius of Christianity*, Philadelphia 1871; original French text in *Génie du Christianisme*, Paris 1978.

Chu, P. ten Doesschate, 'Nineteenth-Century Visitors to the Frans Hals Museum', in G. P. Weisberg and L. S. Dixon (eds), *The Documented Image. Visions in Art History*, Syracuse (N.Y.) 1987, 111–44.

Cohen, H. F., *The Scientific Revolution. A Historiographical Inquiry*, Chicago 1994.

Cooper, M. P., *Robbing the Sparry Garniture. A 200-Year History of British Mineral Dealers*, Tucson (Ariz.) 2006.

Craandijk, J., 'Pieter Teyler van der Hulst en zijne stichting te Haarlem', *Eigen Haard* 11 (1885), 116–22.

Cuvier, G., *Recherches sur les ossemens fossiles, où l'on rétablit les caractères de plusieurs animaux dont les révolutions du globe ont détruit les espèces*, vol. 5, Paris 1823.

Daalder, R., 'Haarlem en de Democratische Revolutie. Haarlem van Patriottentijd tot Bataafse Revolutie (1787–1795)', *Jaarboek Haerlem* 1975, 129–229.

Dackerman, S. (ed.), *Prints and the Pursuit of Knowledge in Early Modern Europe*, Cambridge/New Haven/London 2011.

Dam, M. van, 'J. van Maanen Adriaansz. en de kunst', *Oud Rhenen* 21/3 (2002), 38–51.

Daston, L., and P. Galison, *Objectivity*, New York 2007.

Daston, L., and K. Park, *Wonders and the Order of Nature: 1150–1750*, New York 2001 (1998[1]).

Dekkers, D., 'De bedevaart der jonge kunstenaars. Achtergronden van de kunstreis der Noordnederlandse schilders naar Rome omstreeks 1800', in *Reizen* 1984, 25–43.

Delbourgo, J., *Collecting the World. Hans Sloane and the Origins of the British Museum*, London 2017.

Dethmar, F. W., *Freundliche Erinnerung an Holland und seine Bewohner*, Rotterdam 1839.

Deugd boven geweld. Een geschiedenis van Haarlem, 1245–1995, Hilversum 1995.

BIBLIOGRAPHY

Dézallier d'Argenville, A. J., *La conchyliologie, ou, Histoire naturelle des coquilles de mer, d'eau douce, terrestres et fossiles: avec un traité de la zoomorphose, ou, représentation des animaux qui les habitent, ouvrage dans lequel on trouve une nouvelle méthode de les diviser*, Paris 1780[3].

Dhombres, N. and J., *Naissance d'un nouveau pouvoir: sciences et savants en France 1793–1824*, Paris 1989.

Dibner, B., *Early Electrical Machines. The Experiments and Apparatus of Two Enquiring Centuries (1600 to 1800) that led to the Triumphs of the Electrical Age*, Norwalk (Conn.) 1957.

Diderot, D., and J. le Rond d'Alembert, *Encyclopédie ou Dictionnaire raisonné des sciences, des arts et des métiers*, 28 vols, Paris 1751–72.

Dietz, B., 'Making Natural History: Doing the Enlightenment', *Central European History* 43/1 (2010), 25–46.

Dijksterhuis, F. J., *Wereld van Vernuft. Denken over kennis in de vroegmoderne tijd* (Oration, Faculty of the Humanities, VU (Free University)), Amsterdam 2017.

Directorium der Franckeschen Stiftungen, *Die Stiftungen August Hermann Franckes zu Halle. Festschrift zur zweiten Säcularfeier seines Geburtstages*, Halle 1863.

Dixhoorn, A. van, 'Nature, Play and the Middle Dutch Knowledge Community of Brussels in the late Fifteenth and Early Sixteenth Centuries', in B. Noak (ed.), *Wissenstransfer und Auctoritas in der frühneuzeitlichen niederländischsprachigen Literatur*, Göttingen 2014, 99–122.

Dixhoorn, A. van, 'De Rederijkerskamers', in J. Jansen and N. Laan (eds), *Van Hof tot Overheid. Geschiedenis van literaire instituties in Nederland en Vlaanderen*, Hilversum 2015, 67–92.

Dixhoorn, A. van, and B. de Munck, 'Working Bodies, Matter and the Performance of Knowledge: The Mechanical and Liberal Arts in the Civic Community', in S. Dupré et al., *Embattled Territory. The Circulation of Knowledge in the Spanish Netherlands*, Ghent 2015, 255–78.

Dolezel, E., *Der Traum vom Museum. Die Kunstkammer im Berliner Schloss um 1800 – eine museumsgeschichtliche Verortung*, Berlin 2019.

Driedger, M., 'Anabaptists and the early state: a long-term view', in Roth 2007, 507–44.

Driessen-van het Reve, J. J., *De Kunstkamera van Peter de Grote. De Hollandse inbreng, gereconstrueerd uit brieven van Albert Seba en Johann Daniel Schumacher uit de jaren 1711–1752*, Hilversum 2006.

Driessen-van het Reve, J. J., and O. P. Bleker (eds), *Geloof alleen je eigen ogen: een actuele kijk op de anatomische preparaten van Frederik Ruysch (1638–1731)*, Hilversum [2017].

Druten, T. van, 'Een Atelier in het Museum', in Jonkman/Geudeker 2010, 76–77.

Druten, T. van, 'Teylers Museum en de aquarel. Museaal verzamelen en presenteren in de negentiende eeuw', in Druten/Dijk/Sillevis 2015, 70–87.

260 BIBLIOGRAPHY

Druten, T. van, M. van Dijk and J. Sillevis, *De aquarel. Nederlandse meesters van de negentiende eeuw*, Bussum 2015.

Du Bos (or Dubos), J.-B. called abbé Du Bos, *Réflexions critiques sur la poésie et sur la peinture*, Paris 1719, repr. Geneva 1967.

Duin, P. van (ed.), *Collector's Cabinet with Miniature Apothecary's Shop*, Amsterdam 2017.

Dumas, C. (ed.), *Een koninklijk paradijs. Aert Schouman en de verbeelding van de natuur*, Dordrecht/Zwolle 2017 [exh. Dordrechts Museum, Dordrecht].

Eijnatten, J. van, 'The turning of the tide. German-Dutch intellectual influences at the interface of Pietism and Enlightenment', in Jost/Zaunstöck 2012, 128–39.

Engel, J. J., *De kunst van nabootzing door gebaarden* [Dutch transl. by J. Konijnenburg], Haarlem 1790[1].

Engel, J. J., *De kunst van nabootzing door gebaarden* [Dutch transl. by J. Konijnenburg], Utrecht 1807[2].

Engel, J. J., *Practical illustrations of rhetorical Gesture and Action, adapted to the English drama*, London 1822.

Engel, H., 'The life of Albert Seba', *Svenska Linnésällskapets årsskrift* 20 (1937), 75–100.

Engel, H., 'The sale-catalogue of the cabinets of natural history of Albertus Seba (1752)', *Bulletin of the Research Council of Israel, Section B, Zoology* (1961), 119–31.

H. Engel's Alphabetical List of zoological cabinets and menageries, 2nd, enlarged edn by P. Smit, with the assistance of A. P. M. Sanders and J. P. F. van der Veer, Amsterdam 1986 (*Nieuwe Nederlandse bijdragen tot de geschiedenis der geneeskunde en der natuurwetenschappen*, 19; originally published in *Bijdragen tot de dierkunde* 37 (1939)).

Evers, M., *Begegnungen mit der deutschen Kultur. Niederländisch-deutsche Beziehungen zwischen 1780–1920*, Würzburg 2006.

Eynden, R. van, *Antwoord op de vraag van Teylers Tweede Genootschap te Haarlem, voor den jaare MDCCLXXXII uitgeschreven over den nationaalen smaak der Hollandsche school in de teken- en schilderkunst*, Haarlem 1787 (*Verhandelingen, uitgegeeven door Teyler's Tweede Genootschap. Vyfde stuk, bevattende een antwoord op de vraag in de teken- en schilder-kunde, uitgeschreeven voor den jaare MDCCLXXXII en waaraan de gouden eer-prys is toegeweezen in den jaare MDCCLXXXIII*).

Eynden, R. van, and A. van der Willigen, *Geschiedenis der vaderlandsche schilderkunst, sedert der helft der XVIII eeuw*, 4 vols (1, 1816; 2, 1817; 3, 1820; 4, 1840 (appendix)), Haarlem 1816–40.

Faujas de Saint-Fond, B., *Histoire Naturelle de la Montagne de Saint-Pierre de Maestricht*, Paris 1798.

Findlen, P., 'The Museum: its Classical Etymology and Renaissance Genealogy', *Journal of the History of Collections* 1 (1989), 59–78.

Findlen, P., *Possessing Nature. Museums, Collecting, and Scientific Culture in Early Modern Italy*, Berkeley 1994.

BIBLIOGRAPHY

Findlen, P., 'Anatomy Theatres, Botanical Gardens, and Natural History Collections', in K. Park and L. Daston (eds), *The Cambridge History of Science*, III, *Early Modern Science*, Cambridge 2006, 272–89.

Fitz, O., 'Eine Sammlung Erzählt. Beitrag zu Inhalt und Geschichte der Mineralien- und Gesteinssammlung an der Abteilung Baugeologie des Institutes für Bodenforschung und Baugeologie, Universität für Bodenkultur, Wien', *Mitteilungen des Institutes für Bodenforschung und Baugeologie, Universität für Bodenkultur*, 1993, 1–80.

Forbes, R. J., E. Lefebvre and J. G. de Bruijn (eds), *Martinus van Marum, Life and Work*, 6 vols, 1969–76, Haarlem (R. J. Forbes ed. (vols 1–3): 1, 1969; 2, 1970; 3, 1971; E. Lefebvre and J. G. de Bruijn eds (vols 4–6): 4, G. L'E. Turner and T. H. Levere, *Van Marum's scientific instruments in Teyler's Museum*, 1973; 5, *Martinus van Marum, Life and Work*, 1974; 6, *Martinus van Marum, Life and Work*, 1976).

Fox, R., *The Savant and the State. Science and Cultural Politics in Nineteenth Century France*, Baltimore 2012.

Freylinghausen, J. A., *Ausführlicher Bericht von der Lateinischen Schule des Waysenhauses zu Glaucha vor Halle. Zum Dienst derer die Nachfrage zu thun pflegen*, Halle 1736.

Fuchs, W., '160 Jahre Mineralien-Kontor: Dr. F. Krantz im Spiegel von Etiketten', *Mineralien Welt* 3 (1983), 4–5.

Geerlings, J., 'Hoe verlicht waren de genootschappen? De achttiende-eeuwse sociabiliteit in recent historisch onderzoek', *Tijdschrift voor geschiedenis* 127/2 (2014), 189–209.

Gelder, R. van, 'Liefhebbers en geleerde luiden. Nederlandse kabinetten en hun bezoekers', in Bergvelt/Kistemaker 1992a, 259–92, 309–12, 335–37.

Gelder, R. van, 'Paradijsvogels in Enkhuizen. De relatie tussen Van Linschoten en Bernardus Paludanus' in Gelder/Parmentier/Roeper 1998, 30–50.

Gelder, R. van, J. Parmentier and V. Roeper (eds), *Souffrir pour parvenir. De wereld van Jan Huygen van Linschoten*, Haarlem 1998.

Grafton, A., 'Isaac Vossius, Chronologer', in Jorink/Miert 2012, 43–85.

Grijzenhout, F., and C. van Tuyll van Serooskerken (eds), *Edele eenvoud. Neo-classicisme in Nederland 1750–1800*, Zwolle 1989 [exh. Frans Halsmuseum/Teylers Museum, Haarlem].

Grijzenhout, F., and H. van Veen (eds), *De Gouden Eeuw in perspectief. Het beeld van de zeventiende-eeuwse schilderkunst in later tijd*, Heerlen 1992 (English transl.: *The Golden Age of Dutch Painting in Historical Perspective*, Cambridge 1999).

Gronovius, J. F., *Index supellectilis lapideae: quam collegit, in classes & ordines digessit, specificis nominibus ac synonymis illustravit*, Leiden 1740[1] (1750[2]).

Grotius, H., *Poemata*, Leiden 1639.

Grundmann, G., 'Fundort-Etiketten aus Freiberg', *Lapis* 11 (1986), 61–62.

Haar, C. van de, 'G. W. van Oosten de Bruyn, stadshistorieschrijver van Haarlem', *Tijdschrift voor geschiedenis* 67 (1954), 209–23.

BIBLIOGRAPHY

Haarlems Dagblad and Ijmuider Courant, 29 Feb. 1996, 17 (Appendix).

Hamm, E., 'Mennonite Centres of Accumulation: Martyrs and Instruments' in Roberts 2011, 205–30.

Hampsher-Monk, I., K. Tilmans and F. van Vree (eds), *History of Concepts; Comparative Perspectives*, Amsterdam 1998.

Harkness, D., *The Jewel House. Elizabethan London and the Scientific Revolution*, New Haven 2008 (2007[1]).

Haüy, R.-J., *Essai d'une théorie sur la structure des cristaux, appliquée à plusieurs genres de substances crystallisées*, Paris 1784.

Heij, J. J. (ed.), *Een vereeniging van ernstige kunstenaars. 150 jaar maatschappij Arti et Amicitiae 1839–1989*, Amsterdam 1989.

Heiningen, T. W. van, *The Correspondence of Sebald Justinus Brugmans (1763–1819)*, The Hague 2010.

Heiningen T. W. van (ed.), *Wouter van Doeveren and Petrus Camper in Paris. Travel diaries, kept in the years 1752–1753, 1777 and 1787 and related correspondence*, The Hague 2014 (*Tools and sources for the history of science in the Netherlands*, 4).

Helsloot, P. N., *Het NUT in Haarlem: twee eeuwen volksontwikkeling 1789–1989*, Haarlem 1989.

Hendriksen, M., ' "Art and Technique Always Balance the Scale": German Philosophies of Sensory Perception, Taste, and Art Criticism, and the Rise of the Term Technik, ca. 1735–ca. 1835', *History of Humanities* 2 (2017), 201–19.

Henket, H.-J., *Waar nieuw en oud raken. Een pleidooi voor houdbare moderniteit in architectuur*, Eindhoven 2013.

Heumakers, A., *De esthetische revolutie. Hoe Verlichting en Romantiek de Kunst uitvonden*, Amsterdam 2015.

Holthuis, L. B., 'Albertus Seba's "Locupletissimi rerum naturalium thesauri ..." (1734–1765) and the "Planches de Seba" (1827–1831)', *Zoologische Mededelingen* 43 (1969), 239–52.

Hommel, K., 'Physico-theology as mission strategy. Missionary Christoph Samuel John's (1746–1813) understanding of nature', in A. Gross, Y. V. Kumaradoss and H. Liebau (eds), *Halle and the Beginning of Protestant Christianity in India*, III, *Communication between India and Europe*, Halle 2006, 1115–33.

Hommel, K., 'Kunst und Naturaliensammlungen', in D. Döring (ed.), *Geschichte der Stadt Leipzig*, II, *Von der Reformation bis zum Wiener Kongress*, Leipzig 2016, 431–42.

Hoogstraten, D. van, *Groot algemeen historisch, geographisch, en oordeelkundig woordenboek*, The Hague 1723.

Hoorn, M. van, 'De prijsvragen en Verhandelingen van Teylers Tweede Genootschap (I)', *Teylers Museum Magazijn* 7/3 (Autumn 1989), no. 24, 7–11.

Hoorn, M. van, 'De prijsvragen en Verhandelingen van Teylers Tweede Genootschap 1778–1866 (II): natuurkunde', *Teylers Magazijn* 8/1 (Winter 1990), no. 26, 9–13 [NB no. 25 was the last issue called *Teylers Museum Magazijn*].

BIBLIOGRAPHY

Hoorn, M. van, 'De prijsvragen en Verhandelingen van Teylers Tweede Genootschap 1778–1866 (III): historiekunde', *Teylers Magazijn* 9/4 (Winter 1991), no. 33, 13–17.

Hooykaas, R., 'La correspondance de Haüy et de van Marum', *Bulletin de la Société française de minéralogie et de cristallographie* 72 (1949), 408–48.

Hooykaas, G. J. (ed.), *Thorbecke op de romantische tour*, Amsterdam 1991.

Hornemann, D., and C. Veltmann, ' "Zur Erziehung der Jugend". Die Naturalienkammer August Hermann Franckes in der Tradition der frühneuzeitlichen Sammlungs- und Bildungskultur', in Zaunstöck/Müller-Bahlke/Veltmann 2013, 129–43.

Horst, I. Buckwalter, 'De vroege bloei van Teylers Godgeleerd Genootschap', in *'Teyler'* 1978, 112–18.

Hovens, D., *Lesboek voor de kinderen der christenen; by den aenvang der vatbaerheit voor onderwys. Behelzende de voornaemste gronden van godsdienst en zedekunde*, Leiden 1787 (1794²).

Huisman, T., *The Finger of God. Anatomical Practice in 17th-Century Leiden*, Leiden 2009.

Hunt, L., M. Jacob and W. W. Mijnhardt, *The Book that Changed Europe: Picart and Bernard's Religious Ceremonies of the World*, Cambridge (Mass.) 2010.

Ibelings, H., 'The architecture of Teylers Museum', in Scharloo 2010 (Dutch edn 2009), 30–39.

Impey, O., and A. MacGregor (eds), *The Origins of museums. The cabinet of curiosities in sixteenth- and seventeenth-century Europe*, Oxford 2017² (1985¹).

Janse, G.-J., 'Out of curiosity and for instruction', in Scharloo 2010 (Dutch edn 2009), 10–29.

Jensen, L., 'Loosjes [Pz.], Adriaan', in *Biografisch Woordenboek van Nederland*, see http://resources.huygens.knaw.nl/bwn1780-1830/lemmata/data/Loosjes (accessed 28 Oct. 2018).

Jong, E.A. de, *Nature and Art. Dutch Garden and Landscape Architecture, 1650–1740*, Philadelphia 2000.

Jonge, A. D. de, 'Het Haarlems genootschapsleven en de rol van de Doopsgezinden daarin', *Teylers Museum Magazijn* 7/4 (Winter 1989), no. 25, 8–13.

Jonge, A. D. de, 'Gezelschappen in Haarlem rond 1800', in Sliggers 1995, 16–25.

Jonge, A. D. de, 'Pieter Teylers testamentaire benoemingen. "Doopsgezinden, zo die daartoe bequaam zijn" ', in Sliggers 2006, 115–25.

Jongste, J. A. F. de, *Onrust aan het Spaarne. Haarlem in de jaren 1747–1751*, Dieren 1984.

Jonker, M., 'Cornelis Apostool (1762–1844), cultureel ambtenaar', *Bulletin van het Rijksmuseum* 25 (1977), 97–112.

Jonkman M., and E. Geudeker (eds), *Mythen van het Atelier. Werkplaats en schilderpraktijk van de negentiende-eeuwse Nederlandse kunstenaar*, The Hague/Zwolle 2010.

Jorink, E., *Het Boeck der Natuere. Nederlandse gheleerden en de wonderen van Gods Schepping 1575–1715*, Leiden 2007. See also Jorink 2010.

Jorink, E., *Reading the Book of Nature in the Dutch Golden Age, 1575–1715*, Leiden 2010 [English transl. of Jorink 2007].

Jorink, E., 'Sloane and the Dutch Connection', in A. Walker, M. Hunter and A. MacGregor (eds), *From Books to Bezoars. Sir Hans Sloane (1660–1753) and his Collections*, London 2012, 50–67.

Jorink, E., *De Ark, de Tempel, Het Museum, Veranderende modellen van Kennis in de Eeuw van de Verlichting* [Inaugural lecture, Leiden University], Haarlem 2015.

Jorink, E., and A. Maas, *Newton and the Netherlands. How Isaac Newton was fashioned in the Dutch Republic*, Leiden 2012.

Jorink, E., and D. van Miert (eds), *Isaac Vossius (1618–1689) between Science and Scholarship*, Leiden/Boston 2012.

Jorink, E., and B. Ramakers (eds), *Art and Science in the Early Modern Low Countries* (*Netherlands Yearbook for History of Art/Nederlands Kunsthistorisch Jaarboek*, 61), Zwolle 2011.

Jost, E., '"... alles ist darin zu finden, nur keine Natur." Holländische Gärten in der Wahrnehmung mitteldeutscher Reisender um 1800', in Jost/Zaunstöck 2012, 154–67.

Jost, E., and H. Zaunstöck (eds) with W. Savelsberg, *Goldenes Zeitalter und Jahrhundert der Aufklärung. Kulturtransfer zwischen den Niederlanden und dem mitteldeutschen Raum im 17. und 18. Jahrhundert/Gouden Eeuw and Age of Reason. Cultural Transfer between the Netherlands and the Mid-German Territories in the 17th and 18th Century*, Halle 2012.

Kersten, M., 'Een schilderijenzaal of een gehoorzaal. De polemiek tussen Directeuren en Genootschappen over de bestemming van de ruimte onder de leeszaal van Teylers Stichting (1824–1829)', *Teylers Museum Magazijn* 4/4 (Autumn 1986), no. 13, 9–12.

Kikkert, P., 'Verhandeling ter beantwoording der vraag: wat is de reden, dat de Nederlandsche school, zoo wel voorheen ten tyde van haren grootsten bloei, als hedendaags, zoo weinig meesters in het historisch vak heeft opgeleverd; daar zy zoo uitnemend slaagde en nog slaagt in alles wat de eenvoudige navolging der natuur, of de meer beperkte kring van het huisselyk leven het vermogen der kunst aanbiedt: en welke zyn de middelen, om in dit land uitmuntende historieschilders te vormen?', *Verhandelingen uitgegeven door Teyler's Tweede genootschap. Zeventiende stuk, opgevende de redenen van het klein getal der Nederlandsche historieschilders, en de middelen om in dit gebrek te voorzien* 17 (1809), 1–246.

Klosterberg, B. (ed.), *Licht und Schatten. August Hermann Niemeyer – ein Leben an der Epochenwende um 1800*, Halle 2004a (*Kataloge der Franckeschen Stiftungen*, 13).

Klosterberg, B., 'Zwischen Preußen und Westphalen. Niemeyer als "Diplomat"' in Klosterberg 2004b, 142–53.

Kneppelhout, J., and G. Bilders, *Gekleurd grijs. Johannes Kneppelhout (1814–1885) en Gerard Bilders (1838–1865). Brieven en dagboek. Bezorgd door Wiepke Loos*, Zwolle 2009.

Knolle, P., 'De Amsterdamse stadstekenacademie, een 18de-eeuwse "oefenschool" voor modeltekenaars', *Nederlands Kunsthistorisch Jaarboek* 30 (1979), 1–41.

BIBLIOGRAPHY

Knolle, P., 'Het departement der tekenkunde van Felix Meritis', *Documentatieblad Werkgroep achttiende eeuw* 15/2 [59–60] (1983), 141–96.

Knolle, P., 'Cornelis Ploos van Amstel als pleitbezorger van de "Hollandse" iconografie', *Oud Holland* 98/1 (1984a), 43–52.

Knolle, P., 'De waardering voor het landschapstuk in de Nederlandse kunsttheorie van de 18de en vroege 19de eeuw', in *Reizen* 1984b, 101–23.

Knolle, P., 'Tekenacademies in de Noordelijke Nederlanden: de 17de en 18de eeuw', in M. van der Kamp, P. G. J. Leijdekkers, J. L. Locher and J. B. H. Vierdag (eds), *De Lucaskrater. Historie en analyse van en meningen over het beeldende-kunstonderwijs aan de kunstacademies in Nederland*, Assen 1984c, 19–33.

Knolle, P., ' "Edele eenvoudigheid". De waardering voor klassieke kunst bij Nederlandse kunsttheoretici 1750–1800', in Grijzenhout/Tuyll van Serooskerken 1989a, 33–43.

Knolle, P., 'Dilettanten en hun rol in 18de-eeuwse Noordnederlandse tekenacademies', in *Academies of Art between Renaissance and Romanticism*, The Hague 1989b, 289–301 (*Leids Kunsthistorisch Jaarboek* 5–6 [1986–87]).

Knolle, P., ' "Het kunstkarakter onzer schildernatie". Nationale èn internationale oriëntatie bij het stimuleren van de `Hollandse school" 1750–1820', *Documentatieblad Werkgroep achttiende eeuw* 24 (1992), 121–39.

Knolle, P., and H. Stroomberg, ' "The most amusing studies". Thomas Rowlandson en Nederland', *Leids Kunsthistorisch Jaarboek* 12 (2002), 177–204.

Knolle, P., and R. Vlek, 'Aquarellen van vogels en andere dieren en planten', in Dumas 2017, 230–75.

Konijnenburg, J., *De kunstverdiensten van Angelika Kauffmann, en Raphaël*, Amsterdam 1810. See also Engel 1790 and 1807.

Kooijmans, L., *Death Defied. The Anatomy Lessons by Frederik Ruysch*, Leiden/Boston 2010.

Koolhaas-Grosfeld, E. A., 'Nationale versus goede smaak. Bevordering van nationale kunst in Nederland: 1780–1840', *Tijdschrift voor geschiedenis* 95 (1982), 605–36.

Koolhaas-Grosfeld, E., 'Op zoek naar de Gouden Eeuw. De herontdekking van de 17de eeuwse Hollandse schilderkunst', in Tilborgh/Jansen 1986, 28–49.

Kraayenga, A. E., 'Martinus van Marum en de bevordering van kunsten en wetenschappen in de aanvang van Teylers Stichting', *Teylers Museum Magazijn* 3/4 (Autumn 1985), no. 9, 12–15.

Krebel, G. F., *Die vornehmsten Europäischen Reisen, wie solche durch Deutschland, die Schweitz, die Niederlande, England, Frankreich, Italien, Dännemark, Schweden, Hungarn, Polen, Preussen und Rußland, auf eine nützliche und bequeme Weise anzustellen sind; mit Anweisung der gewöhnlichen Post- und Reise-Routen, der merkwürdigsten Oerter, deren Sehenswürdigkeiten, besten Logis, gangbaren Münz-Sorten, Reisekosten etc. auch einer neuen Sammlung von Post- und Bothen-Charten, Post-Verordnungen, Post-Taxen etc.*, Hamburg 1775.

Kristeller, P. O., 'The modern system of the arts', in P. O. Kristeller, *Renaissance Thought*, II, *Papers on Humanism and the Arts*, New York 1965, 163–227.

Kuby, E., 'Über Stock und Stein – August Hermann Niemeyer unterwegs in Europa', in Soboth 2007, 37–55.

Kurzer Bericht von des Pädagogii regii zu Glaucha vor Halle gegenwärtiger Verfassung, nebst einem Verzeichnisse der Kosten nach verschiedenen Fällen, Halle 1774.

Laan, K. ter, *Letterkundig woordenboek voor Noord en Zuid*, The Hague/Jakarta 1952[2]. See also https://www.dbnl.org/tekst/laan005letto1_01/colofon.php.

Lange, A. de, and G. Schwinge, 'Een snoer van tanden uijt Indien', in A. de Lange and G. Schwinge (eds), *Pieter Valkenier und das Schicksal der Waldenser um 1700*, Heidelberg 2004 (*Waldenser Studien*, 2).

La Peyrère, I., *Prae-adamitae – systema theologicum*, Amsterdam 1655.

Lasius, O., *Lasius' Beobachtungen über die Harzgebirge, nebst einer petrographischen Karte und einem Profilriss – Beiträge zur mineralogischen Naturkunde*, 2 vols, Hanover 1789–90.

Laslett, P., *The World We Have Lost: England Before the Industrial Age*, London 1995 (1965[1]).

Laube, S., 'Privilegierte Dinge für Unterprivilegierte? Die Kunstkammer im Waisenhaus', in E. Dolezel, R. Godel, A. Pečar and H. Zaunstöck (eds), *Ordnen – Vernetzen – Vermitteln. Kunst- und Naturalienkammern der Frühen Neuzeit als Lehr- und Lernorte*, Halle 2018 (*Acta Historica Leopoldina*), 49–72.

Lee, P. Young, 'The Musaeum of Alexandria and the formation of the Muséum in eighteenth-century France', *The Art Bulletin* 79 (1997), 385–412.

Leerrede ter aanprijzing van eensgezindheid in de Gemeente ter gelegenheid van de eerste zamenkomst der Vereenigde Doopsgezinde Gemeente te Haarlem 7 Nov. 1784 (over Hand. IV:32) [about Acts 4:32], Haarlem [1784].

Leeuw, R. de, J. Reynaerts and B. Tempel (eds), *Meesters van de Romantiek: Nederlandse kunstenaars 1800–1850*, Zwolle 2005 [exh. Kunsthal, Rotterdam].

Linnebach, A., *Das Museum der Aufklärung und sein Publikum. Kunsthaus und Museum Fridericianum in Kassel im Kontext des historischen Besucherbuches (1769–1796)*, Kassel 2014 (*Kasseler Beiträge zur Geschichte und Landeskunde*, 3).

Long, P. O., *Artisan/Practitioners and the Rise of the New Sciences, 1400–1600*, Corvallis (Ore.) 2011.

Loosjes, P. Azn., *De Republiek der Vereenigde Nederlanden, zinds de Noord-Americaansche onlusten, behelzende al het meerkwaardige voorgevallen in de Vereenigde Nederlanden, tot op den tegenwoordigen tyd*, vol. 26 (76th book) [NB: the series was started by J. Wagenaar], Amsterdam 1801.

Luc, J. A. de, *Lettres physiques et morales sur l'histoire de la terre et de l'homme: adressées à la Reine de la Grande Bretagne*, The Hague 1779–80.

BIBLIOGRAPHY

MacGregor, A., *Curiosity and Enlightenment. Collectors and Collections from the Sixteenth to the Nineteenth Century*, New Haven 2010.

Margócszy, D., *Commercial Visions. Science, Trade and Visual Culture in the Dutch Golden Age*, Chicago 2014.

Marcuard, F. von, *Die Zeichnungen Michelangelos im Museum Teyler zu Haarlem*, Munich 1900.

Marum, M. van, 'Beschryving eener ongemeen groote electrizeer-machine, geplaatst in Teyler's Museum te Haarlem, en van de proefneemingen met dezelve in 't werk gesteld. Description d'une très-grande machine électrique, placée dans le Museum de Teyler, à Haerlem, et des expériences faites par le moyen de cette machine', *Verhandelingen van Teyler's Tweede Genootschap* 3 (1785).

Marum, M. van, 'Eerste vervolg der proefneemingen, gedaan met Teyler's electrizeer-machine. Première continuation des expériences, faites par le moyen de la machine électrique Teylerienne', *Verhandelingen van Teyler's Tweede Genootschap* 4 (1787).

Marum, M. van, 'Beschryving der beenderen van den kop van eenen visch, gevonden in de St. Pietersberg by Maastricht, en geplaatst in Teylers Museum', *Verhandelingen van Teyler's Tweede Genootschap* 8 (1790), 383–89.

Marum, M. van, 'Tweede vervolg der proefneemingen gedaan met Teyler's electrizeermachine. Seconde continuation des expériences, faites par le moyen de la machine électrique teylerienne', *Verhandelingen van Teyler's Tweede Genootschap* 9 (1795).

Marum, M. van, 'Beschryving van het bekkendeel van een jongen walvisch, geplaatst in het naturaliencabinet van deeze maatschappy', *Natuurkundige Verhandelingen van de Hollandsche Maatschappij der Wetenschappen* 1/2 (1801), 199–202.

Marum, M. van, 'Waarnemingen betreffende den vegetalen oorsprong der steenkolen', *Verhandelingen Ie Klasse Koninklijk Nederlandsch Instituut van Wetenschappen* 3 (1817), 230–45 (lecture, 12 May 1814).

Marum, M. van, *Catalogus der bibliotheek van Teylers Stichting*, Haarlem 1826.

McClellan, A., *Inventing the Louvre. Art, Politics, and the Origins of the Modern Museum in Eighteenth-Century Paris*, Berkeley/Los Angeles/London 1994.

Meeker, N., *Voluptuous Philosophy. Literary materialism in the French Enlightenment*, New York 2006.

Meer, G. van der, 'De prijsvragen en Verhandelingen van Teylers Tweede Genootschap 1781–1866 (IV): numismatiek', *Teylers Magazijn* 10/1 (Spring 1992), no. 34, 9–15.

Meijer, B. W., *The Famous Italian Drawings at the Teyler Museum in Haarlem*, Milan 1984.

Meijers, D. J., 'Het "encyclopedische" museum van de achttiende eeuw', in Bergvelt/Meijers/Rijnders 1993[1], 205–24.

Meijers, D. J., 'Sir Hans Sloane and the European Proto-Museum', in R. G. W. Anderson, M. L. Caygill, A. G. MacGregor and L. Syson (eds), *Enlightening the British. Knowledge, discovery and the museum in the eighteenth century*, London 2003, 11–17.

Meijers, D. J., 'Het "encyclopedische" museum van de achttiende eeuw', in Bergvelt/Meijers/Rijnders 2005[2], 153–78.

Meijers, D. J., 'Het "encyclopedische" museum van de achttiende eeuw', in Bergvelt/Meijers/Rijnders 2013[3], 169–94.

Meijers, D. J., 'A classification based on schools of art? The picture galleries of Sanssouci (Potsdam 1763) and Vienna (1781) as seen through the eyes of the Berlin publisher, book dealer and writer Friedrich Nicolai', in Generaldirektion der Stiftung Preußische Schlösser und Gärten Berlin-Brandenburg (ed.), *Die Bildergalerie Friedrichs des Grossen. Geschichte – Kontext – Bedeutung*, Regensburg 2015, 135–52.

Meijers, D. J., 'Das Galeriepublikum: Momente seiner Genese 1625–1800', in A. Husslein-Arco and T. G. Natter (eds), *Fürstenglanz: die Macht der Pracht*, Vienna 2016, 35–45.

Meijers, D. J., 'Magnets, minerals and books for Teyler's Museum. Martinus van Marum's Russian aspirations in the period c. 1800', *Journal of the History of Collections* 29/2 (2017), 291–308.

Meijers, D. J., 'Das Papiermuseum der St. Petersburger Akademie der Wissenschaften – revisited', in E. Dolezel, R. Godel, A. Pecar, H. Zaunstöck (eds), *Die Ordnungen der Dinge*, Halle/Stuttgart 2018, 355–82 (*Acta Historica Leopoldina*, 70).

Meijers, D. J., 'Gnade, Vergünstigung oder Recht. Die Zugänglichkeit der k.k. Hofsammlungen in Wien und das Publikum, 1765–1825', in N. Fischer and A. Mader-Kratky (eds), *Schöne Wissenschaften. Sammeln, Ordnen und Präsentieren im josephinischen Wien*, Österreichische Akademie der Wissenschaften, Vienna 2021.

Mencfel, M., *Skarbce natury i sztuki. Prywatne gabinety osobliwości, kolekcje sztuki i naturaliów na Śląsku w wieku XVII i XVIII*, Warsaw 2010.

Mérian, J.-B., *Mémoires sur le problème de Molyneux*, ed. F. Markovits, Paris 1984.

Meusel, J. G., 'Zeichnungen von Michael Angelo', *Neues Museum für Künstler und Kunstliebhaber* 3 (1794), 361–64.

Meyer A., and B. Savoy (eds), *The Museum is Open. Towards a Transnational History of Museums 1750–1940*, Berlin 2014 (*Contact Zones*, 1).

Mijnhardt, W. W., 'Veertig jaar cultuurbevordering: Teylers Stichting 1778–1815' in 'Teyler' 1978, 58–111.

Mijnhardt, W. W., *Tot Heil van 't Menschdom. Culturele genootschappen in Nederland, 1750–1815*, Amsterdam 1988 [NB according to the Amsterdam University Library this book was published in 1987].

Mijnhardt, W. W., 'Les sciences en révolution: une affaire d'état', in A. Jourdan and J. Leerssen (eds), *Remous révolutionnaires: République batave, armée française*, Amsterdam 1996, 200–219.

Mijnhardt, W. W., 'De Zeeuwse burger en zijn Teeken Collegie' in K. Heyning and G. van Herwijnen (eds), '*Om prijs en plaats'. De Middelburgse Teeken Akademie 1778–2003*, Middelburg 2004a, 9–26.

Mijnhardt, W. W., 'De Akademie in het culturele landschap rond 1900', in K. van Berkel (ed.), *De Akademie en de Tweede Gouden Eeuw*, Amsterdam 2004b (*Bijdragen tot de geschiedenis van de Koninklijke Nederlandse Akademie van Wetenschappen*, 6), 15–41.

Mijnhardt, W. W., 'Verlichtingsidealen', *De Gids* 169 (2006), 817–20.

Miles, J., 'General Introduction', in *The Norton Anthology of World Religions*, 3 vols, New York 2015, II, 23–39.

Molhuysen P. C., and K. H. Kossmann (eds), *Nieuw Nederlandsch biografisch woordenboek*, IX, Leiden 1933.

Moritz, K. P., 'Versuch einer Vereinigung aller schönen Künste und Wissenschaften unter dem Begriff des In sich selbst Vollendeten', *Berlinische Monatsschrift* 1785; also published in Moritz 1997–99, II, 943–49. (For English transl. see Moritz 2012).

Moritz, K. P., H. Hollmer and A. Meier (eds), *Werke*, 2 vols, Frankfurt am Main 1997–99.

Moritz, K. P., intr. and transl. E. Schreiber, 'An Attempt to Unify All the Fine Arts and Sciences under the Concept of "That Which Is Complete in Itself"', *PMLA* 127/1 (2012), 94–100. See also www.jstor.org/stable/41616796.

Müller-Bahlke, T. J., 'Die Einzigartigkeit der Kunst- und Naturalienkammer in den Franckeschen Stiftungen' in U. Troitzsch (ed.), '*Nützliche Künste'. Kultur- und Sozialgeschichte der Technik im 18. Jahrhundert*, Münster/New York/Munich/Berlin 1999 (*Cottbuser Studien zur Geschichte von Technik, Arbeit und Umwelt*, 13), 219–38.

Müller-Bahlke, T., *Die Wunderkammer der Franckeschen Stiftungen*, Halle 2012[2] (1998[1]).

Munck, B. de, *Guilds, Labour and the Urban Body Politic: Fabricating Community in the Southern Netherlands, 1300–1800*, London 2017.

Naamlyst des oeconomischen taks van de Hollandsche Maatschappye der Weetenschappen voor het jaar 1778, Haarlem 1778.

National Museums and National Identity, seen from an International and Comparative Perspective, c. 1760–1918. An Assessment by D. J. Meijers, E. Bergvelt, L. Tibbe and E. van Wezel, since 23 January 2012. See http://hdl.handle.net/11245/1.351258.

Niemeyer, J. A., *Chronologischer Abriß der Hauptveränderungen und Erweiterungen der Anstalten des Pädagogii regii und Waisenhauses von 1695 bis 1764*, Halle 1764.

Niemeyer, A. H., *Grundsätze der Erziehung und des Unterrichts für Eltern, Hauslehrer und Erzieher*, Halle 1796 (for Dutch transl. see Niemeyer 1799–1810).

Niemeyer, A. H., *Grondbeginselen van de opvoeding en het onderwijs voor ouders, leermeesters en opvoeders. [...] Uit het Hoogduitsch vertaald door Josué Teissèdre l'Ange*, 2 vols, Haarlem 1799–1810.

Niemeyer, A. H., *Beobachtungen auf Reisen in und außer Deutschland. Nebst Erinnerungen an denkwürdige Lebenserfahrungen und Zeitgenossen in den letzten funfzig Jahren*, I, Halle/Berlin 1820.

Niemeyer, A. H., *Beobachtungen auf einer Reise durch einen Theil von Westphalen und Holland. Nebst Erinnerungen an denkwürdige Lebenserfahrungen und Zeitgenossen in den letzten funfzig Jahren*, Halle 1824a[2] (1823[1]).

Niemeyer, A. H., *Waarnemingen op reizen in en buiten Duitschland, met herinneringen van merkwaardige levensgevallen en tijdgenoten in de laatste vijftig jaren*, III, Haarlem 1824b.

Nieuwenkamp, W., 'The Geological Sciences', in Forbes/Lefebvre/Bruijn, III, 1971, 192–238.

Nozeman, C., and M. Houttuyn, *Nederlandsche vogelen; volgens hunne huishouding, aert, en eigenschappen beschreven. Alle naer 't leeven geheel nieuw en naeuwkeurig getekend, in 't koper gebragt en natuurlyk gekoleurd*, IV, Amsterdam 1809.

[Obituary Klaas van der Horst], *Algemeene Konst – en Letterbode* 1825, vol. 1, 282–83.

Oddens, J., *Pioniers in schaduwbeeld. Het eerste parlement van Nederland 1796–1798*, PhD, University of Amsterdam, 2012. See https://pure.uva.nl/ws/files/1873341/111959_thesis.pdf.

Oddens, J., *Pioniers in schaduwbeeld: het eerste parlement van Nederland 1796–1798*, Nijmegen 2013.

Offerhaus, J., 'Van Isaac en Apollo. De prijswinnende tekeningen van de Amsterdamse stadstekenacademie', *Nederlands Kunsthistorisch Jaarboek* 30 (1979), 43–78.

Olsen, N., *History in the plural. An Introduction to the Work of Reinhart Koselleck*, New York/Oxford 2012.

Oprechte Haerlemsche Courant, 22 Nov. 1722, 24 June 1728.

Ouwerkerk, A., *Romantiek aan het Spaarne. Schilderijen tot 1850 uit de collectie van Teylers Museum Haarlem*, Amsterdam 2010.

Paarlberg, S., and H. Slechte (eds), *Willem II. De koning en de kunst* [also in French and Russian editions], Zwolle/Dordrecht/Luxemburg 2014 [exh. Hermitage, St Petersburg/Dordrechts Museum, Dordrecht/Villa Vauban – Musée d'Art de la Ville de Luxembourg, Luxemburg 2013–14].

Palm, L., 'Martinus van Marum 1750–1837', in K. van Berkel *et al.* (eds), *A History of Science in The Netherlands. Survey, Themes and Reference*, Leiden 1999, 519–22.

Peters, M., *De wijze koopman. Het wereldwijde onderzoek van Nicolaes Witsen (1641–1717), burgemeester en VOC-bewindhebber van Amsterdam*, Amsterdam 2009.

Picart, B., *Cérémonies and coutumes réligieuses de tous les peuples du monde*, 9 vols, Amsterdam 1723–43 [in several languages].

Piechocki, J., and C. Soboth, 'Gebildete Geselligkeit um 1800. Die Niemeyerei am Großen Berlin Nr. 432, Halle a. d. Saale', in Klosterberg 2004a, 218–27.

Pieters, F., 'Natural history spoils in the Low Countries in 1794/95: the looting of the fossil Mosasaurs from Maastricht and the removal of the cabinet and menagerie of Stadholder William V', in Bergvelt/Meijers/Tibbe/Wezel 2009, 55–72.

Pietist und Preussenkönig. Ein Dialog aus dem Jahr 1713, Halle 2005 (*Kleine Schriften der Franckeschen Stiftungen*, 10).

Plomp, M. C., *The Dutch Drawings in the Teyler Museum*, II, *Artists born between 1575 and 1630*, Haarlem/Ghent/Doornspijk 1997.

BIBLIOGRAPHY

Plomp, M. C., *Hartstochtelijk Verzameld. 18de-eeuwse Hollandse verzamelaars van teke-ningen en hun collecties*, Paris/Bussum 2001.

Ploos van Amstel, G., *Portret van een koopman en uitvinder Cornelis Ploos van Amstel maatschappelijk, cultureel en familieleven van een achttiende-eeuwer*, Assen 1980.

Pomian, K., *Collectionneurs, amateurs et curieux. Paris, Venise: XVIe–XVIIIe siècle*, Paris 1987.

Porte, E. J. de la, 'Verlichte verhalen. De omgang met het verleden in de Nederlandse verlichting', PhD, University of Amsterdam, 2019.

Prak, M., *Gezeten burgers. De elite in een Hollandse stad. Leiden 1700–1780*, The Hague 1985 (*Hollandse Historische Reeks*, 6).

Previtali, G., *La fortuna dei primitivi dal Vasari al Neoclassici*, Turin [1964] (*Saggi*, 343).

Previtali, G., *La fortune des primitifs de Vasari aux néo-classiques*, Paris 1994 (French transl. of Previtali 1964).

Quatremère de Quincy, A.-C., *Considérations morales sur la destination des ouvrages de l'art*, Paris 1815.

Quay, P. P. de, *De genoegzaamheid van het natuurlijk gezond verstand. Prijsverhande-lingen over godsdienst, zedenkunde en burgerlijke maatschapij in Nederland aan het eind van de 18e eeuw*, The Hague 2000 (*Nederlandse cultuur in Europese context; monografieën en studies*, 19).

Rees, J., and W. Siebers, *Erfahrungsraum Europa. Reisen politischer Funktionsträger des Alten Reiches 1750–1800. Ein kommentiertes Verzeichnis handschriftlicher Quellen*, Berlin 2005 (*Aufklärung und Europa*, 18).

Regteren Altena, C. O. van, 'Achttiende-eeuwse verzamelaars van fossielen te Maastricht en het lot hunner collecties', *Publicatiereeks IX, Natuurhistorisch Ge-nootschap Limburg* (1956), 83–112.

Regteren Altena, C. O. van, 'Nieuwe gegevens over achttiende-eeuwse verzamelaars van fossielen te Maastricht', *Natuurhistorisch Maandblad* 52 (1963), 28–32.

Regteren Altena, J. Q. van, *Les dessins italiens de la reine Christine de Suède*, Stockholm 1966 (*Analecta Reginensa*, II).

Regteren Altena, I. Q. van, J. H. van Borssum Buisman and C. J. de Bruyn Kops, *Wybrand Hendriks, 1744–1831: keuze uit zijn schilderijen en tekeningen*, Haarlem 1972.

Reich, M., A. Böhme *et al.*, ' "Preziosen jeglicher Couleur". Objektdigitalisierung der naturhistorischen Sammlungen von Johann Friedrich Blumenbach (1752–1840)', *Philippia* 15/2 (2012), 155–68.

Reizen naar Rome. Italië als leerschool voor Nederlandse kunstenaars omstreeks 1800 / Paesaggisti ed altri artisti olandesi a Roma intorno al 1800, Haarlem/Rome 1984 [exh. Teylers Museum, Haarlem / Istituto Olandese, Rome].

Reynaerts, J., 'Het karakter onzer Hollandsche school'. De Koninklijke Akademie van Beel-dende Kunsten te Amsterdam, 1817–1870, Leiden 2001.

Reynolds, J., ed. H. Zimmern, *Sir Joshua Reynolds' Discourses*, London 1887.

272 BIBLIOGRAPHY

Rickert, H., *Kulturwissenschaft und Naturwissenschaft*, Freiburg 1899.

Rieke-Müller, A., 'Die außereuropäische Welt und die Ordnung der Dinge in Kunst- und Naturalienkammern des 18. Jahrhunderts – das Beispiel der Naturalienkammer der Franckeschen Stiftungen in Halle', in H.-J. Lüsebrink (ed.), *Das Europa der Aufklärung und die außereuropäische Welt*, Göttingen 2006 (*Das achtzehnte Jahrhundert. Supplementa*, 11), 51–73.

Roberts, L., 'Going Dutch: Situating Science in the Dutch Enlightenment', in W. Clark, J. Golinski and S. Schaffer (eds), *The Sciences in Enlightened Europe*, Chicago/London 1999, 350–88.

Roberts L. (ed.), *Centres and Cycles of Accumulation in and around the Netherlands during the Early Modern Period*, Berlin 2011 (*Low Countries Studies on the circulation of natural knowledge*, 2).

Roemer, B. van de, 'Neat Nature. The Relation between Art and Nature in a Dutch Cabinet of Curiosities from the Early Eighteenth Century', *History of Science* 42 (2004), 47–84.

Roemer, G. M. van de, 'De geschikte natuur. Theorieën over natuur en kunst in de verzameling van zeldzaamheden van Simon Schijnvoet (1652–1727)', PhD, University of Amsterdam, 2005.

Roemer, B. van de, 'Het lichaam als borduursel: kunst en kennis in het anatomisch kabinet van Frederick Ruysch', in A.-S. Lehman and H. Roodenburg (eds), *Body and Embodyment in Netherlandish Art* (*Nederlands Kunsthistorisch Jaarboek/Netherlandish Yearbook of the History of Art*, 58), Zwolle 2008, 216–40.

Roemer, B. van de, 'Regulating the arts. Willem Goeree versus Samuel van Hoogstraten', in Jorink/Ramakers 2011, 184–207.

Roemer, B. van de, 'Art opens the Book of Nature: Skilfulness and knowledge in Dutch Curiosity Cabinets around 1700', in G. Seelig (ed.), *Medusa's Menagerie. Otto Marseus van Schrieck and the Scholars*, Munich 2017, 127–70.

Roemer, B. van de, 'Von Uffenbach's visits. Disclosing the cultural industries of Amsterdam in the early eighteenth century' [forthcoming]

Roth, J., and J. Stayer (eds), *A Companion to Anabaptism and Spiritualism, 1521–1700*, Leiden 2007.

Rousseau, J.-J., *Émile, ou De l'éducation*, 4 vols, Amsterdam 1762.

Rudwick, M., *The Meaning of Fossils. Essays in the History of Paleontology*, Chicago 1985.

Rudwick, M. J. S., *Bursting the Limits of Time. The Reconstruction of Geohistory in the Age of Revolution*, Chicago/London 2005.

Rudwick, M., *Earth's Deep History: How It Was Discovered and Why It Matters*, Chicago 2014.

Ruhland, T., 'Objekt, Parergon, Paratext. Das Linné'sche System in der Naturalia-Abteilung der Kunst- und Naturalienkammer der Franckeschen Stiftungen', in K.

BIBLIOGRAPHY

273

Knebel, C. Ortlieb and G. Püschel (eds), *Steine rahmen, Tiere taxieren, Dinge insze-nieren. Sammlung und Beiwerk*, Dresden 2018 (*Parerga und Paratexte*, 1), 72–105.

Saeys, W., 'Haüy's Kristalmodellen in Teylers Museum', *Grondboor & Hamer* 57/1 (2003), 12–16.

Savoy, B., 'Zum Öffentlichkeitscharakter deutscher Museen im 18. Jahrhundert', in B. Savoy (ed.), *Tempel der Kunst. Die Entstehung des öffentlichen Museums in Deutschland 1701–1815*, Mainz 2006, 9–23.

Scharloo, M. (ed.), *Teylers Museum 1784–2009. Een reis door de tijd*, Haarlem 2009.

Scharloo, M. (ed.), *Teylers Museum. A journey in time*, Haarlem 2010 [English transl. of Scharloo 2009].

Schiller, F. von, *Sämtliche Werke* [based on the edn of H. G. Göpfert, ed. by P.-A. Alt *et al.*], 5 vols, Munich 2004.

Schlegel, A. W., *Geschiedenis der Tooneelkunst en Tooneelpoëzij. Uit het Hoogduitsch ver-taald door N. G.* [*Nicolaas Godfried*] *van Kampen*, I, Leiden 1810.

Schloms, A., *Institutionelle Waisenfürsorge. Im Alten Reich 1648–1806. Statistische Analyse und Fallbeispiele*, Stuttgart 2017 (*Beiträge zur Wirtschafts- und Sozialgeschichte*, 129).

Schlosser, Julius von, *Die Kunst- und Wunderkammern der Spätrenaissance: ein Beitrag zur Geschichte des Sammelwesens*, Leipzig 1908.

Schmid, P., 'Erzieherische Praxis und Bildungstheorie. Der Pädagoge Niemeyer', in Klosterberg 2004, 184–93.

Schmidt, F., *Paleizen voor Prinsen en Burgers. Architectuur in Nederland in de achttiende eeuw*, Zwolle 2006.

Schmidt, F., *Passion and Control: Dutch Architectural Culture of the Eighteenth Century*, Farnham/Burlington 2016.

Schneider, R., *Quatremère de Quincy et son intervention dans les arts (1788–1830)*, Paris 1910.

Schuller tot Peursum-Meijer, J., and W. R. H. Koops (eds), *Petrus Camper (1722–1789), onderzoeker van nature*, Groningen 1989.

Schulze, J. L., C. G. Knapp and A. H. Niemeyer, *Beschreibung des Hallischen Waisenhau-ses und der übrigen damit verbundenen Frankischen Stiftungen nebst der Geschichte ihres ersten Jahrhunderts. Zum Besten der Vaterlosen*, Halle 1799.

Seba, A., intro. by I. Musch, *Cabinet of Curiosities*, Cologne 2011.

Shapin, S., and S. Schaffer, *Leviathan and the air pump: Hobbes, Boyle and the experi-mental life*, Princeton 1985.

Sheehan, J. J., *Museums in the German Art World: From the End of the Old Regime to the Rise of Modernism*, Oxford 2000.

Shipman, P., *The man who found the missing link: Eugène Dubois and his lifelong quest to prove Darwin right*, New York 2001.

Sierstorpff, C. H. von, *Bemerkungen auf einer Reise durch die Niederlande nach Paris im eilften Jahre der grossen Republik*, II, Hamburg 1804.

Skinner, Q., 'Meaning and Understanding in the History of Ideas', *History and Theory* 8 (1969), 3–53.

Sliggers, B. C., 'Honderd jaar natuurkundige amateurs te Haarlem', in Wiechmann/ Palm 1987, 67–102.

Sliggers, B. C., *Augustijn Claterbos 1750–1828. Opleiding en werk van een Haarlems kunstenaar*, Zwolle 1990a.

Sliggers, B., 'Teyler, Teylers Stichting en het Haarlemse tekenonderwijs', *Teylers Magazijn* 8/1 (Winter 1990b), no. 26, 14–17.

Sliggers, B. C., 'De kwalen van Van Marum. Uit het dagboek van Adriaan van der Willigen (1831–1839)', *Teylers Magazijn* 9/4 (Winter 1991), no. 33, 6–10.

Sliggers, B. (ed.), *De verborgen wereld van Democriet. Een kolderiek en dichtlievend genootschap te Haarlem 1789–1869*, Haarlem 1995.

Sliggers, B. (ed.), *Hoogtepunten uit Teylers Museum: Geschiedenis, Collecties en Gebouwen*, Haarlem 1996a.

Sliggers, B. (ed.), *Highlights from the Teyler Museum: History, Collections and Buildings*, Haarlem 1996b [English transl. of Sliggers 1996a].

Sliggers, B., *et al.* (eds), *De idealen van Pieter Teyler. Een erfenis uit de Verlichting*, Haarlem 2006.

Sliggers, B., 'Een biografische schets van Pieter Teyler. Niets bij zijn leven, alles na zijn dood', in Sliggers 2006a, 15–45.

Sliggers, B., 'De verzamelingen van Pieter Teyler. Een bescheiden collectie voor eigen genoegen', in Sliggers 2006b, 75–91.

Sliggers, B. C., 'De verzamelwoede van Martinus van Marum (1750–1837) en de ouderdom van de aarde. Herkomst en functie van het Paleontologisch en Mineralogisch Kabinet van Teylers Museum', PhD, Leiden University, 2017.

Sliggers, B., and M. H. Besselink (eds), *Het Verdwenen Museum. Natuurhistorische Verzamelingen 1750–1850*, Blaricum 2002.

Smith, P., *The Body of the Artisan: Art and Experience in the Scientific Revolution*, Chicago 2004.

Smith, P., and B. Schmidt (eds), *Making Knowledge in Early Modern Europe. Practices, Objects and Texts 1400–1800*, Chicago 2007.

Snelders, H. A. M., 'Martinus van Marum 1750–1837', in A. J. Cox and M. Chamalaun (eds), *Van Stevin tot Lorentz. Portretten van Nederlandse Natuurwetenschappers*, Amsterdam 1980, 107–21.

Snelders, H. A. M., 'Martinus van Marum en de natuurwetenschappen', in Wiechmann/ Palm 1987, 155–82.

Soboth, C. (ed.), *'Seyd nicht träge in dem was ihr tun sollt'. August Hermann Niemeyer (1754–1828): Erneuerung durch Erfahrung*, Halle 2007 (*Hallesche Forschungen*, 24).

Stelter, M., *Zusammentragen von Wissen – Naturgeschichtliches Sammeln als geteilte Handlung am Beispiel der Kunst- und Naturalienkammer der Glauchaschen Anstalten*, Master Thesis, Potsdam University, 2014.

BIBLIOGRAPHY

Stikkelorum, M., 'De joodse gelijkberechtiging en de "verlichte" praktijk. De Maatschappij tot Nut van 't Algemeen onder de loep 1796–1798', in Wall/Wessels 2007, 358–73.

Streefland, A., 'Jaap Kistemaker en uraniumverrijking in Nederland 1945–1962', PhD, Leiden University, 2017.

Steur, A. G. van der, 'Haarlemse patriotten in 1795', *Jaarboek Haarlem* 1970, 182–203.

Sturm, A., *Die Oratorische Bibliothek des Königlichen Pädagogiums zu Halle*, Halle 2017 (*Kleine Schriftenreihe der Franckeschen Stiftungen* 16), 69–79.

Swan, C., 'Ad Vivum, Naer Het Leven, from the Life: Defining a Mode of Representation', *Word & Image* 11/4 (1995), 353–72.

Tex, E. den, 'Was basalt derived from water or from fire? Dutch contributions to an 18th-century controversy', in Touret/Visser 2004, 33–42.

'Teyler' 1778–1978 – studies en bijdragen over Teylers Stichting naar aanleiding van het tweede eeuwfeest, Haarlem/Antwerp 1978.

Teylers in Haarlem. Nomination by the Kingdom of the Netherlands for inscription on the UNESCO World Heritage List, 3 vols, Haarlem 2012 [vol. 1: Nomination file; vol. 2: Management plan; vol. 3: Appendices].

Theunissen, B., *Eugène Dubois en de aapmens van Java*, Amsterdam 1985.

Theunissen, B., 'Martinus van Marum, 1750–1837. "Ten nutte en ten genoegen der ingezetenen" ', in Wiechmann/Palm 1987, 11–32.

Tibbe, L., and M. Weiss (eds), *Druk bekeken, collecties en hun publiek in de negentiende eeuw*, Hilversum 2010 (*De Negentiende Eeuw* 34/3 (2010)).

Tilborgh, L. van, 'Dutch Romanticism: a provincial affair', *Simiolus: Netherlands Quarterly for the History of Art* 14 (1984), 179–88.

Tilborgh, L. van, and G. Jansen (eds), *Op zoek naar de Gouden Eeuw. Nederlandse schilderkunst 1800–1850*, Zwolle 1986.

Tilmans, K., and W. Velema, s.d. *Towards A European History of Concepts*: https://karintilmans.nl/pdf/concepts.pdf.

Touret, L., 'De betrekkingen van Georges Cuvier en Teylers Museum', *Teylers Museum Magazijn* 1/1 (Autumn 1983), no. 1, 8–12.

Touret, L., 'Een onverwachte museumschat: Etiketten', *Teylers Museum Magazijn* 3/1 (1985), no. 6, 4–7.

Touret, L., 'Crystal models: milestone in the birth of crystallography and mineralogy as sciences', in Touret/Visser 2004, 43–58.

Toussaint von Charpentier, J. F. W., *Mineralogische Beschreibung der chursächsischen Lande*, Leipzig 1778.

Trempler, J., *Karl Friedrich Schinkel, Baumeister Preussens. Ein Biographie*, Munich 2012.

Trijp, D. van, The development of ichthyology as a scientific discipline between the late seventeenth and early nineteenth century (working title; PhD Leiden, work in progress).]

Tuyll, C. van, 'Aanwinst: Het Teekencollegie te Haarlem door Wybrand Hendriks', *Teylers Museum Magazijn* 6/3 (1988), no. 20, 17–18.

Tuyll van Serooskerken, C. van, *The Italian Drawings of the 15th and 16th Centuries in the Teyler Museum*, Haarlem/Ghent/Doornspijk 2000.

Vaccari, E., 'Mining academies as centers of geological research and education in Europe between the 18th and 19th centuries', *De Re Metallica* 13 (2009), 35–41.

Veen, J. van der, ' "Dit klain Vertrek bevat een Weereld vol gewoel". Negentig Amsterdammers en hun kabinetten', in Bergvelt/Kistemaker 1992a, 232–58, 313–34.

Velden, F. van der, 'De prijsvragen en Verhandelingen van Teylers Tweede Genootschap 1781–1866 (VI): tekenkunde', *Teylers Magazijn* 13/1 (Spring 1995), no. 46, 11–15.

Veltmann, C., and H. Zaunstöck, 'Soziabilität, Printmedien und sozialfürsorgerische Praxis in Halle zwischen dem Siebenjährigen Krieg und dem Ende des Alten Reiches', in K. Stukenbrock and J. Helm (eds), *Stadt und Gesundheit. Soziale Fürsorge in Halle vom 18. bis zum 20. Jahrhundert*, Halle 2006 (*Forschungen zu hallischen Stadtgeschichte*, 9), 41–63.

Verhandelingen, rakende den natuurlijken en geopenbaarden Godsdienst, uitgegeeven door Teyler's Godgeleerd Genootschap (Transactions, regarding natural and revealed Religion, published by Teyler's Theological Society), vols 1–36 (1781–1860); new series, vols 1–30 (1868–1967).

Verhandelingen, uitgegeeven door Teyler's Tweede Genootschap (Transactions, published by Teyler's Second Society), vols 1–28 (1781–1857); new series, vols 1–19 (1873–1975).

Verheus, S. L., *Naarstig en Vroom. Doopsgezinden in Haarlem 1530–1930*, Haarlem 1993.

Vermij, R., *Secularisering en natuurwetenschap in de zeventiende en achttiende eeuw: Bernard Nieuwentijt*, Amsterdam 1991.

Vincent, L., *Wondertooneel der nature: geopent in een korte beschryvinge der hoofddeelen van de byzonder zeldsaamheden daar in begrepen*, Amsterdam 1706.

Vincent, L., *Het tweede deel of vervolg van het Wondertooneel der Nature*, Amsterdam 1715.

Visser, R. P. W., *The Zoological Work of Petrus Camper (1722–1789)*, Amsterdam 1985.

Visser, P., 'Teyler en liefdadigheid. Onbeperkte verdraagzaamheid en zedelijk gemak', in Sliggers 2006, 127–46.

Visser, P., 'Mennonites and Doopsgezinden in the Netherlands, 1535–1700', in Roth 2007, 299–346.

Vogel, J., 'Koopman en rentenier. Wat deed Teyler met zijn geld?', in Sliggers 2006a, 47–59.

Vogel, J., 'Pieter Teyler en een bedrijfstak in verval. Zijdefabrikeur te Haarlem', in Sliggers 2006b, 61–73.

Vries, J. de, 'Een bezoek aan Teyler', *Eigen Haard* 1 (1875), 204–7.

Vries, L. de, ' "De gelukkige Schildereeuw". Opvattingen over de schilderkunst van de Gouden Eeuw in Nederland, 1700–1750', in Grijzenhout/Veen 1992, 55–77.

Vuyk, S., 'Pleidooien voor de scheiding van kerk en staat: Teylers Godgeleerd Genootschap en de prijsvraag van 1795', in Wall/Wessels 2007, 348–57.

BIBLIOGRAPHY

Wackenroder, W. H., *Werke und Briefe*, Berlin [1938], repr. Heidelberg 1967.

Wall, E. van der, and L. H. M. Wessels (eds), *Een veelzijdige verstandhouding: religie en Verlichting in Nederland 1650–1850*, Nijmegen 2007.

Wegen, D. H. van, et al., *Wie was De Mol? Ambities in Hollands porselein*, [Loosdrecht] 2019.

Weiss, M., 'De gang naar toegankelijkheid. Publiek gebruik van Teylers Museum in de negentiende eeuw', *De Negentiende Eeuw* 34 (2010), 269–85.

Weiss, M. P. M., 'The Masses and the Muses. A History of Teylers Museum in the Nineteenth Century', PhD, Leiden University, 2013a. See also Weiss 2019a.

Weiss, M., ' "Monuments of Science": how Teyler Museum's Instrument Collection Became Historical', in Bennett/Talas 2013b, 195–214.

Weiss, M. P. M., *Showcasing Science. A History of Teylers Museum in the Nineteenth Century*, Amsterdam 2019a (*History of Science and Scholarship in the Netherlands*).

Weiss, M., 'The Lorentz Transformation of a Museum', in F. J. Dijksterhuis, A. Weber, H. J. Zuidervaart (eds), *Locations of Knowledge in Dutch Contexts*, Leiden 2019b, 232–61.

Weringh, N. M. van, 'De prijsvragen en Verhandelingen van Teylers Tweede Genootschap 1781–1866 (V): dichtkunde', *Teylers Magazijn* 10/4 (Winter 1992), no. 37, 8–13.

Werner, A. G., *Von den äusserlichen Kennzeichen der Fossilien*, Leipzig 1774 (French transl. by Mme Guyton de Morveau, Paris 1790; English transl. by Weaver, *Treatise on the External Characters of Fossils*, Dublin 1805).

Wezel, E. van, 'Die Konzeptionen des Alten und Neuen Museums zu Berlin und das sich wandelnde historische Bewußtsein', *Jahrbuch der Berliner Museen* 43 Beiheft (2001), 7–244.

Whitmer, K. J., *Halle Orphanage as Scientific Community. Observation, Eclecticism, and Pietism in the Early Enlightenment*, Chicago 2015.

Wiechmann, A., and L. C. Palm (eds), *Martinus van Marum 1750–1837. Een elektriserend geleerde*, Haarlem 1987.

Wiechmann, A., and L. Touret, 'Frappez, Frappez Toujours! Van Marum als verzamelaar en bezieler van het geleerde bedrijf in Haarlem', in Wiechmann/Palm 1987, 103–54.

Wiesenfeldt, G., 'Politische Ikonographie von Wissenschaft: die Abbildung von Teylers "ungemein großer" Elektrisiermaschine, 1785/87', *NTM International Journal of History & Ethics of Natural Sciences, Technology & Medicine* 10/4 (2002), 222–33.

Winkler, T. C., *Musée Teyler: catalogue systématique de la collection paléontologique*, 6 vols, Haarlem 1863–67; 5 supplements 1868–96.

Wyka, E., 'Collections of Experimental Natural Philosophy in Eighteenth-Century Poland', in Bennett/Talas 2013, 173–93.

Yale, E., *Sociable Knowledge: Natural History and the Nation in Early Modern Britain*, Philadelphia 2016.

278 BIBLIOGRAPHY

Youngs, T., 'Travel and telling', in F.-L. Kroll and M. Munke (eds), *Deutsche Englandreisen / German Travels to England 1550–1900*, Berlin 2014 (*Prinz-Albert-Studien/Prince Albert Studies*, 30).

Zappey, W. M., *et al.*, *Loosdrechts porcelein*, Zwolle 1988 [exh. Rijksmuseum, Amsterdam].

Zaunstöck, H., 'Das "Werck" und das "publico". Franckes Imagepolitik und die Etablierung der Marke Waisenhaus', in Zaunstöck/Müller-Bahlke/Veltmann 2013, 258–71.

Zaunstöck, H., T. Müller-Bahlke and C. Veltmann (eds), *Die Welt verändern. August Hermann Francke. Ein Lebenswerk um 1700*, Halle 2013 (*Kataloge der Franckeschen Stiftungen*, 29).

Zijpp, N. van der, 'Hovens, Daniel (1735–1795)', in *Global Anabaptist Mennonite Encyclopedia Online*, 1956, from https://gameo.org/index.php?title=Hovens,_Daniel_(1735–1795)&oldid=146495.

Zuidervaart, H. J., *Van 'konstgenoten' en hemelse fenomenen. Nederlandse sterrenkunde in de achttiende eeuw*, Rotterdam 1999.

Zuidervaart, H. J., 'Cabinets for Experimental Philosophy in the Netherlands', in Bennett/Talas 2013, 1–26.

Websites

Biografisch portaal van Nederland (Biographical Portal of the Netherlands):
    http://www.biografischportaal.nl/persoon/11607802 (Josué Teissèdre l'Ange).
    http://www.biografischportaal.nl/persoon/44287831 (Adriaan van den Ende).
Center for the Study of Egodocuments and History:
    http://www.egodocument.net/egodocumententot1814-2.html, no. 241 (Jacob Barnaart jr).
    http://www.egodocument.net/egodocumententot1814-2.html, no. 293 (Vincent van der Vinne).
    http://www.egodocument.net/egodocumententot1814-3.html, no. 456 (Adriaan van der Willigen).
Delpher: https://www.delpher.nl/nl/platform/results?query=teylers&coll=platform.
Digitale Bibliotheek voor de Nederlandse Letteren (DBNL):
    https://www.dbnl.org/tekst/_tst001199901_01/_tst001199901_01_0013.php.
    https://www.dbnl.org/tekst/laan005lett01_01/colofon.php.
Encyclopedie Nederlandstalige Tijdschriften (Encyclopedia Dutch-language magazines): https://www.ent1815.nl/a/algemeene-konst-en-letterbode-1788–1861/.
Global Anabaptist Mennonite Encyclopedia Online (GAMEO): https://gameo.org/index.php?title=Hovens,_Daniel_(1735–1795)&oldid=146495.
History of Concepts: http://www.historyofconcepts.org/node/17394.

BIBLIOGRAPHY

Huygens Institute for the History of the Netherlands (Huygens ING): http://resources.huygens.knaw.nl/bwn1780-1830/lemmata/data/Loosjes.

ICOM: https://icom.museum/en/resources/standards-guidelines/museum-definition/.

IISG (International Institute of Social History), Amsterdam: https://iisg.amsterdam/en/research/projects/hpw/calculate.php?back-link=1.

The Journal of the History of Ideas: https://jhiblog.org/2015/01/09/back-in-the-sattlezeit-again/.

Koninklijke Bibliotheek (Royal Library), The Hague: https://www.kb.nl/themas/boek-geschiedenis/meer-bijzondere-boeken/vaderlandsche-letteroefeningen.

Lehmann, Ann-Sophie: https://rug.academia.edu/AnnSophieLehmann.

Ma Page: http://mapage.noos.fr/xgen/roglo/ga.lestevenon.jpg.

Oxford Dictionaries: https://en.oxforddictionaries.com/definition/museum.

Parlement.com: https://www.parlement.com/id/vgo9llviinui/w_a_lestevenon.

    https://www.parlement.com/id/vigfgov2wpxl/staten_generaal_1588_1795.

Teyler's Foundation and Museum:

    http://beeld.teylersmuseum.nl/digital_library/Webs-Gastenboek/Gastenboek-en/Gastenboeken.htm.

    http://beeld.teylersmuseum.nl/Digital_Library/Emags/34d_61.

    https://www.teylersmuseum.nl/nl/collectie/boeken-overzicht.

    https://www.teylersmuseum.nl/nl/collectie/gebouw-en-geschiedenis/gebouw/geschiedenis.

    https://www.teylersmuseum.nl/en/about-the-museum/organisation/who-we-are/the-ideals-of-pieter-teyler/the-ideals-of-pieter-teyler.

    https://adcs.home.xs4all.nl/varia/hmw/teyler.html.

Karin Tilmans: https://karintilmans.nl/pdf/concepts.pdf.

University of Amsterdam: https://pure.uva.nl/ws/files/1873341/111959_thesis.pdf (J. Oddens).

Woordenboek der Nederlandsche Taal (Dictionary of the Dutch Language): http://gtb.inl.nl.

ww-Person, a data base of the titled nobility in Europe: http://ww-person.com/.

Photo Credits

Allard Pierson, Amsterdam   5.2, 5.3

Amsterdam City Archives   4.1, 4.6

Bibliothèque nationale de France, Paris   11.2, 11.3

bpk/Das Gleimhaus, Halberstadt   11.1 (Ulrich Schrader)

Castle Museum Sypesteyn, Nieuw Loosdrecht   4.4 (J. G. Pascoe), 4.5 (Johan van der Veer)

Frankesche Stiftungen, Halle   10.1–10.3, 10.4 (Thomas Meinicke), 10.5–10.8

Leiden University Library   9.1

National Museum Boerhaave, Leiden   4.8

National Museum Twenthe, Enschede (on loan from Frans Hals Museum, Haarlem)   7.1 (R. Klein Gotink)

Noord-Hollands Archief, Haarlem   7.2, 7.3, 8.7

Rijksmuseum, Amsterdam   4.2, 4.3, 4.7, 5.4–5.6, 7.4

Royal Library, The Hague   5.1

Teyler's Museum, Haarlem   1.1, 1.3, 1.4, 2.1–2.5, 3.1, 3.2, 3.3, 3.6, 3.7, 3.12, 3.13 3.15, 3.16, 3.17, 5.7, 6.2–6.11, 7.5–7.9, 8.1, 8.2, 8.4–8.6, 9.2–9.7; 1.2, 3.4, 3.5, 3.8–3.10, 3.18, 3.19, 6.1 (Kees Hageman); 3.11, 3.14 (Sybolt Voeten Architectuur Fotografie).

The Walters Art Museum, Baltimore, Maryland   8.3

Index

NB: Numbers in **bold** refer to illustrations.
TM = Teyler's Museum.

Abrams, Meyer Howard (1912–2015),
American literary critic   241
Academy (drawing)   13, 70, 71, 73. *See also*
Amsterdam; Haarlem
Academy/academies of science   10, 15, 16, 73
Academy. *See* Berlin, Academy of Science;
Freiberg, Mining Academy; Paris,
Academy (of art), Academy of Science;
Philadelphia, Academy of Science;
Royal Society in London; St Petersburg,
Academy of Science
Achilles, figure from Greek mythology
*Achilles among the daughters of
Lycomedes. See* Franco, Giovanni Battista
Adam   39
Adams, George (1750–1795), English optician,
writer, mathematical instrument
maker to George III   15
Aesthetic Revolution   239–51 (*passim*)
Air(s)   8, 37, 39, 40n68. *See also*
Phlogiston theory
Air pump   Table 7.1 (18a, 18b)
Aldrovandi, Ulisse (1522–1605), Italian
naturalist   91
Alembert, Jean-Baptiste le Rond d' (1717–
1783), French philosopher   11, 89, 106.
See also Diderot, Denis
Alexandria   108
*Algemeene Konst- en Letterbode, Weekblad
voor min en meer Geoefenden,
Behelzende Berichten uit de Geleerde
Wereld van alle Landen (General
messenger of art and literature, a
weekly for the more or less learned, with
reports from the scholarly world in all
countries),* Haarlem weekly (1788–
1861)   30, 31n40, 179, 180n28, 181, 193,
194n10, 195
Allebé, August (1838–1927), Dutch artist,
visited TM (19/9/1854)   Table 9.1
Alliance of Early Universal Museums
(2020)   65n24
American(s), native   93n22

American War of Independence
(1775–1783)   20n4
Amsterdam   15, 21n6, 29, 37, 46n13, 78, 82
(**4.6**), 85, 93n22, 94n29, 114, 136, 172, 177,
184, 203, 206n49, 230, 237n68
Amsterdams Historisch Museum (1926;
since 2010 Amsterdam Museum)   91
Arti et Amicitiae, artists' society in
Amsterdam (1839)   190
Blaauw Jan Menagerie (17th–18th
century)   93n22
Drawing academy of the city   70 (**4.1**),
136, 177, 183, 184
Felix Meritis, cultural society (1777–1888)
21n6, 177, 184, 201n29
'Tekenzaal' (Drawing Gallery)   83 (**4.7**)
'Zaal der Natuurkunde' (Physics
Room)   82 (**4.6**)
International Art-historical Congress
(1898)   55n13, 181n33
International Institute of Social
History   169n5
Koninklijk (Royal) Museum (1808–1810),
predecessor of the Rijksmuseum   83
Rijksmuseum (in Trippenhuis 1817–1885;
in the building by P. J. H. Cuypers since
1885)   36n54, 49n6, 97, 183n42, 196,
201, 206n49
Synagogue of the Portugese (Sephardic)
Jews (1675)   79 (**4.3**)
Town Hall   70 (**4.1**)
Trippenhuis (location of Rijksmuseum
1817–1885). *See* Amsterdam,
Rijksmuseum
Anatomy/anatomical/anatomist   27, 37n57,
92, 93, 128, 177n13, 221
Ancién Regime   81
Ancient(s) *See* Antique/antiquity
Andriessen, family of artists   196
Andriessen, Anthonie (1746–1813), Dutch
artist, visited TM (5/6/1791)   Table 9.1
Andriessen, Christiaan (1775–1846), Dutch
artist, visited TM (3/9/1799)   Table 9.1

282   INDEX

Andriessen, Jurriaan (1742–1819), Dutch artist,
    visited TM (5/6/1791)   Table 9.1
Anglo-Dutch War, Fourth (1780–1784)   20n4
Anti-French   31
Anti-Orangism/anti-Orangist(s)   20n4,
    35n51. *See also* Patriot
Antique/Antiquity   91, 105n56, 145, 177, 183,
    184, 185, 187, 239, 243n9, 245n10
Anthropology   16n28
Antwerp
    St Luke's Guild   77
Apol, Louis (1850–1936), Dutch artist, visited
    TM (8/5/1894)   Table 9.1
Apostool, Cornelis (1762–1844), Dutch artist,
    first director of the Rijksmuseum
    Amsterdam (1808–1844)   183
Archimedes, Greek mathematician (288–212
    before Chr.)/Archimedean   248
Archives du Musée Teyler (1866–1953)   55n12
Ardea purpurea (*Purpere reiger*)   Table 7.1 (26)
Ark   90
Arti et Amicitiae. *See* Amsterdam
Artificialia   77
Arts, personification of the   35 (2.4)
Astronomy/astronomical   17, 27, 102, 221n7,
    226, 241
Atheism/atheist(ic)   44n84, 97
Audubon, John James, born Jean Rabin
    (1785–1851), American ornithologist,
    naturalist, and painter
    Birds of America (1827–1838)   106
Austria/Austrian   14 (1.4)
Austrian Netherlands (Southern
    Netherlands)   20
Austrian War of Succession (1740–1748)   20
Autonomy (aesthetic)   18, 239–51 (*passim*)
Azzolino, Cardinal Decio (1623–1689),
    Rome   170n6
Azzolino, Marchese Pompeo (1654–1705),
    Rome   170n6

Bacon, Francis (1561–1626), English
    philosopher and scientist   75, 76
Bakker, Barent de (*c.* 1762–1805), Dutch
    artist   147n36, 148n37, 153, Table 7.1
    after Wybrand Hendriks
        *Apparatus for experiments on
        the composition of water and the*

*decomposition of carbonated hydrogen
gas* (1798), print   Table 7.1 (11b)
*Apparatus for experiments on
the oxidation of mercury* (1798),
print   Table 7.1 (17b)
*Apparatus for producing phosphoric
acid* (1798), print   Table 7.1 (12b)
*Apparatus for the production of carbon
dioxide* (1798), print   142 (7.7), Table
7.1 (13b)
*Apparatus for studying the products
of the combustion of oils* (1798),
print   Table 7.1 (14b)
*Big battery with the large electrostatic
generator in the background* (1795),
print   Table 7.1 (5b)
Bill of a platypus (1803), print   Table
7.1 (20b)
Design for an air pump (1798),
print   Table 7.1 (18b)
*Detail of an electrometer attached to
the large electrostatic generator* (1787),
print   Table 7.1 (2b)
*Large electrostatic generator:
situational view of the Oval Room* (1787),
print   142 (7.6), Table 7.1 (1b)
*New design for an electrostatic
generator* (1791, 1795), print   Table
7.1 (7)
*Schematic outline of part of an
apparatus for studying the products
of the combustion of oils* (1) (1798),
print   Table 7.1 (15b)
*Schematic outline of part of an
apparatus for studying the products
of the combustion of oils* (2) (1798),
print   Table 7.1 (16b)
*Schematic outline of a setup for
experiments using a gasometer* (1)
(1791), print   Table 7.1 (8d)
*Setup for experiments using a
gasometer* (1) (1791), print   Table
7.1 (8c)
*Setup for experiments using a
gasometer* (2) (1798), print   Table
7.1 (9b)
Side view of a platypus (1803),
print   Table 7.1 (21)

INDEX

Bakker, Job Augustus (1796–1876),
Dutch artist, visited TM (August
1817) Table 9.1
Bakker Korff, Alexander Hugo (1824–1882),
Dutch artist, visited TM (1845)
Table 9.1
Balmakers, Petrus Antonius (1831–
1903), Dutch artist, visited TM
(1867) Table 9.1
Baltic Sea 20n2
Bandini, Giovanni (c. 1540–1599), Italian
artist 172
Barbiers, Pieter (1749–1842), Dutch artist. See
Vinkeles, Reinier
Barnaart, Haarlem family of Mennonites 23
Barnaart, Jacob jr (1726–1780), Haarlem
merchant and one of the first five
Directors of Teyler's Foundation 26,
27n25, 27n26, 28, 30n39, 46, 102
Barnaart, Jacob sr (1696–1762), silk
manufacturer and collector 27n26,
102n46
his collections 27
Basire, J. (1730–1802), English artist 148n37
and Michael Angelo Rooker
A View of the Apparatus and part of the
Great Cylinder in the Pantheon (1778),
print 149 (7.9)
Bastert, Nicolaas (1854–1939), Dutch artist,
visited TM (3/6/1892) Table 9.1
Batavian Republic (1795–1806) 24n19,
28n29, 31, 33, 174n9, 176
Batavian Revolution (1795) 25n23, 175. See
also Patriot Revolution
Batteux, Charles (1713–1780), called abbé
Batteux, French philosopher 18,
241, 242
Les beaux-arts réduits à un même principe
(1746) 241, 242
Bauer, Ferdinand (1769–1826), Austrian artist,
visited TM (14/9/1814) Table 9.1
Bauer, Marius (1867–1932), Dutch artist,
visited TM (11/6/1889) Table 9.1
Baumann, Charles, visited TM (22/5/
1819) Table 9.1
Baumgarten, Alexander Gottlieb (1714–1762),
German philosopher 18, 241
Aesthetica (2 vols, 1750–1758) 241

Bayersdorfer, Adolf (1842–1901), German art
historian, at the German Institute in
Florence 55n13, 181n33
Beekman, Isaac (1588–1637), Dutch naturalist,
engineer and meteorologist 73
Beets, Nicolaas (1814–1903), Dutch
author, visited TM (8/8/1829; 9/4/
1891) Table 9.1
Berchem, Nicolaes (1621–1683), Dutch
artist 196, 197 (9.1). See also under
Hendriks, Wybrand
Landscape with shepherds near a
ruin (Brederode?; c. 1670–1683),
drawing 198 (9.3)
Berlage, Hendrik Petrus (1856–1934),
Dutch architect, visited TM (28/12/
1898) Table 9.1
Berlin 249
Academy of Science, Prussian 15, 70
Altes Museum 248, 249
Berlinische Monatsschrift 242
Bernard, Jean Frederic (1683–1744),
French bookseller and publisher in
Amsterdam 78. See also Picart, Bernard
Berneman, W.F., visited TM (1862) Table 9.1
Berthollet, Claude-Louis (1748–1822), French
chemist 6n28, Table 7.1 (8a–d, 9a)
Bible/biblical 17n30, 32 (2.2), 77, 90, 91,
93, 105, 113, 227
Old Testament 127
Genesis 90, 93, 127
Bilderdijk, Willem (1756–1831), Dutch author,
visited TM (1813) Table 9.1
Bilders, Johannes Warnardus (1811–
1890), Dutch artist, visited TM
(1854) Table 9.1
Blau-Lang, Tina (1845–1916), Austrian artist,
visited TM (1875) Table 9.1
Bloemen, Pieter van (1657–1720), Dutch
artist 196, 197 (9.1). See also under
Hendriks, Wybrand
Two horses and an open carriage
(undated), drawing 197 (9.2)
Blumenbach, Johann Friedrich (1752–1840),
German naturalist 16n28, 121n25
Bologna, capital of the North Italian region of
Emilia-Romagna 138n17
University 91

Bonnat, Léon (1833–1922), French artist and collector, visited TM (July 1883) Table 9.1

Boom, Mathijs, Dutch historian 105n54

Borch, Gerard ter (1617–1681), Dutch artist 186

Borchardt, Felix (1857–1936), German artist, visited TM (Sept. 1883) Table 9.1

Borssum Buisman, Jan Hendrik van (1919–2012), the last *kastelein* of Teyler's Museum (1952–1980) 43n82, 63 (**3.17**)

Bosboom, Johannes (1817–1891), Dutch artist, visited TM (19/8/1887) Table 9.1

Bosch, Jan (1713–1780), publisher, member of Teyler's Second Society 34, 35n49

Boshamer, Johannes (1800–1852), Dutch artist, visited TM (1822) Table 9.1

Botany/botanical/botanist 16, 77, 90, 92, 108, 111, 133n2, 221, 233

Bottelier, H., visited TM (25/4/1892) Table 9.1

Bouilly, Julien-Léopold (1796–1874), French artist

 Portrait of Antoine-Chrysostome Quatremère de Quincy (1820), print 244 (**11.2**)

Bourgeois, Isidore, visited TM (2/4/1900) Table 9.1

Brabant, a region in the Northern and Southern Netherlands 111

Brahe, Tycho (1546–1601), Danish astronomer 225 (**10.5**)

Brand, Isaäc (?– in or after 1782), one of the first Directors of Teyler's Foundation 25, 26

Brandenburg-Prussia 111, 221. *See also* Prussia

Breda, Jacob Gijsbertus Samuël van (1788–1867), curator and director of Teyler's Museum (1839–1864) 50 (**3.3**), 51, 56, 60n18, 110n3

Breda, Joanna van, wife of Levinus Vincent 94n29

Brederode (?), ruin(s) of. *See* Berchem, Nicolaes

Brentano, Josephus Augustinus (1753–1821), Dutch art collector 183

Breslau, Marie Louise Catherine (1856–1927), French/Swiss artist, visited TM (July 1883) Table 9.1

Bressler, Reinhold (1868–1945), German artist, visited TM (5/7/1893) Table 9.1

Brockhaus, Heinrich (1858–1941), German art historian 55n13

Brondgeest, Albertus (1786–1849), Dutch artist and art dealer, visited TM (1846) Table 9.1

Brouwer, Jan (1760–1822), pastor at the Mennonite Congregation in Leeuwarden, winner of two silver medals (1793 and 1799) and two gold medals (1794 and 1796) of Teyler's Theological Society, winner of the gold medal of Teyler's Second Society (1800) 40n67

Brouwers, A., visited TM (2/5/1892) Table 9.1

Brown, Ethelbert W. (1870–1946), American artist, visited TM (24/10/1900) Table 9.1

Brown, William Laurence (1755–1830), Scottish minister and professor, lived in the Netherlands until 1795, winner of the gold medal of Teyler's Theological Society (1784) 32 (**2.2**)

Brussels 40n69, 77

Bunck, H. J. J., visited TM (22/7/1872) Table 9.1

Burg, Pieter van der (1840–1890), Dutch artist, visited TM (March 1875) Table 9.1

Burtin, François Xavier (de) (1743–1818), mineralogist, physician, physicist, writer on art, Brussels, winner of the gold medal of Teyler's Second Society (competition of 1783, published 1790), participant in the competition of Teyler's Second Society (competition of 1806, published in 1809) 40n69, 41n72, 105n54

 'De algemeene omkeeringen, welke de aarde aan haare oppervlakte ondergaan heeft, en de oudheid van onzen aardkloot / 'Les renversements génerales, qu'a subies la surface de la terre, et sur l'ancienneté de notre globe' (The general reversals that the earth has undergone on its surface, and the antiquity of our earth). *See* Burtin 1790 in the Bibliography

INDEX

'Wat is de reden, dat de Nederlandsche school, zoo wel voorheen ten tyde van haren grootsten bloei, als hedendaags, zoo weinig meesters in het historisch vak heeft opgeleverd? (What is the reason for the small number of Dutch history painters?)' 40n69, 41n72. *See* Burtin 1809 in the Bibliography

Calimero complex 75n12

Calisch, Moritz (1819–1870), Dutch artist, visited TM (1862) Table 9.1

Calkoen, Joan, (?– 1814), Dutch writer about birds Table 7.1 (20a, 20b, 21)

Calvin, John, born Jehan Cauvin (1509–1564), French-Swiss theologist and reformer 34

Camper, Adriaan Gilles (1759–1820), Dutch mathematics, physics professor and collector 116

Camper, Petrus Camper (1722–1789), Dutch physician, naturalist and collector 27, 38, 116

Campi, Bernardino (1522–1591), Italian artist 172

Carbon dioxide 142 (7.7), Table 7.1 (13a, 13b)

Carboniferous Period 128

Carracci, Annibale (1560–1609), Italian artist 183

Cartesius. *See* Descartes

Cate, Anne-Marie ten, restoration consultant 118n21

Catholic (Roman Catholic) 24n19, 25n21

Charlet, Frantz (1862–1928), Belgian artist, visited TM (May 1886) Table 9.1

Chateaubriand, François René vicomte de (1768–1848), French author and politician
Génie du Christianisme (1802) 245n10

Chemnitz 122n27

Chijs, Pieter Otto van der (1802–1867), coin expert, winner of the gold medal of Teylers Second Society (1846) 35 (2.4, 2.5)

Chodowiecki, Daniel Niklaus (1726–1801), Polish, later German artist
Les adieux de Jean Calas, à sa famille (1767), print 186

Christ/Christian/Christianity 17n30, 21, 24n18, 30, 32, 33n47, 34, 78, 245n10, 246

Christina (1626–1689), Queen of Sweden 169, 170n6, 181, 193n9, 194n10

Church-fathers, four (of the first four centuries AD) 106

Civitavecchia 170

Clarke, Samuel (1675–1729), English philosopher and Anglican clergyman 79

Classical 34, 72, 81, 97, 103, 104, 183, 185, 240, 248

Classicism/Classicist 13, 18, 145n29

Claude Lorrain (1600–1682), French artist working in Rome 168, 170
View in Rome (c. 1630–1635), drawing 170 (8.1)

Clé, Jean la (1738–1802) 35n51, 36n53, 42n79

Collector's Cabinet. *See Simpliciakast*

Columbus, Christoforus (1451–1506), Italian explorer, working for Spain 251

Constitution of 1798, First Dutch 24n19, 33, 35

Cook, James (1728–1779), British explorer 226

Cooper, Michael P.
Robbing the sparry garniture. A 200-year history of British mineral dealers (2006) 112

Copenhagen 223

Cornet, Jacobus Ludovicus (1815–1882), Dutch artist, visited TM (1854) Table 9.1

Correggio, Antonio da (1489–1534), Italian artist 187, 251

Couriard, Pelagia Petrowna (1848–1898), Russian artist, visited TM (3/10/1895) Table 9.1

Coutant, J. L. D. (1776–after 1831), French artist 138/139n18

Creator (Divine) 39, 40, 74, 79, 90, 113

Cretaceous 116n19

Crocodile 104, Table 7.1 (4a, 4b)

Crystal(s)/crystallographic 15, 107, 109, 120 (6.7), 120n24, 122, 123, 144n26

Curiosities, cabinet(s) of 9n9, 76, 91. *See also* Impey, Oliver; Rariteitenkabinetten

Cuthbertson, John (1743–1821), English instrument maker, lived in Amsterdam (1768–1796), built the electrostatic generator for Teyler's Foundation (1784) 15, 37

Cuvier, Georges (1769–1832), French naturalist 128, 138/139n18, Table 7.1 (23, 24, 25)

Dal(l)iphard, Edouard (1833–1877), French artist, visited TM (April 1859) Table 9.1

Danekes, Andreas (1788–1855), Dutch artist, visited TM (1845) Table 9.1

Danish-Halle mission 223

Danz, Georg Friedrich (1733–1813), German dealer in minerals and fossils 112

Danzig, German city, nowadays in Poland (Gdańsk) 20n2

Darwin, Charles (1809–1882), English naturalist, geologist and biologist
The Origin of Species (1853) 105

Daston, Lorraine (1951), American historian of science 12

Dekker, Hendrik Adriaan Christiaan (1836–1905), Dutch artist, visited TM (Sept. 1885) Table 9.1

Dekker, J., visited TM (1838) Table 9.1

Delanoy, Jacques (1820–1890), French artist, visited TM (Sept. 1884) Table 9.1

Deluc. *See* Luc, Jean André de

Demont, Adrien-Louis (1851–1928), French artist, visited TM (February 1880) Table 9.1

Demont-Breton, Virginie-Elodie (1859–1935), French artist, visited TM (February 1880) Table 9.1

Descartes, René or Renatus Cartesius (1596–1650), French philosopher/ Cartesian(s) 73, 75, 78

Description des arts et métiers published by the Paris Academy of Science 11

Deterding, Sir Henry (1866–1939), director of Shell and art collector 36n54

Deville, Maria, Swiss mineral dealer 118

Dézallier d'Argenville, Antoine-Joseph (1680–1765), French writer about art and natural history
La Conchyliologie (1780) 36

Dhont, J., visited TM (1811) Table 9.1

Diaghilev, Sergei (1872–1929), Russian impresario, visited TM (10/6/ 1895) Table 9.1

Diderot, Denis (1713–1784), French philosopher, art critic, and writer with Jean le Rond d'Alembert
Encyclopédie(28 vols; 1751–1772) 11, 89, 106

Divine Architect 78, 97, 100 (5.6)

Divine Creator. *See* Creator (Divine)

Dijk, Jan van (1730–1790), Dutch collector of drawings, auction 1791 179

Dixhoorn, Arjan van (1973), Dutch historian 77

Doeveren, Wouter van (1730–1783), Dutch collector, auction in 1785 112

Dou, Gerard (1613–1675), Dutch artist 186

Drawing, personification of 35 (2.4)

Dresden
Gemäldegalerie 249

Dublin
Chester Beatty Library 94n28, 102n46

Dubois, Eugène (1858–1940), palaeontologist and curator of the Palaeontological and Mineralogical Cabinet of Teyler's Museum (1898–1928) 55n14, 110n3

Du Bos (or Dubos), Jean-Baptiste (1670–1742), called abbé Du Bos, French philosopher 18
Réflexions critiques sur la poésie et sur la peinture (1719) 240n3

Dupré, Daniel (1751–1817), Dutch artist 184

Dutch/Dutchman 8n9, 11, 13, 14, 17, 18, 20n4, 31, 38, 43, 49, 63n23, 71 (4.2), 72n4, 73, 74n10, 77, 81, 82, 89, 91, 101, 104, 116, 117, 131, 150, 157, 168, 172, 175, 177, 179–183, 185n55, 186n56, 187–189, 193–195, 202, 205, 219, 221n4, 228, 230. *See also* the Netherlands

Dutch Reformed Church, the official Dutch church 24n19, 27, 29, 33, 34, 35, 36, 44, 105

Dutch Republic (of the Seven United Netherlands; 1588–1795) 20n4, 22n9, 28n29, 37n58, 39, 73, 74, 77, 80, 82, 89, 90, 91, 93, 106, 117, 194, 249

Dutch Revolt 96

INDEX 287

Earth/age of the Earth   8, 10, 37, 40, 48, 81, 109, 110, 113, 116, 119, 122, 125, 126, 128
Eberhardt, Johann August Gottlob (1739 – 1809), German artist
    View from the city wall of Halle to the west (c. 1800), painting   225 (**10.5**)
Ebbinge, Erik (1940), director of Teyler's Museum (1983–2001)   60n18, 63 (**3.17**)
Edam   21n6, 23n17
Ede   136n7
    Village of Manen near Ede (1783)   135 (**7.4**)
Education/educational   17n30, 18, 24n17, 31n40, 61, 65, 69, 70, 77, 87, 88n2, 90, 124, 127, 128, 177, 178, 182, 183, 189, 219, 221, 222, 224, 228, 230n38, 236, 237, 238, 239, 247, 248, 249, 251
Education Law, Dutch (1806)   17n30, 230n38
Eeckhout, Jacob Joseph (1793–1861), Belgian artist, visited TM (1858)   Table 9.1
Eeden, Frederik van (1860–1932), Dutch author and amateur artist, visited TM (16/8/1900)   Table 9.1
Eeden, Nicolas Van den (1856–1918), Belgian artist, visited TM (March 1886)   Table 9.1
Eerelman, Otto (1839–1926), Dutch artist, visited TM (Sept. 1887)   Table 9.1
Egyptology   92
Eigen Haard (short for *Eigen haard is goud waard* (my home is my castle)), Dutch periodical 1875–1941   205, 206
Electric(al)/electricity   8, 37, 42n79, 65n24, 104, 128, 141, 143 (**7.8**), 147, 148, 229
Electrostatic (generator)   27, 36, 61 (**3.16**), 139. *See also* Haarlem, Teyler's Museum, Oval Room
Elizabethan   76
Elout, Cornelis (1714–1779), member of Teyler's Second Society, collector   36
Empirical/empiricism   21n8, 81, 84
Encyclopédie. See Diderot/d'Alembert
Encyclopaedic/*encyclopedisch*   5n3, 10, 11, 25n21, 37, 38n64, 39, 41, 43, 73, 74, 77, 83, 91, 94, 113, 128, 239, 242
Ende, Adriaan van den (1768–1846), Dutch pastor and educational innovator   17, 37n58, 230n38, 230n39, 232n45, 233, 236, 237

Engel, Johann Jakob (1741–1802), German author   150
    Ideen zu einer Mimik (1785; in Dutch: *De kunst van nabootzing door gebaarden*, 2nd edn in 1807)   150
Enlightenment/Enlightened   30, 40, 44n86, 45, 63n23, 71, 73, 88, 105, 106, 133n4, 135, 241
England/English(man)   15, 19, 20n4, 37n57, 84, 111, 112, 121, 127, 139n19, 150n44, 174n9, 181, 186, 230, 236, 239n11, 242n6, 245n10
Enschedé, Johannes (1708–1780), member of Teyler's Second Society, son and partner of the founder of the famous printing house in Haarlem   23n15, 34, 35n49, 36n53, 176 (**8.7**)
    his collections   36
Erfurt   227, 228
    Lutheran orphanage
    Collection of curiosities   228
Escher von der Linth, Hans Conrad (1767–1823), Swiss statesman and geologist   112
Europe/European   10, 15, 16, 17, 69, 73, 76, 89, 91n16, 94, 101, 108, 109, 118, 122, 136, 138n17, 144, 145, 230n38, 236, 238, 240
Eynde, Petrus van den (1787–1840), Dutch artist, visited TM (1813)   Table 9.1
Eynden, Roeland van (1747–1819), Dutch artist and author   177, 178, 180
    Over den nationaalen smaak der Hollandsche school in de teken- en schilderkunst (1787)   178, 185–7
    with Adriaan van der Willigen
    Geschiedenis der vaderlandsche schilderkunst (4 vols, 1816–1840)   177, 182, 201

Faraday, Michael (1791–1867), British scientist
    Faraday cage or shield   61 (**3.16**)
Faujas de Saint-Fond, Barthélemy (1741–1819), French geologist   112, 124 (**6.9**), 155, 165
    Histoire Naturelle de la Montagne de Saint-Pierre de Maestricht (1798)   Table 7.1 (3, 19)
Feith, Rhijnvis (1753–1824), Dutch author   82
    Visited TM (28/6/1797)   Table 9.1

Felix Meritis. *See* Amsterdam
Flanders/Flemish   19, 29, 179
Flood. *See* the Great Flood
Florence/Florentine(s)   181n33, 187
  Palazzo Pitti
    Studiolo of Francesco de' Medici   91
Flushing (Vlissingen). *See* Zeeuwsch
  Genootschap
Fokker, Adriaan Daniel (1887–1972), Dutch
  physicist; Teyler Professor at the
  University of Leiden and curator
  of the Teyler Cabinet of Physics
  (1928–1955)   65n25
Fontana, Felice (1730–1805), Italian
  physicist   37n57
Forster, Jacob, English dealer in minerals and
  fossils   112
Forster, Johann Reinhold
  (1729–1798)   226, 227
Fossil(s)/*fossilia*   8, 9, 11, 37n57, 47, 49n8,
  90, 93, 102, 104, 105n56, 107, 108,
  109–28 (*passim*), 131, 137n10, 138, 139n18,
  139n20, 140 (7.5), 141, 146, Table 7.1 (3,
  19, 22, 24, 25), 177n13, 192, 205, 226
France/French   15, 18, 20n2, 28n29, 31, 36, 38,
  55, 73, 74, 81, 87n11, 122, 128n35, 138n17,
  168, 172, 173, 175, 176, 177, 178, 179, 183,
  187, 199n22, 242, 243n8, 243n9, 245n10,
  246n13, 247, 248, 249
Francesco de' Medici I, Grand Duke of
  Tuscany (1541–1587)   91. *See also*
  Florence, Palazzo Pitti
Francke, August Hermann (1663–
  1727), German theologian and
  pedagogue   221, 222, 223n12, 228,
  232
Francke, Gotthilf August (1696–
  1769), German theologian and
  pedagogue   222n7, 223
Franco, Giovanni Battista, called il Semolei
  (1498–1561), Italian artist   172
  *Discovery of Achilles among the daughters
  of Lycomedes* (*c*. 1545–1550),
  drawing   172, 175 (8.6)
Francq van Berkhey, Johannes le (1729–1812),
  Dutch naturalist, collector, auction in
  1785   112, 114 (6.2), 115 (6.3)
Frankfurt   20n2

Freedlander, Arthur R. (1875–1940),
  American artist, visited TM (24/10/
  1900)   Table 9.1
Freedom, personification of   32 (2.2)
Freemason(s)   176
Freiberg   125
  Bergakademie/Mining Academy   112n10,
  121, 122n27, 125
French Revolution   247
Friedrich III (1657–1713), Elector of
  Brandenburg   221
Friedrich Wilhelm I (1688–1740), King of
  Prussia   222
Friedrich, Casper David (1774–1840), German
  painter   82
Friesland (one of the seven provinces of the
  Dutch Republic)   20
Frikke, Longin (1820/21–1893), Russian artist,
  visited TM (1841)   Table 9.1

Gabriël, Paul Joseph Constantin (1828–1903),
  Dutch artist, visited TM (1848; 19/5/
  1892)   Table 9.1
Galison, Peter (1955), American historian of
  science   12
Gareis, Franz (1775–1803), German painter
  Portrait of August Hermann Niemeyer
  (1800), painting   220 (10.1)
  *Portrait of Agnes Wilhelmine Christiane
  Niemeyer, née von Köpken* (1800),
  painting   220 (10.2)
Gas   Table 7.1 (11a, 11b)
Gasometer Tabel 7.1 (8a–d, 9a, 9b)
Gebirgsarten   92, 104, 105
Gelder, Roelof van (1948), Dutch
  historian   94n28, 104
Geology/geological   39, 92, 104, 105
Germany/German   13, 15, 16n27, 18, 20n2,
  40n68, 55n13, 55n15, 73, 75, 82, 111, 112,
  114, 123, 179, 180n33, 181n33, 219, 223,
  226, 228n30, 239, 240, 241, 242n6,
  246n13, 249, 251n19
Gesellschaft freiwilliger Armenfreunde
  (Society of Voluntary Friends of the
  Poor)   232n45
Giambologna or Giovanni da Bologna (1529–
  1608), Southern Netherlandish sculptor
  working in Italy   171 (8.2)

INDEX 289

Giant's Causeway 127

Gildemeester, Jan (1744–1799), Dutch art collector, auction 1800 179

God 32, 34, 78, 90, 91, 94, 96, 97, 100 (5.6), 104, 105, 108, 224, 246. *See also* Creator; Divine Architect

Goeree, Willem (1635–1711), Dutch art theoretician, author and bookseller *Inleydinge tot de alghemeene teyckenkonst* (Introduction to the Practice of General Painting; 1668) 76

Goethe, Johann Wolfgang von (1749–1832), German writer, naturalist and collector 112

Golden Age 182

Goltzius, Hendrick (1558–1617), Dutch artist 168, 170n6, 193 *Portrait of Giovanni da Bologna* (1591), drawing 171 (**8.2**)

Gotha 227

Gothic 14 (**1.4**)

Graadt van Roggen, Johannes (1867–1959), Dutch artist, visited TM (August 1880; Sept. 1884; 28/3/1890; 26/2/1891; 9/3/1891; 11/4/1893; 1/2/1898) Table 9.1

Graaff, Frederik Carel de (1819–1897), Dutch artist and photographer, visited TM (3/8/1892) Table 9.1

Grand Tour 77

Grande machine Teylerienne. See Haarlem, Teyler's Museum, Oval Room, Electrostatic generator

Grandjean, Jean (1752–1781), Dutch artist 184n50

's-Gravesande, Willem Jacob (1688–1742), Dutch philosopher, mathematician and physicist 73

Great Britain 73. *See also* England/English

Great Flood 90, 93, 106n58, 125, 127

Greek/Greece 242, 243n9, 248

Greenland 93n22

Greive, Johan Conrad (1837–1891), Dutch artist *The First Paintings Gallery of Teyler's Museum* (1862), drawing 204 (**9.6**)

Greuze, Jean-Baptiste (1725–1805), French artist 186, 187

Groningen (city) 27 University 101

Groningen (one of the seven provinces of the Dutch Republic) 20

Gronovius, Johannes Frederik (1686–1762), Leiden physician and collector 114

Grotius, Hugo (1583–1645), Dutch jurist 90

Grootveld, Jan David Geerling (1821–1890), Dutch artist, visited TM (1856) Table 9.1

Gründler, Gottfried August (1710–1775), German artist 223

Gruijter, Jacob Willem (1856–1908), Dutch artist, visited TM (15/2/1886) Table 9.1

Gruyter, Willem (1817–1880), Dutch artist, visited TM (1833) Table 9.1

Guercino, or Giovanni Francesco Barbieri (1591–1666), Italian artist 13, 168, 184

Guyon, Jeanne-Marie Bouvier de la Motte- (1648–1717), French mystic 246n13

Haak, Johannes Andries Martinus (1831–1903), Dutch artist, visited TM (9/11/1858) Table 9.1

Haanen, Adriana (1814–1895), Dutch artist, visited TM (1849) Table 9.1

Haarlem *passim*, 32 (**2.2**) Burgersociëteit, a patriot society 31. *See also* Hendriks, Wybrand, *De kamer van de voormalige Burgersociëteit* City Council 22, 28, 35, 175 Damstraat 21 23n16, 56 (**3.10**) Democriet, 'poetry-loving, nonsensical' society (1789–1869) 22 Drawing school/academy ('Teekenacademie'; 1772–1795) 22n11, 23, 100, 101n39, 136, 177, 178, 181, 182, 192 Drawing college ('teekencollegie'). *See* Haarlem, Kunstmin en Vlijt Frans Hals Museum 16n29, 205 Freemasons' Lodge 176 Gouden Leeuw, a guest house on Zijlstraat in Haarlem. *See* Hendriks, Wybrand, *De kamer van de voormalige Burgersociëteit* Grote Houtstraat 38n62, 232n48 Gro(o)te Kerk. *See* Haarlem, St Bavo Gro(o)te Markt 94n29, 96n31 Guild of St Luke 94n29 Hollandsche Maatschappij der Wetenschappen, Haarlem, since

290 INDEX

Haarlem (*cont.*)

1752 (since 2002 Koninklijke (Royal) Holland Society of Sciences and Humanities) 16n28, 16n29, 21n6, 22n9, 23, 27, 28, 38n62, 41n71, 43n83, 73n6, 74, 84, 101, 116n19, 120, 131, 153, 176, 184, 188, 227

Cabinet of natural curiosities 27, 38n62, 102, 116n19, 136, Table 7.1 (20a, 20b. 21, 26)

Natuurkundige Verhandelingen (Physical Transactions), periodical 41n71, 133, 153

Oeconomische Tak (Economic Branch; 1777) 22, 23n15, 37n57, 101n40

Hulst, De, Pieter Teyler's house before he moved to Damstraat 21 23n16

Kaasmarkt (Cheese market) 14 (**1.4**)

Kunstmin en Vlijt (Love of art and diligence), Haarlem drawing society ('teekencollegie'; 1796–1826) 13, 22n11, 136, 181, 182, 200 (**9.5**), later Kunst zij ons Doel. *See* Kunst zij ons Doel

Leerzaam vermaak (Instructive entertainment), theatrical society (1785–1816) 22

Nut van 't Algemeen (Society for the Promotion of Public Welfare), Haarlem Branch 21n6, 23n17, 31n40

Paviljoen (Pavilion) Welgelegen 49n6, 204n42, 206n49

Museum of Living Dutch Masters, later of 19th-century Dutch Masters (1838–1885) 49n6

Remonstrant Church 37n58

Rozenprieel 94n31

St Bavo (or Grote) church (1370–1520) 14 (**1.4**), 25n23

St Lucas Guild. *See* Haarlem, Guild of St Luke

Teyler's *Hofje* (almshouse) 25n22, 88, 101, 228

Teylers Fundatiehuis (Teyler's Foundation House; originally Pieter Teyler's dwelling house 1740–1778; recently renamed as the 'Pieter Teyler House') 3, 11, 19, 31, 42, 43, 46, 47 (**3.1**), 49, 50 (**3.3**), 53 (**3.7**), 56 (**3.10**), 57 (**3.12**),

62/63 (**3.17**), 63, 64 (**3.18**), 88, 196n17, 237n66. *See also* Teyler's Foundation

Corridor 47 (**3.1**), 50 (**3.3**), 53 (**3.7**), 62/63 (**3.17**)

Courtyard 47 (**3.1**), 50 (**3.3**), 53 (**3.7**), 62/63 (**3.17**)

'Large Room' 47 (**3.1**), 50 (**3.3**), 53 (**3.7**), 62/63 (**3.17**), 63, 64 (**3.18**)

'Small Room' 47 (**3.1**), 50 (**3.3**), 53 (**3.7**), 62/63 (**3.17**)

Teyler's Museum *passim*

Art collections 51n11, 102, 108

Collection prints and drawings 48, 49, 89

Collection (contemporary) paintings 18, 49, 83, 179, 181, 190–216 (*passim*), 204n42, 249

Astronomical observatory. *See* Observatory

Auditory/Auditorium (*gehoorzaal*; 1885) 49, 53 (**3.7**), 54 (**3.8**), 62/63 (**3.17**), 88

'Betalab' for School Education (1996) 62/63 (**3.17**)

Book and Art Room (*Boek- en Konstzael*; 1784; now Oval Room) 3, 4, 5, 6 (**1.2**), 7, 8, 10, 11, 19, 24, 27, 42n79, 45, 47 (**3.1**), 49, 50 (**3.3**), 57 (**3.7**), 62/63 (**3.17**), 64 (**3.18**), 65, 87–108 (*passim*). *See also* Oval Room

Cabinet of Drawings 194

Cabinet of Physics 51n11

Café (1996) 58 (**3.13**), 61, 62/63 (**3.17**)

Castelei(j)n. *See* Keeper

Coins and Medals Cabinet. *See* Numismatic cabinet

Director 17, 37, 51, 57, 60n18, 74, 81, 105, 107, 109, 133, 137n12, 150, 169, 219, 226, 230, 231, 235

Instruction for the Director of Teyler's Museum (1784) 89, 107, 237n66

Exhibition Gallery (1996) 62/63 (**3.17**)

Exhibition Room for paintings (the former Lecture Room; 1829–1839) 49n7

Exhibition Room (1990–1996) 56 (**3.11**)

INDEX 291

Exhibition Room for Books (1996) 62/63 (**3.17**)

Exhibition Room for Drawings and Prints (1996) 62/63 (**3.17**)

First Fossil Room 49, 53 (**3.7**), 62/63 (**3.17**)

(First) Paintings Gallery (1839) 11, 12n17, 18, 49, 50 (**3.3**), 51 (**3.4**), 53 (**3.7**), 57 (**3.12**), 62/63 (**3.17**), 204 (**9.6**), 205

Fossil gallery (1824–1826) 48

Geology department. *See* Palaeontology and Mineralogy collection

Instrument Room (1885) 49, 52 (**3.6**), 53 (**3.7**), 62/63 (**3.17**)

Kastelei(j)n. *See* Keeper

Keeper (*Castelein* or *Kasteleijn*) 41–3 (*passim*), 47 (**3.1**), 49, 50 (**3.3**), 53 (**3.7**), 56 (**3.10**), 131, 133, 136–8, 169, 174n9, 179, 182n38

Instruction for the Keeper (*Castelein*) of Teyler's Museum (1785) 41n73, 137n12, 14, 191n3, 196n17, 237n66

Laboratories 47 (**3.1**), 50 (**3.3**), 53 (**3.7**), 60 (**3.15**), 63, 84, 131

Lecture Room (1824–1829) 11, 48, 49n7, 50 (**3.3**)

Library (*boekerij*) 6 (**1.2**), 11, 15, 16n26, 28n30, 33, 42, 47 (**3.1**), 48, 49, 50 (**3.3**), 53 (**3.7**), 54 (**3.9**), 62/63 (**3.17**), 81, 102, 103 (**5.7**), 105, 106, 107, 108, 127, 137n12, 202, 205, 229

Extension (1885) 48, 49, 53 (**3.7**), 54 (**3.9**), 62/63 (**3.17**), 106

Lorentz Lab (2017) 55n14, 60 (**3.15**), 61, 62/63 (**3.17**)

Copy of the original electrostatic generator (1784) 61 (**3.16**)

Luminescence Room, (1938), a presentation of luminiscent minerals, i.e. minerals emitting light not caused by heat 62/63 (**3.17**)

New wing (1878–1885) 14, 49n8, 128n36, 190, 192, 206

Façade on the Spaarne 14 (**1.4**), 49, 53 (**3.7**), 57 (**3.12**), 62/63 (**3.17**), 66 (**3.19**), 88, 190, 206, 207 (**9.7**)

New wing (1990–1996) 56 (**3.11**), 57 (**3.12**), 58 (**3.13**), 59 (**3.14**)

Numismatic Cabinet (1888) 53 (**3.7**), 62/63 (**3.17**), 205n43

Observatory 47 (**3.1**), 50 (**3.3**), 51 (**3.7**), 53 (**3.7**), 58 (**3.13**), 62/63 (**3.17**), 102

Oval Room (*Ovale zaal*; 1784) 4, 6 (**1.2**), 10, 12n17, 13, 19, 25n22, 26 (**2.1**), 27, 42n79, 43, 46, 47 (**3.1**), 48 (**3.2**), 49n9, 50 (**3.3**), 53 (**3.7**), 57 (**3.12**), 62/63 (**3.17**), 63, 64 (**3.18**), 87–108 (*passim*), 103 (**5.7**), 109, 110 (**6.1**), 118, 119, 124, 137, 141. 142 (**7.6**), 146, 147n35, 147n36, 149, 151, Table 7.1 (1a, 1b), 196, 202, 204, 205, 228, 231

Electrostatic generator (1784) 15, 37, 39, 47, 48 (**3.2**), 63, 88, 89, 102, 104, 107, 137, 138, 141, 142 (**7.6**), Table 7.1 (1a, 1b, 2a, 2b, 5a, 5b, 6a, 6b, 7, 10a–c). *See also* Bakker, Barent de; Haarlem, Teyler's Museum, Lorentz Lab, Copy of the original electrostatic generator; Wit, Isaak de

Palaeontological and Mineralogical collection/Cabinet 43, 50 (**3.3**), 51n11, 55, 116n19

Physics and chemistry laboratory 47 (**3.1**), 50 (**3.3**)

Reading Room (1824) 16, 48, 50 (**3.3**), 53 (**3.7**)

Room for education (1996) 62/63 (**3.17**)

Second Fossil Room (1885) 52 (**3.6**), 53 (**3.7**), 62/63 (**3.17**)

Second Paintings Gallery (1893) 12n17, 49, 52 (**3.5**), 53 (**3.7**), 57 (**3.12**), 62/63 (**3.17**)

Shop (2001) 61, 62/63 (**3.17**)

R. van Stolk Room, a presentation of the scientific optical phenomena and static electricity magicians used to perform parlor tricks (1996) 62/63 (**3.17**)

Storage space 47 (**3.1**), 50 (**3.3**), 53 (**3.7**)

Visitors' books 16n29, 42, 55n13, 105n57, 181, 196n20, 205n44, 206n50, Table 9.1

Watercolour Gallery 49, 53 (**3.7**)

INDEX

Haarlem (*cont.*)
  Teylers Stichting. See Teyler's
    Foundation
  Waag (Weighhouse) 14 (**1.4**)
  Zegelwaarden building 61n20, 62/
    63 (**3.17**)
Haarlemmerhout 133
  Spanjaardslaan 134 (**7.2, 7.3**), 151, Table
    7.1 (27a, 27b)
Hagemeister, Karl (1848–1933), German artist,
    visited TM (1873) Table 9.1
Hague, The 94n29, 169
  Buitenhof (with the Gallery of Stadholder
    Willem V, 1774–1795, which was
    reconstructed in the 1970s) 87
  Royal Cabinet of Paintings,
    Mauritshuis 49n6, 87n1, 196
Hahn, Johann David (1729–1784), collector,
    auction in 1785 112
Halle (since 1680 part of Brandenburg-
    Prussia; since 1815 part of the Prussian
    Province of Saxony; 2020: part of
    Saxony-Anhalt in Germany) 16, 17,
    219–38 (*passim*), 225 (**10.5**)
  Franckesche Stiftungen (Francke
    Foundations; 1695) 16, 17, 65n24, 219,
    221, 223n13, 225 (**10.6**), 232, 233, 236
    Orphanage 16, 17, 219, 221, 222 (**10.3**),
    223n13, 224 (**10.4**), 227, 228, 237
      Cabinet of Anatomy 221
      Cabinet of Natural Curiosities
        (founded 1698; since 1741
      Cabinet of Artefacts and Natural
        Curiosities) 17, 219–38 (*passim*)
      Kunst- und Naturalienkammer
        (Room for art and *naturalia*) 225
        (**10.5**). *See also* Cabinet of Natural
        Curiosities
      Latina grammar school 226
      Mechanical Cabinet 222
      Royal Pädagogium 17, 221, 226,
        233n51, 234 (**10.8**)
  Fridrichsuniversität 219
  Glaucha 227n25
  Leipziger Tor 225 (**10.6**), 227
Hamburger, Johan Coenraad (1809–1871/
    91), German/Dutch artist, visited TM
    (1838) Table 9.1

Hamilton, Sir William (1730–1803), British
    diplomat, antiquarian, archaeologist
    and volcanologist
  *Collection of Etruscan, Greek, and Roman
    antiquities from the cabinet of the
    Honble. Wm. Hamilton* (1766–67) 106
  Campi Phlegraei [on the eruption of the
    Vesuvius] (1776) 106
Harkness, Deborah (1965), American author
    and historian 76
Hartman or Hurtman, Hendrik (active 1875–
    1914), Dutch photographer, visited TM
    (1879; 18/7/1890?) Table 9.1
Hartman van Groningen, Barend (before
    1745–1806), Mennonite teacher and
    one of the first six members of Teyler's
    Theological Society 29n34
Harz 122
Haüy, René-Just (1743–1822), French
    mineralogist 15, 112, 119, 120, 121,
    123, 144
  Crystal models 120 (**6.7**), 144n26
Hazen, A. C., visited TM (1886) Table 9.1
Heidelberger Mineralien Comptoir 125,
    126 (**6.11**)
Heijmans, Jan Hendrik (1806–1888), Dutch
    artist, visited TM (1875) Table 9.1
Heijmans, Willem George Frederik (1799–
    1867), Dutch artist, visited TM
    (1850) Table 9.1
Hemert, Paulus van (1756–1825),
    liberal reformed preacher, later
    Remonstrant, winner of the gold
    medal of Teyler's Theological Society
    (1788) 33n46
  'How to explain the founding principle
    of Protestantism, that every Christian
    [...] is justified and bound [...] to judge
    for himself in matters of Religion
    [...]?' 33
Hemert, P. van, visited TM (March
    1875) Table 9.1
Hendriks, Wybrand (1744–1831), *castelein* or
    kasteleijn (caretaker of the house) and
    keeper of the art collection of Teyler's
    Museum (1785–1819) 11, 12n19, 38n64,
    41n73, 43, 47, 107, 131–67 (*passim*),
    Table 7.1 (*passim*), 169, 170n7, 172,

174n9, 177, 179n23, 27, 182n38, 183n45, 184, 191n3, 193n9, 196n17, 199n26, 200n27. *See also* Bakker, Barent de; Schwegman, Hendrik

The Directors and Members of the Haarlem Drawing College Kunstmin en Vlijt (1799), painting   200 (**9.5**)

Dune landscape with ruins (undated), drawing after Pieter van Bloemen, Nicolaes Berchem and Herman Saftleven   197 (**9.1**)

Group portrait of five Directors of Teyler's Foundation (1786), painting   26 (**2.1**)

De kamer van de voormalige Burgersociëteit in De Gouden Leeuw (The chamber of the former Burgher Society in the Golden Lion; 1795), drawing   174n9, 176 (**8.7**)

The Oval Room of Teyler's Museum (c. 1810), painting   26 (**2.1**), 48 (**3.2**)

Path through the Village of Manen near Ede (1783), drawing   135 (**7.4**)

Self portrait (1807), painting   132 (**7.1**), 200 (**9.5**)

Wonder tree (1819), drawing   134 (**7.2**), Table 7.1 (27a). *See also* Varelen, Elias van

Hendriksen, dr. M. M. A. (Marieke), Dutch historian   70n1, 72n5

Henket, Hubert-Jan (1940), architect (Bureau Henket)   56 (**3.11**), 57 (**3.12**), 58 (**3.13**), 59 (**3.14**), 61n21

Herding(h), Jan (1747–1822), Director of Teyler's Foundation (c. 1782–1822)   26 (**2.1**)

Heyboer, W., visited TM (March 1875)   Table 9.1

Hijner, Arend (1866–1916), Dutch artist, visited TM (9/2/1893)   Table 9.1

History, personification of   7, 35 (**2.4**)

Hodges, Charles Howard (1764–1837), English/Dutch artist

Portrait of Martinus van Marum (1826), painting   9 (**1.3**)

Hodshon, Johanna (1761–1780), wife of Willem Anne Lestevenon   176

Hofstra, Jacob (1805–1875), Dutch amateur artist, visited TM (1854)   Table 9.1

Holland   183, 221, 228, 232, 249–251. *See also* Low Countries; the Netherlands

Holland (one of the seven provinces of the Dutch Republic)   20. *See also* States of Holland

Holland, Kingdom of (1806–1810)   28n29

Hollandsche Maatschappij der Wetenschappen. *See* Haarlem, Hollandsche Maatschappij der Wetenschappen

Holstein, Johann Georg von (1662–1730), Danish minister of state   223n12

Holtzhey, Johan(n) George (1726 or 1729–1808), Dutch medallist and mint master

Prize medal of Teyler's Theological Society, awarded in 1784 to William Laurence Brown in Utrecht (design 1778)   32 (**2.2, 2.3**)

Prize medal of Teyler's Second Society, awarded in 1846 to Pieter Otto van der Chijs (design 1778)   35 (**2.4, 2.5**)

Homo diluvii testis (the man who witnessed the Flood)   90, 106n58, 139n18, Table 7.1 (24)

Hoogbruin, W., visited TM (15/9/1886)   Table 9.1

Hoogstraten, David van (1658–1724), Dutch author

Groot algemeen historisch, geographisch, en oordeelkundig woordenboek (1723)   89

Hopman, Nicolaas (1794–1870), Dutch artist and conservator, visited TM (1848)   Table 9.1

Horst, Klaas van der (1731–1825), Mennonite pastor, one of the first six members of Teyler's Theological Society   29n34, 29n35

Horstink, Warnaar (1756–1815), Dutch artist, visited TM (14/1/1800)   Table 9.1

Houttuyn, Martinus (1720–1798), Dutch naturalist, collector, auction in 1789   112, 114 (**6.2**), 115 (**6.3**), 124 (**6.10**). *See also* Nozeman/Houttuyn

Natuurlyke Historie of uitvoerige beschrijving der dieren, planten en mineralen volgens het samenstel van den Heer Linnaeus, Amsterdam, 37 vols, 1761–1785, vol. 33 (1783, p. 200, pl. 46, fig. 5)   115 (**6.4**)

294 INDEX

Hovens, Daniel (1735–1795), Mennonite minister in Leiden, winner of the first gold medal of Teyler's Theological Society (competition of 1778, published 1781) 32
'The distinguishing characteristic of Christian Revelation and its relation to natural and Judaic religion', *Verhandelingen van Teyler's Godgeleerd Genootschap* 1 (1781) 32
Hovens, Koenraad (1737–1817), first secretary of Teyler's Foundation 25n23, 26 (2.1), 36n53
Hoytema, Theo van (1863–1917), Dutch artist, visited TM (August 1881) Table 9.1
Hugaart, Gerard jr (?–in or after 1791), one of the first Directors of Teyler's Foundation 26 (2.1)
Huguenot(s) 78
Hulst, Maria van der (?–1721), mother of Pieter Teyler (van der Hulst) 19
Humbert de Superville, David Pierre Giottino de (1770–1849), Dutch artist 169n2, 184, 188
Humphrey, William, English dealer in minerals and fossils 112, 127
Hunck, H. J., visited TM (11/8/1891) Table 9.1
Hurtman. *See* Hartman

ICOM. *See* International Council of Museums
Immerzeel, Christiaan (1808–1886), Dutch artist, visited TM (1838) Table 9.1
Immerzeel, Johannes (1776–1841), Dutch artist and biographer, visited TM (1841) Table 9.1
Imperato, Ferrante (1525? –1615?), apothecary in Naples
Dell'historia naturale di Ferrante Imperato napolitano Libri XXVIII (1599) 92 (5.1)
Impey, Oliver (1936–2005), curator of the Ashmolean Museum, Oxford
with Arthur MacGregor
The Cabinet of Curiosities (1983), conference 91
The Origins of Museums (1985), book 91n16
India 223

Ingenhousz, Jean (1730 –1799), Dutch physiologist, biologist and chemist Table 7.1 (7)
Institut de France 81
Instruments 11, 12, 15, 23, 36, 37, 42n76, 47, 89, 104, 105, 108. *See also* Haarlem, Teyler's Museum, Instrument Room
International Council of Museums (ICOM) 10, 87/88n2, 128
Museum definition 10, 87/88n2
Ireland/Irish 119, 127
Israëls, Jozef (1824–1911), Dutch artist, visited TM (1866; May 1879) Table 9.1
Italy/Italian 15, 37n57, 75n12, 92, 137n14, 175, 177, 178, 184, 188, 196n22, 243
Italian drawings 7n7, 13, 137, 168–89 (*passim*), 193, 195

Janssens, René (1870–1936), Belgian artist, visited TM (23/8/1900) Table 9.1
Janus, personification of History 7
Japanese 75n12
Java 55
Jelgersma, Taco Hajo (1702–1795), Dutch artist
Portrait of Pieter Teyler van der Hulst as Collector (c. 1760), drawing 4 (1.1)
Jena 16n27, 111, 227
Jew/Jewish 24n19, 25n21, 78, 79 (4.3). *See also* Judaic
Jorink, Eric (1963), Teyler Professor at the University of Leiden (since 2013) 65n23, 76
Josephson, Ernst (1851–1906), Swedish artist, visited TM (1876) Table 9.1
Judaic 32. *See also* Jew/Jewish

Kamerlingh Onnes, Heike (1853–1926), Dutch scientist and Nobel Prize-winner (1913) 73
Kamphuijsen, Jan (1760–1841), Dutch artist 184
Kant, Immanuel (1724–1804), German philosopher 18, 241
Kritik der Urteilskraft (1790) 241
Karsen, (Johann) Eduard (1860–1941), Dutch artist, visited TM (Sept. 1882) Table 9.1

INDEX

Karsten, Wenceslaus Johann Gustav (1732–
1787), German mathematician 227
Kassel
Museum Fridericianum (1777) 11, 106
Kate, Herman Frederik Carel ten (1822–
1891), Dutch artist, visited TM (15/10/
1875) Table 9.1
Kauffman(n), Angelica (1741–1807), Swiss
artist, working in London and Rome
Farewell of Abelard and Héloise (1780),
painting 186
Kaufman, Aug. B., visited TM (13/5/
1892) Table 9.1
Kieser, Dietrich Georg (1779–1862), German
physician in Northeim (today in Lower
Saxony), from 1812 in Jena, winner
of the gold medal of Teyler's Second
Society's (1808)
l'Organisation des plantes 16n27
Kikkert, Pieter (1775–1855), Dutch artist and
author, winner of the gold medal of
Teyler's Second Society (competition of
1806, published in 1809) 41n72, 185–7
'Wat is de reden, dat de Nederlandsche
school, zoo wel voorheen ten tyde van
haren grootsten bloei, als hedendaags,
zoo weinig meesters in het historisch
vak heeft opgeleverd? (What is the
reason for the small number of Dutch
history painters?)', 185–7. *See* Kikkert
1809 in the Bibliography
Kirwan, Richard (1733–1812), Irish
physicist 119
Elements of Mineralogy (1784) 119
Kistemaker, Jacob (1917–2010), Dutch atomic
physicist, Teyler Professor at the
University of Leiden and curator
of the Teyler Cabinet of Physics
(1956–1984) 65n23
Klerk, Willem de (1800–1876), Dutch artist,
visited TM (21/9/1829) Table 9.1
Kloos, L., visited TM (October
1829) Table 9.1
Knip, Augustus (1819–1859), Dutch artist,
visited TM (1840) Table 9.1
Knolle, Paul (1952), Dutch art historian 5n3
Konijnenburg, Jan (1757–1831), Dutch
preacher and author

'Over het kunst-schoone in Raphaël, als
voorbeeld ter navolging' (1810) 184
Koning, C. H., Dutch printmaker
Print of a large electrical spark
(1787) 143 (7.8)
Koninlijk Nederlandsch Instituut (Royal
Netherlands Institute, 1808–1851;
predecessor of the Koninklijke
Nederlandse Akademie van
Wetenschappen (Royal Netherlands
Academy of Sciences), since
1851) 199n23
Society of Arts (since 2014) 86n31
Kops, Haarlem family of Mennonites 23
Koselleck, Reinhart (1923–2006), German
historian 5
Sattelzeit 5, 7n6, 10, 45
Koster, Anton Lodewijk (1859–1937), Dutch
artist, visited TM (3/6/1892) Table 9.1
Krämer, Johann Victor (1861–1949), Austrian
artist, visited TM (6/7/1896) Table 9.1
Krantz, Adam August (1808–1872), German
mineral and fossil trader
Mineralien Kontor 121n25
Krebel, Gottlob Friedrich
*Vornehmsten Europaeischen
Reisen*(1792) 227
Kruseman, Cornelis (1797–1857), Dutch
artist 196, 251
Visited TM (8/5/1818) Table 9.1
Kruseman, Frederik Marinus (1816–
1882), Dutch artist, visited TM
(1837) Table 9.1
Kruseman, Jan Theodoor (1835–1895), Dutch
artist, visited TM (June 1857) Table 9.1
Kruseman van Elten, Hendrik Dirk (1829–
1904), Dutch artist, visited TM (1852; 1/
9/1897) Table 9.1
Kuits, Antoni (1718–1789), one of
the first Directors of Teyler's
Foundation 23n15, 25, 26 (2.1), 26n24,
27, 28, 30n39, 36n53
Kunstbeschouwing(en) (art appreciation
gathering(s)) 13n21, 182n38, 199n25,
200, 201n29
Kunstkamer(s) (art room(s)) 10
Kunstmin en Vlijt. *See* Haarlem, Kunstmin
en Vlijt

296 INDEX

Kunst zij ons Doel (That art may be our goal), Amsterdam drawing society 181n36, 184

Kunst zij ons Doel (That art may be our goal), Haarlem drawing society ('teekencollegie'; since 1821) 22n11, 177n14, 181n36, 181n37, 200n28

Kuyper, Ja(c)ques (1761–1808), Dutch artist. *See* Vinkeles, Reinier

Lairesse, Gerard de (1641–1711), Dutch artist 186n56

Lamanon, Robert de (1752–1787), French naturalist 139n18

Lambertini, Prince De, possibly Giovanni Lambertini (1739–1806) 138n17, Table 7.1 (10c)

La Peyrère, Isaac (1596–1676), French scholar *Prae-Adamitae - systema theologicum* (1655) 39n65, 128n35

Lasius, Georg Sigmund Otto (1752–1833), German mineralogist 122

Laslett, Peter (1915–2001), Cambridge historian 84
The World we have lost. England before the Industrial Age (1965) 7, 84

Latin 77, 89, 105n56, 241

Laurillard, C. L. (1783–1853), French artist 138n18

Lavoisier, Antoine (1743–1794), French scientist 8, 15, 37n59

Leeuwarden 40n67

Leiden 21n8, 32, 33n47, 219
Museum Naturalis (Naturalis Biodiversity Center) 93
Rijksmuseum Boerhaave 93
Rijksmuseum van Oudheden (National Museum of Antiquities) 92/93
University 33n47, 65n25, 92, 116
Anatomical Theatre (1597) 92
Board of Trustees 176
Botanical Garden (Hortus Botanicus) *Gallerij* 90, 92, 108

Leighton, John (1822–1912), British artist, visited TM (1861) Table 9.1

Leipzig 20n2

Lelie, Adriaan de (1755–1820), Dutch artist *The Drawing Gallery of the Felix Meritis Society* (1801), painting 83 (4.7)

Lenz, Johann Georg (1748–1832), German mineralogist 112, 119

Leonardo da Vinci (1452–1519), Italian artist 183n46

Leonhard, Karl Cäsar Ritter von (1779–1862), German mineralogist 125, 126 (**6.11**)

Lestevenon, Mattheus (1715–1797), father of Willem Anne, secretary and *schepen* of Amsterdam and Dutch ambassador in Paris 172

Lestevenon, Willem Anne (1750–1830), director of the Haarlem drawing academy (1778–1795), member of Teyler's Second Society (1780–1797) 15, 23n15, 36n52, 53, 37n57, 38, 43, 168–89(*passim*), 187 (**8.7**)

Leyden jars 147

Lieder, Friedrich Johann Gottlieb (1780–1859), German artist, visited TM (7/4/1804) Table 9.1

Liefhebber(s)/Liefhebberij(en) 28n32, 42, 77, 203n37

Liernur, Alexander (1770–1815), Dutch artist 184

Lieste, Cornelis (1817–1861), Dutch artist, visited TM (1835) Table 9.1

Linden, David van der, Dutch historian 94n29

Linnaeus, Carl (1707–1778), or Carl von Linné, Swedish botanist, zoologist, and physician 114, 115 (**6.4**), 144
Systema Naturae (1735) 144, 223

Lion Cachet, Carel Adolph (1864–1945), Dutch artist, visited TM (1/7/1897) Table 9.1

Locke, John (1632–1704), English philosopher 75

London 76, 111
British Museum (1753, open 1759) 11, 90, 101, 106, 111, 183n46, 239, 242
Pantheon 148, 149 (**7.9**)
Royal Society. *See* Royal Society
Society for the Encouragement of Arts, Manufactures and Commerce (1754; since 1908 Royal Society for the Encouragement of Arts, Manufactures and Commerce. Today known as Royal Society of Arts – RSA) 22

Loosdrecht 79
porcelain (1774–1782) 79, 80 (**4.5**)

INDEX

Loosjes, Adriaan (1761–1818), son of Petrus, poet, publisher and founder of the *Algemeene Konst- en Letterbode,* member of Teyler's Theological Society (from 1813) 22n12, 30, 31

Gedenkzuil, ter gelegenheid der vry-verklaaring van Noord-America (Memorial column on the occasion of the declaration of independence of North America; 1782) 31

Loosjes, Cornelis (1723–1792), half-brother of Petrus, Mennonite minister, member of Teyler's Theological Society (from 1778) 29n34, 30, 36n53, 97

Loosjes, Petrus Adriaanszoon (1735–1813), half-brother of Cornelis, father of Adriaan, Mennonite minister, member of Teyler's Theological Society (from 1788) 30, 31, 33, 36n53, 194/195

Looy, Jacobus van (1855–1930), Dutch artist 190n1, 199n23, 208

Jacob van Looy Foundation (Frans Hals Museum) 190n1

Lorentz, Hendrik Antoon (1853–1928), Dutch scientist and Nobel Prize-winner (1902), curator of the Teyler Cabinet of Physics (1909–1928) 53 (**3.7**), 55n14, 60 (**3.15**), 61, 65n25, 73, 84, 85 (**4.8**)

Louis Napoleon (1778–1846), King of Holland (1806–1810) 28n29, 184

Louyot, Edmund (1861–1920), German artist, visited TM (29/7/1892) Table 9.1

Low Countries 28n29, 76, 77, 78. *See also* the Netherlands

Lubbers, Wessel (1755–1834), Dutch artist, visited TM (8/5/1817) Table 9.1

Luc, Jean-André de or Deluc (1727–1817), Swiss geologist 127n34

Lunteren, Frans H. van (1958), Dutch historian, Teyler Professor at the University of Leiden (since 2007) 65n25

Lyell, Charles (1797–1875), Scottish geologist

Principles of Geology (1830–1833) 105

Lycomedes

Daughters of. *See* Franco, Giovanni Battista

Maastricht 90, 104

'Maastricht Creature' 90, 104, 105, 106n58, 107. *See also* Mosasaur(us)

St Pietersberg (Mount St Peter) 104

Maatschappij tot Nut van 't Algemeen (Society for the Promotion of Public Welfare; founded in 1784) 21n6, 23n17, 31n40, 33n47, 71 (**4.2**), 232. *See also* Haarlem, Nut [...]

MacGregor, Arthur (1941), curator of the Ashmolean Museum, Oxford. *See* Impey, Oliver

Malacca/Malakka 124 (**6.10**)

Malmström, August (1829–1901), Swedish artist, visited TM (1875) Table 9.1

Manen Adriaanszoon, Jacob van (1752–1822), Dutch Patriot and author, silver medal of Teyler's Second Society (competition of 1806, published 1809) 'Wat is de reden, dat de Nederlandsche school, zoo wel voorheen ten tyde van haren grootsten bloei, als hedendaags, zoo weinig meesters in het historisch vak heeft opgeleverd? (What is the reason for the small number of Dutch history painters?)', *Verhandelingen van Teyler's Tweede Genootschap* 17 (1809) 41n72

Mantegna, Andrea (1431–1506), Italian artist 180

Mar, David de la (1832–1898), Dutch artist, visited TM (17/7/1890) Table 9.1

Marcus, Jacob Ernst (1774–1826), Dutch artist *Interior of the Drawing Academy at the Amsterdam Town Hall* (between c. 1790 and 1822), drawing 70 (**4.1**)

Maris, Jacob (1837–1899), Dutch artist 190/191n1

Visited TM (1869; 26/10/1871) Table 9.1

Maris, Willem Jbzn (1872–1929), Dutch artist, visited TM (8/11/1897) Table 9.1

Marum, Martinus van (1750–1837), director and curator of Teyler's Museum (1784–1837) 8, 9 (**1.3**), 10, 12, 15n23, 16, 17, 23n15, 27n27, 28n30, 28n31, 36n53, 37n58, 37n59, 38, 39n65, 39n66, 40n68, 41n71, 42n79, 42n80, 43, 46, 47 (**3.1**), 48n7, 49n7, 51, 60m18, 61 (**3.16**), 63, 74, 81, 83, 89, 90, 93, 101, 102, 104n52, 105n56, 106, 107,

298 INDEX

Marum, Martinus van (*cont.*)
109–28 (*passim*), 117 (**6.5**), 123 (**6.8**),
131–67(*passim*), 169, 174n9, 177n13, 178,
196, 219, 221, 225 (10.6), 226, 227, 228,
230, 231n48, 232n48, 235, 236n60,
237n69
'De Geschiedenis van de oprigting van
Teijler's Museum' (1823–1833)   89n11,
118n19
'Journaal van mijne verrichtingen ter
verkrijging eener Verzameling van
Fossilia in Teyler's Museum'   118n19
Mastenbroek, Jan van (1827–1909),
Dutch artist, visited TM (28/8/
1885)   Table 9.1
Mathematics/mathematical   17, 29n35, 75,
81, 84, 85, 111, 136, 221, 226, 227
Mauritius, Johann Georg (active first half 18th
century), German artist
Das Hällische Waysenhaus (The
Orphanage in Halle; 1740),
print   222 (10.3)
Mauve, Anton (1838–1888), Dutch artist,
visited TM (22/1/1857; 24/2/
1862)   Table 9.1
Mawe, John, English dealer in minerals and
fossils   112
Medici. *See* Francesco de' Medici and
Raphael, drawing
Meer Cz., P. v.d., visited TM
(1862)   Table 9.1
Meirelles de Lima, Victor (1832–1903),
Brasilian artist, visited TM
(1881)   Table 9.1
Melis, Henricus Joannes (1845–1923), Dutch
artist, visited TM (Nov. 1880)
Table 9.1
Mendes da Costa, Joseph (1863–1939),
Dutch artist, visited TM (16/10/
1885)   Table 9.1
Mengs, Anton Raphael (1728–1779), German
artist   187, 188
Mennonite(s)   3, 5, 10, 19, 22n12, 23, 24n18,
24n19, 25n21, 25n22, 25n23, 27, 29,
30, 31n41, 32, 33n46, 34, 36, 40n67,
44, 93, 97, 100, 101, 102, 104, 105, 195,
205, 228
Mennonite church

Congregation of Flanders and
Waterland   29
Congregation in Leeuwarden   40n67
Seminary in Amsterdam   29
Vereniging (Unification)   29
Mercury   Table 7.1 (17a, 17b)
Mérian, Johann Bernhard (1723–1807), Swiss
philosopher   70, 76
Mesdag, Albertine or Tine (1859–1936), Dutch
artist, visited TM (16/2/1894)   Table 9.1
Mesdag, Hendrik Willem (1831–1915), Dutch
artist and collector, visited TM (24/6/
1852; 10/9/1888)   Table 9.1
Mesdag, Taco (1829–1902), Dutch artist
and collector, visited TM (24/6/
1852)   Table 9.1
Meteorological/meteorology   21n8, 27
Metsu, Gabriël (1629–1667), Dutch artist   186
Meulen, Willem van der (1714–1808); Dutch
collector, auction in 1782   112
Meusel, Johann Georg (1743–1820), German
author   180
Michaëlis, Gerrit Jan (1775–1857), *kasteleijn*
(caretaker of the house) and keeper of
Teyler's art collections (1820–1856)   11,
43, 200n27, 203n37, 251
Landscape at Vogelensang (1824),
painting   248 (11.4)
Michel, Émile François (1818–1909),
French artist, visited TM (June
1886)   Table 9.1
Michelangelo Buonarotti (1475–1564), Italian
artist   13, 65n24, 168, 172, 180, 183n46,
187, 189, 193, 199n23, 251
Figure study of a walking man (*c.* 1527–
1560), drawing   173 (**8.4**)
Michielsen, G., visited TM (1811)   Table 9.1
Mieris, Frans van I (1635–1681), Dutch
artist   186n57
Mineral/mineralogy/mineralogical/
mineralogist   8, 9, 11, 15, 17, 28, 37,
43, 47, 49, 51n11, 63, 77, 100 (**5.6**), 102,
105n56, 107, 109–28 (*passim*), 110
(**6.1**), 126 (**6.11**), 131, 137n10, 144, 146,
164, 165, Table 7.1 (19), 192, 226, 229,
231, 233n51
Mining academy/academies   112n10,
122n27, 125

INDEX 299

Moerenhout, Joseph (1801–1875),
    Belgian artist, visited TM (1840,
    1844) Table 9.1
Mol, Joannes de (1726–1782), Protestant
    minister at Loosdrecht, who started a
    porcelain factory 79, 80 (**4.4**)
Molijn, François Adriaan (1805–1890), Dutch
    amateur artist, visited TM (1840,
    1841) Table 9.1
Mont Blanc 106, 108, 117 (**6.5, 6.6**), 118
Morandi, Giorgio (1890–1964), Italian
    artist 56 (**3.11**)
Moritz, Karl Philipp (1756–1793), German
    philosopher 18, 239, 240n2, 242–243,
    244 (**11.1**), 245, 246, 247
    *Reisen eines Deutschen in England im Jahr
    1782* (Journey of a German in England
    in the year 1782) 239n1
    'Versuch einer Vereinigung aller schönen
    Künste und Wissenschaften unter dem
    Begriff des In sich selbst Vollendeten'
    (An Attempt to unify all the Fine Arts
    and Sciences under the Concept of
    That which is Complete in Itself; in
    Berlinische Monatsschrift 1785) 242
    'Über die bildende Nachahmung des
    Schönen' (About the pictorial
    imitation of the beautiful;
    1788) 246n12
Mosasaur(us) 90, 104, 128, 139n18, 139n20,
    140 (**7.5**), 141, 146, Table 7.1 (3, 22, 25). *See
    also* Maastricht, 'Maastricht Creature'
Mount St Pieter. *See* Maastricht, St
    Pietersberg
Mozart, Wolfgang Amadeus (1756–1791),
    composer
    Don Giovanni (1787) 251
Munck, M. de, visited TM (July
    1883) Table 9.1
Muslim 78
Musschenbroek, Petrus van (1692-1761),
    Leiden physicist
    Beginselen der Natuurkunde (Principles of
    Physics; 1736) 21n8

Naples/Napoli 92n50
Napoleon Bonaparte (1769–1821), French
    general and Emperor 28n29, 243

National Assembly 25n23
Naturalia 38, 77, 88, 89, 90, 93, 95 (**5.2**), 96
    (**5.3**), 97, 100, 101, 102, 111, 117n20, 139,
    225 (**10.5**), 239
Natuurkundig College (Physics
    society), founded *c.* 1737 in
    Haarlem 21n6, 27, 33
Natuurkundige Verhandelingen. See Haarlem,
    Hollandsche Maatschappij der
    Wetenschappen
Neoclassical 63, 188, 199n22
Neo-Renaissance 49
Netscher, Caspar (1639–1684), Dutch
    artist 186
Netherlands, the 3, 7n7, 10, 13, 16, 17n30,
    18, 21n6, 23n17, 30, 33, 37, 60, 73, 87n1,
    91, 104, 113, 116, 117, 136, 145n29, 168,
    180n28, 182–185, 190, 199n22, 219n2,
    230n38, 232, 233, 234 (**10.8**), 237, 240,
    249, 251n22
*Neues Museum für Künstler und
    Kunstliebhaber*, German
    periodical 180
Newton, Isaac (1643–1727), English scientist/
    Newtonian(s) 78, 85
Niemeyer, August Hermann (1754–
    1828), German theologian and
    pedagogue 16, 17, 219–38 (*passim*),
    220 (**10.1**)
    Grundsätze der Erziehung (Principles of
    Education) 17, 228
    *Beobachtungen auf einer Reise durch einen
    Theil von Westphalen und Holland*
    (Observations on a journey through
    a part of Westphalia and Holland;
    1823) 221n4, 228, 229 (**10.6**)
Niemeyer, Agnes Wilhelmine Christiane,
    née von Köpken (1769–1847) 16, 220
    (**10.2**), 232, 233n49, 238
Nieuw-Loosdrecht. *See* Loosdrecht
Nieuwenhuijzen, Jan (1724–1806),
    Mennonite pastor and founder of the
    Maatschappij tot Nut van 't Algemeen
    (1784) 23n17
Nieuwenhuijzen, Martinus (1759–1793),
    son of Jan and co-founder of the
    Maatschappij tot Nut van 't Algemeen
    (1784) 23n17

Nieuwenhuizen, Peter van (1938), Dutch mathematician and theoretical physicist, Teyler Professor at the University of Leiden and curator of the Teyler Cabinet of Physics (1985–1990) 65n25

Nobel prize 55, 73. *See also* Kamerlingh Onnes, Heike; Lorentz, Hendrik Antoon; Waals, Johannes Diderik van der; Zeeman, Pieter

Noot, Thomas van der, bookseller in Brussels 77

North-America 31

Noster, Ludwig (1859–1910), German artist, visited TM (5/7/1893) Table 9.1

Novalis, pseudonym of Georg Friedrich Philipp Freiherr von Hardenberg (1772–1801), German poet 82

Nozeman, Cornelius (1720–1786), Dutch naturalist
 with Martinus Houttuyn
 Nederlandsche Vogelen (vol. IV, 1809) Table 7.1 (26)

Numismatics 34, 39, 41n72, 42, 44, 88, 102

Numismatics, personification of 35 (2.4)

Odescalchi, don Livio (1655–1713) 169, 170n6, 171 (8.3), 178
 his collection and his heirs 170 (8.1), 171 (8.2), 173 (8.4), 174 (8.5), 175 (8.6), 178, 181, 182, 183, 185

Oets, Pieter (1720–1790), Dutch artist
 Portrait of Joannes de Mol(c. 1750), drawing 80 (4.4)

Oils, combustion of Table 7.1 (14a, 14b, 15a, 15b, 16a, 16b)

Oosten de Bruyn, Gerrit Willem van (1727–1797), city historian of Haarlem, member of Teyler's Theological Society, reformed later Walloon, director of the Haarlem drawing academy (1788–1792) 19, 34, 35n51, 36n53, 39, 42n79, 174n9, 178
 his collections 36

Oppenoorth, Willem Johannes (1847–1905), Dutch artist, visited TM (February 1882) Table 9.1

Oprechte Haerlemsche Courant (literally, the sincere, or honest, Haarlem newspaper) 34, 94n29, 94n30

Orange (Oranje-Nassau), House/Family of, family from which since the 16th century the Dutch Stadholders were chosen until 1795, since 1815 the Royal Family of the Netherlands 174

Orangist, supporter of the family Orange-Nassau 15, 35n51, 36n53, 39, 44

Orangist Restoration/Revolution (1787) 15, 39, 44, 175

Orbis in domo (the world at home) 91, 108

Ornithorhynchus paradoxus (now *Ornithorhynchus anatinus*). *See* Platypus

Os, Pieter Frederik van (1808–1892), Dutch artist, visited TM (1848; 1881) Table 9.1

Overijssel (one of the seven provinces of the Dutch Republic) 20

Oxford
 Ashmolean Museum (1683) 90, 91. *See also* Impey, Oliver

Oyens, David (1842–1902), Dutch artist, visited TM (31/5/1853) Table 9.1

Palaeontology/palaeontological/ palaeontologist 8, 27, 38, 43, 51, 55, 116n19, 118, 121

Paludanus, Bernardus (1550–1633), Dutch physician and collector 90n15, 117n20

Panini, Giovanni Paolo (1691–1765), Italian artist
 Capriccio with ruins, drawing 183n45

Paris 111, 119, 166, 172, 177, 178, 188, 233, 234 (10.8)
 Academy (of art) 243
 Academy of Science 15
 Description des arts et métiers (1761–1782) 11
 École des Mines 112
 Louvre 183n46, 243
 Muséum d'histoire naturelle 15
 Jardin des Plantes 112, Table 7.1 (23–25)

Parmigianino (1503–1540), Italian artist 168, 172, 183

Patriot (or anti-Orangist) movement in the 18th century 15, 20, 22n12, 25n23, 28n29, 28n30, 30n37, 31n41, 35, 36n52, 36n53, 39, 44, 174n9, 177

INDEX

Patriot Revolution (1795)   20, 25n23, 35,
  36n52, 174n9
Persia/Persian   30
Peter the Great, Tsar of Russia
  (1672–1725)   93
Pettenkofen, August Xaver Karl, Ritter von
  (1822–1889), Austrian artist, visited TM
  (1875)   Table 9.1
Peyrère. *See* La Peyrère
Pfannschmidt, Ernst Christian (1868–1949),
  German artist, visited TM (13/10/
  1893)   Table 9.1
Pharmacy/pharmacist   8n9, 93, 99 (5.5). 113,
  114, 227
Philadelphia
  Academy of science   16
Philology/philologist(s)   84, 190, 206
Philosophy/philosophical/philosopher(s)   5,
  30, 34, 70, 71, 73, 74, 75, 78, 79, 80, 81, 101,
  127, 133, 135, 136, 144, 150n44, 153, 239,
  241, 243
Philosophical Transactions of the Royal Society.
  See Royal Society
Phlogiston theory   40n68. *See also* Air(s)
Phosphoric acid   Table 7.1 (12a, 12b)
Phrygian   32 (2.2)
Physician   16n28, 27, 101, 113, 114
Physico-theology   10, 33, 39n65, 40n70,
  41n72, 97, 105, 113, 127, 221
Physics/physical/physicist   8, 15, 17, 21n8, 23,
  27, 30, 34, 36, 37, 39, 40, 43, 47, 48, 51,
  55, 60 (3.15), 65n25, 81, 82 (4.8), 85, 86,
  111, 119, 127, 128, 131, 147n36, 221, 222n7,
  226, 227, 228, 232, 235, 236
Physics, personification of   35 (2.4)
Picart, Bernard (1673–1733), French/Dutch
  printmaker   25, 78
  Cérémonies et coutumes religieuses de
  tous les peuples du monde (9 vols,
  Amsterdam 1723–1743; in several
  languages: Ceremonies and Religious
  Customs of the various nations of
  the known world; published by J. F.
  Bernard)   25n21, 78, 79 (4.3)
Pieneman, Jan Willem (1779–1853), Dutch
  artist   196
  Visited TM (March 1820; 23/8/1849)   Table 9.1
Pieneman, Nicolaas (1809–1860), Dutch artist,
  visited TM (1834)   Table 9.1

Pieterse, Gijsbertus (1847–1878), Dutch artist,
  visited TM (August 1877)   Table 9.1
Pietist(ic)/ pietism   16, 17, 221, 222, 226, 228
Pirou, Eugène (?–?), Louvain, visited TM
  (1854)   Table 9.1
Pithecanthropus erectus (the upright
  ape-man)   55
Pitloo, Antonie Sminck (1790–1837),
  Dutch artist, working in Italy since
  1811   184n50
Planetarium   36
Plantijn, family of printers in Antwerp   77
Plantlust, country estate of Martinus van
  Marum   230
Plato (428/427–348/347 before Chr.), Greek
  philosopher/Platonic   81
Platypus   Table 7.1 (20a, 20b, 21)
Plomp, Michiel (1958), Dutch art
  historian   182
Ploos van Amstel, Cornelis (1726–1798), Dutch
  printmaker and collector, auction
  1800   179, 182, 183, 184
Poetry, personification of   35 (2.4)
Polder model(consensus
  decision-making)   186
Portielje, Gerard (1856–1929), Belgian artist,
  visited TM (1874; 1876)   Table 9.1
Portman, Christiaan Julius Lodewijk (1799–
  1868), Dutch artist, visited TM (16/4/
  1836)   Table 9.1
Posilippo, Scuola di (School of), art
  movement in Naples in the beginning
  of the 19th century   184n50
Praetorius, Pieter Ernst Henk (1791–1876),
  Dutch artist and collector, visited TM
  (1838; 10/9/1853)   Table 9.1
Pra(e)-Adamite/pra(e)-Adamism   39n65,
  127n35, 128n35
Prix de Rome   184
Provinciaal Utrechtsch Genootschap van
  Kunsten en Wetenschappen. *See*
  Utrechtsch Provinciaal [...]
Prussia/Prussian   20n2, 70, 219, 221, 222, 237.
  See also Brandenburg-Prussia

Quatremère de Quincy, Antoine-
  Chrysostome (1755–1849), French
  arts administrator and writer on
  art   243–8, 244 (11.2)

Quatremère de Quincy, Antoine-Chrysostome
(*cont.*)
*Considérations morales sur la destination
des ouvrages de l'art* (1815) 243,
245 (**11.3**)
Querelle des Anciens et des Modernes 240n3
Quietism 246n13

Rademaker, Gerrit (1671–1711), Dutch artist
*The Cabinet of Levinus Vincent
in Amsterdam* (*c.* 1680–1709),
drawing 98 (**5.4**)
Radermacher, Jacob Cornelis Matthieu
(1741–1783), Dutch botanist and
author 124 (**6.10**)
Ralli, Théodore Jacques (1852–1909), French/
Greek artist, visited TM (20/8/
1897) Table 9.1
Ramakers, Bart (1961), historian of Dutch
Literature 76
Raphael, Raffaello Sanzio da Urbino (1483–
1520), Italian artist 13, 65n24, 168,
172, 175 (**8.6**), 180, 183n46, 184, 187, 189,
193, 251
Putto carrying the Medici ring (*c.* 1513–
1514), drawing 174 (**8.5**)
Rapin, Aimée (1869–1956), Swiss artist, visited
TM (19/10/1898) Table 9.1
Rariteitenkabinet(ten) (cabinet(s) of
curiosities) 10. *See also* Curiosities,
cabinet(s) of
Ravenzwaay, Johannes Gijsbertzn van (1815–
1849), Dutch artist, visited TM (1834,
1836) Table 9.1
Reekers, Hendrik (1815–1854), Dutch artist,
visited TM (1833) Table 9.1
Reekers, Johannes (1790–1858), Dutch artist,
visited TM (1833) Table 9.1
Reekers, Johannes (1824–1895), Dutch
artist, visited TM (August 1881; Sept.
1885) Table 9.1
Regteren Altena, Iohan Quirijn van (1899–
1980), professor of art history of the
University of Amsterdam, curator of
the art collections of Teyler's Museum
(1952–1973), after the positions
of *kastelein* and curator of the art

collections had been separated in
1951 43n82
Regteren Altena, Marinus van (1866–1908),
Dutch artist, visited TM (April
1884) Table 9.1
Religion, personification of 32 (**2.2**)
Remonstrant(s) 24n19, 29n34, 33n46, 34,
37n58
Renaissance 91n17, 92, 104, 108, 184, 185, 187
Reni, Guido (1575–1642), Italian artist 172
Rensing, Carl (1826–1898), Dutch artist,
visited TM (1856) Table 9.1
Renkewitz, Theodor (1833–1913), Swiss artist,
visited TM (July 1892) Table 9.1
Repin, Ilja (1844–1930), Russian artist, visited
TM (18/5/1883) Table 9.1
Republic. *See* Dutch Republic
Reynolds, Joshua (1723–1792), British
artist 145
Richard, L., visited TM (1856) Table 9.1
Rickert, Heinrich (1863–1936), German
philosopher 75
Rijk, James de (1806–1882), Dutch artist,
visited TM (1835) Table 9.1
Ritsema, Coenraad (1834–1916), Dutch artist,
visited TM (1848) Table 9.1
Ritsema, Jacob Coenraad (1869–1943), Dutch
artist, visited TM (4/8/1898) Table 9.1
Robin, Louis (born 1845), French artist, visited
TM (June 1882) Table 9.1
Rochussen, Hendrik (1779–1852), Dutch artist,
visited TM (1/6/1801) Table 9.1
Rochussen, Henri (1812–1889), Dutch artist,
visited TM (May 1884) Table 9.1
Rocks 8, 9, 102, 109–28 (*passim*), 110 (**6.1**),
126 (**6.11**)
Roelofs, Willem (1822–1897), Dutch artist,
visited TM (February 1880) Table 9.1
Romantic/Romanticism 16n27, 18,
239–51 (*passim*)
Rome/Roman 14, 15, 38, 43, 48, 55, 168,
169n3, 170 (**8.1**), 172 (**8.2**), 173 (**8.3**), 174
(**8.5**), 175 (**8.6**), 181, 184n50, 243n9
Romen, Guillaume, visited TM (Sept.
1883) Table 9.1
Romé de l'Isle, Jean-Baptiste Louis (1736–
1790), French mineralogist 119, 123

INDEX

Roode, Nicolaas Johannes Wilhelmus de (1814–1884), Dutch artist, visited TM (1840)   Table 9.1

Rooker, Michel Angelo (1742/1743–1801), English artist. *See* Basire, J.

Roosenboom, Nicolaas Johannes (1805–1880), Dutch artist, visited TM (1840)   Table 9.1

Roodenburg, Johannes Carolus (1852–1928), Dutch artist, visited TM (4/7/1893)   Table 9.1

Rotterdam   179n23, 230

Rousseau, Jean-Jacques (1712–1778), Swiss/French philosopher   69, 70, 76, 82
Émile (1762)   69

Royal Netherlands Academy of Sciences   86n31. *See also* Koninklijk Nederlandsch Instituut

Royal Society, learned society in London (since 1660)   11, 15, 93, 101
Philosophical Transactions of the Royal Society (1665)   11, 149 (7.9)

Russia/Russian   16, 55n15, 111n4

Russian Revolution   55n15

Rutgers, Antoni (1695–1778), Dutch collector, auction 1778   182

Ruysch, Frederik (1638–1731), Dutch anatomist and collector   93n23, 94, 108

Rydberg, Gustaf Fredrik (1835–1933), Swedish artist, visited TM (1875)   Table 9.1

Sade, Donatien Alphonse François, Marquis de (1740–1814)   81, 82

Sadée, Philip (1837–1904), Dutch artist, visited TM (31/8/1887)   Table 9.1

Saftleven, Herman (1609–1685), Dutch artist   196, 197 (9.1). *See also* under Hendriks, Wybrand
Ruins (1649), drawing   198 (9.4)

St Petersburg
Academy of science   16
Kunstkamera (1728), later Museum of Anthropology and Ethnography (Kunstkamera 'Peter the Great')   11, 65n24

Saleh, Raden Sarief Bastaman (1811–1880), Indonesian artist, visited TM (1837)   Table 9.1

Sannack, Jean, visited TM (22/5/1819)   Table 9.1

Sattelzeit. See Koselleck, Reinhart

Saussure, Horace-Bénédict de (1740–1799), Swiss naturalist   112, 117 (6.5, 6.6), 118

Saussure, Théodore de (1767–1845), son of Horace-Bénédicte   117 (6.5, 6.6), 118

Saxony   111, 122n27

Saxony-Anhalt   16

Scale models   63, 106, 107, 108

Schaalstein   126 (6.11)

Schaeken, H. H., visited TM (1874)   Table 9.1

Schalbroeck, Eduard (1853–1935), Dutch artist and conservator, visited TM (August 1887)   Table 9.1

Scharloo, Marjan, director of Teyler's Museum since 2001   60n18

Schelfhout, Lodewijk (1881–1943), Dutch artist, visited TM (8/9/1897; 7/6/1898; 5/7/1898; 20/10/1899; 5/2/1900; 27/2/1900; 11/10/1900)   Table 9.1

Scheltinga, Frederik (died 1781), one of the first six members of Teyler's Theological Society   23n15, 29n34

Scherbatov, Sergei Alexandrovich (1875–1962), Russian artist, visited TM (13/4/1896)   Table 9.1

Scheuchzer, Johann Jacob (1672–1733), Swiss scholar   117

Schiller, Johann Christoph Friedrich (von) Schiller (1759–1805), German playwright, philosopher and poet   18, 240n2, 247–9, 251
Über die ästhetische Erziehung des Menschen in eine Reihe von Briefe (About the aesthetic education of man in a series of letters; 1795)   248n15

Schindler, Emil Jacob (1842–1892), Austrian artist, visited TM (1875)   Table 9.1

Schinkel, Karl Friedrich (1781–1841), German architect   248, 249

Schlegel, August Wilhelm (von) (1767–1845), German critic
Vorlesungen über dramatische Kunst und Literatur (Lectures on dramatic art and literature; 1809) 251

Schlosser, Julius Alwin Franz Georg Andreas Ritter von (1866–1938), Austrian art historian
  Kunst- und Wunderkammern der Spätrenaissance (1908) 91n17
Schmarsow, August (1853–1936), German art historian, University of Leipzig 55n13, 181n33
Scholten, Hendrik Jacobus (1824–1907), artist and curator of Teyler's art collections (1863–1907) 55n12, 190n1, 191, 192, 201n29, 202, 203, 208
  Musée Teyler à Haarlem. Catalogue raisonné des dessins des écoles française et hollandaise (1904) 55n12
Schotel, Johannes Christiaan (1787–1838), Dutch marine painter 251
  Calm water (1829), painting 250 (**11.6**)
  Storm at sea (c. 1825), painting 250 (**11.5**)
Schouman, Aert (1710–1792), Dutch artist, auction 1792 179n25
Schuch, Carl (1846–1903), Austrian artist, visited TM (1873) Table 9.1
Schumann, Karl Franz Heinrich (1767–1827), German artist
  Portrait of Karl Philipp Moritz (1791), painting 244 (**11.1**)
Schumann, Paul (1855–1927), German art historian 55n13
Schwartze, Thérèse (1851–1918), Dutch artist, visited TM (Sept. 1882) Table 9.1
Schwegman, Hendrik (1761–1816), Dutch artist 153, 154
  after Wybrand Hendriks
    Mosasaur fossil (1790), print 140 (**7.5**), 153, Table 7.1 (3)
Sciences de parlage 74
Scientific Revolution 71, 72, 73, 75
Seba, Albertus (1665–1736), pharmacist and collector in Amsterdam 8n9, 93n23, 114n16, 117n20
  Thesaurus (vol. 1, 1734) 114
Semolei, Il. *See* Franco, Giovanni Battista
Sepp, Jan Christiaan (1739–1811), Dutch artist and publisher 153
  after Wybrand Hendriks
    Ardea purpurea/Purpere reiger (1809), print Table 7.1 (26)

Serra Porson, Josep (or José Serra y Porson; 1824–1910), Spanish artist, visited TM (August 1883) Table 9.1
Sierstorpff, Caspar Heinrich von (1750–1842), German statesman 233n49, 235
  Bemerkungen auf einer Reise durch die Niederlande nach Paris, vol. 2 (1804) 233, 234 (**10.8**)
Simpliciakast (Collector's cabinet with a miniature pharmacy) 97, 99 (**5.5**), 100 (**5.6**), 113n12
Six, collection 36n54
Sloane, Sir Hans (1660–1753), British physician, naturalist and collector 90, 93n24, 101
Smirke, Richard (1778–1815), British artist, visited TM (27/7/1801) Table 9.1
Smirke, Robert (1780–1867), British architect, visited TM (27/7/1801) Table 9.1
Smith, Pamela (1957), American historian 76
Smith, W. O., probably American, visited TM (24/10/1900) Table 9.1
Smits, Jan Gerard (1823–1910), Dutch artist, visited TM (August 1865) Table 9.1
Sociability/sociable 22n12, 38, 76, 97, 237
Spaarne 14 (**1.4**), 49, 57 (**3.12**), 66 (**3.19**), 88, 190, 206, 207 (**9.7**), 233, 236
Spinoza, Baruch or Benedictus de Spinoza (1632–1677), Dutch philosopher 73
Spruyt, Charles (1769–1851), South-Netherlandish/Belgian artist, visited TM (May 1808) Table 9.1
Squarcione, Francesco (c. 1395–after 1468), Italian artist 180
Stadholderless Age, Second (1702–1747) 20
Stahl, Georg Ernst (1659–1734), German doctor and chemist 40n68
Staring, Maurits Lodewijk Christiaan (1840–1914), Dutch artist, visited TM (1864) Table 9.1
Stasov, Vladimir (1824–1906), Russian author, visited TM (18/5/1883) Table 9.1
States General, the Dutch Parliament 175
States of Holland 22n9, 175
Statius Müller, Johan Wilhelm (1767–1836), Dutch Lutheran pastor 228n30

INDEX

305

STCN (Short-Title Catalogue Netherlands)
106n58
Steen, Jan (1626–1679), Dutch artist   186n57
Stengelin, Alphonse (1852–1938),
French artist, visited TM (28/7/
1890)   Table 9.1
Steur jr, Adrianus van der (1836–1899), Dutch
architect, designed the Instruments
Room, Fossil Room I and Fossil Room
II, Auditory and extension of the
Library (1880–1885)   50, 59 (3.14)
Stock, Johann Christian, German dealer in
minerals and fossils   112
Stolp, Jan (1698–1753), Leiden merchant,
founder of the Stolpian Legacy   33n47
Stolpiaansch Legaat (Stolpian
Legacy)   33n47, 34
Stoop, W.B,, visited TM (1840)   Table 9.1
Stortenbeker, A. W., visited TM
(1886)   Table 9.1
Stortenbeker, Johannes (1821–1899), Dutch
artist, visited TM (August 1875;
1885)   Table 9.1
Stortenbeker, Willem (1789–1882),
Dutch artist, visited TM (August
1875)   Table 9.1
Struyk, Cornelis, visited TM (1/6/
1789)   Table 9.1
Suitensammlung(en)   125, 126 (6.11)
Sweden   169, 181
Swinden, Jean Henri (also Jan Hendrik;
1746–1823), Dutch scientist   82 (4.6)
Swiss/Switzerland   15, 70, 111, 112, 114, 117, 118

Tak, Jan (1729–1780), Dutch collector of
drawings, auction 1780   179
Teekenacademie (drawing academy). See
Amsterdam, Drawing academy of
the city; Haarlem, Drawing school/
academy
Teerlink, Abraham (1776–1857), Dutch
artist, working in Rome since
1810   184n50
Teissèdre l'Ange, Josué (1771–1853), Dutch
Walloon minister and school reformer,
member of Teyler's Second Society
(from 1798)   17, 31n40, 228n30,
230n39, 232, 237

Grondbeginselen (1799–1810), translation
of Niemeyer's Grundsätze der
Erziehung   17, 228
Teyler, Isaac (1669–1750), father of Pieter
Teyler (van der Hulst)   19, 100
Teyler van der Hulst, Pieter (1702–1778),
Dutch cloth merchant, banker and
philanthropist, founder of Teyler's
Foundation   3n1, 4 (1.1), 11n16, 19–25
(passim), 25n21, 27, 29, 30, 34, 36, 41,
46, 47 (3.1), 49, 50 (3.3), 69, 87–108
(passim), 177, 179, 189, 192n4, 193n7, 195,
196, 228, 237n66, 249
his collections   3, 11n16, 27, 42, 47n4, 88,
100, 102, 104, 106
his cabinet of coins and medals   11n16,
27, 42, 47n4, 88, 100, 102
his will   3n1, 3n2, 20, 21n5, 24, 25, 26n24,
32n42, 33, 39, 41, 42n74, 43, 46, 69, 86,
88n4, 89, 101, 102, 137n11, 190, 192, 193, 249
Teyler Chair at Leiden University   65n25.
See also Fokker, Adriaan Daniel; Jorink,
Eric; Kistemaker, Jacob; Lunteren,
Frans H. van; Nieuwenhuizen, Peter
van; Visser, Robert W. P.
Teyler's Challenge   65n23
Teyler's Foundation (Stichting) passim. See
also Haarlem, Teylers Fundatiehuis;
Haarlem, Teylers Museum
Directors   3n2, 9, 19, 22, 23n15, 25, 26 (2.1),
27–9, 30, 37, 38n64, 39n66, 41, 42n80,
44n84, 46, 51n11, 81, 88, 89, 101, 102, 104,
127, 137, 169, 180, 182n38, 183, 190, 191,
194, 195, 199, 201, 202, 203, 208, 224,
231n42, 235
Teylers Godgeleerd Genootschap/Teyler's
Theological Society   3–5, 7, 19–45
(passim), 32 (2.2, 2.3), 65n25, 78n19,
90n12, 105, 106, 192, 195, 232
Annual competition   3n2, 16, 19, 31–4
(passim), 38, 41n72, 88, 108, 178n18
1778 (a comparison between revealed
and natural religions)   31, 32, 33n45,
40, 101
1780 (about human moral freedom)   33
1783 (about the relation between
true philosophy and Christian
revelation)   32n43

INDEX

Teylers Godgeleerd Genootschap/Teyler's
Theological Society, Annual
competition (*cont.*)
1784 (about the middle way, in
religious matters, between doubt and
determination) 32 (2.2)
1788 (about the right to self-
determination as the founding
principle of Protestantism) 33n46
1793 (about the proof of the divinity of
the teachings of Jesus) 40n67
1794 (can people, by using their reason
alone, come to the right ideas about
God and divine matters?) 40n67
1795 (about whether and how
the civil authorities may exercise
some influence in matters of
Religion) 33n46
1796 (is self-love the governing
principle of humankind?) 40n67
1799 (are religious concepts and
practices necessary conditions for
virtue and good morals) 40n67
Teylers Tweede Genootschap (or 'collegie')/
Teyler's Second Society (for Arts and
Sciences) 3–5, 7–9, 13, 15, 19–45
(*passim*), 88, 101, 102n48, 104–6, 110, 138,
153, 168n1, 172, 176 (8.7), 178, 179, 185,
192, 201, 203, 205, 228, 230, 232
Annual competition 3n2, 16, 31, 38, 39–41
(*passim*), 41n72, 88, 108, 178n18
1778 (physics: about phlogisticated
air) 40, 101, 102
1781 (drawing/painting: about the
national taste of the Dutch school in
drawings and paintings; published in
1787) 101n42, 178, 185n54, 187, 188
1783 (physics: about the Age of the
Earth) 40, 104, 107
1787 (numismatics: an inventory of
Dutch coins since 1579) 39
1797 (numismatics: about the use of
gold and silver) 40n72
1800 (history: about characteristics of
the 18th century, compared to the 17th
century) 40n67
1801 (physics: about physics as proof
of the Creator's existence) 40,
41n72

1806 (drawing/painting: about the
reasons for the small number of
Dutch history painters; published in
1809) 40n69, 41n72, 101n42, 187
1808 (physics: *l'organisation des
plantes*) 16n27
1811 (drawing/painting: an overview
of the present state of painting and
drawing in what used to be the Dutch
Republic) 41n72, 101n42
Thorbecke, Johan Rudolph (1798–1872), Dutch
liberal statesman 251
Thorenfeld, Anton Erik Christian (1839–1907),
Danish artist, visited TM (August
1885) Table 9.1
Thors, Joseph (active c. 1835–1920), Dutch/
British artist, visited TM (August
1880) Table 9.1
Tieck, Johann Ludwig (1773–1853), German
author and critic 247
Titian (c. 1487–1576), Italian artist 187
Toorop, Jan (1858–1928), Dutch artist,
visited TM (August 1882;
1888) Table 9.1
Toussaint von Charpentier, Johann Friedrich
Wilhelm (1779–1847), German
mineralogist at the Freiberg Mining
Academy 112, 122
Tranquebar (now Tharangambadi, southern
India) 223
Trimolet, Anthelme (1798–1866),
French artist, visited TM (28/9/
1855) Table 9.1
Truth, personification of 32 (2.2)
Tuyll van Serooskerke, Carel van (1950),
Dutch art historian 180, 181

Uilenbroek, Gosuinus (? –1740), Dutch
collector, auction in 1741 182
Ulrich, Christian (1836–1909), Austrian-
Hungarian architect, designed the
façade on the Spaarne of Teyler's
Museum 14 (1.4), 49, 66 (3.19)
UNESCO 57n17
United States (US) 16
Utilitarian 13, 18, 36, 39, 43, 74, 81, 127, 192,
194, 238
Utrecht (city)
Union of Utrecht (1579) 39

INDEX

Utrecht (one of the seven provinces of the Dutch Republic) 20

Utrechtsch Provinciaal Genootschap van Kunsten en Wetenschappen (Provincial Utrecht Society of Arts and Sciences; 1773) 21n6, 22n9, 73n6, 84

Vaarzon Morel, Willem (1868–1955), Dutch artist, visited TM (June 1885; Dec. 1886) Table 9.1

Vaderlandsche Letteroefeningen (Literary essays for the benefit of our fatherland; 1761–1876), Dutch literary-cultural magazine, founded by Cornelis and Petrus Adriaanszoon Loosjes 30n37, 39, 31n40, 32n42, 33

Valckenier, Pieter (1641–1712), Dutch collector 114, 117n20

Varelen, Jacob Elias van (1757–1840), artist 133n3, 153

after Wybrand Hendriks
The Wonder Tree on the Spanjaardslaan in the Haarlemmerhout, Haarlem (1819), print 133, 134 (7.3), Table 7.1 (27b)

Velvet Revolution (1795) 174n9

Ven, Elisa van der (1833–1909), mathematician and physicist, curator of the Cabinet of Physics of Teyler's Museum (1878–1909), secretary of Teyler's Second Society 53 (3.7)

Venice/Venetian(s) 187

Verbeek, Jan (died 1788), Remonstrant preacher and one of the first six members of Teyler's Theological Society 29n34, 34

Vereenigde Oost-Indische Compagnie (VOC); United East Indian Company) 93

Verhandelingen van Teyler's Tweede Genootschap (Transactions of Teyler's Second Society) 15n24, 16n27, 31, 37n59, 40n67, 40n69, 88, 138, 140 (7.5), 142 (7.7), 143 (7.8), 153

Verhandelingen, rakende den natuurlijken en geopenbaarden Godsdienst, uitgegeeven door Teyler's Godgeleerd Genootschap (Transactions, regarding the natural

and revealed Religion, published by Teyler's Theologian Society) 31, 33n45, 88

Verlinden, Eric, Dutch physicist 85

Vermeer, Johannes (1632–1675), Dutch artist *Straatje* (Little street), painting, Rijksmuseum Amsterdam, SK-A-2860 36n54

Verschuur, Gerrit Pieter (1830–1891), Dutch artist, visited TM (16/3/1852; 1852) Table 9.1

Versteegh, Dirck (1751–1822), Dutch collector and mecenas, auction 1823 182, 184

Veth, Jan (1864–1925), Dutch artist, visited TM (21/8/1895) Table 9.1

Vienna/Viennese 14 (1.4), 49, 121
Vienna Circle 84

Viervant, Leendert (1752–1801), Dutch architect, designed the Oval Room of Teyler's Museum 25n22, 26 (2.1), 37n60, 46, 58 (3.13), 102, 103, 147n36, 149, 151, 155
Longitidunal section and ground plan for the Oval Room (1779?), drawing 103 (5.7)

Vincent, Levinus (1658–1727), Dutch designer and trader of silk textiles, collector in Amsterdam and Haarlem 8n9, 10, 93, 94n29, 97, 98 (5.4), 104, 105
Collection 93, 94, 97, 102, 104, 108, 117
Visitors' book 94n28, 29, 100, 102n46, 105n57
Wondertoneel der nature (Wonder-theatre of nature; 2 vols, 1706 and 1715) 94, 95 (5.2), 96 (5.3)

Vinkeles, Reinier (1741–1816), Dutch painter and engraver
After Jacques Kuyper and Pieter Barbiers *A public presentation by the Amsterdam professor Jan van Swinden for the Felix Meritis company in Amsterdam* ('Physica'; 1801), print 82 (4.6)

Vinne, Vincent van der III (1736–1811), the first *custos* (keeper) of Teyler's Museum (1778–1785) 41n73, 42n75, 42n80, 43, 179

Visitors' books 16n29. *See also* Haarlem,
Teylers Museum, Visitors' books;
Vincent, Levinus, Visitor's book
Visser, Robert P. W. (1942), Dutch historian
of science, Teyler Professor
at the University of Leiden
(1997–2007) 65n25
Visser Bender, J. A. (active 1800–1849), Dutch
artist, visited TM (1811) Table 9.1
Vlugt, Bartel Willem van der (1763–1839),
Director of Teyler's Foundation
(1789–1839) 199n26
Vlugt, Willem van der sr (?–in or after 1807),
one of the first Directors of Teyler's
Foundation 25, 26 (**2.1**)
Vlugt, Willem van der (1787–1849), Director of
Teyler's Foundation (1817–1849) 202,
203n37, 203n40
Vlissingen (Flushing). *See* Zeeuwsch
Genootschap [...]
VOC. *See* Vereenigde Oost-Indische
Compagnie (VOC)
Voet, Jakob-Ferdinand (1639–*c.* 1700), South-
Netherlandish artist
Portrait of Livio Odescalchi
(1676–1677) 171 (**8.3**)
Vogel, Cornelis Johannes de (1824–
1879), Dutch artist, visited TM
(1868) Table 9.1
Voigt, Johann Gottfried, German dealer in
minerals and fossils (Weimar) 112
Voigt, Johann Karl Wilhelm, dealer in
Weimar 122
Volta, Alessandro (1745–1827), Italian
scientist 8, 15
Voorhelm Schneevoogt, George (1775–1850),
Haarlem botanist 233
Vos, Koenraad (Coen; 1990), Dutch art
historian 5n3, 107
Voogd, Hendrik (1768–1839), Dutch
artist 184n50
Vos, Hubert (1855–1935), Dutch/
American artist, visited TM (Sept.
1883) Table 9.1
Vosmaer, Carel (1826–1888), Dutch artist,
collector, art historian, visited
TM (5/10/1882; Sept. 1883; Sept.
1885) Table 9.1

Vriends, Bernardus (1727–1791), member of
Teyler's Second Society, collector 36
Natural history collection 36
Vries, E. J., visited TM (1856) Table 9.1
Vries, Jeronimo de (1838–1915), member of
Teyler's Second Society 205

Waals, Johannes Diderik van der (1837–1923),
Dutch scientist and Nobel Prize-
winner (1910) 73
Wackenroder, Wilhelm Heinrich (1773–1798),
German jurist and writer 246,
247, 249
*Herzensergießungen eines kunstliebenden
Klosterbruders* (Outpourings from
the heart of an art-loving monk;
1797) 246
Wagenaar, Jan (1709–1773), Dutch
historian 194
Waldorp, Antonie (1803–1866), Dutch artist,
visited TM (1834) Table 9.1
Wallerius, Johann Gottschalk (1709–
1785), Swedish chemist and
mineralogist 119
Walloon 34, 35
Walraven, Isaac (1686–1765), Dutch collector,
auction in 1765 182
Walré, Jan van (1759–1837), Dutch poet 150
Waning, Carolus Lambertus (1844–1928),
Dutch artist, visited TM (May
1888) Table 9.1
Wap, P. W. M., visited TM (1863) Table 9.1
Washington, D.C.
Smithsonian Libraries 159
Waterland 29
Watson, White, English dealer in minerals
and fossils 112
Wax models 37n57
Weeshoff, Dirk (1825–1887), Dutch artist,
visited TM (1864) Table 9.1
Weimar 111, 122, 227
Weiss, Martin Paul Michael (1985), German
historian 235n53
Weitsch, Friedrich Georg (1758–1828),
German artist, visited TM (26/7/
1811) Table 9.1
Wereld binnen Handbereik, De (Distant
worlds made tangible), exhibition

INDEX

at Amsterdam Historical Museum (1992)   91. *See also* Bergvelt/Kistemaker 1992a and 1992b in the Bibliography

Werff, Adriaen van der (1659–1722), Dutch artist   186n56

Werner, Abraham Gottlob (1749–1817), German mineralogist, Freiberg Mining Academy   112, 119n23, 128

West, Benjamin (1738–1820), Anglo-American artist   186
The Death of General Wolfe (1770), painting   186

Wiebeking, Carl Friedrich von (1762–1842), German architect and hydraulic engineer   16n28

Wieringa, J. C., visited TM (May 1888)   Table 9.1

Wijnalda, Age (1712–1792), one of the first six members of Teyler's Theological Society   29n34

Wijnands Verschaave, Helena (?–1754), wife of Pieter Teyler van der Hulst   19n1, 20, 100

Wijngaerdt, Petrus Theodorus van (1816–1893), Dutch artist, visited TM (23/7/1887)   Table 9.1

Wijst, Marijke van der (1940), Dutch interior designer   56 (**3.11**), 61n21

Wikipedia   63n23

Wilcock, Matthew, from Manchester, entrepreneur   37n57

Willem I (1772–1843; son of Willem V), King of the Netherlands (r. 1814–1840)   183n42

Willem II (1792–1849; son of Willem I), King of the Netherlands (r. 1840–1849)   183n46

Willem IV (1711–1751), Prince of Orange, Stadholder of the Dutch Republic (1747–1751)   20

Willem V (1748–1806), Prince of Orange, Stadholder of the Dutch Republic (1766–1795)   20n4, 28n29, 35, 40, 87n1
Collections   87n1
Gallery   87n1

Willigen, Adriaan van der (1766–1841), Dutch author, silver medal of Teyler's Second Society (competition of 1806,

published 1809), member of Teyler's Second Society since 1812   41n72, 177, 181, 182, 201, 202n36, 203, 205. *See also* Eynden, Roeland van
Visited TM (25/5/1791; 30/3/1798)   Table 9.1

'Wat is de reden, dat de Nederlandsche school, zoo wel voorheen ten tyde van haren grootsten bloei, als hedendaags, zoo weinig meesters in het historisch vak heeft opgeleverd? (What is the reason for the small number of Dutch history painters?)', *Verhandelingen van Teyler's Tweede Genootschap* 17 (1809)   41n72

Willigen, Volkert S. M. van der (1822–1878), curator of the Cabinet of Physics of Teyler's Museum (1864–1878)   51n11, 53 (**3.7**), 55n12

Winckelmann, Johann Joachim (1717–1768), German art historian and archaeologist   188

Winkler, Tiberius Cornelis (1822–1897), curator of the Palaeontological & Mineralogical Cabinet of Teyler's Museum (1864–1897)   51n11, 110n3
Musée Teyler: catalogue systématique de la collection paléontologique (6 vols and 5 supplements, 1863–1896)   53n12

Winter, collection Van   36n54

Wit Jansz., Isaak de (1744–1809), Dutch artist   153
after Wybrand Hendriks
Schematic outline of the updated design of the big electrostatic generator (1795), print   Table 7.1 (10b, 10c)
Updated design of the big electrostatic generator (1795), print   Table 7.1 (10a)

Wit, Jacob de (1695–1754), Dutch artist   186n56

Witsen, Jonas (1705–1767), Dutch collector of drawings, auction 1790   179

Witsen, Nicolaes (1641–1717), Amsterdam burgomaster and collector   8n9, 93n23, 117

Witsen, Willem (1860–1923), Dutch artist, visited TM (14/4/1899)   Table 9.1

World War One (1914–1918)   24, 25n20, 55

WorldCat   106n59

Wolfe, General James (1727–1759), British army officer. *See* West, Benjamin

Wyttenbach, Jakob Samuel (1748–1830), Swiss naturalist and collector   112

Zeebergh, Adriaan van (1746–1824), one of the first Directors of Teyler's Foundation (1780–1824), appointed president of that board in 1807, but acting as such since 1788/89   23n15, 26 (2.1), 26n24, 27, 28n29, 30, 30n39, 32, 36n53, 38n64, 43, 105, 168n1, 169

Zeeland (one of the seven provinces of the Dutch Republic)   20

Zeeman, Pieter (1865–1943), Dutch scientist and Nobel Prize-winner (1902)   73

Zeeuwsch Genootschap ter bevordering van Nuttige Kunsten en Wetenschappen (Zeeland Society of Useful Arts and Sciences), Vlissingen (Flushing) 1768; since 1769 known as Zeeuwsch Genootschap der Wetenschappen (Zeeland Society of Sciences); since 1801 in Middelburg   21n6, 22n9, 40n67, 73n6

Zoology/zoological   16, 133n2, 141, 230, 232n48, 233

Zwolle   249

Printed in the United States
By Bookmasters